SACRED MANDATES

JAMES A. MILLWARD, SERIES EDITOR

The Silk Roads series is made possible by the generous support
of the Henry Luce Foundation's Asia Program. Founded in 1936,
the Luce Foundation is a not-for-profit philanthropic organization
devoted to promoting innovation in academic, policy, religious, and
art communities. The Asia Program aims to foster cultural and
intellectual exchange between the United States and the countries of
East and Southeast Asia, and to create scholarly and public resources
for improved understanding of Asia in the United States.

SACRED MANDATES

ASIAN INTERNATIONAL RELATIONS
SINCE CHINGGIS KHAN

Edited by Timothy Brook,
Michael van Walt van Praag,
and Miek Boltjes

The University of Chicago Press   *Chicago and London*

The University of Chicago Press, Chicago 60637
The University of Chicago Press, Ltd., London
© 2018 by Timothy Brook, Michael van Walt van Praag, Miek Boltjes
Published 2018
Printed in the United States of America

27 26 25 24 23 22 21 20 19 18   1 2 3 4 5

ISBN-13: 978-0-226-56262-9 (cloth)
ISBN-13: 978-0-226-56276-6 (paper)
ISBN-13: 978-0-226-56293-3 (e-book)
DOI: https://doi.org/10.7208/chicago/9780226562933.001.0001

Library of Congress Cataloging-in-Publication Data
Names: Brook, Timothy, 1951– editor. | Walt van Praag, M. C. van,
editor. | Boltjes, Miek, editor.
Title: Sacred mandates : Asian international relations since
Chinggis Khan / edited by Timothy Brook, Michael van Walt
van Praag, and Miek Boltjes.
Other titles: Silk roads (Chicago, Ill.)
Description: Chicago ; London : The University of Chicago Press,
2018. | Series: Silk roads
Identifiers: LCCN 2017053371 | ISBN 9780226562629 (cloth :
alk. paper) | ISBN 9780226562766 (pbk. : alk. paper) | ISBN
9780226562933 (e-book)
Subjects: LCSH: Asia—Foreign relations.
Classification: LCC DS33.3.S337 2018 | DDC 327.5—dc23
LC record available at https://lccn.loc.gov/2017053371

♾ This paper meets the requirements of ANSI/NISO Z39.48–1992
(Permanence of Paper).

Cover calligraphies by Yondonrinchin Munkhbat, Jamyang Dorjee
Chakrishar, and Hsiao Hung-Wen depict core Mongol, Tibetan
Buddhist, and Chinese Confucian concepts of legitimate rule:
törö, *chos srid zung 'brel*, and *tianxia*, respectively.

CONTENTS

PREFACE

This book is the culmination of five years of collaborative research, discussion, and reflection on the nature of sovereignty, rulership, legitimacy, state formation, and interpolity relations in Inner and East Asia from the early thirteenth century to the early twentieth. This research has led us to doubt the modernist paradigm that informs the generally shared understanding of the contemporary international system as a world of equal independent states exercising exclusive sovereignty within their borders and engaging in equal relations with each other. Whether that paradigm may usefully be applied to the analysis of states outside Inner and East Asia we leave to other analysts, but in Asia it is a fiction with shallow historical depth. In the regions of Asia we examine in this book, state sovereignty and interpolity relations have been shaped around quite a different paradigm. It is undeniable that Asian states have been conspicuous in performing many of the protocols of modern international relations since World War II, some of them starting as early as the late decades of the nineteenth century. But these performances have not obscured the deeper practices that mark state sovereignty and interpolity relations even today.

Our ambition in this book is not to present an analysis of Asian international and intrastate relations as these are conducted today. Rather, our approach is to foster an improved appreciation of Asia's past to aid in understanding the deep context of current discussions of what those relations are and should be. Our purpose in doing so is to introduce overlooked sources of historical influence that contribute to today's tensions and conflicts in the vast region covered in this book, which may benefit efforts to resolve them and to prevent others from arising. By looking back from the present and inquiring into the conceptual frameworks and actual practices through which rulers and political elites in Inner and East Asia have conducted their relations with each other over the eight centuries leading up to the twentieth, we seek to develop an awareness of the different, often conflicting, perceptions that are held of those relations and that have an impact on policies today. Our working hypothesis is that Inner and East Asian rulers and polities conducted their relations on the basis of expectations and principles that differed not just from those that derive from an idealized version of European international relations but from each other. Despite the formation of vast territorial empires under Mongol, Chinese, and Manchu rulers, distinctive Mongol, Chinese, and Tibetan traditions persisted, and these rulers acknowledged, invoked, and deployed them simultaneously as they sought to construct their legitimacy, pursue their imperial projects, and interact with other rulers. This book presents our findings based on this hypothesis.

Michael van Walt van Praag and Miek Boltjes initiated the project from which this book arises through the support of Kreddha, a conflict resolution organization that has been involved in the facilitation of intrastate peace processes in many parts of the world as well as in research on the causes of conflicts and obstacles to their resolution. The research that underpins the findings of this book was developed through a series of five international roundtables at which seventy-four historians, political scientists, anthropologists, Sinologists, Mongolicists, Tibetologists, and specialists on Central Asia from North America, Asia, and Europe discussed their most recent work based on a broad range of Asian sources. The first roundtable, held in April 2010 at the Institute of Asian Research of the University of British Columbia (UBC), examined political and spiritual relations among East and Southeast Asian rulers and polities from the fourteenth to the eighteenth century. Much of the discussion circled around the impact of tributary relations between Ming China and the polities surrounding it. The second roundtable, held in November 2010 at the Centre for Studies in Asian Cultures and Social Anthropology and the Institute for Iranian Studies of the Austrian Academy of Sciences (OAW), focused on the Mongol empire and its legacy across Inner and East Asia up until the eighteenth century. We asked participants to examine how power was established, maintained, and administered by the Mongol khans and to consider the significance and impact of spiritual and political bonds among Mongol, Tibetan, and Manchu leaders. The third roundtable, held in April 2011 at the Nalanda-Sriwijaya Centre of the Institute of Southeast Asian Studies at the National University of Singapore (NUS), looked at how interpolity relations in Inner, East, and Southeast Asia changed between the eighteenth and early twentieth centuries as a consequence of the transition from multiple Asian systems to the modern single system of relations prescribed by European norms of international law. The fourth roundtable was hosted by the Asia Institute at the University of California at Los Angeles (UCLA) in May 2012. Discussion at this roundtable focused on the role of Tibet and Tibetan hierarchs in the political and spiritual dimensions of relations among Asian leaders and polities within a greater Tibetan Buddhist world. The fifth roundtable, hosted by the School of Historical Studies at the Institute for Advanced Study (IAS) at Princeton in November 2012, addressed the nature of the Manchu Qing empire and its relations with polities within and beyond its reach. We are immensely grateful to those who participated in the roundtables: their collective knowledge and wisdom have assisted us enormously in seeing the direction in which we decided to go and the arguments we have needed to make. We are grateful in particular to Tsering Shakya (UBC), Florian Schwarz and the late Helmut Krasser (OAW), Tansen Sen and Geoffrey Wade (NUS), and Bin Wong (UCLA) for hosting us on these occasions and for contributing intellectual leadership. A special thanks is due to the IAS not only for hosting the fifth roundtable but also for its support of the project during Michael van Walt van Praag's tenure on the faculty of its School of Historical Studies. We are particularly grateful to Nicola Di Cosmo and his colleagues at the school for recognizing the project's value and supporting it. We also thank the Institute of Social Sciences at the University of California at Davis for hosting Michael during the final stages of the preparation of the manuscript.

The opening chapter of the book lays out the approach that we have developed to understand the principles and practices of sovereignty and of the conduct of relations among rulers and polities in Inner and East Asia. We define this vast region loosely as the zone of Eurasia that stretches north and east from the southern slopes of the Himalayas, so as to include the Himalayan states and exclude Islamic Central Asia. To speak of "Inner and East Asia" is to use a cumbersome and inelegant term that cobbles together leftovers from the geographical imaginaries of the so-called Great Game of the nineteenth century and the Cold War of the twentieth. Whenever for the sake of brevity and euphony we contract the term to "Asia" or use the adjective "Asian"—as in the book's title—we mean this to be understood as an explicit reference to Inner and East Asia, which does not include the zones conventionally referred to as South and West Asia.

Following a presentation of this new approach for conceptualizing Inner and East Asian historical polities and relations in chapter 1, we take the reader in turn to three distinct worlds from which principles of lawful rule and protocols of interpolity relations flowed, and each of which we regard as seminal in creating the world of Asian relations. To respect the layering of historical experience that has shaped the norms and practices of relations among rulers and polities in Inner and East Asia, we have arranged our inquiry as a sequence of chapters that broadly reflects our sense of the chronology of state formation in this large region, though each chapter is more an exploration of distinct traditions of rule and its legitimation, state formation, and systems of interpolity relations than it is a survey of a period. We begin in chapter 2 with the Mongol empire and the nature of its Chinggisid rule and administration, which had a lasting impact on state formation and governance in eastern Eurasia and beyond. In chapter 3, we proceed to the Chinese civilizational world at the time of the Ming dynasty, organized on Confucian principles of legitimacy, hierarchy, and order. In chapter 4, we turn to the Tibetan Buddhist world and its notions of spiritual supremacy and the role of worldly rulers in relation to it, which shaped both forms of governance and interpolity relations throughout the period of our inquiry. Chapter 5 then moves to the Qing empire. Its Manchu rulers dominated much of Inner and East Asia up until the turn of the twentieth century by drawing on the traditions of all three civilizational worlds in its modes of rule and interaction. These chapters are followed by a panoptic chapter, which considers the ascendancy within Inner and East Asia of what is regarded as the modern interstate system enunciated around certain European (Westphalian) norms in the nineteenth and early twentieth centuries. A concluding chapter points to the continued presence and impact on political behavior of some of the assumptions and principles at the heart of the three civilizational worlds and legal orders we explore in the book.

The compelling subject matter and purpose of this book demand a breadth of scholarship beyond the competence of any one author. The result accordingly is a book that is both authored and edited, yet not entirely either. We have woven contributions from sixteen specialists into our narrative, or stated differently, we have excerpted their work into our narrative in order to draw faithfully upon the excellent, specialized work that these scholars presented at the roundtables. The unconventionality of the multivocal, multiperspectival format we have adopted is, we believe, especially suited to the broad subject matter and argument of this book, predicated, as it must be, on such diverse fields of knowledge. Needless to say, the contributors are responsible only for the views they express in their sections, and not for the views expressed by the coauthors.

As coauthors and editors of this volume, we bring different perspectives to the task of constructing an extensive history of the cultures of political rulership and spiritual authority in Inner and East Asia and revealing its importance to today's theory and practice of international relations and conflict resolution. We come from different cultures, have had different training and life experience, have worked in different types of institutions, and are engaged in projects aligned to different ends. One of us is a Canadian historian of China who has specialized on the Ming dynasty and whose more recent work has taken on the challenge of situating China in a global context. Another is a European specialist in international law and a practitioner in the field of international relations and conflict resolution who has worked extensively in Asia and undertaken years of research on Inner Asian political history. The third is a Dutch mediator with an international relations background who has facilitated, and written about, peace processes in Asia, Africa, and the South Pacific. Rather than pull us in opposite directions, we found that our differences of background and experience were productive for this project, for each of us asked questions the others might not have considered, and each was willing to consider answers the others would not have proposed. What bound us together in this project are the concerns we hold in common: that there is great need to recognize the logic that drives every story that is told about the past of this part of the world, no matter how widely these stories diverge; that none of the tensions threatening international and domestic peace in Inner and East Asia can be resolved by suppressing some stories in favor of others; and that the past can be both a reservoir of conflict and a resource for its resolution, depending on the wisdom with which we choose to approach it.

We wish to acknowledge the considerable financial support that this project has received from the Triodos Foundation, the Thyssen Foundation, the Austrian Academy of Sciences, the Nalanda-Sriwijaya Centre, the Asia Institute at UCLA, the Institute for Advanced Study, Princeton, the Princeton Foundation for Peace and Learning, and Kreddha. Finally, and most important, a special thanks goes to all the scholars who participated in this extensive project. None of what we may have achieved would have been possible without their invaluable engagement.

CHAPTER ONE

THREE WORLDS; THREE BODIES OF INTERNATIONAL LAW

Once upon a time, the world was not as it is. The patterns of inclusion and exclusion we now take for granted are historical conventions. The principle of state sovereignty is the classic expression of those patterns, an expression that encourages us to believe that . . . those patterns are permanent.

R. B. J. WALKER, *Inside/Outside*

A discipline that is often overlooked in the study of international relations in Asia, yet intrinsically connected to it, is history. Specialists in contemporary international affairs are aware of the historical depth on which Asian states act, but few seek to engage with this rich past to explicate and understand the conduct of states today.[1] This nonengagement is reflected in the models on which many rely to explain how states interact, models derived from a different place of origin, western Europe to be precise, and a shallower past, going back no further than the seventeenth century, and more often no further than the twentieth. Of course, most of humanity has been neither European nor modern, so we offer this study to join those who seek to broaden the analysis of international relations by taking Asian historical experience into account. We do so by bringing to light the multiple international legal orders that predated the modern system of international relations and international law in Inner and East Asia, because understanding them is critical to comprehending not only historical relations in Asia but relations within and among states in that region today. It is this broader experience—in particular from Asia—that this book seeks to incorporate into the analysis of international relations.

Historians of Asia have for some time now observed that the reigning theoretical models of political, social, and economic theory, based narrowly on European experience, fall short of guiding us in developing an analysis of today's realities that pertain across much of Asia.[2] A number of scholars are already applying this insight from within the international relations field. We join these efforts from our own areas of specialization, so that the field might evolve to become more global in its foundations and, more important, to enable political leaders to draw from deeper understandings of Asian history when called upon to develop policies and make decisions affecting human welfare.

THE PAST IN ASIA'S PRESENT

History is a powerful medium to explain the world and our place in it. How the past is perceived and narrated profoundly informs the attitudes of ordinary people as well as the decisions of political leaders. Nowhere is the tenacity of historical perception more immediately apparent than in situations of conflict, both international conflicts and conflicts within existing states, especially identity-based ones. Here, perceptions of history animate the positions of parties, the claims they make, and the sense of entitlement and righteousness they feel in relation to those positions and claims. Some are prepared to go to war to enforce their claims. Yet the paradigms, concepts, and terminologies used to analyze and explain the past are mostly those of modern international relations and international law. This practice prevents us from appreciating past realities and events on their own merits and within their spatial and temporal contexts, which inevitably augments existing conflicts and hinders their resolution.

To cite an instance currently in the public eye, the People's Republic of China, Taiwan, and Vietnam assert competing claims of sovereignty over islands and expanses of the South China Sea using selective historical narratives, some of them going back centuries.[3] To argue their respective cases, they interpret events and behavior from earlier and very different contexts through the lens of sovereign rights as understood today. They are not the only ones to do so. Many parties to conflicts—states and nonstate actors alike—invoke twenty-first-century concepts of sovereignty, statehood, and territorial integrity and project them onto a very different past, in which those concepts and the paradigms to which they belong have no place. Doing so creates warped understandings of past relations and exacerbates tensions. Today in our single international legal system, sovereignty is exclusive, territorial, and all-encompassing. Observers today commonly associate sovereignty and statehood with exclusive territorial and jurisdictional rights and presume states to be equally sovereign actors. Such concepts obscure Asian historical realities before, and even during, the nineteenth century. Polities and their rulers in Asia were never presumed equal; indeed, relationships were typically unequal. Rulers exercised authority over other rulers who owed allegiance to them and possibly to other stronger rulers as well. "Sovereignty," when the term is applied in Asian history, was mostly divisible, layered, and relative, as were allegiance, loyalty, and subjection. So the package that comes with the modern concepts and language of sovereignty, statehood, legitimacy, and the like impedes real understanding of the past and often only serves to legitimize political agendas in the present.

This book is intended to draw attention to the existence of these problems and to encourage a more effective approach to understanding how Inner and East Asian polities have conducted their relations. Ours is far from the first call for a new approach to international relations theory and practice for reasons of history. The critical wing of international relations theorists has been here before us, as our opening citation from Robert Walker acknowledges.[4] To the extent that our approach is unique, it is because we are coming at the question not from within international relations theory, nor from a single national case, but from as wide a historical base in Asia as we can encompass.

The basic premise of Europeanist international relations theory is that states relate to each other as equal actors coexisting in a state of anarchy. According to this theory, every state is deemed formally equal to every other state, and each is regarded as engaging in relations with other states in pursuit of its interests without deferring or being subordinate to another power. States are territorially defined, and sovereignty is exclusive in relation to that territory and the state's subjects. This theory of state status and interstate relations is regarded as an adequate description of the modern world. It is loosely known as the Westphalian system or theory of international relations because it draws from principles enunciated in the Peace of Westphalia, a set of treaties negotiated in 1648 to bring an end to the Thirty Years' War. Because this moment in European history is considered to have been decisive in terms of the appearance of the modern state and its corresponding system of international relations—"the founding moment of an internationalized modernity," as Robert Walker tags it—theorists have been unable to conceive of what lay before and beyond Europe except in relation to or as opposed to it. As Walker has noted, this Westphalian orientation has "worked to efface more complex histories, and to legitimize a claim about the origins of modernity that resonates with so many other accounts of what must be excluded so as to affirm modern accounts of the achievements and costs of modern inclusions and exclusions."[5]

The modernist term "international relations" is inextricably bound up in a particular teleology attached to European concepts of the nation and the state. This teleology has been one of the obstacles to developing an alternative approach to the conduct of historical states and rulers. For this reason, we prefer the more precise term of "interpolity relations" instead, which we use from time to time so as not to predetermine the entities—"polities," not "nations"—whose relations we analyze. As a model to understand historical interpolity relations in Asia, modern international relations theory is hobbled by three shortcomings. The first is its inability to take account of the persistent, inescapable presence of hierarchy in the conduct of interstate relations or, indeed, to recognize hierarchy as a principle by which states may legitimately relate to each other. The second is its inability to theorize empire, a type of political formation that has erupted regularly throughout history and that has overridden many of the assumptions of international relations theory regarding the capacity and autonomy of polities to act in their own interests—and that may be causatively tied to the ideologies that Europeans subsequently invented to justify the creation of new colonial empires overseas. The third shortcoming is the misfit of the Westphalian model when applied to states that pre-existed the Peace of Westphalia in 1648, not just in Europe but all over Eurasia—in fact, when applied to most of history in most parts of the world. Looking for Westphalian ideals or their absence in the past induces misunderstanding of the forms and constitutions of historical states, dressing up such states as botched or inferior versions of the modern state—and, in so doing, confirming the rightness, indeed inevitability, of the modern state to the exclusion of all others.

Asian states today operate broadly within the mechanisms that have been shaped around Westphalian principles, not least by virtue of their participation in the United Nations system, which embodies and codifies them. We hold, however, that focus on these principles alone restricts the possibilities for analyzing the conduct of contemporary Asian states and impedes our understanding of historical Asian states and their relations. Our reservation arises not because of some indelible cultural difference between East and West but because the actual historical experience of state rule has varied so widely between the parts of western Europe that produced the Peace of Westphalia and the rest of Eurasia. We need to bear in mind that Westphalia was a solution to problems particular to conditions that prevailed in Hapsburg Europe at the end of the Thirty Years' War. The intention of its framers was that it be a "universal peace," though in practice it was entirely embedded in the political circumstances prevailing at that moment in the history of the Holy Roman Empire and extended no further. No one at the time pretended to prescribe the rules of state conduct beyond the states they represented at the negotiations at Westphalia. To state our case bluntly, the rules that emerged from those negotiations had no integral relationship to practices governing interpolity relations beyond Europe and indeed had limited salience for much of the conduct of actual interstate relations in Europe. Westphalia's salience for Asian states began only with the imposition of European diplomatic protocols

and international law in the wake of Europe's military and economic penetration of Asia during the age of empires in the eighteenth and nineteenth
centuries.[6]

The Westphalian model does not establish the only norms for a coherent
theory of international relations. Every historical regime based in China,
to offer the obvious example, conducted its relations according to a coherent system that was explicitly hierarchical and centered on that regime as
the system's apex and hegemon. To the extent that the study of international relations is the study of states relating horizontally to each other,
can there be a history of international relations of the Sinic world within
"international relations"? If there can, it cannot impose the expectation
that the same rules apply. Rather than relegate Inner and East Asia to a
condition of exceptionalism or dismiss the region as being of "merely"
historical interest, we want to take that archive of political and legal experience seriously: first, by broadening the definition of what constitutes
a state and, second, by elevating the rules through which states and rulers
have interacted to the status of law. We are not merely seeking to rescue
historical states from misrecognition and thereby open up a new path for
theorizing interstate relations in Asia. On a practical level our ambition is
to provide new insights for international relations practitioners to enable
them to appreciate and take account of the diversity of historical experience in Inner and East Asia and the role this experience continues to play
in decision-making in that region today.

BEYOND CHINA

We are not the first to plead for the inclusion of Asian historical experience
in our analyses: John Fairbank was an eloquent proponent of this inclusion half a century ago. Fairbank, the impresario of China studies in North
America through the third quarter of the twentieth century, published *The
Chinese World Order: Traditional China's Foreign Relations* in 1968.[7] For this
ambitious volume, which students of Chinese foreign relations still read,
Fairbank solicited essays on aspects of the history of China's foreign relations from thirteen of the finest scholars of his and the next generation. The
opening paragraph of his introduction makes explicit to readers that the
project worked from the concept of the tribute system, an interpretation
he absorbed from his colleagues in the Chinese scholarly world, which was
this: that by virtue of its size and power, China imposed a system of tribute submission on other states. This system was developed from practices
originally imposed some two millennia ago to manage regional subordination within an expanding Chinese state, but it came to provide a mecha-

nism for organizing international relations as a hierarchy of which the emperor of China occupied the apex. This hierarchy constituted a world order extending across a considerable part of Asia, reaching its height during the Qing dynasty and collapsing under the pressure of the new world order that the European powers imposed through the course of the nineteenth and early twentieth centuries.

To his credit, Fairbank regarded his approach as offering "a preliminary framework," to use the title of the introduction to his book, and nothing more. The tribute system was taken as a starting point for this enterprise, but this was a concept, as he notes in his opening paragraph, burdened with "hoary stereotypes." The intention of his team of colleagues was to scrutinize the system "both in theory and in practice, from without as well as from within." The tribute system gave them a place to begin, but this paradigm did not necessarily provide a complete model for understanding how China has related to the world without. Although some critics invoked the tribute system to disparage China's foreign policies at the turns of the twentieth and twenty-first centuries, returning to that history "opens the door a bit further on a system that handled the interstate relations of a large part of mankind throughout most of recorded history," according to Fairbank. He did not have his eyes trained solely on the past, however, but went on to propose that the "political experience" of managing relations through this system "even has some indeterminate relevance to the world's China problem of today." He declined to sketch out the implications of Qing foreign policy for the People's Republic, though as China had been effectively closed to all but the socialist world for two decades at the time he was writing, it was clear that something needed to be explained, and that perhaps the tribute system had within it the seeds of that explanation.

It was not our purpose when we set out on this project either to perpetuate Fairbank's approach or to overturn it. But through the course of our inquiry, we became increasingly struck by resemblances in intention, if less in program, between this book and *The Chinese World Order*. Fairbank's desire to incorporate Asia's experience into the history of how some states have handled their relations with each other is not unlike our concern to develop an Asian-based analysis of interpolity relations that might enlarge current approaches to international relations, at least in Asia. His sense that his interpretation was preliminary is a caution we acknowledge as suitable also for this volume. Significantly, we share with him the sense that what we have found may be relevant to understanding the tensions between China and much of the region today. We live, as did he, in troubled times and would not likely have taken up the questions this project raises were the world otherwise; but then perhaps all times are troubled.[8]

Having conceded that common ground of concern, we suggest that this book departs from the Fairbankian model in several significant ways, of which two deserve immediate notice. The first regards Fairbank's focus on China as what he called the "natural center" of the East Asian world. The second regards his focus on the study of Chinese-language sources on the Qing dynasty, when much of this region was under the sway of the Manchus.

China is not an unreasonable place from which to launch an inquiry into the relations among rulers and states in that region, given its size and role. Although increasingly there are demurrals from this point of departure, centering the analysis of interpolity relations in East and also Inner Asia on China continues to shape much of the scholarship.[9] But however large China must loom in any such project, including ours, it is necessary to bear in mind that it has been, and is, one polity among many. China has not been the only, or even the largest, player shaping interstate relations in this region of Asia. To grant it too much centrality is to assign the other players reactive positions when they have in fact taken the lead much of the time.

Another limit on Fairbank's vision of the world order of East and Inner Asia is that he derived it from his study of the Qing dynasty on the basis of Chinese-language sources. Working from that documentary base encouraged scholars of his generation to conceive of Inner and East Asia as constituting a unified "Chinese world order." It was not unreasonable at the time to attempt to identify what distinguished that part of the world in terms of a China-based totality, yet the illusion of a unity led scholars to conflate political and cultural categories, with the unintended effect of flattening differences across cultural traditions and setting aside political and other distinctions that may have had much greater influence on the making of the order that formed under Manchu dominance.

In this volume we adopt a different approach, one that originates from a quest to understand the diverse perceptions of an often-shared historical past held today by peoples and leaders of Inner and East Asia. These perceptions, which are reflected in national sentiments and official national narratives as well as in scholarship in and beyond the region, inform and influence political decision-making, particularly in situations of tension and conflict. To understand the diversity of perceptions and their origins, we asked what a broader array of sources—Mongolian, Tibetan, Manchu, Chinese, Vietnamese, and Persian—might tell us about polities and the conduct of relations among them from the thirteenth century to the early twentieth. In the course of doing so, the existence and critical roles of three major centers of civilizational and legal authority rather than just the one from which Fairbank and others have worked imposed themselves on us. Each of these three centers was based in a different environmental and political ecology, each projected a different model of rulership and statehood, and each anchored a distinctive system of legitimation of rule, political governance, and state administration, as well as protocols for conducting relations with other polities. Each was the center of a world of peoples, rulers, and polities that shared a common understanding of the features that were felt to define it. Each of the three influenced and overlapped with the other two and in numerous ways was shaped by their coexistence, yet each managed in the past millennium to remain distinctive as a source of legitimacy and in part to define its distinction in terms of not being either of the other two. For narrative convenience we refer to these three centers as Chinese, Mongol, and Tibetan Buddhist.[10] If there was a "world order" that spanned the Asian continent from the Pamirs to Pusan, it was constituted not from one center alone but from three.

Once we move into the Qing dynasty, the examination of Manchu, Mongol, and Tibetan sources reveals that, even as Manchu imperialism absorbed polities into the body of the Qing state and exercised varying degrees of authority and influence over others, the distinctness of Inner Asian polities and their governance was mostly maintained. And so were their worldviews and corresponding political and diplomatic protocols, which the Qing court adopted as its own to form a world order characterized by a continuing political, cultural, religious, and legal diversity. The Manchus were not original in doing so. Inner Asian rulers who, before the Qing, centered their states in China employed the same conceptual sleight of hand to obtain legitimacy in the Sinic, Mongol, and Tibetan Buddhist worlds. Toward the Chinese and others in the Sinic world, the Manchus successfully invoked the imperial concept of "all-under-Heaven" to secure for their political project legible foundations within Chinese culture. It was this trend to which Fairbank drew attention, attributing the geographical enlargement of the "Chinese" state to a tendency "for exterior vassals of one period to become interior vassals of a later period," resulting in a unified world order organized not "by a division of territories among sovereigns of equal status but rather by the subordination of all local authorities to the central and awe-inspiring power of the emperor." Although Fairbank was aware that "the Chinese world order was a unified concept only at the Chinese end and only on the normative level, as an ideal pattern," he allowed the Manchu empire to fill the picture of what he sought to describe—particularly the normative picture. This he did in a way that ignored, perhaps even effaced, the equally significant Inner Asian faces of the empire and their corresponding world orders.

Our approach to the Qing state is to recognize it as a highly complex Manchu polity that exerted varying levels of authority over other polities, some of which it regarded as within its boundaries, some without. Its repertoire for conducting its relations with these polities varied. With some polities, the Manchu rulers conducted "Chinese" modes of tributary relations; with others, they asserted authority through Chinggisid norms (so called for having been derived from the traditions and bloodline of Chinggis [Genghis] Khan); and with yet others they adopted modes of communication, legitimation, and relation from the Tibetan Buddhist world. What mattered to the Manchus was that they obtain support for and compliance with what they perceived to be the interests of their empire, and they wielded a broad variety of means to bring this about.

As the story we tell is dense with people and events, and complex in the relationships of its parts, allow us to begin by focusing on one moment that reveals some telling features of the workings of interpolity relations and international law at one site within the western edge of the Mongol empire in the first of the centuries covered in this book.

MARCO POLO AND THE PROTECTION OF EMISSARIES

The moment is recorded in Marco Polo's account of his adventures in the Mongol empire between 1271 and 1295.[11] In the prologue, Polo casts forward to the return voyage he made with his father and uncle back to Europe after seventeen years in the service of Khubilai Khan. They traveled as members of an official delegation from Khubilai to his great-nephew Arghun, ruler of the Il-khanate in Persia. The Il-khanate was one of the four polities into which the empire of Chinggis Khan was disaggregated after the ascension of his grandson Khubilai to the position of Great Khan in the 1260s. Arghun was the fourth Il-khan and, like his great-uncle Khubilai, shared descent from Chinggis Khan, without which he could never have become a legitimate khan in this empire. Arghun wished to take a wife from within the Mongol aristocracy and sent envoys to the imperial capital, Daidu (now Beijing), asking the Great Khan to send a Mongol bride. Khubilai selected seventeen-year-old Kökečin for this duty and sent her by sea, attaching the Polos to her retinue.

When the envoys arrived in Tabriz in 1293, they discovered that Arghun had died. The Il-khanate was in the hands of his brother Gaykhatu, who had declared himself the fifth Il-khan. Messengers were sent back to Khubilai for instructions. Perhaps concerned that the succession had been disorderly, the Great Khan directed that Kökečin be given not to the new

Il-khan but to Arghun's twenty-year-old son Ghazan. Within two years, Gaykhatu was garroted by his own military commander, and Ghazan became the seventh Il-khan by defeating the man who replaced Gaykhatu. Ghazan subsequently took the name of Mahmud and oversaw Persia's conversion from Buddhism to Islam, but that takes us past the Polos' story and beyond the scope of this inquiry.

What interests us here is not the internecine struggle among the claimants to the Il-khanate throne. It is the remark with which Marco Polo ends his account of the mission. He tells us that when the Polos left Gaykhatu's court for Europe, the Il-khan gave them each a golden tablet three inches thick declaring them to be under his protection until they left his realm. Impressive as those tablets may have been, far more useful, in Polo's entirely practical view, was the bodyguard of two hundred horsemen that Gaykhatu assigned "to escort them and ensure their safe passage from one district to another." This was "a necessary precaution" because, Polo notes, Gaykhatu "was not a lawful ruler and the inhabitants might have molested them, as they would not have had they been subject to a lord to whom they owed allegiance."[12]

This segment of Marco Polo's account enunciates four basic legal principles that governed relations between states in Asia at that time. The first is that the legitimacy of rulers is derived in accordance with the principles of lawfulness governing the particular civilizational world to which the ruler belongs, in this case the Chinggisid Mongol world. Wielding power without such legitimacy brings into question the allegiance and obligations of subjects and opens the door to conduct deemed unlawful according to that world's norms, rules, and protocols of interstate behavior.

The second principle operates under the canopy of the first but is of narrower scope. It is that emissaries of a sovereign are entitled to protection when they are within the jurisdiction of another sovereign.[13] The capacity of the second sovereign to provide protection may in practice depend on the actual resources he makes available, but the principle is attested to the extent that Polo is conscious that it may fail under the particular ruler he is visiting because of his illegitimacy.

Marco Polo's story shows that relationships between states were mediated by relationships between sovereigns. This principle was not unique to the Mongol world, although it was particularly pronounced in it, since the Chinggisid empire was a strictly family enterprise built vertically on direct descent from Chinggis Khan and horizontally on intermarriage within the Mongol aristocracy. This is a third principle of the international order of the time.

A fourth principle, linked to the third, is that the subjects that Ching-gisid law brings into being are hierarchically ordered. It is possible for kinship relationships to mediate interpolity relationships because states, like families, operate within hierarchies. International relations in this world—to the extent that we wish to apply this concept to the thirteenth century—were hierarchical. Khubilai was acknowledged as the Great Khan of the entire Mongol empire; Arghun, as the khan of one part of that empire. As we shall note in the next chapter, the Il-khanate had become, in practice, autonomous as a political realm from the rest of the empire, evidenced by the fact that successions there were determined independently of the wishes of the Great Khan. Though it was still the rule that the Great Khan had the rightful authority to appoint successors, enforcing that rule became increasingly problematic as polities diverged. Even so, in the particular matter that concerned him, Arghun chose to turn to Khubilai to determine his marriage partner, a request that Khubilai as Great Khan could not refuse and still maintain his position at the apex of the empire. The obligation was not reciprocal, for the Great Khan would never have asked the Il-khan for a marriage partner. For his part, so long as the Il-khan conceived of himself as being within the hierarchy of Mongol khans, he would not have turned to anyone else for a wife. The relationship between the two sovereigns was based on a mutually recognized difference of position, the sovereignty of the first (Khubilai) exceeding and overlapping the sovereignty of the second (Arghun). Each was legitimate within his jurisdiction and understood the other to be so within his.

What would Marco Polo have made of these principles? Did he recognize the conduct of the rulers among whom he shuttled on these matters as lawful, in the sense of being bound by a set of norms that all rulers would have accepted and to which there was general compliance beyond? Did he regard what he encountered as peculiarly Asian? He does not say so, but he does the next best thing: he reports that conduct without registering surprise or expressing demurral. His tone indicates that this was simply how relations between states in the Mongol world were managed. It was how the world as he knew it in the 1290s worked. Traversing the Eurasian continent from Venice to Khubilai's court in Daidu, he ran into strange customs to absorb, odd beliefs to accommodate, and difficult people to deal with; but the rules by which Asian sovereigns ruled, and the protocols by which they managed their relations with other sovereigns, did not fall outside the expectations of someone for whom the Mediterranean civilizational world was the norm.

INTERNATIONAL LAW BEFORE
"INTERNATIONAL LAW"

Is "law" relevant for theorizing the rules by which the embassy bearing Kökečin to Arghun was conducted? We propose that it is and accordingly approach the rules and protocols that governed relations among rulers and polities in historical Inner and East Asia since Chinggis Khan, and the world orders of which they were a part, as systems of law. The notion of law—"the idea that order is necessary and chaos inimical to a just and stable existence"—has played a central role in all human societies.[14] If we define law as "a series of rules regulating behavior, and reflecting, to some extent, the ideas and preoccupations of the society within which it functions," as the eminent international jurist Malcolm Shaw does, we find it in operation at different levels of society and at different times and places in world history.[15] At the interstate or interpolity level, the law in operation mostly reflects the ideas and preoccupations—or the ideologies and projects—of the rulers and elites of the dominant polities in distinct civilizational worlds.

Today we have a single system of international law based on a more or less universally agreed notion of statehood defined by the concept of an exclusive territorial sovereignty and the formal equality of states. But before this "modern" international law was made universally applicable, in large part through its imposition by European imperial powers in the nineteenth century, there existed multiple systems of international law corresponding to different interpolity orders in various regions of the world. Communities in these regions possessed their own understandings of the known world and of the place, status, and role of rulers, subjects, and polities within it. These understandings, and the corresponding values, rules, and protocols that regulated the behavior of rulers and polities toward one another and that emanated from their respective centers of civilizational authority, can, in our view, be considered systems of international law. They were not universal in the sense that all communities in the world recognized or adhered to them, for no civilizational center was in a position to impose its laws globally. But they were often universalistic in their claims. Rules regulating interpolity behavior need not be universal in their application for them to be considered as systems of international law. After all, European "international law," or "law of nations" as it has also been called, though universal in its philosophical claims, was for the longest time accepted and adhered to only by European rulers and their polities.

In this book we shall discover rulers relating to each other hierarchically in situations in which sovereignties overlapped and full autonomy was not always possible. The existence of such situations does not imply that their polities were absorbed into others, somehow dissolved underneath them, nor does it imply that the relations their polities had with others lacked legal foundation, even legal guarantees. Quite the contrary: interpolity relations conformed to the norms and realities of those places and those times, just as the relations among states in our time conform to our international norms and realities.

Included in the concept of law is the set of rules that determines the legitimacy of rulers and their regimes in relation to their subjects and to each other: the set of rules used to render the subjects of a given polity or ruler as legal subjects and, at the interpolity level, the set of rules by which rulers recognize each other as rulers. The dependence on what was lawful—or legitimate, in the language we tend to use in this study—within hierarchical relationships did not mean that the obligations between "legal" superiors and "legal" inferiors were always upheld. Khubilai had to stave off military challenges from kinsmen who sought to usurp his power. So long as his troops prevailed in battle, as they always did, he could reassert the legality of his rule by condemning each of them as "a traitor who broke faith with his liege lord" and punishing them accordingly, and to his mind legally, for the injury their rebellions did to his authority.[16] Khubilai was often under threat. Besides the Mongol aristocrats who dreamed of seizing the khanate, Chinese had a quite separate urge to rebel against their overlord. Khubilai Khan claimed Chinese as his lawful subjects when he proclaimed the Yuan dynasty, but from the Chinese perspective—which held that a ruler was legitimate to the extent that he received a mandate from Heaven to rule—his claim was not sufficient to establish the lawfulness of the power he wished to exercise over China. The Great Khan had merely conquered China by force, and conquest did not automatically endow legitimacy. Khubilai of course understood this and addressed it by stationing Mongol armies outside all large Chinese cities to forestall armed insurrection.[17] The willingness of many to offend against the legal order to which they were subject does not detract from the proposition we offer here: that wherever Marco Polo traveled under the aegis of the Great Khan, he found himself within a legal universe that guided the conduct of rulers, subjects, and polities in ways that made sense to him as they did to others within it.

What was understood as law at the time of Khubilai Khan is not necessarily what we think of when we use the word "law" in our twenty-first-century context. Terms such as "international law" and "international relations" as we use them today derive from Westphalian assumptions, banishing alternative conceptualizations in order to sustain the coherence of the modernist paradigm.[18] We will make use of these concepts when examining norms and practices that prevailed in Inner and East Asia before the nineteenth or twentieth century, but as much as possible we will fill them with *their* content rather than ours. A more traditional approach might insist on excluding the use of either term for conceptualizing the thirteenth-century world, on the grounds that they denote modes of interstate activity defined by the modern treaty-based context within which we expect to find international law. This restriction may satisfy standards of internal coherence within international relations as a modern academic discipline or even as a field of contemporary legal practice, but we find it of no salience for our project, which is to understand how rulers and states interacted prior to the installation of the modern international regime. Their polities do not have to look like members of the United Nations, interacting with each other anarchically within a regime of formal equality, in order to be deemed to have the capacity to act like states, interact with other states, and seek conformity to legal norms that require certain prior conditions of state legitimacy to be upheld.[19]

We are not the first to theorize that a legal order grounded in principles different from those of modern international law governed relations among Asian polities. In their 1999 edited volume, *Religion and International Law*, Mark Janis and Carolyn Evans explore how religions throughout the world, including ancient Hindu, Judaic, and Islamic thought, nourished principles of international law. Similarly, with respect to East Asia, comparative legal historian Teemu Ruskola speaks of "an East Asian law of nations, roughly similar to the European tradition of *ius gentium*," "the law of nations." He observes that "both traditions claimed universality, though each embodied a particular set of imperial norms—Roman and Chinese, respectively."[20]

Pursuing this line of approach is not just a tactical move for us. Accepting a more broadly conceptualized law of nations entails understanding that intercourse between all polities is rule sensitive and therefore predictable on that basis, and that this is not just valid for relations among polities operating under Westphalian rules of interstate conduct. Rather than propose a unified law of nations for all of Inner and East Asia that might constitute "a legally ordered inter-state system which on its own merits persisted over a long period of time alongside the mere use of force," to quote the standard set of features given by a leading historian of international law of the last century, Wolfgang Preiser,[21] we identify three legally ordered systems of norms, protocols, obligations, and expectations that correspond to three distinct worlds and emanated from their respective centers of civilizational authority: the Mongol Chinggisid world, the Sinic world, and the Tibetan Buddhist world. Three bodies of international law: three laws of nations. Each contained its own rules for determining the legitimacy of rulers and extending recognition to them and their polities. Each consisted of a body of norms and conventions that were understood to guide the conduct of relations with others and to fashion the interpretation of those relations in line with its respective worldview. Not only did rulers and elites acknowledge their counterparts outside their own world as presumptively legitimate according to the norms applicable in the relevant foreign systems, but they also extended recognition to rulers with whom they interacted, frequently projecting their own norms across system boundaries and endowing these foreign rulers with a legitimacy that made sense in the recognizers' system.[22] This book thus traces not just how these discrete international legal systems operated but how they intersected and coexisted as rulers used their corresponding systems of international law to advance their own objectives.

SOVEREIGNTY IN ASIA BEFORE THE MODERN ERA

The concept of sovereignty in today's system of international law is not transferable to earlier periods and different contexts. Although the word "sovereignty" gets used differently in international and in domestic law contexts, and in political science and sociology, these usages largely agree in tying the concept to a defined territory and associate it with the independence of states, considering it the right of a state to exercise authority over its territory and population without external interference. Some authors consider sovereignty to be "a political entity's externally recognized right to exercise final authority over its affairs."[23] Others define sovereignty in terms of power, as Antonio Cassese does when he identifies sovereignty as "the power to wield authority over all the individuals living in the territory."[24] These notions of sovereignty reflect the Westphalian international order and modern international law, which define states territorially and as formally equal. The concepts of exclusive territorial sovereignty and "sovereign equality," which are, as we pointed out earlier, central to the modern international order and are core principles of modern international law, have no place in historical Asia—and none, for that matter, in pre-Westphalian Europe either. Applying them to Asia's past is fundamentally misleading.[25]

Before the advent of modern international law, sovereignty—defined simply as *the lawful authority of a ruler to wield power over his subjects*—was tied to the person of the ruler and not to a specific territory. Sovereignty was not necessarily exclusive and did not always imply that there was no

greater authority than the sovereign prince, khan, king, sultan, or hierarch. Unlike in the world of equally sovereign states, sovereignty in historical Eurasia was usually layered or shared and rarely supreme. It most
often derived from material power that was legitimized by a variety of
ideologies, usually sacred in reference, placing its source in higher divine
spheres—be it the sky, heaven, god, or enlightened beings—and by recognition by other rulers. This is how we use the concept of sovereignty in
most of this book. Only in the last two chapters, where we discuss the transition to modern international law in Asia, do we also use "sovereignty"
with the meanings attributed to it by the modern legal system.

The challenge for historians, political scientists, and practitioners alike
is to utilize a concept of sovereignty that best fits the historical reality they
examine. In Inner and East Asia, polities that displayed state-like qualities regularly experienced sovereignty as a condition of ruling that was
constrained by, submissive to, or overlapped with a higher authority with
which those polities regularly had to deal but into which they did not disappear. Our approach in this book is, therefore, not to work downward
from standards that today's international law sets for a very different time,
but to work upward from the record of how rulers in Inner and East Asia
claimed sovereignty and conducted relations with other rulers according
to one or more sets of protocols and expectations of lawful behavior. In
that world, sovereignty was always vulnerable to challenge from above
and below, which is why a strong, widely recognized claim to legitimacy
was essential and a sacred mandate to rule fundamental. A ruler was lawful to the extent that his rulership conformed to established expectations
of who could be a ruler and what a ruler had to do. The legitimacy of a ruler
was also exposed in relation to his dealings with other rulers.

The further idea that the lawfulness of subjects depended on the legitimacy of their ruler, a condition that concerned Marco Polo when he worried about what Gaykhatu's dissatisfied subjects might do to the embassy
he was part of, was about as universal as any principle could be in the thirteenth century, yet this understanding is foreign to us in the twenty-first.
We no longer define our legal obligations in terms of personal allegiance.
We do not establish our personal state of lawfulness by declaring fealty to
a ruler, nor would we tolerate a legal regime in which laws are applicable
only to the extent that they impose or confirm relationships of overlordship
and subjugation. Detached from the person of the sovereign, our notion
of sovereignty has been reattached to an abstract concept of the state that
imposes its legal regime on citizens without a differentiation of status. We
are required to be loyal to the state through treason laws, but we are not
bound in loyalty to a particular ruler. Not so in Khubilai's day—or for that

matter in the time of the Great Fifth Dalai Lama (1617–1682), the Qianlong emperor (1711–1799), or even the last Manchu emperor, Puyi (1906–1967), and his contemporary, the Thirteenth Dalai Lama (1876–1933). Leaders, subjects, and even nonsubjects on a realm's frontier were bound to their rulers in particularized ways. Sovereignty was neither abstract nor universal: it happened in particular places and under particular circumstances. Stated differently, whereas the primary legal actors of modern international law (somewhat confusingly also called "subjects" of international law) are abstract entities, that is, "states" defined as equal and independent of one another, the actors in the international legal orders we deal with in this book are the rulers who wielded authority over their subjects and who were neither equal nor independent.

We focus on how authority was constituted as legitimate, sovereign, and therefore law-giving and also on how it was negotiated not just with subjects but with other rulers. We need therefore to consider the form of the state within which this sovereignty was declared and in relation to which laws of nations came into being. The political landscape of Inner and East Asia has been the site of states for at least three millennia, but a major shift occurred in 1206, which is why we have chosen this moment as the point of departure for this study. That was the year in which Chinggis Khan took the title of Great Khan (*khagan*, also *qaghan, qa'an*) and declared the founding of what the Mongols would come to call the Mongol Great State. Chinggis's subsequent campaign to bring the known world under his rule remade the political space of Eurasia; it also remade the very idea of rulership as an assertion of authority that could potentially claim universal sovereignty. Other imperial traditions, notably China's, had declared a right to rule universally on the basis of the idea that the ruler enjoyed Heaven's mandate to rule "all-under-Heaven" (*tianxia*). Buddhist monarchs had claimed universal rule as *chakravartins* on the basis of enlightened wisdom. But the new Great Khan, who regarded himself as having been singularly blessed by what the Mongols called the Blue Sky Above, interpreted the idea of universal rule literally and imposed it on an unsuspecting world. Thus, having achieved mastery over his own and other surrounding peoples, he sent his armies in all directions to bring all under his command.

The Great State that Chinggis Khan ruled became a dominant political form of this phase of Inner and East Asian history and was adopted by Chinese, Oirat (western Mongol), and Manchu rulers in naming, if not crafting, their subsequent imperial projects. It corresponds most closely to the European concept of "empire" and, like that concept, has proven as difficult to define as "nation" or "state." We use the word in its broadest sense to mean a large, hierarchical polity with an expansionist history, particularly in its Inner and East Asian form, the Great State. The Great State was itself a state under the supreme sovereignty of the Great Khan, but it was also a form of dominion in which other sovereigns could coexist with him as subordinate rulers. The Chinggisid legal order, as it is called, relied on the kinship of subordinate rulers and tolerated quasi-autonomous jurisdictions within its outer bounds. The Mongol Great State proved unprecedentedly expansive, eventually extending over more of Eurasia than any political entity had ever done or indeed would ever do again.[26]

The histories written of Inner and East Asia have tended to focus on the dominant empires of the Mongols, the Chinese (the Ming), and the Manchus (the Qing). Often these Great States are placed under the headings of "Chinese dynasties," and much of Asia is then subsumed under the dynastic timeline that results. Although this can be viewed as simply a convenient periodization tool, it generates a perspective on Inner and East Asia that privileges one view based on the presumed unvarying centrality of the Chinese civilizational world. That view proposes the existence of one constant principal agent—the Chinese state, however vulnerable to dynastic change—which it places center stage, relegating other polities to the periphery. The political ramifications of this paradigm have been felt throughout Inner and East Asia and beyond to this day and animate tensions between the PRC and numerous countries and peoples of the region. Working with the three civilizational centers as we do in this book, on the other hand, reveals the coexistence of different centers of power, authority, legitimacy, and even international law. This approach recognizes the distinctness of the Great States and the civilizational worlds from which they emerged as well as the agency of peoples, polities, and sovereigns other than those of these Great States. It moreover helps to explain the diversity of credible perceptions of history by recognizing that they are the products of distinct worldviews that continue to be of critical importance to the shaping of Inner and East Asia.

All three centers of civilizational authority produced orders of politics and ideas that governed their own worlds and also became influential with the other two. These orders expressed the norms understood to prevail in eliciting the loyalty of subjects and the recognition of other rulers. The first was the body of laws and rituals that guided right conduct within the realm of the sovereign, and the second was the system of what we are calling international law, by which a ruler sought to organize and maintain relations with other rulers. This system varied from one center to another in accordance with the theology that authorized the sovereign's claims and invoked the sanctions that would follow if those claims were not respected, although these could repeat and overlap with each other. These worlds remained distinct, and their interstate rules of conduct persisted even after the coming of the Qing empire. Indeed, the Manchus mobilized all three traditions to establish their predominance. Europeans approaching the Qing state from the water encountered what they perceived to be an imperial state operating by rules, different from their own, that they identified as "Chinese." This was of course true of the way the Manchus ruled their Chinese subjects. The Europeans were unaware of the other worlds in which the Qing also operated, on the basis of very different sets of rules, and simply called the Qing empire "China." Only toward the end of the nineteenth century did some of the polities of Inner and East Asia shed the principles of their centuries-old international legal orders as they found themselves obliged to enter into the new "universal" order regulated by its single international law.

THE STRAITJACKET OF THE MODERN LAW OF NATIONS

The aggressive incursion of European state power into Asia in the nineteenth century brought a different international legal order, producing tensions that had not existed before. Finding their laws of nations ignored or scorned and then supplanted by a different set of norms emanating from Europe, Asian rulers struggled to reinvent their states to conform, to some degree at least, with these unfamiliar principles of statehood, territorial sovereignty, and interstate relations in order to assert themselves in the new order. Their resulting actions created not only tensions within states but also conflict between them, as demands and expectations no longer followed well-trodden paths. The multiplicity of international legal systems had required a degree of respect and accommodation for differences in worldviews and for the consequences attached to the actions of rulers and the nature of relations between their *polities*. The new system was a straitjacket in which the preexisting diversity of systems had no place and the accommodation to which Asian polities had been accustomed was absent. As state sovereignty came to be defined as an exclusive right in relation to territories delimited by precise geographic borders, borderlands that had been ruled autonomously or whose local rulers owed allegiance to more than one sovereign now became objects of contested sovereignty claims and at times armed conflict.

An early feature of the introduction of the European system was the signing of treaties, whether for trade or for peace.[27] This constituted another source of tension. What the signing of treaties did, before the Westphalian system actually replaced the Asian systems we present in this book,[28] was to produce first Qing "China" and later Korea and Vietnam and eventually Tibet and Mongolia as diplomatic subjects purportedly acting in their own interests in partnership with the European states with which they entered into agreements. As regards the Qing Great State, it was, interestingly, conceptualized by the Europeans, not as an imperial Manchu suzerain, but as a modern-seeming state they called China. But what looked from a distance like entry into the European "family of nations" was something else entirely. Neither the Qing court nor its Chinese officials were fully cognizant of the contradictions between the complex and hierarchical interpolity order in which that court occupied the most elevated place and the new system of international law that posited treaties as agreements between formally equal partners. Moreover, in practice, only European nation-based empires such as the British, Dutch, Portuguese, Spanish, Russian, and French really counted in this mono-legal order. Most other states were determined by them to fall short of the criteria required to be subjects of their law of nations. This justified the annexation and colonization of Asian polities and their subjugation to the authority of European empires. It similarly justified their exploitation through self-serving treaties that often included extraterritorial rights and jurisdiction. In addition, most Asian rulers were introduced to the European protocol of treaty making at gunpoint, as happened to the Qing at the conclusion of the Opium Wars in 1842 and 1860 and to the Dalai Lama's court following the British invasion of Tibet in 1904.

Not surprisingly, then, the new international system did not persuade most Asian states on the strengths of its merits. Most experienced the coming of the European system, not as the arrival of the equality of states it purported to be, but as the imposition of colonial rule. Using the gunboat diplomacy of free trade and treaties that were later deemed, and repudiated by some, as "unequal," European states forced most Asian rulers to surrender a measure of their sovereignty, at the same time withholding the rights and privileges of the new form of state sovereignty the Westphalian system granted to European states.[29]

Asian rulers strove, sometimes successfully but often not, to respond to the challenges to their sovereignty—and by extension to that of their states—by attempting to refashion their polities along the lines of the new state/diplomatic model presented to them. These challenges precipitated political crises that spawned reform movements across Asia, from the Meiji Restoration in Japan in 1868 to the Hundred Days' Reform under the Qing in 1898. The upstart leaders of these movements set their sights on strengthening their polities on national lines, even at the cost of abandoning civilizational norms that had stood the test of time. The arrival of aggressive foreign powers altered the Asian elites' agenda, for only by meeting foreign expectations could they demonstrate that unequal treaties were no longer needed to protect foreign interests, which was the reason they were imposed in the first place. In the struggle to regain the sovereignty that had been taken from them, the older dynastic regimes collapsed and were replaced by constitutional monarchies and republics, forms that were judged acceptable to the new international "family of nations." In this harsh context, the Qing state found its entry into the family of nations significantly delayed compared with Japan.[30] As political leaders at the end of the Qing discovered, turnover in political forms did not necessarily lead to cancellation of the unequal treaties. Abrogating such treaties, which is to say, removing the limitations that these formal agreements imposed on state sovereignty, was in most cases not feasible until World War II weakened most European powers' capacity to perpetuate colonial control beyond Europe.

The experiences of Inner and East Asian states were far from uniform, and threats to sovereignty came as much from one another as from the European powers. Korea asserted its independence only to find itself subject to expanding Japanese imperial authority. Japan claimed a place for itself in the modern interstate system by becoming an imperial power to be reckoned with at the expense of other Asian polities such as Ryukyu, Taiwan, and Korea. Sikkim and Bhutan came under British imperial authority as protectorates of its Indian empire. Dai Viet, renamed Annam, succumbed to French colonialism, and the Qing Great State was erased by Chinese nationalists. As that empire dissolved in 1911–1912, Chinese, Mongolians, and Tibetans took steps to assert themselves as modern nation-states on the European model, invoking some of the boundaries in use at the time or in earlier historical periods. The nationalistic Chinese republic was eager to claim its place in the new international order but unable to mobilize the economic, political, or military power to do so. It claimed Tibet and Mongolia as part of its state territory on the theory that its new state inherited Manchu dependencies but was unable to exercise any measure of authority in or over either state. Both Inner Asian states, for their part, rejected China's contention, arguing that whatever the nature of their relations may have been with the Manchu court and its Qing state, these ended with the demise of both.[31] In the new order there could be no allowance for multiple constructs and interpretations, and there was little room for ambiguity. So claims were absolute, even if in practice they could not always be made to stick on the ground where demonstrable effective control was necessary to make good a claim. In the contests for control, conflicts ensued, borders were redrawn, and states were seized and absorbed.

The transition to the new international order was thus tumultuous and difficult to manage, with no outcomes assured. Some rulers and regimes, most notably Tokugawa Japan and the Qing, were toppled by lesser elites who took advantage of weakness at the center. These lesser elites reorganized the state by adopting forms imitating European models and writing constitutions that invested sovereignty not in the actual sovereign but in the abstract collectivity of the "people" or the "state." The great challenge facing the men who gambled on these newly constituted polities was how to assert the legitimacy of the new forms. If the bid for sovereign authority is the expectation of being obeyed, that authority has to be believed. This is never an easy task when people are asked to change what they believe the state is and why they should accept a new form of rulership; and it is even harder when states are conquered by others. Political transitions and contested territorial expansions invariably involve legitimacy deficits, whether on the part of the departing regime or on the part of the regime that replaces it, which may be why most new polities end up repeating the legitimacy appeals of previous regimes to create a comforting illusion of continuity.

As we know from today's political geography, at the end of World War II Japan was pushed out of the mainland. Korea, though becoming formally independent, was effectively partitioned. Mongols ended up divided, with so-called Inner Mongolia becoming a part of the PRC and Outer Mongolia becoming independent only after decades of serving as a satellite of the USSR. Manchuria disappeared into China. Soon after the PRC proclaimed its founding, it sent armies into Tibet and East Turkestan (Xinjiang). As a result, both are today entirely incorporated as nominally autonomous jurisdictions of an expanded Chinese state. Vietnam became a united and independent state only after France and the United States withdrew their military forces. Bhutan and Nepal emerged as independent states (although the future autonomy of both may now be in jeopardy), whereas Sikkim ended up being annexed by India. Despite today's political realities, national identities remain and nationalist sentiments persist among the peoples of these polities, keeping alive visions of the restoration of boundaries and states from an earlier time in history. Contemporary states and imagined ones do not necessarily correspond to what they claim as their historical antecedents, but their clashing perceptions of history animate their claims to territory and legitimacy as well as their determination to pursue them.

Nationalist history is committed the world over to the illusion of continuity, usually for the purpose of inserting solid ground underneath the legitimacy claims of modern regimes and suppressing the competing histories of those who have chosen not to subscribe to the dominant state narrative, which treats the past as though it were a rehearsal for an inevitable present. Our purpose in this regard is not to celebrate or challenge national boundaries but to understand better how the modern system of international law came to override earlier systems of law and practice. Among other things, this orientation encourages us to approach this part of Eurasia not as a culturally flat space that for eight centuries was filled by a sequence of Chinese dynasties and its tributaries, as many have done, but as a complex, rifted space in which rulers and subjects—operating within and across distinct conceptual worlds drawing from their own civilizational centers and invoking mutually recognizable norms of international law—found themselves in constant negotiation over authority, influence, and, at times, identity.

This approach allows us to understand the persistence of very different perceptions of the historical past of Inner and East Asia among its peoples: perceptions based on the divergent historiographies informed by the specific worldviews emanating from the different centers of civilizational authority, perceptions that have been reinforced and manipulated by the development of national historical narratives that project present political geographies and aspirational ones and twenty-first century political, as well as legal, concepts into a history where they do not at all belong. The European law of nations may have deauthorized norms and beliefs that once guided interpolity relations in Inner and East Asia, but these norms and beliefs have not entirely dissipated and now animate nationalist claims to territory and legitimacy. Ongoing tensions in Asia, notably within the PRC and between the PRC and almost every one of its neighbors, and even some states farther afield in the South China Sea, might have a better chance of being eased were it possible to produce a fuller and franker account of the assumptions that Asian polities and their rulers make regarding the appropriate ordering of their worlds. These assumptions continue to generate friction, often in the absence of sound historical evidence.

Paradoxically, turning to history may help to diffuse the hold history has on people. Our goal is not to determine anew what happened and to impose one narrative as representing the sole truth; even less is it to reimpose unwelcome hegemonies and reignite old animosities. It is to make clearer where the diverse historical narratives come from and to appreciate their relative and necessarily selective nature. A heightened awareness of this kind may enable a renewed coexistence of these otherwise-contested histories. In this way we hope to make a contribution to the fields of history and international relations. On a more immediate, practical level, we encourage practitioners of international relations, including those concerned with the prevention, management, and resolution of conflicts in Asia, to consider the insights the pages of this collaborative book provide, not just for encountering the past, but for appreciating the dynamics of Inner and East Asian political realities today.

CHAPTER TWO

CHINGGISID RULE AND THE MONGOL GREAT STATE

The mountains, high grasslands, and deserts of the Mongolian Plateau occupy the eastern part of the great Eurasian steppe zone from the Altai Mountains in the west to the Greater Khingan range in the east, covering approximately 3.2 million square kilometers (1.2 million square miles). Today most of this territory is broadly divided north–south between the independent state of Mongolia and the Autonomous Region of Inner Mongolia in the People's Republic of China. Starting late in the twelfth century, from a base in the upstream regions of the Onon and Kelüren Rivers in the mountains of the eastern Mongolian Plateau, a man of the Kiyad Borjigid lineage or clan named Temüjin unified the pastoral peoples of the Mongolian Plateau. A Mongol *ulus*, or state, was formed. In 1206 a *khuriltai*, or assembly, of Mongol nobles elected Temüjin as their supreme ruler after he emerged victorious against rival Mongol leaders allied against him. On that occasion they gave him the title of Chinggis (Genghis) Khan and inaugurated a new political formation that would take the name Mongol Great State, commonly referred to as the Mongol empire.[1] After consolidating his rule over the peoples loosely identified as Mongols, Chinggis Khan embarked on an endless campaign to extend his dominion beyond the Mongolian Plateau. He died in 1227 while on campaign in the Tangut empire in the northeastern part of the Tibetan Plateau. To distinguish imperial rulership from that of a traditional khanate, the term *khagan* (*qa'an*, "ruler of rulers," which we translate as "Great Khan") was later coined and applied retroactively to Chinggis.[2]

The Mongol conquest of much of Eurasia in the thirteenth century marks a watershed in human history. Chinggis Khan conquered more territory than had any previous steppe ruler, created the largest continental empire of all time, stretching from the eastern Mediterranean shores to the Pacific Ocean, and animated Mongol ideas and precedents about conquest, sovereignty, legitimacy, governance, administration, and interpolity relations that have influenced every subsequent empire or Great State in

Asia.[3] No successor state escaped the shadow of these innovations. Mongol imperial expansion thus had powerful consequences for eastern Eurasia.[4]

The empire Chinggis Khan created was an extensive rather than intensive political formation. Though he set up a centralized administration, the empire was administered through a structure of interlocking units of ten, starting at the bottom with ten households and scaling up to ten thousand. Each larger unit was ruled on behalf of the Great Khan by a lord bound to him by personal fealty, usually based on kinship.[5] The Great Khan gave his lords inheritable estates, and in return they gave him loyalty and a lifetime of active military service. The decimal system bound every man and household into a strictly regulated hierarchy that climaxed at its apex in the person of the Great Khan. This structure proved to be durable and had the advantage of being expandable when a new polity was added to the empire.

The weak links in a system that depended so heavily on the person of the Great Khan were those that existed not across space but over time. This weakness was most sharply exposed during leadership successions when the death of the Great Khan removed the linchpin that connected his position to those who had sworn themselves loyal. Formally at least, succession to this supreme position was decided by election at a *khuriltai*, an assembly of the senior Mongol lords. In practice, the outcome was predetermined by tradition and legal norms or determined by political competition, at times violent, among the ruler's sons and nephews aspiring to take his position, through a process that Joseph Fletcher called "bloody tanistry."[6] Although Fletcher's characterization may overstate the use of violence in these processes, khanal succession was not always orderly. But it had its logic, even its predictability. Chinggis Khan recognized the tension between stabilization and reinvigoration that struggles might bring about and, like many monarchs, sought to control the succession after him. Legend has it that he summoned his sons on his deathbed in 1227 and told them a fable of a cart that was bearing down on two snakes, one with a thousand heads and a single tail, the other with a thousand tails and a single head. The first was crushed because the heads pulled in different directions, while the second, directed by a single head, slithered away to safety.[7] However they were persuaded, Chinggis's sons agreed that the third son, Ögedei, should succeed without a challenge, allowing the empire to survive into the next generation.

Ögedei was succeeded as Great Khan by his son Güyük in 1246, but Güyük reigned for less than two years before he died. The next two successions turned violent. After a round of fighting among the cousins, another of Chinggis Khan's grandsons, Möngke, was elected Great Khan in 1251. He assigned Khubilai, his younger brother, the rule of the conquered Jin state in today's northern China. Möngke entrusted his youngest brother, Ariq Böke, with the Great Khan's seal when he embarked on his military expedition to conquer the Southern Song state. When he died on campaign in 1259, Ariq Böke was elected Great Khan at a *khuriltai* he had duly convened near Karakorum. Khubilai, however, called his own *khuriltai* away from the Mongolian heartland and close to his own power base and had himself elected Great Khan. Only by defeating and capturing Ariq Böke in 1264 was his position secure.[8] Khubilai then moved the center of the empire to his own power base in the former Jin state, building a first capital, Shangdu (Xanadu), at the southeastern edge of the steppe and then, further south, a second, known as Khanbaliq (City of the Khan) or Daidu (Great Capital), which would be renamed Beijing in the Ming era.

In 1271, seven years after the defeat of his main challenger and a year before announcing his grand project of conquering the Southern Song state, Khubilai declared the founding of a dynasty in the Chinese tradition. He called it Da Yuan, or Yuan Great State. Khubilai and his Chinese advisers were thereby able to present his realm in eastern Asia as the legitimate successor dynasty to previous dynasties that had ruled China. This construct, calculated to correspond to the Chinese conceptualization of legitimate rule and succession, applied only to the Sinic part of the Mongol empire and its tributary relations, not to the Mongol empire as a whole. This distinction is sometimes lost in Chinese historiography, which regards the Yuan dynasty as a Chinese political formation. Contrary to the standard textbook account of Chinese history, Khubilai Khan and his successors did not become "Chinese" but remained politically and culturally Mongol, and the Mongol empire remained a thoroughly Chinggisid project.[9] Mongols themselves understood the distinction between the East Asian polity under Khubilai Khan's direct rule and the much broader Eurasian empire they continued to regard as the Mongol Great State. We follow this distinction but use Yuan, as did the Chinese, only in reference to the eastern part of the Mongol empire that encompassed the former Jin and Southern Song territories, the Mongolian Plateau, and the conquered Dali and Tangut kingdoms.[10] When referring to the Mongol empire in its entirety, we use Mongol Great State or Mongol empire.

Unlike the preceding Great Khans, Khubilai Khan and his successors were overlords of an empire that was in practice increasingly partitioned, although it remained structurally intact. It comprised four major zones ruled by the close descendants of Chinggis Khan. Each constituted its own polity but remained, at least formally, under the ultimate sovereignty of the Great Khan. The Chagatai khanate in Central Asia (which later subdivided), the Il-khanate of the Hülegü dynasty in western Asia, the Kip-chak khanate centered in what is today western Russia, and the Great Yuan in eastern Asia—which Mongols referred to mostly as "the Great Khan's own realm"—were all ruled by Chinggisid khans who also participated in some ways in the governance of the Mongol Great State led by the Great Khan, who was concurrently the emperor of the Yuan.

In addition, since the subjugation of Tibet under Möngke Khan, the Mongols ruled over much of Tibet, in part through Tibetan Buddhist hier-archs. Despite the unique religiopolitical features of the Mongol authority there, the regime in Tibet displayed many of the characteristics of other states subjugated by the Mongols. In standard Chinggisid fashion, Möngke allotted parts of Tibet as fiefs to the brothers Khubilai, Hülegü, and Ariq Böke and their cousin Köten, while keeping a portion for himself. By the 1270s most of these fiefs had come into Khubilai's possession, chiefly by inheritance, but the Il-khan (the head of the Il-khanate), who had also inherited Möngke's portion, maintained a degree of authority in signifi-cant parts of Tibet for a considerable time. Although according to Tibetan sources these parts eventually also came under Khubilai's dominion, Yuan sources nowhere refer to Tibet as a part of the Yuan Great State, suggest-ing that Tibet was not incorporated into or administered under the Yuan dynasty, much less "China," as is sometimes assumed.[11]

After roughly a century in this pattern, the empire fractured into re-gional successor states under the pressures of rebellion, civil war, and an insurgent Islam. The Chinggisid aura did not diminish, however. It persisted in some of these successor states, and no Mongol leader who dreamed of rebuilding the lost empire—and many were those who allowed themselves to be consumed by this ambition—neglected to claim succes-sion from (and even the title of) Chinggis Khan or to offer sacrifices at the shrine of his cult, even if he was not a lineal descendant.

Historians have invoked a wide range of social, material, and technical factors—from climate change to horse breeding to the stirrup—to explain why the Mongols were able to accomplish their unprecedented conquest of so much of Eurasia. In this chapter, concerned as we are with the proto-cols and institutions through which rulers asserted their sovereignty and organized their relations with other rulers, we highlight instead the spiri-tual and conceptual resources that Inner Asian traditions made available to these conquerors to endow their expansion with moral or religious au-thority and invest them with legitimacy to rule. Ideologists of the regime made concerted efforts to generate unimpeachable legitimacy for the founder. As late as 1346, one surviving stone inscription represents Ching-gis's accomplishment as not just unprecedented but a new beginning: "The world and its people having been in chaos from time immemorial to the present, Chinggis Khan was born and vanquished the idle sovereigns of foreign realms." In other words, Chinggis transformed a world made chaotic by rulers lacking legitimacy. He did so by vanquishing those who had failed to earn the moral right to rule and by unifying their dispersed polities into a single sovereignty. So great was the moral force of his conquest that, or so the inscription suggests, it happened effortlessly: "[Having founded] the Mongol Great State and [grasped the pivot of Heaven and Earth, he stooped to] pick up [the myriad countries] as if they were fallen leaves."[12] Never before in history, it was claimed, had so perfect a transformation occurred.

The building of the Mongol empire was anything but effortless, of course. By the time the endeavors of those who opposed Chinggis's grand imperial project had failed, the new state declared it impossible to imagine that there could have been any other outcome. Such is the force—and necessity—of the myths through which every state, modern or historical, declares the rightness of its ascendancy over opposing forces. The need to assert legitimacy never dwindled, however, so that generations after Chinggis Khan, as we shall see, the protocols and institutions binding lesser polities to the Mongol empire continued to aim at producing the legitimacy of the Chinggisid model.

THE EMERGENCE OF THE CHINGGISID STATE

· *Lhamsuren Munkh-Erdene* ·

Chinggis Khan rose to power and built his imperial state on the strength of a long history of Inner Asian empires on the Mongolian Plateau. The post he first seized to launch his project was that of khan of the Kereyid kingdom. The Kereyid kingdom had been part of the Khitan empire, known in the Chinese tradition of dynastic succession as the Liao. The Khitans had established their empire on the Mongolian Plateau in the tenth century by first conquering neighboring nomadic polities and investing their leaders with royal and administrative titles and then challenging Chinese authority north of the Yellow River. When the Khitan empire collapsed in the twelfth century under pressure from the Jurchens, the rulers of the administrative units into which the Khitans had reorganized those they had conquered competed for dominance, and the Kereyid kingdom emerged hegemonic. When the Jurchens absorbed much of the Khitan realm into their Jin state, they invested the Kereyid khan with the Chinese title of Wang (king). The Kereyid leader thus became known in Mongolian as

Ong Khan, literally King Khan. Temüjin, as the young Chinggis was called, pledged his allegiance to Ong Khan in the turbulent 1190s, but when Ong Khan turned against him once he felt threatened by Temüjin's ambition, the latter strategized a brilliant countercampaign that would eventually bring all Mongols, as well as the Kereyids and many other entities, into a new polity that he would rule as Chinggis Khan.[13]

It has been supposed that the Chinggisid state emerged from a tribal order of egalitarian kinship society in premodern Inner Asia. It is difficult to understand, however, how one man could, in three years and over an area as big as today's Mongolia, have built a political community and centralized government out of tribesmen scattered among a multitude of clans and tribes splintered along segmentary lineage lines and in constant friction. More recent scholarship has challenged the notion that Inner Asia was a kinship society, proposing instead the political form of a headless order of myriad aristocratic houses that, at times, gave way to a centralized state like that of the Chinggisid.[14] This newer scholarship is unable to explain, however, where the aristocratic houses came from or how they actually functioned within a single headless state. We propose instead to take a historical approach and argue that the Chinggisid power structure and political community were built upon the Kereyid kingdom, which is to say, on Khitan administrative divisions. In other words, Chinggis Khan's great empire and the ideas and institutions that he invoked to sustain it—khan, Heaven (*tengri*), and the decimal system and other distinctive elements of sociopolitical organization—came out of a long-standing tradition of Inner Asian statecraft and political culture.[15]

We offer this interpretation in part on the basis of the language by which thirteenth-century Mongols themselves understood the political and cultural entities of which they saw themselves to be a part. To do so we consider the surviving contemporary Mongol sources on their own terms rather than turn, as most scholars have done, to the more numerous Chinese and Persian sources. The principal Mongol concepts of collectivity are *ulus* and *irgen*. In modern Mongolian, *ulus* means a "state" or "nation"; *irgen* now means "citizen" or "subject." In Chinggis's time, *ulus* was understood as a community of the realm, a political entity, a state, while *irgen* was a community of language, custom, and descent, or an ethnocultural entity, to give it a modern framing.[16] The two were complementary: an *irgen* could also be a political community. This means that Mongol *ulus* and Mongol *irgen* were two different conceptualizations of the same body, one political and the other ethnocultural. The idea that the people of the Mongolian Plateau should constitute a single realm under one ruler was widely held by Mongol aristocrats before the establishment of the Chinggisid state, but it was only with the rise of Chinggis Khan and the establishment of his new state that their sense of constituting a distinct Mongol *ulus* gained strength.[17]

By the time the official chronicle of the Chinggisid state, the *Secret History of the Mongols*, was written in the mid-thirteenth century to confirm the legitimacy of rule by Chinggis's heirs, the only *ulus* existing in the contemporary world, from the Mongol perspective, was the Mongol *ulus* (*mongqol ulus*). There had been other *ulus*es, but they had existed in the past. Mongol scribes acknowledged that China had had its Shang, Zhou, and Song *ulus*es, as India had had its Magadha *ulus*; even the Pure Land presided over by the Buddha was called the Sukhavati (Western Paradise) *ulus*. But with the rise of the Mongol *ulus*, at least from the Mongol point of view, no contemporary polity could be thought of as constituting an *ulus*, or state. Instead, these polities were reduced to communities, or *irgens*. The Jin state of the Jurchens (1115–1234) was referred to as the *kitat* (Cathay) *irgen*; the Abbasid caliphate of Baghdad (750–1258), as the Baghdad *irgen*. Europeans belonged to the *virangud* (Frank) *irgen*. Even the Mongols constituted their own *irgen*, yet the political state that rose above them all was the sole *ulus*, the Mongol *ulus*.

According to the *Secret History*, 1206 marks the moment at which Chinggis Khan "established" (*bayi'uluqsan*) the Mongol *ulus* to encompass the entire Mongolian Plateau. This was the point at which the Mongol state transitioned from being one *ulus* among many to being the only legitimate *ulus*. By then Chinggis's sovereignty extended beyond the "original" Mongol people to the larger body of people that Mongol sources speak of as the felt-tent dwellers (*sisgei to'urgatu*).[18] This group of people on the Mongolian Plateau, constituting his new subjects, was much broader than the original Mongol *ulus* he had ruled. Having completed this "unification" (*quriyaldun* or *qamtutqaju*) of the felt-tent dwellers, he imposed massive reforms over the next years to construct a state administration through which to rule an extensive empire. By 1206, when the great *khuriltai* was held to enthrone Temüjin as Chinggis Khan and reorganize his rulership of the realm, his state had already grown to include most of the felt-tent dwellers. The *Secret History* captures this process as "having completed the task of setting the Mongol people in order."[19] The format by which Chinggis Khan did so was to reorganize them into ninety-five *mingqans* ("thousands," one of the interlocking decimal units that the Mongols inherited from the Kereyids) and appoint a lord to rule each one of them. The whole realm then was divided into central and right- and left-wing *tümens* (units of ten thousand households). Mongol terminology quite explicitly calls this process "*ulus* building" (*ulus-i bayi'ulurun*).

From the Mongol sources it becomes clear that the idea that the peoples of the Mongolian Plateau were to constitute a single realm was already well established before 1206, and that the Mongol *ulus* was the realization of this idea. This *ulus* did not expand beyond its boundaries after that date in order to embrace newly conquered peoples and territories, however. The latter remained distinct from the Mongol *ulus*, and for the larger political formation that came into being to include these imperial conquests, a different term was created, Yeke Mongqol ulus, the "Mongol Great State," which we also call the Mongol empire.

Once incorporated into the Mongol Great State, conquered peoples were placed in *irgen*[20] and put under the authority of a Chinggisid lord. Thus, the Great State consisted of the core Mongol *ulus*, on the one hand, and numerous *irgen*, or distinct ethnocultural communities, under the Great Khan's authority, on the other. Administratively, Chinggis apportioned the peoples and territories to the west of the Mongol *ulus* to his elder sons and those to the east to his brothers as *ulus*-appanages, leaving the Mongol *ulus* itself undivided.[21] As a result, the Chinggisid state was transformed into an empire that consisted of the "core *ulus*" and left- and right-wing *ulus*-appanages, all under the sway of the *Yeke Mongqol ulus-un dalay-yin qan*, that is, the "Universal Khan of the Mongol Great State."[22]

The chief source for the account of this transformation is the *Secret History*, the official imperial reconstruction—or, more precisely, the ex post facto imposition—of the post-1206 Mongol imperial framework onto the historical past. Although the concepts of *ulus* and *irgen* were well established among pre-Chinggisid Mongols, the author of the *Secret History*, speaking in the language of his time, knowingly or unwittingly revised the narrative of the past by reducing all non-Mongol polities to *irgen* because, at the time of writing, they were merely peoples of the empire. By the same logic, he even used the word *irgen* to designate the pre-1206 polities of the Mongolian Plateau, including those of Mongols, to distinguish them from the Mongol *ulus* of imperial times.[23]

The *Secret History* refers to the Chinggisid empire in its initial years simply as Mongqol ulus, the "Mongol State," but the inscription known as the Stele of Yesüngge calls it *Qamuq Mongqol ulus*, the "All-Mongol State." By 1240 or possibly earlier the term *Yeke Mongqol ulus* came into use, *yeke* meaning "great." *Yeke Mongqol ulus* has been translated variously as State of the Great Mongols, Nation of the Great Mongols, Great Mongol Empire, and Great Mongol State. None of these is quite accurate, as *yeke* modifies *ulus* rather than *mongqol*. The confusion arises from the fact that it is syntactically impossible to place *yeke* between *mongqol* and *ulus*; that is to say, it is not the Mongols who are designated as great but the state. *Yeke*

Mongqol ulus thus should be understood as Mongol Great State. The first use of this title is hard to pinpoint. *Yeke Mongqol ulus* is attested on the seal of Güyük Khan imprinted on his 1246 letter to Pope Innocent IV. A Turkic rendering of this title—Ulugh Manqul ulus—was minted on a coin in Transcaucasia some two or three years earlier.[24] Chinese sources suggest that the name may have been in use even earlier than this, as a Song envoy in 1221 reported that the Mongols called their state Da Menggu guo, which would appear to be a word-for-word translation into Chinese of Yeke Mongqol ulus.[25]

As of this date, an empire well beyond the Mongol *ulus* had already emerged to encompass the conquered Khwarezmid empire (comprising southern Central Asia and most of Iran and Afghanistan), parts of the Jin state, and the Uighur and Tangut states, whose leaders had submitted to Chinggis. "Yeke Mongqol ulus" gave a name to this new reality, reflecting the scale of Chinggis Khan's project, and remained in use among the Mongols for the empire's duration. Even after the empire mutated into the four Chinggisid khanates in the 1260s, the larger framework of the Mongol Great State remained intact, and the use of that name continued through Khubilai's and Toghön Temür's reigns (1260–1294 and 1333–1370, respectively) and beyond, either standing alone or inflected with the addition of the name Khubilai adopted for his regime in 1271, Great Yuan (Dai Ön in Mongolian), as in "Dai Ön Yeke Mongqol ulus" (Great Yuan Mongol Great State) or "Dai Ön kemekü Yeke Mongqol ulus" (so-called Great Yuan Mongol Great State).[26]

IMPERIAL ALLOCATION OF FIEFS AND THE RESILIENCE OF CHINGGISID LAW

· *Koichi Matsuda* ·

After establishing the Mongol Great State, Chinggis Khan distributed fiefs on the Mongolian Plateau among his sons and brothers and kept the central part of it for himself. Three of his sons, Jochi, Chagatai, and Ögedei, were each given a fief with troops along the Altai range on the plateau's western border, while the fief of his youngest son, Tolui, was closer to his father's domains, in the region stretching from Karakorum to the upper Yenisei River.[27] Chinggis Khan's three brothers, Jochi Khasar, Khachiun, and Temüge Odchigin, were each given a domain with troops along the Greater Khingan range, now known as the Daxing'anling Mountains, on the plateau's eastern border.[28] The fiefs comprised thousands of soldiers' households and land to pasture their horses. This parceling out of land and allocation of households within the Mongol Great State was based on the idea that the state was the common property of all members of Chinggis Khan's family. This principle applied not only to the Mongol *ulus* but to the newly conquered territories as well. Thus, in the sedentary regions of the empire, such as the traditionally Chinese areas of the former Jin state (in today's northern China), all fiefs were allotted to Chinggis Khan's family members.[29] Properties not specifically allocated to the nobility remained in the hands of Chinggis Khan.

Succession by heredity to the allotted fiefs, which we shall call inheritance so as not to confuse it with the succession to the imperial throne, occurred according to different principles or rules than did succession to the position and title of Great Khan. The inheritance of fiefs—domains, including soldiers and their households—was regulated according to the principle of ultimogeniture, succession by the youngest son. A customary inheritance pattern among Turks and Mongols, this practice was confirmed as one of the *yasa*, or laws, of the Mongol empire by Chinggis.[30] Compliance with Chinggis Khan's *yasa*, especially regarding the allotment of fiefs and the inheritance of domains, persisted throughout the Chinggisid imperial era and across the vast expanse of the empire.

The resilience of these principles and laws provides a lens through which to appreciate the coherence of the Chinggisid empire even after it fractured into largely autonomous khanates in central, eastern, western, and northwestern Eurasia in the latter part of the thirteenth century. The Great Khan may no longer have had a major role in the governance of any but his own part of the empire, but he continued to preside over the Mongol empire as Great Khan, and the khan of each part continued to fulfill his prescribed role in the governance of the whole as a member of the Chinggisid ruling family. Despite rivalries and even wars between brothers, cousins, uncles, and nephews, the examples we present below demonstrate the tenacity of tradition, principles, and laws that Chinggis Khan established for the allocation to his family of the property and resources of the Mongol *ulus* and of the conquered territories that constituted their empire. To provide the context for the examples we present, we must first briefly recapitulate the events that followed Chinggis Khan's death in 1227.

Upon his death, Chinggis Khan was succeeded as Great Khan by his son Ögedei, but it was his youngest son, Tolui, who inherited his properties. Tolui's legacy, including several fiefs in the conquered territories of the Jin dynasty, was distributed among his sons, Möngke, Khubilai, Ariq Böke, and Hülegü. In accordance with the principle of ultimogeniture his youngest son, Ariq Böke, received the main legacies of both his father and his mother.[31] When Ögedei died in 1241, he was succeeded by his son Güyük for two years (r. 1246–1248), after which his cousin Möngke became Great Khan in 1251. Möngke dispatched his brother Hülegü west to Baghdad to defeat the caliphate and complete the conquest of West Asia (the Middle East). In the east he put his other brother, Khubilai, in charge of former Jin territories and the expansion south into Song territory.

In 1257 Möngke set out to personally lead the campaign against the Song, entrusting the Mongol Great State and the imperial seal to his youngest brother, Ariq Böke, who remained in the Mongolian Plateau homeland. Möngke died during his military campaign, as we have noted, and it fell to Ariq Böke as his designated representative to preside over the *khuriltai* convened fifty kilometers west of Karakorum to elect the Great Khan's successor. Sometime between 12 May and 10 June 1260, Ariq Böke was elected by the assembly of nobles to take his brother's place. However, his brother Khubilai had already convened his own assembly in Kaipingfu (later Shangdu), his summer residence on the southern Mongolian steppe, and had himself elected Great Khan on 5 May.[32] Ariq Böke's right to call the *khuriltai* and his possession of the seal rendered Khubilai's assembly illegal. The struggle for succession moved to the battlefield.

Hülegü halted his military campaigns in Transjordan and Palestine and returned to his Persian headquarters upon hearing of Möngke's death in order to participate in the selection of the new Great Khan. Hülegü's son Jumqur found himself in a difficult position in this succession conflict. As Hülegü's representative in the Mongol heartland, he lived and operated in the shadow of the overwhelming forces of his uncle Ariq Böke and felt pressure to support him, but his father instructed him not to oppose Khubilai. Tugged between these pressures, Jumqur nevertheless felt obliged to collaborate with Ariq Böke by going to war on his behalf in Turkestan.

When he set out on his western Asian campaign, Hülegü had expected to return to the Mongolian heartland after the campaign was completed. But after Möngke's death and Khubilai's contested ascendancy, Hülegü decided to remain in Persia. In 1263 he established a de facto independent *ulus* there, declaring himself Il-khan of what had become his West Asian empire, while at the same time accepting the continued overlordship of the Great Khan, Khubilai. When Ariq Böke surrendered to Khubilai in 1264, Jumqur set off on the journey to Hülegü's newly established domain in northern Persia, bringing with him Hülegü's two wives, sons, grandsons, retainers, and households who had remained in his father's domain on the plateau when Hülegü had left for the western campaign. Jumqur died of illness in Samarkand before completing his journey. When Hülegü himself died shortly thereafter, in 1265, it was Hülegü's eldest son, Abaqa, who succeeded, with Khubilai's approval, to his father's position and title as Il-khan. Hülegü's wives, sons, and others who traveled with Jumqur eventually reached the family's Persian headquarters, effectively ending that family's presence on the Mongolian Plateau. Abaqa never returned to his family's Mongolian land, instead sharing with other family members in Hülegü's Persian domain.

What then became of his abandoned domain, his *ordos* (the wives' palaces) and *yurts* (pasturelands) on the plateau? The answer to this question demonstrates the strength of the Chinggisid *yasa* and tradition in determining inheritance in the Mongol imperial world. The fate of Hülegü's Mongolian domain was left to Khubilai to determine, since he was by now unquestionably the Great Khan. Khubilai could easily have appropriated that domain for himself, but he directed that it pass to the family of his erstwhile enemy, Ariq Böke, instead. He did so because, according to Chinggisid legal principle, abandoned domains went to the father of the deceased. When this person was no longer alive (as was the case with Tolui), it was to be passed to his youngest son (in this case, Ariq Böke). After Ariq Böke died in custody the following year, Hülegü's Mongolian *ordos* and *yurts*, together with the rest of Ariq Böke's estate, were transferred to his successors.[33] It may have been the initial illegitimacy of his accession to the throne that persuaded Khubilai to uphold the *yasa* of Chinggis Khan by authorizing that the property go to Hülegü's successor.

The handling of Hülegü's domain in the eastern part of the empire tells a similar story. The Mongol nobility's domains in the conquered Jin state consisted of two elements: personal household properties, which a nobleman was free to dispose of as he chose, and tax allotments received from the Great Khan, which entitled the nobleman to a share of the taxation of a region. Chinese-language records indicate that the subjects of Hülegü's eastern domain consisted of some 7,000 artisanal and hunting households living in the capital, Daidu.[34] The domain was personal property that Chinggis Khan had allotted to him shortly after he was born in 1218. Hülegü also enjoyed two tax allotments, one of which consisted of a portion (around one-third) of the silk thread tax levied annually from 25,056 civilian households registered in Zhangde circuit (in today's Hebei Province).[35] Möngke most likely gave Hülegü these tax allotments to fund his military campaigns when he dispatched him toward Baghdad, just as he gave Khubilai tax allotments around the same time to finance the latter's conquest of the Dali kingdom bordering the Song. Both had the same purpose: to finance campaigns of conquest.[36] After the Mongol conquest of the Song state, each member of the Mongol nobility was again awarded a portion of the tax resources of the newly conquered land. Hülegü's allotment was in Baoqing circuit south of the Yangzi.[37]

After the establishment of the Il-khanate, the nature of the relationship between that part of the empire and Khubilai's court began to change. The Il-khanate, which stretched from present-day central Turkey and northern Syria and Iraq in the west to include Afghanistan and much of Pakistan in the east and the southern Caucasus in the north, became reliant on its own resources and grew materially independent of the Hülegü family domains located in the distant eastern part of the empire. Despite the Il-khanate's effective autonomy from the rest of the empire, however, the Il-khan and his family retained their due participation in the central Mongol imperial institutions. Thus, they appointed representatives to the plenary sessions of the *jarghuchi*, or judges, who gathered in the imperial capital Daidu from all the major fiefs of the Mongol nobility. These plenary sessions were part of the nobility's governance system under the rule of the Great Khan and were chaired by the *yeke jarghuchi*, or great judge, a plenipotentiary dispatched directly by him.[38] Khubilai maintained this joint governance system and incorporated it into his central government structure in 1261 as the Central Secretariat, signaling his commitment to preserving fief-holders' rights in the eastern part of the empire in a bid to sustain his status and legitimacy as Great Khan among his nobles.[39] Khubilai also established a nominal bureaucratic "home" for the Hülegü family's personal household properties in these eastern domains, called the Office of the Supervisor-in-Chief of Hunting, Falconry, and Artisanal Households.

The Hülegü family in the Il-khanate continued to participate in the imperial inspection of accounts carried out every few years, another aspect of the Mongol imperial governance system that Khubilai carefully maintained. This institution involved gathering representatives from each of the empire's princes to inspect the imperial accounts and confirm the correctness of disbursements. As late as 1268, the Il-khan sent two envoys from his capital, Tabriz, to participate in this auditing body.[40] With the outbreak of civil war in Central Asia triggered by Qaidu Khan's rejection of Khubilai Khan's authority, this modest level of interaction between the Il-khan and his eastern domains became impossible. For a quarter of a century, the Hülegü family had no practical means of making contact with their representatives there. The land route was insecure because of war, and the sea route was controlled by the Song dynasty as it battled for survival against the Mongol advance. In 1275 Hülegü's son and successor, Abaqa Khan, dispatched an envoy to request that the personal household properties that had belonged to Hülegü be entrusted to the care of Khubilai's court. Khubilai accepted this request and placed these properties under his Ministry of War. The annual income from the Hülegü eastern domains was also placed in the imperial court's safekeeping.[41]

The final defeat of Song forces in 1279 and incorporation of the Song dynasty's territories into the Mongol empire made it possible to travel by sea between the Il-khanate and the imperial court in Daidu. The first such voyage from the Il-khanate occurred during the reign of the fourth Il-khan, Arghun Khan, in response to his request for a Mongol bride to serve as his new principal wife. As noted in chapter 1, the large delegation Khubilai sent, which included Marco Polo, could travel by sea (1291–1293). With that connection, the income from the Hülegü family's eastern domains could at last be transported to the Il-khan's court. The seventh Il-khan, Ghazan Khan, sent a representative with another delegation a few years later, in 1297, again by sea. When that delegation returned in 1307, it carried with it the income from the Hülegü eastern domains that had accumulated since the reign of Möngke. In addition, a new administrative organ was set up to manage the Hülegü properties in the imperial capital, Daidu.[42]

At least until 1323, the Il-khan's court maintained contact with the center of the Mongol Great State by dispatching some twenty delegations to the imperial court, and it continued to receive income from the Hülegü eastern domains.[43] The principles of Chinggisid rule governing the properties of the Chinggisid nobles and the apportioning of the empire's wealth thus continued to function throughout the Mongol empire. This was true despite the decentralization and disarticulation of the larger empire under Khubilai and his successors. We take this continuing respect for and application of Chinggisid protocols as evidence of their importance in maintaining the legitimacy of the Great Khan and of the Mongol Great State.

IMPERIAL SUBJUGATION OF POLITIES AND EXTENSION INTO TIBET

· Koichi Matsuda ·

The Mongol empire was built by adding domains through war or the threat of war, but each polity submitted in its own way depending on the phase in which it came up against the Mongols and the conditions under which submission was achieved. This section considers the circumstances and process by which the Mongols extended their empire onto the Tibetan Plateau.

Mongol relations with Tibet began about the time of Chinggis Khan's death in 1227, when the final conquest of the Tanguts removed the territorial barrier between the Mongols and the Tibetans. Over the following decades, the Mongol empire gradually expanded its system of governance and asserted control there. The resulting interaction between the two cultures had a deep impact on both. Influences moved in both directions, for the Mongols would come to favor Tibetan Buddhism, and their khans entered into distinctive relationships of patronage with Tibetan religious leaders. At an organizational level, the Mongol conquest of Tibet was not all that different from its conquest of other peoples, yet the religious dimension of the relationship sets it apart. If Mongols today still regard themselves as devout followers of Tibetan Buddhism, it is because of the relationship that Mongol rulers developed with Tibetans at the time of the empire. This makes Tibet something of a special case for analyzing the dynamics of Mongol imperial power.

To understand the extension of the Mongol empire into Tibet, we need to familiarize ourselves with certain features of the Mongol system of governance. The roots of this system were established through Chinggis Khan's great reform in 1206. As noted above, that reform reorganized the population of the newly formed Mongol Great State into a decimal structure of units of ten to ten thousand households. Initially, Chinggis Khan divided it into ninety-five *mingqans*, or groups of a thousand households. These *mingqans* were then combined by tens into units of ten thousand households, called *tümens*, which served as the main administrative units of the Mongol empire. On the frontiers of the Mongolian Plateau, Chinggis was flexible in combining *mingqans* in unfixed numbers into toparchies, or petty states, over which he installed princes: his three brothers (Jochi Khasar, Khachiun, and Temüge Odchigin) on the eastern end of the Mongolian Plateau and his three elder sons (Jochi, Chagatai, and Ögedei) on the western end. Their obligation was to defend the frontiers of the plateau, drawing their military manpower from the households of their *mingqans*. Chinggis Khan himself retained control of the core of his empire, the Mongol *ulus*, which was passed to his youngest son, Tolui, after his death. The military empire of which these toparchies were parts, the Mongol Great State, was the conjoint property of Chinggis's family.

As Chinggis Khan expanded his rule beyond the Mongolian Plateau to build the Mongol empire, he incorporated new areas by applying this same system of administration. But the expansion of the empire demanded a new strategy for implementing it. The first constraint forcing alteration of the original principle of decimal organization was a shortage of manpower. If the Chinggisid state at the time of its founding consisted of ninety-five *mingqans*, we can estimate a total "Mongol" population of something less than a million. Given this scarcity of manpower, the Mongols avoided full-scale battles as much as possible in the course of expanding the empire for fear of losing soldiers. They preferred, instead, to expand the empire by winning the voluntary submission of frontier states. The sheer menace of Mongol military might persuaded many rulers to submit to Mongol authority in exchange for favorable treatment. In 1209, for example, the Uighur ruler Barchuk Art Tegin preemptively sent a mission to Chinggis Khan to express his desire to submit, and two years later he traveled to his court to offer tribute. In response, Uighurs were given preferential treatment, and for generations each successive king of the Uighur kingdom was given a daughter of Chinggis's lineage in marriage to confirm the relationship.

The Mongols also mobilized vassal states in the service of imperial expansion. To guarantee their ongoing submission and to strengthen the power of the empire, Chinggis Khan and his successors extracted military manpower and resources from those states. This is clear from two records that chronicle how Khubilai Khan managed relations with vassals. From these records, we can extract seven rules regarding the obligations imposed on subordinate states.[44] He required (1) that the ruler present himself at the khan's court to submit in person to Mongol overlordship, (2) that he leave a son or brother as a hostage, (3) that he conduct a census and compile a written register of all families, and (4) that he make soldiers available for military service. Further, vassal rulers were expected (5) to submit taxes and (6) to establish and maintain a postal system within their jurisdictions. They had also to (7) accept a Mongol governor (*darugha-chi*) to oversee state affairs. These seven obligations were designed to ensure the incorporation of subjugated states into the Mongol empire and to secure military support from them. New armies were then formed under the command of a member of the Imperial Guard. Known as *tamma* armies, these forces were distinguished by the fact that they consisted of Mongol soldiers as well as soldiers from the subjugated states. The *tamma* armies, most of which had a strength of forty thousand to fifty thousand soldiers, were dispatched to frontier regions to conquer and garrison new territories. In this way, the empire was able to expand while at the same time decreasing the number of Mongol soldiers on campaign.

Manpower scarcity also meant that the Mongols did not seek to intervene in the internal workings of institutions of subjugated states. Manpower was not the only consideration; in most cases Mongol rulers recognized that they were too unfamiliar with local conditions to administer those areas effectively. They consequently preserved institutions that existed in subjugated territories. The policy on religions was much the same. The Mongols believed that *tengri* (Heaven or God) had granted Chinggis Khan the right to rule all territories universally. Any religion that recognized Heaven or God—effectively, every religion—was left intact so that each clergy would pray to its Heaven or God to bless Chinggis Khan and grant him longevity. In exchange for this cooperation, clergy were granted exemption from taxation and a measure of freedom in their activities. All these measures—extending the Mongol administrative system originating on the Mongolian Plateau into conquered areas, conserving Mongol human resources, ensuring continued Mongol military dominance, and incorporating local institutions, including local religions, into the imperial project—enabled the Mongol Great State to expand across much of Eurasia in a few decades.

The policies that supported this inexorable expansion came to affect Tibet. When Ögedei was enthroned as the second ruler of the Mongol empire in 1229, he appointed his second son, Köten, to rule over the Tanguts and gave him the responsibility of conquering adjacent regions, including Tibet. For this task Ögedei Khan granted him four thousand soldiers and ordered him to establish a military base in the eastern part of the former Tangut territories. Köten began his campaign of conquest to the east and southeast in 1235. He soon defeated and absorbed the forces of Wang Shixian, the last surviving military leader of the Jin dynasty. By adding the support of several other Mongol military units stationed in adjacent regions, Köten gained sufficient military power to launch an invasion of Tibet.

Tibetan records state that the first Mongol invasion took place in 1239 or 1240 under the command of General Doorha Darqan, causing the deaths of hundreds and the burning of two monasteries around Lhasa.[45] The troops, most likely a *tamma* army, withdrew soon after the invasion for reasons that are unclear but may have had to do with the death of Ögedei in 1241.[46] Shortly thereafter, Köten invited, or summoned, an influential Tibetan lama of one of the leading schools of Tibetan Buddhism from central Tibet, the Sakya Pandita, who was abbot of Sakya Monastery, to his court in the Tangut city of Xiliangfu, also known as Liangzhou (present-day Wuwei). The Sakya Pandita departed from his monastery in 1244 at the age of sixty-three accompanied by his two nephews, the brothers Drogön Chögyal Phagpa and Chakna Dorjé, and all arrived at the court two years later. Köten was in Karakorum at the time attending the coronation of Great Khan Güyük. When he met the Sakya Pandita upon his return to Xiliangfu the next year, Köten granted him the supreme position of dean of the religious elders.[47] The Sakya Pandita died in 1251 at the age of seventy after five years of promoting Buddhism to the Mongols.

Köten's summons of the Sakya Pandita to his court is unlikely to have been religiously motivated. His intention was rather to establish that this important lama acknowledged Mongol authority over Tibet. Although the Sakya Pandita could not, in fact, claim to exercise ruling power over Tibet at the time, nor even to represent it, the summons should be seen as an attempt by Köten to fulfill the first of Chinggis Khan's seven rules for subjugating new territories, which was that its ruler should accept a summons to the khan's court. By bringing his two nephews with him, the Sakya Pandita appeared to fulfill the second rule of supplying close kinsmen as hostages to the khan's court. Such hostages were supposed to be given positions in the imperial bodyguard, and records suggest that Chakna Dorjé was inducted into Köten's bodyguard, because he was instructed to study Mongolian and to adopt Mongol costume. Tibetan historians later presented the Sakya Pandita's presence at the court and the relationship he developed with Köten as the beginning of the Sakya order's hegemony over Tibet. Actually, no further extension of Mongol influence or Sakya power in Tibet occurred during the Pandita's lifetime. Recent scholarship places the start of Sakya rule over central Tibet a decade later, after Möngke sent troops to establish imperial authority there.[48]

After Möngke became the fourth Great Khan in 1251, he dispatched armies to the southern frontiers of the empire. One of these was sent to Tibet, the central region of which fell after two years of severe fighting.[49] After a census was carried out, the territory was organized into thirteen regions identified as *tümens*, even though these regions did not meet the ten-thousand-household criterion. Twenty-seven postal relay stations were established to connect the central region of Tibet to the frontier with the former Jin territories already under Mongol control. These were placed under the responsibility of the *tümen* commanders, as was the case elsewhere within the Mongol empire.[50]

Ties to the various Buddhist orders in central Tibet then quickly formed. According to Tibetan records, after the census of central Tibet was completed, Möngke, Khubilai, Hülegü, Ariq Böke, and Köten each developed a relationship with a leading lama of one of the Tibetan Buddhist orders and forged a "patron-priest" or "benefactor-*guru*" relationship with him (*yön-chö* or *yön-mchod* in Tibetan). In such a relationship, which we shall discuss in detail in chapter 4, the secular ruler recognized the lama as his spiritual teacher and became his and his order's benefactor.[51] What might appear only as strong religious linkages between Mongol khans and princes and distinct Tibetan Buddhist orders must equally be understood as part of the usual practice of allocating conquered territories among members of Chinggis Khan's lineage.[52] Indeed, studies show that each of these Mongol khans exercised some authority over Tibetan appanages corresponding to the domains of these religious orders.[53] From this perspective, the whole process, from the census to the allocation of territories and people, was a straightforward division of the spoils of war rather than the sign of a more explicitly religious adoption of Tibetan Buddhism. It is not unlikely that Tibetan chroniclers interpreted or presented military defeat and submission to Mongol rule in a manner that accorded with their own traditions of connections between the religious and secular realms.

A new stage in Tibet's relationship with Mongol rulers came in 1253, when Möngke granted Khubilai a fief in the region of Jingzhao (present-day Xi'an in Shaanxi Province) and ordered him to subjugate the Dali kingdom (present-day Yunnan). While thus engaged, Khubilai sent an envoy to the court of Köten, who had since passed away, asking that the Sakya Pandita be transferred to his court as a sign that the territories Ögedei had granted to Köten, which included parts of Tibet, were now his. As the Pandita had already died, his nephew Phagpa was sent to Khubilai's court in his place. This succession accorded with Chinggisid protocols; it also seeded a personal and spiritual relationship that would have significant impact on Tibet's position vis-à-vis the Mongol empire. Khubilai accepted religious instruction from Phagpa and obtained highly coveted tantric empowerments. Once Khubilai became Great Khan, he received on this basis recognition as a *chakravartin*, a universal monarch.

The relationship between Khubilai and Phagpa was symbiotic. When Khubilai sought to extend supervision over the Buddhists throughout his empire, especially in Tibet, in 1264, he appointed Phagpa to head a new institution called the Bureau of General Regulation.[54] He subsequently appointed him imperial preceptor and asked him to create a new Mongolian writing system, which became known as Phagpa script and served as the official script in the empire. By now the Tibetan appanages had been reorganized. While their owners' rights were protected by Khubilai, all of Tibet was controlled by Phagpa and his Sakya order under the Great Khan's authority.

Phagpa was in Tibet from 1264 to 1268, presumably to further Khubilai's efforts to strengthen control there,[55] and again from 1274 until his death two years later. But he was not the only figure Khubilai Khan used to consolidate his ties to Tibet. Khubilai appointed Phagpa's brother, Chakna Dorjé, who had also been Köten's hostage and was married to one of Khubilai's daughters, to rule Tibet as the White Orchid King.[56] When Chakna Dorjé died in 1267, Khubilai appointed the head of Sakya Monastery to be governor-general of central Tibet, consolidating the connection between the imperial court and the Sakya order that enabled the exercise of imperial authority in this part of Tibet. This arrangement would last almost ninety years, until Changchub Gyaltsen of the Pakmodrupa hierarchy seized power from the Sakya order in Tibet in 1350.[57]

While the system of indirect rule in Tibet established by Khubilai through Phagpa was generally successful, conflict did occur with Tibetan vassals of the Il-khan, in particular the Drigung order, whose power might have been infringed upon by the Sakya. In 1275 resistance to the growing influence of Sakya's Mongol patron led to an insurrection by the governor, Kunga Tsangpo, which was put down by Khubilai's armies.[58] When an attack was launched against the Sakya by the Drigung order a decade later, Khubilai again responded by dispatching a large army, which left the Sakya victorious and Khubilai's predominance over central Tibet undisputed.[59]

Phagpa's relationship with Khubilai laid the foundations for an explicitly religious connection between the Mongol rulers and Tibetan Buddhist hierarchs. In 1265, on the occasion of the completion of a Tibetan-style pagoda (chorten) in the imperial capital, Phagpa led prayers for the eternal security of the court. Some years later he conducted extensive Buddhist services at the Temple of the Imperial Ancestors to honor Khubilai's forebears back to Chinggis Khan, thereby attaching a Buddhist aura to the Mongol tradition of ancestor worship. At Phagpa's suggestion, Khubilai had the Buddhist symbol of the White Parasol placed above his throne and also had the image of the Golden Wheel, the Buddhist symbol of the universal ruler, placed above the iron pillars at the entrance to his palace. All this conveyed the powerful image of Khubilai Khan as the legitimate ruler of the Buddhist world.[60] Indeed, under Phagpa's influence, the Mongol capital was thronged with Buddhist temples and pagodas and with people performing Buddhist rites, all centering on the figure of Khubilai as the ideal Buddhist ruler. Khubilai may have accepted this commitment to Tibetan Buddhism for political ends and possibly to counterbalance the influence of Daoism and Chinese Buddhism in the Yuan dynasty. Whatever role political expedience played, an intense devotion to Tibetan Buddhism was fostered and continued under Khubilai's successor Temür Khan and beyond, shaping centuries of close religious and political ties between Mongol rulers and Tibetan hierarchs.[61]

In summary, the Mongols at the beginning of their imperial expansion saw Tibet as one more frontier territory to conquer. To achieve their initial subjection of Tibet and administer it, they implemented the rules prescribed by Chinggis Khan as they would in any other territory they subjugated. Tibet, however, distinguished itself by presenting the Mongols with religious institutions that they could co-opt for political ends. The choice was made not to govern Tibet directly by installing a Chinggisid ruler but mostly to work indirectly through the Sakya hierarchs. This choice, and the religiopolitical relationship it brought about between the Mongols and Tibetan Buddhists, would have a lasting impact.

MONGOL PERCEPTIONS OF "CHINA" AND THE YUAN DYNASTY

· *Hodong Kim* ·

In 1271, prior to launching his conquest of the Southern Song dynasty, Khubilai declared the founding of the Da Yuan, the Yuan Great State. He did so at the time that the Mongol empire was disaggregating into increasingly autonomous regional empires. Khubilai's declaration has been portrayed by Chinese historians as establishing a new Chinese dynasty and reunifying China under it. Understanding the Yuan as a Chinese dynasty reflects the viewpoint of Chinese elites of the fourteenth century, which includes the founder of the Ming dynasty, who expelled the Mongols in 1368. In the *Yuan shi*, the official history that was launched the following year and published two short years later, the new Ming dynasty baptized the Yuan as part of an uninterrupted dynastic succession extending from the Han through Song dynasties to the Ming. To Chinese, Da Yuan was simply the dynasty Khubilai founded in China to succeed the Song and precede the Ming.

This understanding is far from how Mongols perceived it. They regarded Da Yuan as a Chinese way of expressing Yeke Mongol ulus, that is, the entire Mongol empire embracing the Eurasian continent. This was how the term was used in the Mongol-Chinese bilingual title Dai Ön [Da Yuan] kemekü Yeke Mongqol ulus (so-called Great Yuan Mongol Great State). Mongols and others, such as Turks and Persians, did not use "Yuan" to refer to the eastern part of the empire, as they mostly conceived of that domain as the territory and people under the Great Khan's direct rule. For them it was simply Khagan ulus (State of the Great Khan) or Mamlakat-i Qa'an (Kingdom of the Great Khan).[62] The histories of the Mongol empire and of China are thus suspended between conflicting perceptions about the Yuan, the Mongol Great State, and "China" during the century of Mongol rule.

To appreciate these competing readings, it helps to consider a perspective from elsewhere in the Mongol empire. One is readily available in Rashīd al-Dīn's "History of Khitay and Machin," generally though misleadingly referred to in Western translations as the "History of China." Rashīd al-Dīn, who converted from Judaism to Islam to serve as a minister in the court of the Il-khan, was ordered to compile a history of the Mongol empire from the ancestors of Chinggis Khan down to the time of Ghazan Khan (r. 1295–1304), and subsequently to extend it to a history of the known world. In what would become one of the world's most important historical and artistic documents, he included sections on the histories of other peoples and their polities, such as the Indians, the "Franks" (Europeans), Arabs, Jews, Turks, and Chinese.[63] As Rashīd al-Dīn belonged to the ruling group of the Mongol empire, his writings can be said to represent the interests and viewpoints of that group, yet he had to draw on a Chinese source to write the section on the Khitay (Cathay) and Machin, making his "History of Khitay and Machin" an encounter among Persian, Chinese, and Mongol perspectives.[64]

Rashīd al-Dīn uses the name Khitay to designate the territory we know as northern China under the Jin dynasty of the Jurchens. The name is derived from the Khitans, who established the Liao dynasty, later supplanted by the Jurchens. To its south was the Southern Song dynasty, comprising the territory we know as south China; non-Chinese called it Nankiyas, Machin, or Manzi. Rashīd al-Dīn does not use a unified term such as "China" to embrace both regions. It was not that he was avoiding the use of such a term; rather, his lexicon simply did not have such vocabulary, nor did political reality at the time require it. Rashīd al-Dīn was not alone in doing so. Travelers and writers from Europe and West Asia—among them Marco Polo, William Rubruck, and Ibn Baṭṭūta—distinguished Khitay (Cathay) and Machin/Manzi.[65] Accordingly, rather than force the modern concept of China onto the early fourteenth century writing, we shall translate the title as Rashīd al-Dīn wrote it, "History of Khitay and Machin," however cumbersome and unfamiliar that may be to us.

In the preface to this section of his history, Rashīd al-Dīn explains that he used "the names of the big countries in those kingdoms following their own expressions." These "big countries" he knew as Khitay, Machin, Kandahar (the Dali kingdom),[66] Qara Khitai (part of the Mongolian Plateau south and east of the Gobi desert), and Jurche (which we know as Manchuria). He describes these five one by one, giving separate accounts of their inhabitants and dynasties without ever designating the entire territory as a unity. The only thing that unified them was that all were subjects of the Great Khan. According to his usage, Khitay and Machin were, like India, Russia, and Syria, independent and separate "kingdoms" (mamālik) or "countries" (vilāyāt).[67] In his introduction to explain the rules and norms that he followed in writing about the Khitay people, Rashīd al-Dīn explains that he relied on a Khitay historical work.[68] Brought to the Ilkhanate by two Khitay scholars, this work was "a book famous among the

Khitay people and an accurate and trustworthy historical work in which all the wise men and intellectuals put confidence."[69] This source appears to have been a Chinese history of Buddhism.[70]

The "History of Khitay and Machin" enumerates a list of thirty-six dynasties and their emperors. Rashīd al-Dīn numbers them consecutively from the legendary founding figure of Pangu down to the last emperor of the Southern Song dynasty. He calls them in Persian *ṭabaqa-yi aṣlī*.[71] Neither Arabic nor Persian had a word that matched well with the Chinese notion of "dynasty," much less with the Chinese theory of the dynastic cycle based on the mandate of Heaven. In Arabic lexicography, the word *ṭabaqa* means "everything that is related to another and which is similar or analogous to it" or "a layer of things of the same sort." It has been commonly used in Islamic literature and historiography "in the sense of category or class, in particular of society."[72] Having otherwise no word for "dynasty," Rashīd al-Dīn combined *ṭabaqa* with *aṣl* (meaning "origin"), conveying the sense of layers of earth piled up one on top of the other.

Rashīd al-Dīn's thirty-six "original layers" do not correspond to the way that Chinese count their dynasties, for he excludes dynasties founded by northern non-Chinese peoples, such as the Sixteen Kingdoms after the fall of the Han, the Liao dynasty of the Khitans, and the Jin dynasty of the Jurchens. Rather than calling the founders and the successors of these dynasties "original layers," he uses the word *ṭāʾifa*, meaning a "group" or "company of men." Although not a pejorative expression, it sets these dynasties apart. Rashīd al-Dīn derived this distinction from his Chinese source. As he writes of these northern dynasties, "since the renown of *ṭabaqa* belongs to *ṭabaqa-yi aṣlī*, here I would call them not *ṭabaqa* but *ṭāʾifa* and write with a different color of ink. This is because there was a difference between them and their contemporaries."[73]

When he gives names to the dynasties, he calls them by the epithets of their founders (with the exception of the Three Kingdoms of Wei, Wu, and Shu, which he names as such). This device does not seem to have anything to do with his Khitay source. The Han dynasty he calls Han Gaozu (Founding Ancestor of the Han), for example, and the Jin dynasty he calls Jin Wudi (Martial Emperor of the Jin)—in both cases, the titles of their founders. An examination of terminology in contemporary Chinese or Khitay works suggests that it was Rashīd al-Dīn who substituted personal titles for dynastic titles. He must have done so because of an unfamiliarity with the abstract notion of a dynasty separable from its founder. In the Islamic world, the Umayyad and Abbasid dynasties were named after Umayya and ʿAbbās, their respective founders. To him, therefore, the personal names of dynastic founders made sense as the names of their dynasties.

Rashīd al-Dīn compiled the "History of Khitay and Machin" in response to an order from Öljeitü Khan, who wanted one book "that informs about all countries and regions" or "has delved into the history of the ancient kings." Now that "all corners of the earth are under the control of us and of Chinggis Khan's illustrious family, philosophers, astronomers, scholars, and historians of all religions and nations—[Khitay], Machin, India, Kashmir, Tibet, Uighur, and other nations of Turks, Arabs, and Franks [Europeans]—have gathered in droves at our glorious court." Accordingly, it was appropriate that "the histories, stories, and beliefs of their own people" be drawn upon to create "a compendium that would be perfect."[74] Responding to this command, Rashīd al-Dīn observes of Khitay: "While in the past no foreign ruler had ever conquered and occupied the aforementioned country, Chinggis Khan and his illustrious family succeeded in subjugating it and putting it under their command. For that reason, the necessity has emerged to write stories of that country and insert them into this history."[75]

These passages yield two important points. First, Khitay's history was introduced to the Il-khanate only because it was conquered by the Chinggisids and incorporated into their empire. Öljeitü Khan and Rashīd al-Dīn were not among those who ruled that country directly, but they were very much conscious of the fact that Khitay was a part of their Chinggisid empire. Second, the Mongol rulers regarded their conquest of Khitay and Machin as historically unprecedented and therefore worthy of record. Rashīd al-Dīn does note several episodes when foreign peoples, *ṭāīfa*, entered the land of Khitay and established kingdoms there, but he regards the case of the Mongols as completely different. After being ruled by 267 emperors in thirty-six dynasties, the history of Khitay came to an end with "the conquest of the country by the Great Khan's army."[76] The Mongol conquerors did not consider the Great Yuan as the thirty-seventh in the long line of "original dynasties." Their conquest was nothing less than the conclusive suppression of that history of dynasties.

The perspective of the rulers of the Il-khanate suggests that the Mongols and their Chinese subjects maintained different explications of the Mongol empire and its eastern portion, based on fundamentally different worldviews about the legitimacy of the realm and its place in history. The Mongols regarded their realm as apart from Chinese traditions, whereas Chinese—thanks in part to the Mongol endeavor to establish legitimacy in East Asia in Chinese terms—absorbed the Yuan into their orthodox succession of dynasties. For Mongols, as for most other non-Chinese at the time, there was no coherent concept of one geographic or historical "China" nor a belief in a theory of orthodox dynastic succession.

CHINESE LEGITIMATION OF THE MONGOL REGIME
AND THE LEGACY OF "UNIFICATION"

A key term in the ideology that Khubilai Khan's Chinese advisers fashioned to enunciate the logic, and therefore the legitimacy, of his rule over the realm that Chinese knew as Zhongguo (later identified as "China") was "unification" (*tongyi* or *yitong*).[77] The conviction that the Chinese realm should be unified, that unification has always been the goal of those who sought to rule it, sits at the heart of Chinese national consciousness today. It is an idea with a deep and not-uncomplicated past. The founding moment of unification as political goal is conventionally associated with the Qin unification of the Warring States in 221 BCE, though some historians prefigure that event with the Zhou unification in 1046 BCE or go even further back to the founding of "China" by the Yellow Emperor.[78] According to this ideology, China is always best when unified, and in need of unification when it is not. It is a view with which almost no Chinese would argue today. A close examination of Chinese imperial sources reveals, however, that like every political idea, this one has a history. And in that history, as it happens, the Yuan dynasty occupies a curiously important place.

The language of making China one entered the Chinese ideological mainstream via the seven steles that the First Qin Emperor erected on ritual mountain sites around his new realm in the decade between founding his regime in 221 and dying in 210 BCE. In these texts he speaks of having used military power to "amalgamate," or "force together," "all-under-Heaven" (*bing tianxia*). The result was that he "unified all-under-Heaven as [or "under"] one lineage," one text declares; he "made one the great universe," another states; he "pacified and made one all within the universe," according to a third.[79] While these texts reported that the founder assembled a new political unit, all of which he placed under his administration, their language falls short of enunciating a new principle of legitimacy. More significantly, they declined to align the new state with any prior state formation. Conspicuously absent is any suggestion that the Qin was restoring something that the ancestors had achieved, but lost, during the Zhou dynasty. What the founder did was entirely his own accomplishment, without reference to anything in the past. Only after the unity state was securely installed was the Qin boast of unification projected back to the Zhou. "The unity of the Zhou was . . . ephemeral and weak from the very beginning," Yuri Pines has argued. "Careful reading of Zhanguo [Warring States] texts and their pro-unification discussions indicates remarkable lack of interest in the past precedents of political unity."[80] The Qin was unifying, not reunifying.

Not until midway through the Han dynasty would a clear discourse of unification arise. Early elements of this discourse appear in the *Shi ji* (Records of the Grand Historian), the synoptic history that Sima Qian completed just prior to his death in 86 BCE. His account of Chinese state formation tracks the emergence of the Qin without employing the language of unification. He describes the rise of the mythic founder, the Yellow Emperor, in terms of forcing contending warlords to submit to his rule in order to end the suffering that their contention brought to the common people. To designate the extent of that emperor's realm, Sima uses the standard ambiguous phrase, "the four quarters."[81] When he gets to the founding of the Qin dynasty in 221 BCE, known to us as the classic moment of unification, he quotes the First Qin Emperor's comment about "forcing together all-under-Heaven." He then follows this with the first use of the term *yitong*, usually taken to mean "unification," but not here. According to Sima Qian, the founder's advisers declared that under the new dynasty, "the laws and regulations form a single rule" (*faling you yitong*), which they regarded as unprecedented.[82] The Qin in effect unified the territory under Heaven, but it was Qin unification of law that marked that achievement. This is what *yitong* originally meant.

Subsequent official histories track the rise and fall of dynasties that unify the realm, but they decline to identify the idea of "unification" as a civilizational goal. The dynastic history of the Latter Han dynasty (*Hou Han shu*), for example, regretting the rebelliousness throughout the "four quarters" that led to dynastic decline, praises the founder for "stabilizing the realm and spreading his grace over what lies within the seas," but this is not the language of unity. The only time "ruling all as one" (*yitong*) is mentioned is in the context of noting that the warlord Liu Xuan "lacked the means" to do so.[83] The dynastic history of the Song (*Song shi*), compiled under the auspices of the Yuan, praises the founder for "gaining the state," following which "the various states in the four quarters were gradually pacified one by one." Again, the founding of the new dynasty is not written of as an act of unification; it is described in the language of coming to power. Despite the habit of asserting that each dynasty restored the unity of the Chinese empire, this is not how the founding of a dynasty is expressed in the dynastic histories. And so the Song history praises its founder not for unifying the realm but for establishing a dynasty that lasted over three centuries.[84] His virtue consisted in unifying not space but time.

In the Chinese rhetoric of the Yuan dynasty, some of this conceptual structure remains in place, but some has changed.[85] The guiding spatial concept in the Chinese materials is *tianxia*, "all-under-Heaven": an early document from 1233 on the negotiations between the Mongols and the

Song at the fall of the Jin dynasty speaks of "gaining the *tianxia*"—the language of the Song history—and "losing the *tianxia*." The official edict issued on Khubilai's election as Great Khan in 1260 speaks of his ambition in terms of "the great enterprise of *tianxia*"—the language of the Han history. His "Edict of Foundation" issued the same year declares that his ancestors used their military prowess to "pacify the four quarters"—the language of every history since Sima Qian's *Shi ji*.[86] The vocabulary is predictable, unsurprisingly. This was how a new dynasty was expected to declare its emergence.

But the Mongols' conquest presented a difficult challenge for their Chinese advisers. The territory Khubilai ruled was far greater than the territory of earlier dynasties. This posed a problem of historical coherence. "Today the realm has been enlarged beyond the territory of the Han and Tang dynasties," the Chinese official Hao Jing writes in 1260, "and the population has also increased beyond that of the Han and Tang." Hao's concern was that, as the new realm did not by any stretch of the imagination follow the boundaries of the old, his khan might not wish to adopt a Chinese-style administrative system but might instead adopt an Inner Asian format, as some of his Mongol advisers had already advocated. As he delicately weaves his way through this problem, Hao switches in speaking of the realm from *tianxia* to the more neutral term of "territory" (*di*).[87] The spatial coherence of the realm remains general; no one is unifying anything because no Chinese emperor has ever ruled this much territory.

When Khubilai announced the founding of the Yuan dynasty at the end of 1271, he broke with Chinese precedent by overturning the tradition of naming a dynasty after the region in which the founder arose (a tradition to which no subsequent dynasty would return). His new realm would take the name of Yuan, meaning "origin," a keyword in the *Book of Changes*.[88] This choice—which must surely have been made for him by his Chinese advisers—aligned the identity of the new regime with a key text of the Chinese tradition, but the focus on origination was tantamount to declaring that the regime was unprecedented. Lack of precedent is not something to which the Chinese (or any) tradition responds well. A solution began to emerge in the 1270s. The edict of investiture of Khubilai's empress and crown prince in 1273 phrased his legitimacy as "authoring and receiving the *datong*," the "great unity" that was said to link all dynasties to each other in a natural chain.[89] This was a formula designed to meet Chinese expectations regarding the legitimacy of succession. When Khubilai announced the following year that he would invade the south and take over the territory of the Southern Song dynasty, he phrased it in terms of Heaven's having given him the opportunity to "rule universally" or "rule everything as one thing" (*yi tong*), without specifying whether that meant his right to incorporate Song territory into his realm or his right to seize the mandate of the Song as its legitimate successor.[90] As it took the Mongols another five years to crush the south, it was not obvious that Heaven was ready to give the Song mandate to the Mongols.

Succession became a thorny problem, at least for Khubilai's Chinese audience. What was the line of succession that unified the Yuan with earlier dynasties? Did the correct line of succession flow to the Mongols from the Song dynasty, or had it passed to them from the Jin dynasty, which the Mongols had eradicated thirty-seven years before starting their own? What about the Liao, the Khitan dynasty that the Jurchens had conquered before taking over the Northern Song? Should the Yuan claim that regime as part of its inheritance? Khubilai was indifferent to these questions, but they were matters of intense concern to the Chinese who were trying to construct legitimacy for the new regime in terms that would appeal to Chinese, and thus justify their decision to join the Mongol regime. Not until 1343 was a final decision on this business made: the correct succession would flow through all three—Liao, Jin, and Song—making them all ancestors to the Yuan.

This decision threw the Chinese intellectual world into turmoil, for it was assumed that Heaven handed out its mandates only one at a time. The most prominent opponent to this new formula was the eminent scholar Yang Weizhen.[91] By recognizing all three, Yang argued, the Yuan failed to show that there had been only one single line of correct succession leading to itself. Instead of allowing the *zhengtong*, the "orthodox line of succession," to split among multiple channels, Yang proposed the higher concept of *da yitong*, or "great unitary succession." He took this concept from the Gongyang commentary on the revered classic the *Spring and Autumn Annals*. This Warring States idea grew from the then-recent notion that royal succession should adhere to patrilineal descent rather than follow the more ancient pattern of indirect matrilineal succession from uncle to nephew. *Da yitong* was coined to organize the many competing rulers of the pre-Qin era according to a single line of transmission. As Heaven handed out its mandate once at a time, there could be only one line of succession—and therefore only one continuous Chinese polity. Since the Liao had fallen to the Jin and not the Yuan, and the Jin had fallen to the Great Khan Ögedei and not to Khubilai, none of these polities earned the right to be in that line of transmission. Thus, Yang explained, that line should bypass these "illegitimate" regimes and go straight from the Song to the Yuan. "In my view," he wrote to the emperor, "the 'great unitary succession' of our Yuan dynasty should be with the Song and not with the Liao, which lies even further in the past than the Jin." Accordingly, Yang wanted the start of the Yuan dynasty to be retroactively delayed to the final destruction of the Song in 1279. "So long as the mandate of the Song had not been removed for even one day, then the great transmission [*datong*] of our Yuan had yet to coalesce, even for one day." To arrange the past in any other way made it impossible to write the Yuan into "the *da yitong*," the great unitary succession of dynasties. "Why should we be anxious to extend our Yuan back an extra half a century to the founding of the state by the Great Ancestor [Chinggis Khan], or even just seventeen years to the election of the Generational Ancestor [Khubilai Khan], and make that the moment at which the great succession of all-under-heaven [*tianxia*] came into being?" Make it simple: let the Song fall and the Yuan rise in one clean step, and leave out all those other Inner Asian polities that rose and fell along the way. Effectively, pretend that no Inner Asian states had ruled China.

Yang Weizhen's concern was not to produce truthful history. It was to create a history that proved the legitimacy of the dynasty he served in Chinese terms. For Yang, the Yuan was a Chinese dynasty, not a Mongol polity, and it had to be seen as such. The difference in perspective between legitimacy in Chinese terms and legitimacy in Mongol terms remained in place right to the end of the dynasty. The Sino-Mongolian inscription of 1346 cited earlier, characterizing Chinggis Khan's conquest as stooping to pick up lesser polities as if they were fallen leaves, hints at this conceptual divide. The stele on which this text was inscribed is bilingual. The Chinese side speaks of the conquest in conventional Chinese terms as "richly possessing all within the four seas." The Mongolian side uses a different metaphor, stating "that the people have become one [from the place where the sun rises] unto [the place where] the sun sets."[92] The Chinese text stresses the bringing of all territory under Mongol control, whereas the Mongolian text celebrates the bringing of all people under Chinggis's rule. The one expresses the agrarian ideal of possessing all agricultural land and putting it to the plow; the other, the pastoral goal of commanding people. To *da yitong* was to rule everything on a grand scale, not to "unify," much less to reunify, an abstract entity called China.

In the Ming dynasty, the meaning of *yitong* migrated from unitary succession to territorial unity, becoming the catchword of the new dynasty. Founder Zhu Yuanzhang could not boast of his achievement in replacing the Yuan with the Ming without mentioning *yitong*. As a text of 1370 claimed on his behalf, he had "brought together all who dwell within the oceans: warriors east, nomads west, foreigners north and south, Vietnamese and Mongols: all have been brought onto the map."[93] This claim was conspicuously untrue, as his realm did not include any part of the Mongolian Plateau or Vietnam.[94] Still, the new emperor felt that his legitimacy depended on his being able to claim for his Great State whatever regions had been under the control of the Yuan Great State. To declare that he had "reunified" the realm was political rhetoric rather than geographical description, but it became an idée fixe that no subsequent emperor of China could relinquish. What had been the Mongol empire should henceforth be the Chinese empire, even if no Chinese state ever succeeded in "reunifying" the country on quite that scale.

The Ming expulsion of the Great Khan Toghön Temür from Beijing in 1368 did not mark the end of Mongol authority in Eurasia. In the eastern zone of Eurasia, he and his successors continued to rule a smaller but still formidable polity north and west of the Ming, incorporating Liaodong, bordering on the Koryŏ state of the Korean peninsula, and embracing large parts of the Mongolian Plateau. This successor state, referred to variously as the Northern Yuan *ulus*, Northern Yuan dynasty, or Later Yuan (Khoitu Yuwan), maintained relations with Tamerlane's imperial court as well as with the Koryŏ dynasty and continued to exist until shortly after the Manchu defeat of the last Mongol Great Khan, Ligdan, in 1632. Mongol writings of the seventeenth and eighteenth centuries thus tend to present the Chinggisid empire as having spanned more than four centuries, from 1206 to 1636. As Christopher Atwood has noted, Mongol historian Rashipunsug in his 1775 *Dai Yuwan ulus-un bolor erike* (Crystal rosary of the Great Yuan *ulus*) "considered that the legitimate succession of the throne passed from the earlier Yuan to the later Yuan and directly to the [Manchu] Qing dynasty, bypassing the Ming usurpers altogether."[95] Here was a line of unitary succession that was quite different from the Chinese conception of who had been legitimate rulers for all those centuries. Both traditions could survey the same series of events and legitimately understand them entirely differently.

Elsewhere in Eurasia after the Yuan dynasty, Mongols continued to rule large chunks of the continent. The Golden Horde, or the Kipchak khanate, held sway over the Rus (Russian) empire for another two centuries. In Central Asia the Chagatai khanate split into two, each half remaining a dominant force in Transoxania and on the Mongolian steppe, respectively. Descent from Chinggis Khan continued to be the principal legitimizing basis of rule in Central Asia, and Mongols who lacked such ancestry either falsely claimed it or sought to rule in the name of a nominal Chinggisid ruler. In West Asia, the Il-khan Abu Sa'id died in 1335, possibly of the plague, and the Il-khanate broke apart. Most of it was eventually conquered by Temür, better known as Tamerlane, in the 1380s and 1390s.

Temür lacked Chinggisid credentials and so ruled in the name of the Chagatai khan. He asserted his rule over a significant part of the former Mongol Great State and pushed south, attacking Delhi in 1398. His descendant Babur, of Timurid and Chinggisid descent, eventually founded the Mughal empire, which comprised most of the Indian subcontinent and Afghanistan and lasted into the middle of the eighteenth century.[96]

In Tibet, Pakmodrupa hierarchs replaced the Sakya hegemons and by 1358 ended the Great Khan's influence over Tibet.[97] By the mid-fifteenth century, however, Tibetan Buddhist leaders started to establish relations and alliances with Mongol khans again, and for centuries thereafter Tümed, Khoshot, Zunghar, and other Mongol nobles played leading roles as rulers of parts of the Tibetan Plateau and as benefactors and protectors of Tibetan Buddhist hierarchs, including the Dalai Lamas, and their religious orders, a subject we develop further in chapters 4 and 5.

The legacy of the Mongols in the successor polities of their empire was extensive and profound. One such legacy relates directly to the conceptualization of the legitimacy of rulers and their polities, one of the themes of our study. The Mongol Great Khans had deployed multiple concurrent ideologies of legitimacy. These were submission to the will of the highest God or Heaven (*degere tengri*); descent from the founder of the empire, Chinggis Khan; and, since Khubilai's reign, the Tibetan Buddhist sanctification of political authority.[98] These conceptualizations survived in various forms, most notably among the Manchu (Jurchen) rulers who later dominated East Asia and parts of Inner Asia for almost three centuries until the turn of the twentieth century. They adapted the Mongols' multiple approach to legitimacy by emphasizing different credentials to different peoples over whom they claimed authority, establishing a link to the past that was distinct for each civilizational world.

The founders of the Manchu empire, known as the Qing Great State, asserted their Inner Asian identity and invoked Chinggis Khan's legacy to establish legitimacy among the Mongols. Nurhaci had himself recognized in 1616 as the "Enlightened Khan" and demonstrated Heaven's approval through military victory, as did his son and successor, Hong Taiji. They created their own Great State, eventually defeating the last Great Khan in 1632. Manchu emperors, starting with Nurhaci, also presented themselves as righteous Buddhist rulers, seeking and acquiring legitimacy from Tibetan Buddhist leaders by becoming their benefactors.[99] Invoking the idealized model of the Khubilai-Phagpa relationship, they mostly patronized the dominant Gelug order of Tibetan Buddhism (Gelugpa) and in particular the Dalai Lamas, and they were recognized by the latter as incarnations of Manjusri and as *chakravartins*, or universal Buddhist rulers. For the Chinese and the broader Sinic world, Manchu emperors assumed the mantle of the Son of Heaven and claimed uninterrupted succession of their dynasty from the Ming, an indispensable requirement for legitimacy. Like Khubilai, Hong Taiji chose a dynastic name, Qing, not derived from his family's place of origin but representing a core word in the Chinese philosophical tradition meaning "pure" or "clear." In this and so many other ways, the legacy of Mongol rule for generating and propagating the legitimacy of imperial authority remained strong, if not always visible, through both the Ming dynasty and the Manchu Qing empire.[100]

CHAPTER THREE

INTERPOLITY RELATIONS AND THE TRIBUTE SYSTEM OF MING CHINA

China as we know it today could not have been predicted from its ancient past. Through a long process of conflict and collaboration between those who thought of themselves as born to the "cultural magnificence centered on the Yellow River Plain"—to be cumbersomely literal in translating China's literary name, Zhonghua—and those whom they thought of as otherwise situated, what we call China came into being. As a polity, it has waxed and waned, sometimes disappearing altogether, sometimes unifying into one, sometimes splitting into many. As a civilization, it has over the past three millennia drawn on disparate beliefs, institutions, and practices from regions as distantly separated as Siberia and Vietnam, assembling a wide reservoir of political and spiritual resources whose origins may be obscure to most Chinese. Those who identify themselves with the Chinese civilizational world have little difficulty recognizing themselves as Chinese, but exactly what such a world should include has defied most observers—Chinese and non-Chinese—who have attempted to put this into words.

The first authority to whom those who seek to define Chinese civilization usually turn is Confucius. This choice has the unfortunate effect of leaving out the tsunami of influences that have swept across China in the two and a half millennia since the time of Confucius. Still, Confucianism is the point from which most Chinese begin when asked to explain their cultural norms, citing phrases and sentences from the *Analects*, the sayings of Confucius collected by his students after his death. It has also served as the canonical foundation on which all major thinkers in the Chinese tradition have since built their ideas and theories about the proper conduct of life, the obligations of the state, and the requirements that subjects must fulfill for the construction of a durable moral order. Within these parameters has emerged a sense of what may be termed "law": not law in the modern sense of civil law, but law in the sense of the rules governing the relation-

ships through which social and political order is imagined to emerge—
rites as much as rights.

RITUALS OF HIERARCHY

The key concept in the universe that Confucius describes in the *Analects* is
Heaven (*tian*). Heaven is the source and final authority for human actions,
whether the actions of the ordinary person or of the ruler, who was designated "Heaven's son" (*tianzi*) and whose right to rule was understood as
having been given to him by divine mandate. Heaven was the transcendent
source of all that was good in people, so that the worst thing one could
do was to commit an offense against Heaven. This was the context within
which ritual was performed. To offend Heaven, as Confucius put it, left one
"without that to which rites may be addressed." Heaven was also the point
of reference from which the world itself derived, as enunciated in the common expression "all-under-Heaven" (*tianxia*). Quite what this expression
meant in real-world terms fluctuated depending on the reach and ambitions of the Chinese state. It could name the realm that the emperor ruled
on Heaven's behalf, or it could denote the entire world over which Heaven
arched. Heaven presided largely without intervention other than at extraordinary moments, such as nominating a ruler's successor or, more radically in a time of extreme "distress and want," revoking an existing mandate to one ruler and passing it to another. The moral person and the moral
ruler alike were advised to know and stand in awe of Heaven's mandate.[1]

Heaven served as the point of reference from which flowed the moral
principles that Chinese associate with Confucianism. The most basic principle was hierarchy: every person occupied a social position that placed
him or her in relationships of deference to those above and responsibility
to those below. The only relationship of equality in the social hierarchy
was between friends, but that was the exception that proved the rule of
the Confucian moral system, which was inequality. The way Confucianism managed these unequal relationships was to conduct them through
ritual, which choreographed how one should act appropriately in one's relationships. Since ritual intercourse drew the map for social intercourse,
harmony must always result. The ritual management of hierarchy had its
political valence, for Confucius regarded correct relationships within the
family as analogous to the correct relationship between ruler and subject.

At the level of the state, the ritual corpus was paired with the legal code
that every state was expected to promulgate in its first years. The founding
emperor of the Ming dynasty, Zhu Yuanzhang, understood this to be the
case. He opened the 1397 preface to the last edition of the Ming Code pro-

duced during his reign with this statement: "I have the realm and govern it by imitating antiquity. Rituals are manifested to guide the people; law codes are established to restrain the wayward."² If we put this into a modern legal vocabulary, Zhu was making three important announcements to his subjects, and ultimately to the world: that sovereignty, which can only devolve from Heaven, resided in his person; that his respect for antiquity attested to the legitimacy of his authority; and that the rules governing his subjects were enshrined in the dynasty's ritual corpus and its law code. Zhu was not declaring the legal code and the ritual corpus to be the same thing. Both were texts, which is the form in which both have to be formulated, but they were different texts that applied to different areas and were intended to solve different problems. Still, they formed a pair: rituals and laws together brought the Chinese legal subject into being. Behavior that offended against the ritual corpus was just as "unlawful" as offenses against the law code.

The norm of first priority in Confucian law and ritual, hierarchy, imposed a steep gradient between Chinese and non-Chinese. Confucius puts this with striking harshness in verse 5 of chapter 3 of the *Analects*. He declares that non-Chinese, for whom he uses the standard terms *yi* and *di* (both of which are loosely equivalent to the English term "barbarian"), are inferior to Chinese, even when they have rulers and the Chinese don't. The distinction was not absolute in practice, however, for elsewhere Confucius makes the odd declaration that he would like to live among the *yi*. When asked whether this would sully him, he assured his challenger that he had the moral superiority to withstand the pollution; he phrases this same inoculation elsewhere as moral sincerity. Later in the *Analects*, Confucius goes much further by insisting that foreigners who are sincere in their words and honest in their actions can attain moral perfection quite as well as Chinese—which casts some doubt on the wisdom that later became conventional, which is that between Chinese (*hua*) and foreigners (*yi*) lay a moral gulf too wide to be bridged.³

The *Analects* is far from providing a definitive account of the categorical distinction between *hua* and *yi*, between Chinese and non-Chinese. In later eras, the line between the two was a malleable boundary that could move as power shifted and cultural practices changed. It was also a permeable membrane through which Chinese and non-Chinese could pass, depending on the level of charisma (or, in contrast, of border guarding) demonstrated by Chinese civilization at the time. Beyond that border lay *yi* polities whose rulers might choose to acknowledge a theoretically universal order pivoting on the Chinese emperor and peaking in Heaven—which they did by sending envoys bearing tribute to the Chinese court, each time thereby resubstantiating the boundary. Regardless of how that boundary moved over time, the distinction was seen as foundational in asserting the unequal relationship between China and the rest of the world—indeed, as constitutional in determining what the Chinese state considered to be legitimately within its interests.

Central to the management of foreign relations, as for relations within the state and family, was ritual. In the absence of international relations in the modern sense, ritual stood in as the set of rules to guide norms and set expectations of how other states should behave. Chinese wrote ceremonies to manage these relations, reserving "law" for domestic purposes. This is why the Ming Code, the core laws of the dynasty, has almost nothing to say on the question of foreigners, recognizing them as lying beyond the jurisdiction of the Chinese state. Foreigners come up in the code only when it expresses the fear that Chinese might conspire with them against the interests of the state.[4] Ritual was thus the means through which something like a Chinese *jus gentium* found its expression.

The ritual corpus that applied to the conduct of China's relations with other states consisted of two components. The first was the emperor's use of what is termed "investiture" to extend diplomatic recognition in the form of a conferral of inferior status on other rulers. The second component was the "guest ritual," designed to demonstrate the foreign rulers' acknowledgment of this inferiority by dispatching envoys to the imperial court. This protocol required foreign envoys to submit tribute in regulated kinds and amounts and at set intervals, acting out a choreography of deference to the throne. Foreign envoys understood that these were the rules of interpolity communication and largely consented to them. This was simply how matters between states were managed. The only way a state in communication with China could challenge these rules was to decline to send a tribute mission, which was tantamount to withdrawing recognition of China as regional hegemon. The cost of this decision was high, for it rendered trade with China illegal.[5]

It has been argued that Confucianism played a significant role in ruling out the use of force to manage international relations.[6] Certainly the avoidance of force has been a Confucian norm since the time of Confucius himself. When Duke Ling of Wei asked Confucius about military tactics, the philosopher brusquely refused to respond. "With regard to the laying out of ritual vessels," he replied to the duke, "this I have heard something about. As for deploying troops, that I have never studied." The following day he pulled up stakes and left Wei.[7] In fact, no state achieves the territorial extent that China did without the use of force, and most rulers who founded new dynasties in China did so through supremacy in battle.

Whether the philosophical disinclination for war as a policy option has shaped China's international relations is an open question, however, for as we shall see in this chapter, China has often backed its foreign policy with force or the threat of force. In most cases sheer scale ensured compliance. To restrict an assessment of China's use of force to the most obedient states within the larger Confucian zone (Korea, Japan, and Dai Viet—the northern part of today's Vietnam[8]—being the leading cases), as most who regard China's foreign policy as the pursuit of harmony tend to do, misses the larger context within which Chinese states have managed relations beyond the polities that claimed to subscribe to Confucian values. It also neglects the degree to which violence has been used to determine and maintain boundaries within the Sinic zone and dulls our vigilance regarding the threat of military conflict today.

The rules and rites through which China made other polities' relations with it lawful comprise what is known as the tribute system. It was the construct through which China conducted its foreign policy—and presented, interpreted, and recorded it. It was at the same time the architecture with which other states and rulers had to comply in order to have diplomatic and trade relations with China. The roots of the system go back to the time of Confucius or before, when lesser rulers on the North China Plain managed their relationships with greater rulers by submitting tribute to them. This arrangement was formalized into local levies after the centralization of power under the Qin dynasty in 221 BCE, when tribute was imposed on regions within the empire to produce goods for the political center.[9] Subsequently, this model of tribute paying was extended outward to rulers and polities beyond the borders of the realm. Submitting and receiving tribute provided a platform to ritually confirm the Chinese emperor's apical position, mandated by Heaven, in the universal hierarchy of states.

The system permitted the delineation of two categories of foreign status. As noted casually in a Ministry of War document of 1432 preserved in Korea, foreign envoys belonged either to a *wangguo*, a kingly realm, or to one of the *siyi*, or "four tribes." States in both categories enjoyed the privilege (from the Chinese point of view) of submitting tribute.[10] Kingdoms were those polities that China regarded as junior partners in the Confucian world: Chosŏn Korea, Japan, and Dai Viet in the first instance, though rulers in Southeast Asia could be given the designation of *wang* at the emperor's discretion (a designation also used for the imperial princes who held fiefs inside China, with whom these rulers were placed on a theoretical par). The Ming emperors, when they sent copies of the annual Ming calendar to these states, privileged kings over other rulers by sending each a personal copy bound in silk in imperial yellow.[11] The so-called "four tribes" denoted polities that fell short of the Confucian civilizational standard: principally the nomadic states but also less organized entities in the southwest. Their rulers were addressed by titles below "king" and did not receive yellow-bound calendars. Who lay within which category was mutable, as was who remained beyond direct supervision. Many small polities in the southwest were dragged to the Ming side of the border in the early decades of the dynasty as the founding emperor pushed down into Southeast Asia. To be within the bounds was to be subject to rule from Beijing and be levied for taxes and corvée. To be without, and yet still enjoy tributary status, was to be left to the authority of the invested ruler on the expectation that he would send tribute missions on a regular basis. Tributary status was in practice an agreement by the Ming not to invade and by the invested ruler not to launch a military attack.

The Chinese point of view regarded the tribute system as useful for maintaining distance as well as contact, always a difficult balance in foreign relations. A Chinese norm was offered, and foreign states were arranged in a civilizational hierarchy in terms of their willingness to conform to that norm. As Emperor Tianshun explained to Lê Thánh Tông, the ruler of Dai Viet, "We are the Emperor, and having received Heaven's great mandate, We rule the *hua* and the *yi*. One culture provides the norm for all places, its influence transforming all beyond the four quarters. Of all who are vaulted by Heaven and sustained by Earth, there is none who does not submit in heart."[12] Tianshun's claim that he was receiving universal submission rings hollowly, given that he had been taken hostage by Mongols seventeen years earlier during a Ming-Mongol border war. But the tribute system was a modeling exercise, not a description of actual relations, and what was always being modeled was the distinction between *hua* and *yi*. As the *Analects* stated unequivocally, to be foreign was to be not Chinese. That cultural boundary was so strong that Tianshun's grandson in 1500, in response to stories of foreign envoys in the capital getting beaten up, posted a warning that anyone who "dares to gather in the street and stare at the foreigners, make fun of them, throw potsherds or tiles at them, or strike and injure them" would be punished.[13] Xenophobic animosity was a low-grade dynamic of the tribute system, generating disincentives with its own border-maintenance project. But the emperor wished to see foreigners in Beijing—living proof of his charisma in drawing them to China—and wanted street-level hostility staunched.

Scholarship through much of the twentieth century dismissed the tribute system as Sinocentric, archaic, and dysfunctional. At worst it reflected an "imaginary world empire" and was an entirely artificial system in which foreign states colluded to the extent that it served their interests.[14] It was best reduced to functional terms as nothing more than "a cloak for trade," as John Fairbank and Teng Ssu-yü phrased it in 1941.[15] Two decades later, however, Fairbank spearheaded a reinvestigation of the tribute system more on its own terms, focusing his investigation on the Ming's conduct of relations, and concluded that it offered "a repertoire of means available to rulers of the Chinese empire in their relations with non-Chinese . . . along a spectrum that runs from one extreme of military conquest and administrative assimilation to another extreme of complete non-intercourse and avoidance of contact."[16] Scholarly evaluation of the system has since taken a further step with the work of Hamashita Takeshi and his Japanese colleagues, who have argued for bringing the tribute system back to the center of East Asian international relations, on the understanding that states in this part of the world in fact participated in a unified regional system. China was the hegemonic power in the system but did not control or unilaterally determine the diplomatic and trade relations linking this region. With the onslaught of Western imperialism, the game changed.[17]

Our purpose in this volume, as we stated in chapter 1, is neither to deny the salience of the tribute system to a renewed vision of Asian relations nor to bring it back as the central organizing principle. It is to recognize that, under certain circumstances and at certain moments, the rules and expectations of the system guided the judgments shaping interpolity relations, and that the rhetoric of the system made interpolity relations in East Asia legible to those involved. To regard it as a sublimation of other dynamics, particularly of economic relations (which we largely do not address in this study), is to neglect the terms in which some, not all, Asian states made sense of their relations with China, and by which China sought to explain its capacities and contradictions as a hegemonic power at least to itself. Such neglect prevents us from seeing how those states that submitted to the rules of the system calculated their positions as tributaries and understood what they were doing. These states fulfilled their tribute obligations not merely to satisfy China's economic, political, or symbolic needs but to serve their own interests, which were always multiple and can never be derived from China's interests.

The reproduction of the system over many centuries demonstrates that it was in some measure effective in setting and meeting the expectations of state rulers and state envoys on both sides of the relationship. Although in this chapter we focus on the tribute system as applied by the Ming state, the analysis pertains as well to the Yuan and Qing regimes to the extent that they used Confucian norms and the tribute system, as they did, in the conduct of some of their foreign relations. To transpose this system into modern legal rhetoric, the rules of the system could fairly be called the body of Confucian law of nations, designed to put into place what could further be called a Confucian international order.

THE TRIBUTE SYSTEM AND REGIME LEGITIMACY

Most Asian rulers had no difficulty grasping the rules of China's intra-Asian diplomacy. They accepted what might be termed the consensual fiction of Chinese power: that the emperor ruled "all-under-Heaven" (*tianxia*) on Heaven's behalf, and that his ritual jurisdiction extended outward to "all within the four seas" (*sihai zhi nei*) or, sometimes, "all within the four directions" (*sifang*). This fiction rested on the Chinese geographical imaginary of all Earth submitting to Heaven and thus of all rulers prostrating themselves before the emperor. The evident impracticality of managing universal submission was not something the tribute system could acknowledge. This impracticality produced unease, not just for the global geographical imaginary under which China labored but for the emperor's very legitimacy. This was the Achilles' heel of the system, especially at times of regime instability or regime transition in China. What if no tribute envoys arrived? What if at least part of what lay under Heaven chose to ignore the would-be hegemon?

Zhu Yuanzhang, the man who came to power in 1368 by driving out the Mongols and replacing their Yuan dynasty with his own, the Ming, was intensely aware of this vulnerability. During his first year on the throne as Emperor Hongwu, Zhu received tribute from no other ruler.[18] Tribute visits mattered to him because they served as public confirmation of his right to rule. This confirmation was not just for the benefit of potentates beyond his borders; it was a demonstration to his bureaucrats and his subjects that he enjoyed Heaven's mandate and that the Ming was now the legitimate ruling dynasty. But the expectation of confirmation fueled anxiety when foreign acknowledgment of his reign was not forthcoming. This anxiety comes out in Hongwu's first proclamation to Dai Viet, promulgated on 3 February 1369: "Recently the Yuan capital has been overcome and pacified and all within the borders are united, thus constituting our legitimate succession. And now our relations with all both near and far are those of security and freedom from concerns, as we all enjoy the blessings of an era of great peace." Having congratulated himself on his complete success, Hongwu then turned to what was worrying him: "There is only the matter that you foreigners in the four directions, you chieftains and commanders, being far away, have not learned of this. I am thus issuing this proclamation so that you will be fully aware of the situation."[19] To correct this failure, on 26 February envoys were dispatched to Japan, Champa (the southern part of today's Vietnam), Java, and Coromandel to demand tribute; ten days after that (9 March), envoys were sent to Yunnan and again to Japan.[20] Hongwu could only wait for a response, but finally it came. Champa's embassy was the first to arrive, having departed before Hongwu's envoys had reached their destination. Champa's envoy Huduman arrived on 12 March and presented the emperor with tigers, elephants, and Champa products from King Ada Azhe. Hongwu was "greatly pleased," he wrote in his letter back to Ada Azhe, noting that the Mongols had failed to maintain a close relationship between China and foreign countries. As an explicit token of his universal position as Son of Heaven, Hongwu sent Ada Azhe, besides the usual return gift of forty bolts of the finest silk, a copy of the calendar for the second year of the Ming dynasty.[21] Ada Azhe may not have lived within Ming space, but he now lived within Ming time. A delegation from Dai Viet in July also went home with silk and a calendar.[22]

Even though Champa had sent Huduman, in his reply to Ada Azha, Hongwu felt compelled to repeat his concern that, although "All under Heaven is now at peace, foreigners in the four directions have not heard about this."[23] Champa responded by sending a second delegation right away. Less than three months later, however, another delegation arrived from Champa to complain that Dai Viet had attacked Champa and to ask the Ming for support against their ancient enemy. Here for China was a second vulnerability that came with being at the apex of the tribute system: intervening in the affairs of other states without the knowledge or resources to do so effectively. As Hongwu put it in his letters to both parties on 30 December 1370, the situation between them was "difficult to assess" from Nanjing. All he could do was order a ceasefire and send envoys in the hope that they might be able to sort things out.[24] The envoy from Champa was sent home two weeks later—with a full calendar for the third year of Hongwu, plus three thousand copies of an abbreviated calendar. The conflict later proved to be an opening for Ming intervention in Dai Viet, one that would lead eventually, and disastrously, to full-scale invasion under his son, the Yongle emperor.

Having received missions from Champa, Dai Viet, and Korea (Koryŏ), the Hongwu emperor at the end of 1369 ordered the Ministry of Rites to enter the mountains and rivers of these three territories into the register of official sacrifices to the spirits of the Earth alongside China's mountains and rivers: a sort of ritual annexation that advertised at home the extent of Ming authority beyond its borders. It was also an excuse for Hongwu to send envoys to all three countries ordering them to hold Chinese rites on their territory and have his edict on the matter inscribed on stone. This was necessary, as he put it, "to demonstrate Our will of looking on all equally."[25]

In his third year as emperor, impatient at having heard nothing from the rest of Asia, Hongwu dispatched envoys to the rulers of Coromandel, Suoli, and Japan to remind them that Korea, Dai Viet, and Champa had all "recognized themselves as subjects and sent tribute" and that they should do the same.[26] In July 1370 he enlarged the invitation to include Java as well as the Uighur and other polities further west, reminding them that tributary rulers in Southeast Asia had already fallen into line. "In imitation of the way in which the former emperors ruled all under Heaven, I wish only that the people of China and abroad all be happy in their places. We are nonetheless anxious that, secluded in your distant places, you have not yet heard of Our will. Thus, I am sending envoys to go and instruct you so that you will all know of this."[27] By 1371 all had dutifully responded. Hongwu was gratified. The entry for every year in the official chronology of his reign—minus that unfortunate first year—ends with the list of the tribute missions that arrived at the new regime's imperial court in Nanjing.

Even as the tribute system came back into operation, however, Hongwu remained alert to every slight, shortfall, and other breach of propriety. He rejected the Korean mission that showed up in 1379 with a lavish gift of a hundred catties of gold and ten thousand ounces of silver, as these amounts were in excess of what protocol required. The following year he rejected a Japanese mission on the grounds that it did not carry the correct documentation (Japanese regional lords competed with each other over the right to send tribute missions, and one in 1380 stepped in to preempt whoever had official authorization).[28] The system inadvertently provoked a major crisis in October 1379, when an ambassador of Ada Azhe arrived from Champa. It was the prime minister, Hu Weiyong, who received the emissaries, not the emperor. Hongwu learned about the embassy only because his eunuchs saw the elephants the ambassador had brought as tribute.[29] The emperor was furious. Diplomatic theater it may have been for the tribute bearers, but for the emperor this was serious politics. Hongwu charged Hu Weiyong not just with failing to report a tribute mission but with conspiring with hostile foreign forces to assassinate him and replace the Ming dynasty with his own. It is impossible to find any substance to these charges, on which matter the *Ming shi* (History of the Ming dynasty) is uncharacteristically sparse on details.[30] Whatever the truth of the matter, the results were shockingly destructive. Hongwu himself estimated that he put fifteen thousand people to death in the purge that followed. The fury of his reaction suggests that we need to see the tribute system as more than Sinocentric formalism; it was a principal arbiter of regime legitimacy.[31]

With the death of Hongwu, the Ming record of its foreign relations goes blank. Not a single tribute mission is registered in any official document during the unsettled four years of the Jianwen era (1399–1402).[32] Envoys must have arrived, but Jianwen's uncle Zhu Di, who overthrew his nephew and took the reign-era title of Yongle, wanted all mention of the nephew removed from the official record. Every tribute embassy to Jianwen had to disappear in order to show that foreign rulers had never recognized Jianwen and had simply been waiting for the next legitimate emperor to climb to the throne. The stakes were high for Yongle. Diplomatic recognition was the only way he could hope to gain legitimacy, other than threatening his subjects with death if they defied him—which they did, and to which he responded with mass executions. Externally Yongle went on the offensive and in October 1402 ordered the Ministry of Rites, which handled foreign relations, to dispatch envoys to Dai Viet, Ayutthaya (Siam), Java, Ryukyu (Okinawa), Japan, Coromandel, Samudra (northern Sumatra), and Champa. In his letter to the ruler of Champa, he declared that, now that he had taken the throne, "all within the four seas are one family." It was a way of putting other rulers on notice that their deference to the Ming should be submission to him. He went on in the same communication to state: "It is proper that we widely proclaim that there are no outsiders. All countries that wish to express sincerity by coming to offer tribute are to be allowed to do so."[33] For Yongle, anxiously waiting for tribute envoys to arrive and acknowledge him, no foreign ruler could put himself beyond the pale of his suzerainty.

Chosŏn Korea, Ayutthaya, and Sipsongpanna (Cheli in Chinese) sent envoys at the start of the following year, but the hoped-for flood of foreign dignitaries proclaiming Yongle's rulership did not materialize.[34] Through 1403, he sent out more envoys armed with imperial proclamations. On 22 October, the emperor reminded the Ministry of Rites that "the Emperor occupies the central position and cherishes and governs the 10,000 countries. He is as great as Heaven and Earth and there is nothing that he does not cover or support. Those distant people who have attached themselves are all comforted and soothed and thus others wish to follow them." Yongle was able to cite only one case of this having actually happened, but that one case was enough to warrant reminding ministry officials that "from now on, all the people of all countries outside who wish to enter China are allowed to do so," even if few were actually taking up the offer. A week later, he sent eunuch Yin Qing "to take an imperial proclamation for the instruction of the various countries of Melaka and Cochin and to confer upon the kings of these countries gold-spangled silk gauze fabrics and parasols together with patterned fine silks and coloured silks," essentially bribing regional rulers into recognizing his regime.[35]

In Melaka, Yin Qing met with success. Its young king, Parameswara, agreed to send a tribute mission to China.[36] Parameswara's envoy reached Nanjing in 1405 and requested that Yongle not just accept Melaka as a tributary state but enfeoff a local hill as a protector of the Ming realm. The language of the request was that Yongle should treat Melaka as though it were "like an administrative division of China"—not that Melaka should thereby become part of the Ming state, but that it be deemed to be an extension of its ritual geography. The payoff from the Melakan point of view was the entitlement to send tribute on a more frequent basis than usually permitted. Yongle accepted. In his reply, he asserted an all-under-Heaven position by declaring that the virtue of his father, Hongwu, "pervaded the Universe, including all beyond Heaven and Earth. His knowledge encompassed all and he acted with divine understanding. Of all living things within Heaven and Earth, there is none on which his secretly conferred beneficence has not been bestowed." This was more than Hongwu would have claimed for himself, but this was the filial son speaking. Yongle attached a poem that opens with a bolder assertion of China's centrality in the web of tribute:

> To the vast seas south and west, China reaches out,
> Pervading Heaven and encompassing Earth for a hundred million
>   years,
> Washed by the Sun and bathed by the Moon. . . .
> Their king, devoted to all that is good and right, wishes to turn to
>   our Court,
> Wants his country to become like a division of China and follow
>   Chinese ways.[37]

By incorporating a hill in Melaka into China's ritual geography, Yongle was simply doing what his father had already done with mountains in Dai Viet, Champa, and Chosŏn, and what he himself would later do in Brunei. He was not declaring Chinese political sovereignty over Melaka; he was incorporating it into the ritual geography of all-under-Heaven. He was also signaling his willingness to move Melakans closer to the *hua* side of the *hua–yi* spectrum.

This was the language of diplomacy, expressing an arrangement that was accepted because it met needs on both sides. Europeans found the whole business puzzling and, by the nineteenth century, offensive. To be fair to the Manchus, who ruled China at the time, no Qing emperor ever bothered to suggest that Europeans and Chinese were "one family." Our reason for contrasting European and Asian expectations regarding Chinese foreign relations is, first, to note in passing that different diplomatic norms prevailed in different parts of the world and, second, to observe that diplomatic counterparts of the Ming and Qing, East Asian as much as Euro-American, conceived of their relations with those states in terms distinct from the claims of Chinese rhetoric, while leaving both sides relatively free to sort out a modus vivendi. Others have noted the fictionality of the system of hierarchical gift exchange we call tribute by looking through the non-Chinese end of the telescope, where what Chinese regarded as submissive compliance, others treated as evasive hoodwinking.[38] But as we have seen, it is possible to make the same discovery by following the reports of tribute missions in the official *History of the Ming* as well as in the *Veritable Records of the Ming Dynasty*. These sources do not capture the tributaries' point of view, but they do show that the tribute system always had a second, domestic audience. The Ming emperors wanted foreigners to know that the emperor was their suzerain, but they intended that their Chinese subjects should know this as well. The ritual gift exchange was for domestic as much as foreign consumption.

It is in this context that we should understand the flotillas that Yongle sent abroad under the command of palace eunuch Zheng He. The briefest of notes in the *Veritable Records* on 25 May 1403 records what would prove to be the first of a long series of such orders. The entry reads simply, without explanation: "The Fujian Regional Military Commission was ordered to build 137 oceangoing ships." Yongle followed this order three months later with a second to set up a maritime trade administration to handle the goods that he expected envoys from foreign countries to bring, though few such goods had actually arrived.[39] Launched three years later, the armada would be the first of seven led by Zheng to announce Yongle's enthronement to every ruler of the navigable world. These maritime expeditions were impressive, as they had to be in the context of a usurper struggling to get the Southeast and South Asian worlds to accept his usurpation. The first (1405–1407) got as far as the southwest coast of India before deciding it was time to report back to the emperor. Barely a week after Zheng He departed, the planning for the second expedition began with an order to build another 1,180 ships—an extraordinary number.[40]

It is worth noting that Khubilai Khan had done the same. While he was undoubtedly concerned to assert the legitimacy of combining the Chinese throne with the great khanate, he was in fact continuing the Chinggisid project of ruling the world. As an invasion of Southeast Asia proved infeas-

ible, Khubilai chose instead to regard tribute submission as political submission. When an independent ruler refused to send tribute on Khubilai's
order, as Kertanegara, king of the eastern half of Java, did in 1289, Khubilai
was more than prepared to dispatch a large force—a combined Mongol-
Javanese force of over one hundred thousand soldiers, according to the dynastic history—to punish him and force his state into submission.[41] By the
time that force arrived, however, Kertanegara had been assassinated by
one of his own vassals. His son-in-law was able to capitalize on the chaos
and rally local militia to drive the Mongols out. As we shall note later in
this chapter, Zheng He was likewise prepared to use military means to
force Southeast Asian rulers into a tribute relationship when they resisted.

What is to be learned from this survey of the foreign policy initiatives
of the early Ming emperors is that China depended on the international
system of tributary gift exchange for its prestige and its prerogatives. This
may have been political theater, but it mattered to the actors involved,
especially the emperors, for whom diplomatic exchanges broadcast a Sinocentric order made visible by the rituals of tribute submission. Especially
for emperors facing legitimacy deficits, the performance of the rites of
tribute submission demonstrated their claim to authority over all-under-
Heaven. That this theater played to a domestic audience is simply further
evidence of the political complexity of this system of interstate relations.

POWER AND THE USE OF FORCE

· Yuan-kang Wang ·

Although the Ming emperor claimed supremacy or suzerainty over other
polities in East Asia and beyond, China's imperial government did not
function as a central government over them, capable of enforcing agreements or monopolizing the legitimate use of force. Those polities had their
own military forces and governing structures and competed with China for
resources and territories; some even went to war against China when circumstances made war desirable and unavoidable. Like international systems elsewhere, in other words, the structure of political relations in this
part of the world was anarchic, that is, without a central authority capable
of imposing its will on all other states. Tribute submission structured that
system as a hierarchy in which China, or its emperor, was universally acknowledged as occupying the apex, but the history of Asian international
relations was animated in reality by this tension between anarchy and
hierarchy.

Under Ming rule, China's preponderance of power over its neighbors enabled it to impose its tributary system to govern its interactions with other states. It justified its position of dominance in that system using the Confucian ideology of hierarchy. A popular conception of the tribute system takes the pattern of deference in the political interactions between China and other Asian polities as a basis for declaring the system to have been one characterized by harmony and order, and in which these benefits were not based on military coercion. The American political scientist Samuel Huntington was vulnerable to this popularization in asserting that "Asians generally are willing to 'accept hierarchy' in international relations." Because of this, he avers, peace and stability characterize Asia's past.[42] David Kang has similarly asserted that "East Asian regional relations have historically been hierarchic, more peaceful, and more stable than those in the West," although he also noted in his later book that to declare that "stability was the norm in East Asian international relations" is to gaze down from the hegemon's position.[43] "China does not have a significant history of coercive statecraft," agrees David Shambaugh. "The tribute system may have been hegemonic, but it was not based on coercion or territorial expansionism."[44] Writing about the global backlash against America's post-9/11 overreactions, Zbigniew Brzezinski even proposed that there may come a new regional order in Asia, one "with China at the helm," and conjectured that this order would be harmonious by virtue of drawing on the memory of "a deferential tributary system."[45]

This view of a benevolent tribute system, often contrasted with the conflict-ridden balance-of-power politics of the Westphalian system, relies not just on the hegemon's perspective but on a literal acceptance of the Chinese rhetoric of imperial benevolence, impartiality, and other values claimed by Confucianism, and it assumes that the system was monitored by purely cultural factors and Confucian norms. Confucian thinkers may have hoped at one time that obliging foreigners to submit to the rites of gift exchange would transform them into civilized peoples, and that they would internalize that submission so thoroughly as to themselves rule out the possibility of threatening China's position. This casts the system as a "defense mechanism" to protect China from foreign attack, as Morris Rossabi suggested.[46] Our argument is that material power, rather than cultural hegemony, was the decisive factor in the creation and maintenance of the tribute system. We propose that it is analytically more powerful to understand the tribute system as a means that Chinese rulers used, not to Confucianize a benighted barbarian world, but to organize foreign relations in a way that helped their state achieve its security objectives. Cultural and economic factors can supplement the power-based explanation, but they do not replace or refute power as the key to understanding the nature of political relations in historical Asia.

Material capabilities, including military might, enabled China to set the tributary "rules of the game" in ways that disproportionately served its self-interest. Although the Ming regime was not averse to using force to impose compliance on neighboring states, it recognized the high cost of doing so, as is evident from the founding Ming emperor's designation of fifteen countries to the east and south as "not to be invaded."[47] This declaration was motivated not by magnanimity but by strategic necessity, given the new dynasty's ongoing vulnerability on its northern border. This was the zone where the dynasty was at war with the Mongols for most of its first two centuries, and where China found itself least able to impose the protocols of the tribute system. Ming armies marched into Hami in 1391 to prevent that oasis state from being dominated by the Mongols but had to withdraw for logistical reasons. Emperor Yongle nevertheless managed to establish a tributary relationship with the strategically located state, under which Hami's rulers provided intelligence about Central Asia to the Ming court in return for a security commitment.[48]

Under Yongle and his grandson Xuande, the regime's strategy to solve its principal security concern was to take an offensive and expansionistic posture toward the Mongols. Preponderant power allowed them to sustain campaigns against Mongols to the north. Their strategy included relocating the national capital from Nanjing to Beijing and building the Grand Canal to link the two. Between 1410 and 1424 Yongle personally led five large-scale offensive campaigns against the Mongols, allegedly mobilizing as many as half a million troops.[49] These activities suggest that the early Ming rulers aimed to assert irredentist claims on the realm of the former dynasty and conquer the Mongol steppe.[50] Ming troops traveled a great distance and advanced as far as the northern shores of Kerulen River and Tula River in present-day northern Mongolia. These military offensives weakened the dynasty's adversaries but failed to subjugate the Mongols. The Chinese were not accustomed to campaigning on the steppe, at times failing to locate and engage the Mongol main forces. Logistical problems forced them to withdraw.[51]

To the south, Emperor Yongle invaded the tributary state Dai Viet in 1407 to punish a usurper, and after the country was pacified, he decided to expand his war aims and annex it. The Ming was eventually forced to withdraw after twenty years of occupation and revolt. The same reliance on force lurks within the accounts of the Zheng He voyages. The sheer size and armament of these expeditions—a reference in 1427 notes that "ten

thousand crack troops had earlier been sent to the Western Ocean"[52]—
attest that the logic of force was at work on the ocean as it was on land. The
arrival of the fleet at a port was a demonstration of Chinese naval power
sufficient to prompt most coastal rulers to comply with Ming requests to
participate in the tribute system. Even the threat of sending a naval force
could be used to persuade a ruler who was not interested in conforming
to Chinese requirements, a threat the Ming court used against Burma in
1409.[53] To Qing historians of the Ming, the situation was crystal clear:
"Those who did not submit were pacified by force."[54] This occurred most
conspicuously in Palembang in 1407, in Ceylon in 1410, and in northern
Sumatra in 1415.[55] Even minor skirmishing of the sort that happened when
Ming troops "went ashore to trade" in western Java in 1407 and were killed
by Javanese attests that Zheng's forces were perceived as belligerents and
a threat to local security. Lest the local ruler presume that he could remain
independent of Ming demands, he was issued with this order: "Immediately pay 60,000 ounces of gold to compensate for lost lives and atone for
your crime. This is how you will protect your land and your people. Fail to
comply and there will be no option but to dispatch an army to punish your
crime. What happened in Annam"—a blunt reference to the Ming willingness to invade Dai Viet (here referred to as Annam, meaning "the pacified
south") only a few years earlier—"can serve as an example!"[56] The only
region beyond the range of Ming force was West Asia, which was too far
from China to matter to its hegemonic position at the top of the hierarchy
of East Asian states.[57]

Korea is often singled out as the model tributary state, yet the reestablishment by the Ming of its tributary relationship was not smooth, taking
more than three decades to complete. Bilateral tensions were high because
Koryŏ maintained contacts with the Mongols of the Northern Yuan, who
were still militarily active. Sandwiched between the defeated hegemon
(the Mongols) and the up-and-coming hegemon (the Ming), the Koreans
were careful not to antagonize their two powerful neighbors and sought
to maintain friendly relations with both. The Ming court, concerned about
a possible Koryŏ-Mongol alliance, demanded that the Koryŏ break off relations with the Mongols, a demand the Koreans were not able to meet.[58]
Both went to the brink of war in 1388, when the Ming expanded into the
Liaodong peninsula to an area claimed by the Koryŏ. King U of the Koryŏ
mobilized the country and dispatched an expeditionary force of 38,830
soldiers to attack the Ming.[59] Conflict was averted when the Korean general Yi Songgye turned the army back and removed King U from power.
After ruling from behind the scenes for four years, General Yi took the
throne and founded the Chosŏn dynasty (1392–1910). Ming China and Cho-

sŏn Korea then went to the brink of war in 1398 over three Korean memorials that Emperor Hongwu found offensive. Not to be bullied, the Chosŏn
court made a decision for war. A palace coup in Korea and the death of Emperor Hongwu in 1398 averted the impending conflict. When the succession issues were resolved in both countries, Ming-Chosŏn relations were
finally brought into the tributary framework in the early fifteenth century.
In exchange, the Chosŏn court gained security, recognition, and noninter-
vention. Chosŏn's policy of "serving the great" (sadae) was not an easy one.
Ming China's tribute demands for strategic items such as horses turned out
to be no small burden on the Koreans.[60] The reality of asymmetric power
between a hegemon and a weak state determined the content of the tributary relationship.

Beyond Korea lay Japan. There too the threat of military force was on
display in the Ming's effort to bring the island into the tribute system.
Japan's Prince Kanenaga, apparently annoyed by the condescending tone
of a Ming diplomatic letter, imprisoned and executed some of the envoys
sent by Hongwu in 1369 demanding tribute. The Ming court threatened invasion but was reminded by the Japanese of the Mongols' failed attempts
to conquer Japan in 1281. A letter sent by Kanenaga in 1382 explicitly denied the legitimacy of Chinese dominance: "Now the world is the world's
world; it does not belong to a single ruler. . . . I heard that China has troops
able to fight a war, but my small country also has plans of defense. . . .
How could we kneel down and acknowledge Chinese overlordship!"[61] In
response, the Ming denied trade privileges. Eager to trade with the Ming,
the shogun Yoshimitsu sent a mission in 1399 and addressed himself as
"your subject, the king of Japan." Because this departed from Japanese tradition, his successor quickly repudiated the arrangement in 1411. Neither
government, however, was able to stop the flow of trade voyages, and so
the Ming had to "retain the pretence that the voyages were official tribute
missions signifying Japan's acquiescence in China's claim to hegemony."[62]

However tempting it has been for some commentators to treat the tribute system as an all-encompassing framework generating stability for all,
not all of China's foreign relations can be generalized within the tributary rubric.[63] Ming-Tibetan exchanges, for example, were mainly spiritual
and ceremonial. The Ming court invited several Tibetan clerics to perform
Buddhist rituals and awarded titles to them. Some, such as the Fifth Kar-
mapa Lama, rejected Ming titles. Others, notably Tsongkhapa, the founder
of the Gelug school of Tibetan Buddhism, refused to travel to the Ming
court. Though some Tibetan lamas and hierarchs did bring tribute, one can
hardly conclude that Ming relations with Tibet fell neatly within the Chinese tribute system. Indeed, the conduct of Tibetan leaders at the time sup-

ports the view that Morris Rossabi enunciated decades ago, that "neither in the economic nor in the political realms did the Tibetans perceive themselves to be subjects of the Ming court."[64] As for generating stability for all, although long periods of peace did occur in some areas, the Chinese waged protracted wars with the Mongols, invaded Yunnan and Dai Viet, and engaged in power politics that did not correspond to the idealized tributary system.[65]

Rather than seeing the tribute system as a paradigm to explain China's interactions with other Asian polities, we maintain that it is better treated as a historical arrangement that actually needs to be explained.[66] The key to understanding the reality of the tribute system is the fundamental condition within which it operated: the asymmetry of power between China and the tributary polities.[67] Economic interests and cultural considerations were also at play, but it was Chinese preponderance of power that made many Asian polities accept the tributary arrangement. Indeed, in those periods in which China's claim to hegemony was not backed by military power, the system became unsustainable.[68] As Wang Gungwu has pointed out, "There could not surely be a stable [tribute] system without power, sustained power."[69]

Most state ideologies, including Confucianism, evade the moral cost of military success, but submission is only ever forced. The use or threat of force against China's neighbors had to be overwritten at the level of rhetoric as an account of civilizational transformation from barbarism to culture and then choreographed in diplomatic protocol as the willing tendering of tribute upward to the moral apex occupied by the Chinese emperor. But that was not why tributaries acceded to these terms, nor why they sometimes turned against them. To see matters otherwise is to fail to recognize the Confucian state as the military hegemon it had to be.

CIVILIZATIONAL RHETORIC AND THE OBFUSCATION OF POWER POLITICS

· Geoff Wade ·

Confucian political philosophy does not celebrate the use of force, either by the state or between states, and yet as we have noted, coercion and military force were hardly absent from Ming foreign policy calculations and practice. The dissonance between power politics and moral philosophy was addressed via an elaborate web of rhetoric upholding a China-centered worldview. It consisted of a number of components we might collectively call "civilizational rhetoric" that depicted the emperor (and by extension the Chinese state) at the center and apex of a civilizational, geographic, and in some ways cosmological structure. We look at three components of particular importance to understanding the nature of rule and interpolity relations.

The first component of the civilizational rhetoric exalts the peace-loving, virtuous, righteous, and supremely benevolent nature of the emperor and his rule; the second depicts China as the civilized center of the world fulfilling the mission of civilizing and thereby providing moral and behavioral betterment to the peoples who lived outside China and who came in contact with its superior culture; the third presents the emperor as the legitimizer of rulers and the dispenser of benefits to all who submit to him because of his superior virtue. In this vein, as Emperor Yongle noted in 1405, "I manifest the love of the One on High for all living things."[70] His decisions and those of the Ming state were by circular definition correct, since "the Way of Heaven is supremely just and correct in the most minute degree."[71] Strains of this rhetoric were utilized to present the motives and actions of the emperor and the Chinese state in ideological terms that concealed from both foreign and, more important, Chinese audiences the true nature of China's foreign policies and practices. Contrasting this rhetoric, widely reproduced within Chinese historiography, with the actual practice of China's relations with other polities helps us appreciate both the nature of those relations and the constructs developed for that purpose.

Ming sources—official decrees, communications, and declarations as well as the official histories—routinely stress the benevolence and peace-loving nature of the emperor and by extension his state. Regardless of whether the Ming state was invading or withdrawing, acting on its own initiative or being forced to act, the emperor was eternally manifesting his benevolence, grace, and concern to preserve order and maintain peace. When Emperor Hongwu sent armies to invade Yunnan (subsequently incorporated into China) in 1395, for example, he explained:

> China is surrounded by *yi* [non-Chinese] in the four directions and its land adjoins the territories of chieftains and headmen. However, I have never taken advantage of my strength to oppress them, bully them, or eliminate them. The territory of Yunnan is already ours. It may appear that it was taken by force. This is not so. The Liang Prince, who was the grandson of the Yuan Emperor Shizu [Khubilai], using his claim as a descendant of the Yuan court, gave shelter to our criminals, received our fugitives, and lured away our frontier guards. Thus there was no other way but to dispatch an army to punish him.[72]

Intervention was never invasion, only punishment for crimes the emperor deemed that another state ruler had committed.

The most egregious use of force to intervene in the affairs of a tributary state was Yongle's invasion of Dai Viet in 1407 to punish a usurper.[73] Prior to launching the invasion, the emperor promulgated a list of twenty crimes of which the usurper was guilty and for which he had to be punished. In the official declaration of victory, the court announced that seven million Viet had been killed—clearly an exaggeration, though by how much cannot be known.[74] However, upon receiving reports of his armies' successes, Yongle decried the implication that he had been seeking gain from the campaign: "I am the lord of all people under Heaven. Why would I act in a warlike manner in order to obtain some land and people? My concern was only that rebellious bandits not go unpunished and that the suffering of the people not go unrelieved."[75] The conquest of Dai Viet violated the much-publicized "ancestral injunctions" of the founding emperor, Yongle's father, which listed Annam (Dai Viet) as one of the fifteen countries his descendants should never invade. Yongle himself promised that Ming forces would withdraw after imposing punishment on the usurper, but once this had been achieved, he decided the troops should remain. By 1408 an administration of 472 military and civil offices staffed by Chinese had been set up to run the country after local leaders were removed or executed. Grain taxes were levied, salt and mining monopolies imposed, and 7,700 artisans, including gun-founders, were sent to the Ming capital to serve the conqueror. Viet scholars were threatened to make them collaborate and, when they did, were rewarded. Some would later be quoted by Chinese chroniclers as declaring that "Annam was formerly China's territory, but later we sank into non-Chinese ways; now we are able to gaze on the brilliance of Chinese culture."[76] The conquered could thus be made to give voice to the Chinese idea of its right to rule Dai Viet.

Not until the Yongle emperor was dead could his successor, Emperor Xuande, acknowledge defeat in the face of violent revolts against China's twenty-year occupation and withdraw the imperial forces. Anxious nonetheless to place the correct interpretation on this decision, Xuande explained that he was ordering his troops out as a way of "taking pity on the Annamese and choosing not to punish them."[77] Putting a good face on a humiliating defeat, he declared that "We, with a virtue whose power is as great as the universe, are fulfilling the wishes of Our ancestors, resting the troops, and bringing peace to the people."[78] This rhetoric was intended not to depict the true nature of political decisions and actions but to uphold the fiction of the virtue, moral superiority, and infallibility of the emperor essential to his legitimacy as China's ruler and to that of the hierarchical international system of which he was the apex and China the center. Similarly, when the Zhengtong emperor decided *not* to send troops against the Möng Mo Tai when asked to do so by the Yunnan Grand Defender in 1438, he explained his refusal as demonstrating a level of compassion superior to that of his senior officials: "I manifest Heaven's love for all living things and I am convinced that if the imperial army is dispatched, it will be impossible to avoid harming the innocent. Also, my heart could not bear taking persons away from their fathers, mothers, wives, and children."[79]

A principal element of imperial China's historiographical and quotidian rhetoric was its differentiation of Chinese (*hua*) from less-civilized or uncivilized non-Chinese foreigners (*yi*). By couching foreign policies and practices in a civilizational rhetoric not unlike the language of *mission civilisatrice* by which European powers later conceptualized direct intervention in their colonial dependencies, China's actions abroad and in frontier regions could be depicted as consistent with Confucian principles. Endowed with a superiority decreed by Heaven, China occupied a higher cultural and moral level than did any other state or people, according to this rhetoric. The universal desire of all other peoples was that they should rise to that level, and direct contact with Chinese culture would assist that process. The emperor rewarded this aspiration by furnishing foreign rulers with uplifting Confucian texts and investing them with titles that reflected their progress toward acknowledging China as the model to which they should submit, politically and morally. Coming into contact with his divine personality was sufficient to bring uncivilized peoples out of darkness and into line with Chinese norms. Foreign policy decisions were therefore nothing more, and nothing less, than the exercise of Heaven's perfect wisdom benefiting all peoples, even in those cases where some rulers or peoples had to be punished.

The civilizing mission found expression in the language of "transformation," and the emperor was depicted as drawing all peoples toward the center of culture constituted by the Chinese court and state and spreading the influence of Chinese culture so as to transform and civilize them. The Yongle emperor, for example, professed, "I do not differentiate between those here and those there."[80] A century later, the Jiajing emperor echoed this sentiment by declaring: "We are the Emperor and We treat all under Heaven as Our family."[81] The notion also found expression in a strict concept of order and precedence based on the degree of "Chineseness" that outsiders demonstrated, a device used to distinguish foreign polities. Those most closely identified with Chinese culture and morality ("Sinic" East Asia) were given ritual precedence over those considered further removed from it. Thus, Korea's Chosŏn rulers were considered model tributaries and given precedence and more prestigious gifts than those of Dai Viet. When in 1464 the Viet king requested a robe and crown like those that had been conferred upon the Chosŏn king, this was refused, as it would have implied equal status between the two states, thereby negating the carefully structured hierarchy descending from Chinese culture.[82] This concern was stated in no uncertain terms when the same request was refused once again in 1495: "although Annam [Dai Viet] follows the court's calendar and brings tribute to the Court, its people are, in the end, still foreign (*yi*)."[83] *Yi* was but one of many terms (*man, di, mo, fan*) that disparaged the "uncivilized" and "barbaric" peoples beyond the pale of Chinese culture.[84] These depictions reinforced the centrality of Chinese civilization within the hierarchy of the tributary system, serving to validate actions against foreign and frontier polities that would otherwise have been considered immoral, unjust, or inconsistent with professed Confucian values. Political submission to the emperor was therefore, by this logic, a natural consequence of the emperor's moral superiority and the superiority of Chinese civilization. Subject polities should obey his instructions.

One such set of instructions was sent to the king of Ayutthaya by the Yongle emperor in September 1419 in the context of warning him not to interfere in a succession crisis in Melaka. Yongle opens his edict by declaring that, "being rightly disposed to the intention of Heaven and Earth to nurture living things, I rule all with the same compassion, making no distinction between these and those," that is, between Chinese and non-Chinese. "I treat with favor the king who respects Heaven, serves the great (*shida, sadae* in Korean), acts as he is required, and submits tribute." The king of Melaka had submitted tribute to the Ming court since 1405, which "demonstrates his sincerity in serving the great." Accordingly, in Yongle's eyes, he "belongs within [the Chinese realm], and is on that basis an officer of the court." If the king of Ayutthaya has a problem with the king of Melaka, "he should refer the matter to the court for handling. Doing otherwise and launching a military attack is tantamount to denying the existence of the court." By this logic, for one tributary to attack another is treason toward the Ming. Yongle gives the king of Ayutthaya a way out by tactfully proposing that he has been misled in this matter by corrupt advisers. He closes by reminding the king that the duty of a tributary is not just to refrain from invading other tributaries but as well to look out for their mutual welfare.[85]

Yongle's understanding of the tribute system was that it bound all members into a pact of mutual nonaggression. That pact in turn recapitulated the very order of morality that Heaven and Earth created by virtue of giving life. In this arrangement, only "the great" could act. One could argue that moral imperatives here veil the Ming state's interest in projecting its power into the Indian Ocean, as it had been attempting to do during the previous fifteen years by sending eunuch envoys to states throughout maritime Asia—for which the alliance with Melaka, sitting at the "throat" of the passage connecting the South China Sea and the Indian Ocean, was critical. Yongle would consider any interference an act of war. The king of Ayutthaya got the message and called off the plan to attack the port.

The Chinese worldview assumed accordingly that all rulers, near and far, required the emperor's legitimation to rule and owed allegiance to him. This assumption often meant that China's foreign policy was an extension of its frontier policy, the enfeoffment of rulers of foreign states being seen as equivalent to the appointment of hereditary officials in frontier polities. In both cases, the Chinese state or, more precisely, the emperor regarded a ruler's right to rule as dependent on his approval.[86] Thus, when Alakeshvara, the king of Kotte (Ceylon, present-day Sri Lanka), resisted Zheng He's orders during his third expedition to the Indian Ocean in 1410–1411, Zheng understood that he had the right to take him hostage and transport him back to his master, Emperor Yongle, for punishment, and that it was up to Yongle to appoint a new king in his place.[87]

The Ming court's concept of enfeoffment is spelled out in a 1501 dispatch from the Ministry of Rites to envoys from Dai Viet, which blurs the line between enfeoffment and recognition of foreign rulers by subordinating them to China's security needs:

> Annam is secluded far on the southern border and has always admired culture and learning. As its ruler was able to fulfil the duties of a minister, our former Emperor enfeoffed him as king of the country of Annam. The king was instructed to rule the area and act as a screen for China. However, despite having the title of "king," he is still in fact a minister. This title has been inherited for over a hundred years. The post, the level of robes and headwear conferred, and the ritual for banquets provided for tribute envoys by the Court have all been formally stipulated. Whenever a king of that country dies and there is a request for Imperial grace and permission to inherit the throne, the Court graciously concerns itself with the distant peoples and sends an envoy to issue a proclamation and to carry out official sacrifices. The Emperor has conferred upon the king a ceremonial leather hat and a set of formal robes, so that the king will not be without honor as the ruler of his country. He has also conferred a set of first grade ordinary clothing upon the king so that he will not forget the need to respectfully serve

China as a minister. Both grace and ritual are thereby stressed and the status [of the king] is not confused.[88]

Foreign rulers were thus both brought into the Chinese imperial system and yet rigorously excluded from it at the same time. When it came to frontier polities, rulers were named "superintendents" or "commissioners" rather than being enfeoffed as "kings," and they were expected to send "chieftains" rather than "envoys" to the court. But the purported benefits and obligations in relation to the emperor were mostly similar.

The status and treatment of a particular polity as "foreign" or "frontier" could change according to political expediency. For example, in Chinese records and statements, Yunnan's status changed from being a foreign state to being a part of Ming China when the founder of the Ming dynasty, Zhu Yuanzhang, set out to conquer it in the late 1370s. That transposition was veiled by declaring that Yunnan had been a part of China since antiquity, turning conquest into mere recovery, not invasion.[89] Similar declarations were made regarding Dai Viet when the Yongle emperor launched his attack against that polity almost three decades later, in 1407.[90] China's particular advantage throughout this history was its capacity to control the written record, which has in turn influenced how historians have read, and often misread, the documents that the Chinese state left for them to find.

CONVERGENCE AND CONFLICT: DAI VIET IN THE SINIC ORDER

· Liam Kelley ·

Just as Ming literati deployed civilizational rhetoric to fix the historical record in China's favor, so too, curiously, did Viet literati, striking much the same tone. The broader condition of Dai Viet's relationship with China, shaped by their long-shared land border, the constant possibility of direct intervention from the north, and the millennium-long Viet experience of operating within the East Asian Confucian hierarchy, made Dai Viet markedly different from other polities. Korea would be its closest equivalent, though the self-adopted name of Viet Great State (which China declined to use, preferring Annam) signaled, at least to itself, higher ambitions than Korean rulers dared to voice.

An important source for understanding the complex nature of the Dai Viet–China relationship is the documents that passed back and forth in volume between the two dynastic courts. Some documents have been preserved in Chinese sources and some in Viet ones, notably the *Bang giao luc* (Records of interdomainal relations), in which are reprinted in their entirety the letters that Viet rulers exchanged with successive Ming emperors. The language of these documents is the language of inequality. The "Middle Kingdom" (Trung Quoc) or "Cultural Magnificence of the Center" (Trung Hoa) is depicted as the center of the known world, while Dai Viet is portrayed as a small polity on its fringes. The Chinese emperor's grace in granting a Viet monarch the authority to rule is likened to the natural phenomenon of spring rains bringing dormant plants to life.

Viet rulers professed elation and gratitude at having been favored by the Ming emperors through "the brilliant conferral of a benevolent edict" or "the cherishing bestowal of a seal."[91] These phrases come from a letter of thanks that the first monarch of the Lê dynasty, Lê Loi (d. 1433), sent to the Xuande emperor shortly after coming to power in 1428. The letter was sent in response to his having received an edict and seal investing him with the authority to rule over his kingdom. Although Lê Loi's rise to power had come at the expense of the Ming, whose occupation forces he had only just defeated, both sides were inviting each other to put their relationship back nominally on a tributary footing. Lê Loi chose to phrase his response as a vote of thanks rather than a declaration of independence—a modern term that is never used in Viet texts before the twentieth century.

The ease with which Lê Loi returned to the familiar language of tributary relations sits uncomfortably with modern Vietnamese historians. Lê Loi, like most of the elite who conducted the foreign affairs of the kingdom, understood that Dai Viet could exist only in the shadow of the Chinese empire. Not just the tributary relationship as an institution but the very language of tributary status defined the horizon within which the Viet conducted their foreign relations. That language gave voice to a conceptual model that accepted that what gave Dai Viet its existence and significance were its unequal connections to the Chinese empire. The model goes back a long way, for in the earliest texts in which Viet literati recorded information about their land, they declined to emphasize what made it distinct or equal; rather, they imagined and invented countless ways in which Viet was connected to the "Northern Kingdom" (Bac Quoc), often in ways that placed it in an inferior position. At the same time, though, they could refer to the ruler of their own "Southern Kingdom" as an emperor, a term supposedly reserved for the ruler of the Chinese empire. Understanding this seeming contradiction between unequal status and equal rulers is key for appreciating the particular complexity by which the Viet managed their relations with the Ming and later the Qing empires. Rather than explain away this contradiction as rhetoric versus reality, it might be more useful to enter the mental space of Viet literati and consider how they perceived the world.

Prior to the twentieth century, Viet literati were proud to point out the ways in which their land was the same as that of the kingdom to the north, thanks to the efforts of virtuous individuals both Chinese and Viet.[92] Fifteenth-century writers spoke of Dai Viet proudly as a "domain of manifest civility," a land in which prevailed the ideas, objects, and ritual practices that had emerged in Chinese antiquity, from written script and the classics composed in that script to the caps and gowns of government officials. Repeatedly conjoined with this assertion, however, was the lament that their country fell short of matching China. To the condition of manifest civility they attached a history that went back to certain exemplary Chinese officials in the Han dynasty, when the Red River plain was incorporated into the Chinese empire. Through their actions and moral virtue in times of looming chaos, Viet literati later argued, early Chinese officials such as Zhao Tuo of the Qin dynasty and Shi Xie of the Han set the foundation for Viet to become a domain of manifest civility.[93] Prior to their time, as one nineteenth-century chronicler put it, the people in the region "chattered like birds and tattooed their bodies, and their customs were crude"; it was the influence of these moral men, he believed, that began Viet's transformation out of this primitive condition.[94] Later, once Dai Viet became autonomous from Chinese rule in the tenth century, morally upright Viet followed the Chinese model. As they did so, their realm expanded, attesting to Heaven's recognition of their virtue.

Favored in this interpretation is Dinh Bo Linh, who established a dynastic enterprise in the Red River delta in the 960s. He did this not by fighting off the Chinese and declaring his refusal to submit to the new Song dynasty but by allying himself with a Cantonese warlord and defeating other warlords in the region. In the 970s Dinh Bo Linh then dispatched envoys to the Song court to establish relations. The court first granted him the position of military commissioner and then commandery prince, continuing a common Chinese practice of granting titles to individuals who had fought their way to power in the region and over whom China had no effective control. What would be different this time, however, is that the Song eventually elevated the title of Dai Viet's ruler to "king of the state," thereby establishing Dai Viet's position not as Chinese territory but as a tributary state.[95] Viet "independence" thus came in the form of an unequal relationship with China.

The elevation of the Red River delta from a commandery to a tributary kingdom required local legitimation. A few literati took up the task.

Their work reached its completion with the publication of Ngo Si Lien's fifteenth-century chronicle, *Dai Viet su ky toan thu* (Complete book of the historical records of the Viet Great State). While not the first history compiled by a Viet scholar, this chronicle was unique in extending its coverage further back in time than did any of the works by his predecessors. In particular, Ngo connected the emergence of rulers and their polities in the Red River delta through a line of descent from the mythical Chinese sage-ruler Shen Nong, the Divine Farmer. Some scholars have argued that this was an effort to show equivalence to China, yet the story created around this imaginary genealogy was actually based on ideas of inequality, inasmuch as every kingdom to emerge in "the south" was the result of investiture by a Chinese emperor.[96] What the fifteenth-century chroniclers affirmed was that it was natural that their kingdom should exist as a vassal state, and that history to that point had been an imperfect time in which the kingdom had yet to fully develop in a moral sense. Finding evidence in antiquity of an intermarriage practice of which he disapproved, for example, Ngo could write: "I guess this happened because that was still a primordial age and the proper rites and music had yet to become manifest."[97] The proper rites and music had to become manifest, thanks to the labors of certain Chinese moral exemplars, before Dai Viet could achieve its elevated status as a realm of manifest civility.

Thus, we see that Viet literati envisioned the cultural rise of their country as a long, gradual process in which the moral virtue necessary for establishing a separate polity slowly spread southward, first through the efforts of Chinese administrators and then through the efforts of Viet literati. While the end result was the emergence of a separate kingdom, that status was understood to be dependent on that kingdom's deep ties to the empire to its north. As the source of the moral virtue that made the emergence of Dai Viet possible, China was in a category of its own. Dai Viet was not an equal, nor ever could be, so long as this worldview informed the thoughts of educated Viet. This is why the language of the official documents exchanged between the Lê and Ming courts should not be viewed simply as empty rhetoric. On the Viet side, it rested on deeply seated ideas to which the educated elite in both Dai Viet and China subscribed, and by which Dai Viet could position itself legitimately at the edge of the Chinese world.

REPRODUCTION OF THE TRIBUTE SYSTEM

Despite occasional convergence in philosophy and language on both sides of the tribute interaction, China's relations with its tributaries were not always harmonious in terms either of ideas or of political goals. Tributary states might actively buy in to their subordination without China's threatening to intervene, but they could also find ways to resist the hegemon. When that happened, China was not usually in a position to impose conformity to its idea of tribute obligations other than when military resources to do so were in place, either as force or its threat. When threat was not applied, the relationship depended on the willingness of both parties to arrange their relationship consensually, to the extent that each was able to meet what it perceived to be its needs.

How this arrangement played out in practice depended on what issues the Ming court regarded as important to its interests. In the case of Dai Viet, Ming failure to expand into its territory may have induced the court to extend preferential treatment, such as when it sent Chinese envoys to notify that state of the capture by the Mongols of the Zhengtong emperor in 1449, or on the occasions of the installation of new emperors in 1505 and 1521 (other states received notice through their own envoys).[98] Dai Viet was also the only Southeast Asian polity to which the Ming sent Chinese officials to perform sacrifices on the death of its ruler. But there were clear limits to such special recognition, for as we saw earlier in this chapter, the Ming court repeatedly refused the Viet king's request for a ceremonial robe and crown of the kind given to the Chosŏn ruler. The intention on the Viet side in making the request was not to negotiate an equal status but to improve their state's position in the tribute hierarchy, and so, it was hoped, secure greater benefits. The intention on the Chinese side in refusing was a divisive tactic through which it hoped to reassert its own special status at the top of the hierarchy. Dai Viet may have been special, but it was subordinate.

China and Dai Viet tugged at either end of their relationship, each side jockeying for the status and recognition it felt the other owed by virtue of the tributary connection between them. Neither side was prepared to sacrifice the advantages it perceived itself as having by virtue of adhering to the system. Tribute payer and tribute taker were locked in this deal, which explains in part why the system continued to be reproduced by these and other parties and survived as a set of protocols that states across East Asia largely accepted without worrying what they did or did not claim. It furnished the rules by which the lawfulness of the conduct of both participating states could be judged. When the hegemon behaved in a way that a tributary regarded as unlawful, as in the case of the Ming invasion of Dai Viet, the tribute system provided a discursive space in which declarations of just action (on the hegemon's side) and protests against injustice (on the tributary's side) could be voiced, if only by indirection. The Ming state might issue proclamations that explained its actions and excoriated those of its tributaries, as though it alone adhered to the implicit agreements that bound both to the system, but it would not receive such proclamations from tributaries. Under such conditions, asymmetric rhetoric might meet Ming political expectations without eliciting the reciprocation needed for the tributary to join in two-way communication. Even the Xuande emperor had to understand that the only way he was "bringing peace to the [Viet] people" when he withdrew Ming forces in 1427 was by leaving the Vietnamese alone, not by showering more Heavenly blessings on them. The rhetoric of protection and submission continued, but the reality, as all parties understood, was otherwise. When Xuande sent Lê Loi, the new ruler, the letter noted earlier in this chapter to inform him, in effect, that the tributary relationship was on again, he phrased it in a way that pretended nothing had gone wrong. Lê Loi replied in the same mode, praising the Son of Heaven for his "brilliance" and "greatness." This rhetoric signaled that Dai Viet would revert to its role as tribute subject, so long as it was permitted to be a tributary, as it had been, outside the Ming state and not a territory within it, and therefore not subject to intervention. Xuande let the matter rest.

Why did all parties continue to participate in the tribute system, particularly in this case in the immediate aftermath of a brutal and failed military occupation?[99] The answer is embedded in the basic assumption of the power asymmetry by which the tribute system operated, which is that there is no condition under which power symmetry can be achieved. Except at moments of radical disruption, no state in the tribute system will challenge the dominant participant. A tributary ruler may, if he has the resources or option to do so, withdraw from the system and abandon relations with China, as Tokugawa Japan did, but he does so at his own cost. This is why trade is important to the system: it offers direct material benefits that serve as an incentive for the ruler of a lesser polity to remain within the system. Withdrawal from the system, however disincentivized, is more likely to happen than a challenge to unseat the hegemon whose military and economic resources ensure the asymmetry. Most tributaries do not command the resources necessary to oppose the system from a position of strength. Those that do—and they are usually unsuccessful—are rare exceptions that confirm the limits of the operation of the system.

When Hideyoshi invaded Chosŏn in 1592, his intention was to force the Ming to abandon its exclusion of Japan from trade or tribute. That bid failed, at a terrific cost to all three combatants in the ensuing Imjin War. The Manchu conquest of the Ming in 1644 is one of the few cases in which a former tributary replaced the state at the apex of the system. Nurhaci's earlier repudiation of Ming supremacy, in 1616, was in effect an assertion of status parity with the Ming, a parity the Manchu court tested when it commanded Chosŏn to pay tribute, thereby assuming the superior position vis-à-vis Chosŏn that the Ming had enjoyed. Parity between Manchu and Ming would not continue, however. After defeating the Ming in 1644, the Manchus placed their emperor at the apex of the Sinic world and resumed tribute-taking to enforce the system they had taken over. Unipolarity was thus reasserted in East Asia.

It was soon clear to the rulers of East Asian polities that the Qing dynasty was formidable and would remain in power in Beijing. No other state had the resources to seriously contest its position at the apex. Some within the Sinic world might grumble at the humiliation of submitting to an empire that could not assert the civilizational authority the Ming had claimed for itself as the center of a Confucian order, but most East Asian polities agreed to continue the tributary relationships they had had with the Ming. And so in East Asia the system continued. As we shall explore in the next two chapters, Manchu relations with the Mongols and Tibetan Buddhist hierarchs were founded on different, Inner Asian ideological bases.

Chosŏn was the state that understood the predicament of "serving the great" most keenly, for the obligation of tribute submission bound them to a strategy of culturally emulating the Confucian hegemon while at the same time conceding to fairly harsh exactions, including human tribute (in the form of virgins for the emperor's harem). The policy of maintaining this strategy was entirely practical, and centuries in the making. The *Annals of the Chosŏn Kingdom* in an entry in 1554 looks back at the practice of "serving the great" of its predecessor dynasty, Koryŏ (918–1392), with admiration:

> Mencius said that when the small serves the big (*sadae*) it is because of fear of Heaven. What is meant by fear is nothing other than fearing the power of a big nation in order to preserve one's own country's people, so serving the big nations is only to serve the people. . . . In the era of Koryŏ they served the Song in the south and served the Jin in the north. When they paid tribute to the Song, they hid this fact from the Jin. When they paid tribute to the Jin, they hid this fact from the Song. . . . If it were not like this, if they served the Song and broke off with the Jin, then the people of the whole nation would become fish and meat [to be wolfed down by the Jin].[100]

From the Korean perspective, *sadae* allowed the Koryŏ dynasty to survive for five hundred years, and it would go on to stand the Chosŏn dynasty in good stead for even longer. Fear of a stronger power was the major reason Korea accepted its status in the tribute system. When China lodged a threat, as the Hongwu emperor did in the last years of the Koryŏ dynasty, by holding a Korean envoy hostage and declaring the tribute memorial he brought to be "empty text disguising treachery that would someday provoke border conflict," the Korean side had to move carefully.[101] Diplomatic instability was a dangerous game, for it often provoked domestic instability. It certainly did so in this case. The conflict Hongwu predicted in fact erupted eight years later, as we noted earlier in this chapter, when General Yi Songgye led a spirited defense of Korean frontier territories. The upshot, however, was his return to Seoul to overthrow Koryŏ and replace it with his own dynasty, Chosŏn. Yi maintained a vigilant posture against an aggressive Ming court, though after the death of Hongwu, he too recognized the rationality of reestablishing tributary status. After all, so long as Chosŏn complied with its rules, the tribute system tied the Ming to an implicit agreement not to interfere in Korean affairs. Submission brought the new dynasty security and preserved for Korea as much autonomy as it could hope for.[102] As the Hideyoshi invasion two centuries later demonstrated, the relationship could even provide the weaker state with a powerful ally in time of war.

Serving the hegemon without becoming its impoverished slave or, worse, the target of annexation required great care and intelligence under the Ming, and even more under the Qing. From a Korean perspective, despite the occasional flight of diplomatic language praising the wise government of the Son of Heaven, it was difficult to detect the benignity in Chosŏn's relationship with either the Ming or the Qing Great State. Korean intellectuals might admire the wisdom of the Confucian tradition, just as Viet intellectuals expressed themselves to do, and they might aspire to get as close to the sources of Confucian culture as they could, but that was not the same as celebrating the service that the tribute system demanded of their state. On that matter, most were entirely unsentimental. They understood that Chosŏn, however highly ranked in the list of tributaries, occupied a position of weakness and that the cost of noncompliance could be great.

The contribution of Chinese civilization to the creation of an interstate order in East Asia was thus to provide a system of hierarchically ordered relationships that policed regimes on its borders and that was potentially infinitely extendable throughout the known world and even beyond. The system existed as long as the relationships it entailed were regularly reproduced through the extraction and submission of tribute goods and the performance of rituals confirming the unequal status of the two parties.

Its logic of pyramidal power was sustained by an ideology claiming that Heaven invested universal authority in the emperor of China. All rulers who respected Heaven—as all rulers should—were thereby obliged to offer him formal submission. The tribute system thus resonated with the fundamental principle of Confucian morality that the lesser should submit to the greater and that the greater was always in the right when the lesser was punished for withholding submission. Modeled within the patriarchal family, the Confucian belief in benign hierarchy was extrapolated up to the state and in turn relayed out to the world to the extent that China was able to project power beyond its borders.

The system proved relatively durable. That durability rested materially on the difference of scale between the Chinese polity and other polities throughout the region, a difference that translated into unequal resources and an unequal capacity to mobilize military force. It also rested on the willingness of China to impose a loose rather than a tight rein over lesser states most of the time, as well as to provide regular access to Chinese goods and markets. On this dual basis of tolerable autonomy and financial benefit, most tributaries acceded to the terms offered. Some even at times constructed their self-understanding of submission to Chinese civilization as a posture that dignified rather than demeaned them. This could change. When the uneven interstate distribution of wealth and power came under strain and the cost of serving the great seemed higher than the cost of resisting it, lesser polities either exited the system at their peril or, as the Manchus would do in 1644, captured it.

CHAPTER FOUR

THE TIBETAN BUDDHIST WORLD

In this chapter, we shift to Tibet to consider the Tibetan Buddhist world's legal order and the considerable role it and Tibetan Buddhist hierarchs played in the shaping of interpolity relations in Inner and East Asia. Buddhism's place in Tibet can be traced to the Tibetan imperial age of the seventh to ninth centuries. The rulers of this empire not only expanded their political power across the plateau and beyond it,[1] uniting formerly disparate populations, but actively facilitated the introduction of Buddhism into their realm. Buddhism continued to develop and spread after the empire disintegrated, eventually becoming a dominant faith in much of Inner Asia and a potent political force as well. When the Tibetan empire collapsed, its successor polities vied for power, none of them achieving predominance. Not until the Chinggisid imperial expansion in the thirteenth century was most of the Tibetan Plateau again united, this time under the indirect rule of the Mongol Great Khan. Although Tibet was never again a great military power, the pervasive role of Tibetan Buddhism as a spiritual force and as a legitimizing construct for political authority, as well as for interstate relations, turned Tibet into the center of what we refer to as the Tibetan Buddhist world. This world encompassed not only the polities on the Tibetan Plateau but also those on the southern slopes of the Himalayas and the Mongol polities of the Inner Asian steppe. The expansive spiritual and political reach of the Tibetan Buddhist world and its authority as a world-ordering center were implanted at the heart of Mongol and Manchu imperial power. As Matthew Kapstein has observed, "post-imperial Tibet would come to substitute the spiritual potency of its Buddhist traditions for the political and military supremacy it formerly enjoyed, thereby ensuring a continuing Tibetan role in the affairs of China and Inner Asia down to modern times."[2]

The distinctive characteristic of the Tibetan Buddhist world was the singular manner in which spiritual and worldly domains were interwoven. This interweaving existed in the very conception and structure of Tibetan

Buddhist polities and profoundly shaped the relations they maintained with other polities. The transformation this brought about, however, took centuries to complete, so that what we describe in this chapter as the distinguishing features of the Tibetan Buddhist world achieved their fullest expressions only beginning in the seventeenth century.

Tibet was not ruled by Buddhist hierarchs for all of its post-imperial history. At first, local kings and princes exercised power, as did hegemons who emerged from the powerful aristocracy. During this period, which lasted until the advent of the Mongol imperial domination in the thirteenth century, Buddhist culture flourished and the prestige and power of Tibetan religious leaders increased.[3] As the Chinggisid Mongols extended their reach to the Tibetan Plateau, they favored the hierarchs of the Sakya order of Tibetan Buddhism to establish hegemony in Tibet in exchange for their submission. Moreover, in 1264, according to Tibetan sources, Khubilai Khan formally gave his Sakya preceptor, Drogön Chögyal Phagpa, the religious and secular leadership of Tibet, including the regions of Amdo and Kham.[4] As the power of the Mongols and of the Sakya order (Sakyapa in Tibetan) declined in the middle of the fourteenth century, control shifted to the Pakmodrupa hierarchs affiliated with the Kagyu order (Kagyupa). These hierarchs effectively ruled Tibet for over a century, substantially reforming the system of administration and introducing new codes of law based on Buddhist morality. Eventually, internal divisions and the emergence of competing centers of power increased the autonomy of local hierarchs and princes until the kings of Tsang emerged as the most powerful in central Tibet. These lay rulers patronized various schools of Tibetan Buddhism but became most closely associated with the Karma-Kagyu school. They exercised authority over much of central and western Tibet until the Khoshot Mongol leader Gushri Khan defeated them as well as other rivals of the Gelug school (Gelugpa) and proceeded to unite most of Tibet under the rule of the Fifth Dalai Lama, who was enthroned in 1642. From that time, the Tibetan Buddhist civilizational world, with the Tibetan state at its center, developed the distinctive forms that endured, with only moderate change, down to the mid-twentieth century.

The principal source of legitimacy to rule was the idea that emanations of Buddha took on human form out of compassion to lead humans toward enlightenment, and that these divine beings could be recognized and placed in positions of leadership. This conception informed the belief that governance should be based on a symbiosis of spiritual and political authority. It was understood that political authority was at the service of spiritual authority, and that spiritual masters should empower worldly rulers. Just as the otherworldly and the earthly realms were interdependent and intertwined, so were spiritual and political authority. Whether exercised by multiple persons or united in one individual, the interplay of these forms of authority was at the heart of the system.

This conception is key to understanding interpolity relations. Spiritual masters sought support for themselves and their institutions from powerful and wealthy benefactors, including foreign rulers, and the latter obtained special religious teachings, tantric empowerments, and blessings in return and derived prestige and added power from such relationships. In the economic sphere, this meant that Tibetan Buddhist institutions complemented the revenue extracted from their estates with the lavish gifts received from such benefactors. In the political sphere, with the ascent of the Dalai Lamas it meant that local kings and chieftains, powerful Mongol khans, and Manchu emperors offered these hierarchs economic, political, and military support in return for their conferral of sacral legitimacy and transmission of highly coveted spiritual powers, special blessings, teachings, and prayers.

Fundamental to Tibetan Buddhism, which developed in Tibet as a fusion of mostly Mahayana and Vajrayana doctrine and practice, is the belief that the purpose of enlightenment is to benefit other living beings. In the words of Gyalwa Gendun Drub, posthumously recognized as the First Dalai Lama, "If you wish to be of maximum and ultimate benefit in the world, and because only a fully enlightened being can be so, you should aspire to achieve full enlightenment as quickly as possible for the benefit of all that lives."[5] This is the bodhisattva way, the path that leads to becoming a bodhisattva and, eventually, a Buddha, a fully enlightened being. When a fully enlightened being, having attained the realm of the *dharmakaya*, or Buddhahood, chooses to manifest in an "emanated" human body in order to benefit all living beings, that emanation, like those who are aspiring to attain Buddhahood, is referred to as a bodhisattva.[6] Mahayana scriptures mention numerous bodhisattvas, three of which are especially important to understanding the Tibetan Buddhist world: Avalokitesvara, the bodhisattva of compassion, known to Tibetans as Chenrezig; Manjusri, the bodhisattva of wisdom; and Vajrapani, the bodhisattva of power.[7]

Avalokitesvara's central and enduring place in the Tibetan conceptualization of the Tibetan Buddhist world and of the Tibetan nation and its rulers must not be underestimated.[8] According to Tibetan belief as projected onto the early history of Tibet, Avalokitesvara had a special relationship with the Tibetan people, traced back in ancient myth to the very conception of the Tibetan race as an act of the bodhisattva's compassion.[9] The Tibetan Plateau became the seat of the human manifestation of Avalokitesvara, who came to be regarded as the protector of the "land of snows."[10] The bodhisattva who takes on the human form of a ruler becomes a bodhisattva-as-ruler (or, to use David Seyfort Ruegg's term, "bodhisattva-king"). This concept was applied to Tibetan ruling hierarchs, but it was also made available to other rulers, who were thereby recognized as emanations of a bodhisattva. Thus, Khubilai Khan and his successors, as also Hong Taiji and his successors on the Qing throne, were formally recognized as emanations of Manjusri.[11] Zhabdrung Ngawang Namgyal, the founder of Bhutan, was similarly considered an emanation of Avalokitesvara.[12] When the Fifth Dalai Lama in his biography of his predecessor, the Fourth, makes the point that Manjusri rules China, he was speaking of the Manchu emperor as an incarnation of that bodhisattva in just the same way as he spoke of himself as a manifestation of Avalokitesvara.[13]

Add to this phenomenon the Tibetan Buddhist practice of searching for and recognizing reincarnations of deceased Buddhist masters, including the Dalai Lamas, as emanations of bodhisattvas, and you have a unique manner of securing the continuation of this form of sacral rule: the transfer of spiritual and political succession through rebirth. This practice originated in Tibet in the thirteenth century, but it took a couple of centuries for it to replace the prevailing forms of familial succession practiced by the powerful aristocracy. It wasn't until the Fifth Dalai Lama's consolidation of power in the seventeenth century, uniting spiritual and worldly authority in his person, that this divine form of legitimacy and continuity of rule was firmly institutionalized.

In Buddhism, reincarnation is considered to be a self-evident truth. All beings except the fully enlightened ones are reborn in some realm of impermanent existence owing to the forces of cause and effect, without being able to determine where, how, or in what form it happens.[14] According to the Mahayanan emphasis on the practice of compassion and care for all living beings rather than the personal quest for liberation, a being can grow closer to enlightenment in each successive life if motivated to benefit all beings. In the Vajrayana tradition, a bodhisattva has the exceptional ability to determine the conditions of his or her reentry into the world through the overwhelming altruistic desire to benefit others. On the basis of these convictions Tibetan Buddhists conceived and developed the practice of officially recognizing such reincarnations. Since the pursuit of spiritual realization founded on the generation of altruism and compassion was the raison d'être of Tibetan Buddhist practice and institutions, it was presumed that lamas, or higher-status monks and spiritual masters (*gurus* in Sanskrit), who were most accomplished in this endeavor would choose to return and that their reincarnations could be identified. The search for, and official recognition of, reincarnations of important lamas, often abbots of monasteries, became a primary means of determining succession to spiritual and institutional leadership positions and often entailed inheritance of property as well.[15] As the power of the religious establishment increased in the worldly sphere, the system of recognizing incarnations created an alternative to the power of hereditary nobility. Although it was not uncommon for incarnate lamas to be discovered within prominent and wealthy families, they were not necessarily part of the aristocratic establishment.

THE SYMBIOSIS OF SPIRITUAL
AND TEMPORAL AUTHORITY

The symbiosis of the spiritual and the temporal domains informs the nature of polities in the Tibetan Buddhist world and of their interactions with others. At the abstract theoretical level, the Tibetan Buddhist conception of the model polity, of legitimate governance, and of the system of interpolity relations is essentialized in the Tibetan concept of *chö-si*[16] and its Mongolian and Manchu equivalents, *törü shasin* and *doro shajin*. This concept denotes the inextricable connection between the Dharma and politics, which Ishihama Yumiko calls "Buddhist government" in English,[17] but which might be better rendered as "Buddhist governance" or "Buddhist Way." The word *chö* (*chos*) is Tibetan for "Dharma" (sometimes inadequately translated as "religion").[18] *Si* (*srid*) generally refers to "Samsara," our cyclical worldly existence. In this context and in the phrase *chos srid gnyis ldan* it means "dominion" or "temporal authority." Since *gnyis* means "dual" or "twin," the concept signifies one possessed of the twin domains of spiritual and worldly authority.

It would be nice to be able to present a clean theory and a consistent model of the relationship between the two domains and forms of authority to explain the many expressions of the principle, but in reality its invocations and applications varied and shifted depending on the time and place, the power relations between specific holders of authority, and the context in which it was used and explained, so much so that a leading scholar of the subject describes it as "kaleidoscopic."[19] Having said that, we briefly discuss two expressions of the symbiotic relationship most pertinent to understanding the nature of polities in the Tibetan Buddhist world and of Inner Asian interpolity relations. The first is the concept of the Chogyal, the Dharma-king (Dharmaraja in Sanskrit), and its variant when applied to the universal monarch, the *chakravartin*.[20] The second is the *chö-yön* relationship between high lamas and worldly rulers.

Dharma-kings were said to rule in the service of the Dharma. Some of the early *tsenpos* of Tibet, Mongol khans, and the rulers of Sikkim came to be thought of as Dharma-kings. The same was true of Bhutan's early seventeenth-century founder, Zhabdrung Ngawang Namgyal (the Zhabdrung Rinpoché), who was a lama and an accomplished spiritual practitioner, and Bhutan's twentieth-century hereditary kings. Leading Tibetan hierarchs bestowed the *chakravartin* title on Great Khans of the Mongols once they converted to Buddhism; the Dalai Lamas did the same for Manchu emperors. When the Dharma-king was not himself a religious personage, as was often the case, he was generally considered to have a special relationship with one or more spiritual masters whose roles in governance were often institutionalized. In Sikkim this was symbolized by the Chogyal's enthronement ceremony, which was performed by three high lamas. In Bhutan, although the Zhabdrung incarnations were acknowledged as Dharma-kings, they seldom held actual power. Instead, successive lay regents, or *desi* (*sde-srid*), wielded civil authority, while the Je Khenpo acted as the country's highest spiritual authority.

A *chö-yön* relationship between an accomplished lama and a lay ruler consisted of the religious conferral of symbolic authority and thereby legitimacy on the ruler in exchange for the latter's grant of material support. *Chö-yön* is a conflation of the Tibetan terms *chöné* (the object of honor, respect, and worship: the guru, who is the lama) and *yöndag* (the maker of offerings, the giver of alms to the lama and his monastic community).[21] The term expresses traditional Buddhist values of humility and deference, but it mostly refers to the interconnectedness of the spiritual and temporal domains. In English, the *chö-yön* concept has been translated as the "priest-patron," "chaplain-donor," "prelate-disciple," and "officiant-benefactor" relationship.[22] *Chöné* is the *tsawe lama*, or "root guru," the teacher and spiritual guide with whom a disciple has a special connection and from whom he or she receives initiations or empowerments.[23] Here we use the word Teacher in this sense, with a capital *T*, to translate *chöné* into English. As for the *yöndag*, we use "benefactor" or "protector" depending on the context.

Relationships between lamas and their benefactors flourished when leaders of monastic orders looked for external support to maintain and expand their institutions. But the distinctive *chö-yön* relationship embedded in Tibetan religious and political culture existed at a high level of authority.[24] It was particularly important when it served as the foundation for relations among polities and became the construct through which they were conceived, shaped, and interpreted. The relationship between Khubilai Khan and the Tibetan lama Phagpa of the Sakya order was often taken as a model. As part of the assertion of Mongol supremacy over Tibet,

Chinggis Khan's grandson Köten Khan summoned the well-known Tibetan lama and scholar Sakya Pandita to his court in 1244, and the latter brought his nephew Phagpa with him, as discussed in chapter 2.[25] Köten and Sakya Pandita forged a *chö-yön* relationship, but it was the higher-profile relationship between Khubilai Khan and Phagpa after Khubilai became Great Khan in 1260 that has mostly served as the point of reference. In this prototypical relationship, Phagpa provided Khubilai with enhanced legitimacy among Buddhists and gave him coveted tantric empowerments and esoteric teachings that, according to Tibetan Buddhist tradition, can only be transmitted in person by the Teacher to the duly initiated disciple. On his part Khubilai venerated his Teacher and supported the latter's dominant Sakya order and institutions. He made him imperial preceptor, anointing Phagpa as the supreme spiritual authority in the empire. And he gave Phagpa (also considered an incarnation of Avalokitesvara) the authority to rule Tibet, overseeing a state apparatus consisting of both monastic and lay officials. Tibetan historiographers subsequently idealized this *chö-yön* relationship, declaring that "Tibet was happy and the Sacred Doctrine glittered like a mirror because of the Two Laws, the Lama's Command and Emperor's Rule," and that, under the auspices of the two, "the riches of Mongolia and China made Tibet the center of the Sacred Doctrine."[26] This narrative may usefully be juxtaposed alongside Koichi Matsuda's analysis of the Mongol perspective in chapter 2. Matsuda suggests that the extension of Mongol domination over Tibet in the thirteenth and fourteenth centuries was a regular part of the imperial project initiated by Chinggis Khan and displayed important characteristics of the imperial strategy and system of governance of the empire. For our purposes here, the Tibetan rendition uses the *chö-yön* concept as the construct to give shape to political and economic relations within the Tibetan Buddhist worldview.

The support from Mongol Khans for Tibetan lamas and their institutions waned after the shrinking of the eastern Mongol empire and the reestablishment of indigenous Tibetan rule on much of the plateau. Significant *chö-yön* relationships between them were only reestablished some two hundred years later when Altan Khan, ruler of the Tümed Mongols, invited a leading lama of the reformist Gelug order, Sonam Gyatso, to his court. Sonam Gyatso became Altan Khan's Teacher. They exchanged titles, the khan giving him the title Dalai Lama — meaning Ocean Lama, a Mongolian term connoting vastness — that has since been carried by all successive incarnations of Sonam Gyatso.

In 1642 Gushri Khan, the Fifth Dalai Lama's *yöndag* and ruler of the Khoshot Mongols (part of the western Mongols, or Oirats), intervened militarily against the Lama's sectarian rivals and proceded to create a kingdom that encompassed the Tibetan Plateau. In conformity with the *chö-yön* relationship, the victorious khan is said to have given the newly subdued realm as an offering to his Teacher. The Dalai Lama then assumed temporal rule over Tibet in addition to his spiritual role, creating an enduring complementary religious and political governance system referred to as Ganden Phodrang.[27] He consolidated his power through the vigorous expansion of Gelugpa monasticism across the plateau, shaping the Tibetan polity for centuries to come. The *chö-yön* relationship of successive Dalai Lamas with Manchu emperors, dating from 1639, would take on an enhanced political and strategic significance after the latter conquered China and consolidated their power among the Mongols.

Although the *chö-yön* relationship is conceived as personal,[28] these examples show that it was more intricate than that. Implicitly it was also institutional, since the benefactor was expected to support religious institutions and protect not only the Teacher personally but also his position, his power. The relationship was further complicated when the Teacher, the recipient of the *yöndag*'s benefaction and protection, was himself also a worldly ruler, as were the Dalai Lamas from the mid-seventeenth century on. In such cases patronage by a powerful ruler was not limited to financial assistance to the Teacher and to his monastic institutions but could include political and even military support for the polity of which his Teacher was the ruler. The *yöndag* was expected to wield his power in the service of his Teacher and the Tibetan Buddhist faith. Within this religiopolitical framework therefore, Khubilai Khan, Gushri Khan (who even after 1642 retained military power in Tibet), and the Manchu emperors of the Qing were Dharma-kings, some recognized as *chakravartins*. At the same time, they were *yöndags*, the benefactors and protectors of their Teacher and his polity. Some, like the Manchu emperors, were recognized as incarnations of bodhisattvas, recalling a similar recognition of Khubilai Khan as Manjusri centuries earlier. This gave both parties in the *chö-yön* relationship the attributes of both worldly political authority and a sacred source of legitimacy.

Is one superior to the other? Ishihama has demonstrated that Mongols, Tibetans, and the Manchu emperors shared the Tibetan Buddhist understanding of "Buddhist government" and of its expression in the *chö-yön* relationship. In Buddhist theory, the Teacher, the *tsawe lama*, is superior; the worldly ruler who is his benefactor and protector is subordinate.[29] When the ruler is considered a *chakravartin*, this hierarchy may hold in theory but the situation may be more complicated in practice. Ruegg concludes that the answer depended on the exact circumstances prevailing at a given historical time and place and that the relationship was fluid in practice.

"The representatives of the two orders have indeed very often been considered equal—that is, as 'cojoined . . . like sun and moon,'" Ruegg observes. "But on other occasions, in a specifically religious context for instance, it was naturally the preceptor-officiant, the [lama] Hierarch, who has been thought of as superior; while in a secular political situation the lay donor could well be regarded as predominant."[30] At the Mongol courts of Khubilai Khan and Altan Khan, as well as at the Manchu court of the Shunzhi emperor, when these rulers received their Teacher (Lama Phagpa and, in the latter two cases, the Third and the Fifth Dalai Lamas respectively), protocol implied the supremacy of the Teachers in religious matters and of the emperors in worldly affairs. The modified protocol observed by the court of Qianlong at the end of the eighteenth century, as we will see in the next chapter, may have reflected the Qing's brief assertion of greater political power in relation to Tibetan affairs at that time.

RULE BY RELATIONSHIP

The Tibetan Buddhist world was not centrally or uniformly ruled and needs to be understood in terms of relationships rather than territorial authority. The overarching religiopolitical paradigms common to all Tibetan Buddhist polities were not exclusive principles of legitimacy and governance everywhere. For example, whereas the conception of dual religiopolitical governance constituted the foundation of the Tibetan state and the Dalai Lamas' form of government, it was not the only basis for Mongol rulers, who operated within two civilizational worlds simultaneously: the Chinggisid Mongol world as well as the Tibetan Buddhist one. While Mongol rulers and nobles constructed their relationships with one another and their subjects within the norms and laws of the Mongol world, they also acted in accordance with Tibetan Buddhist principles and constructs, deriving legitimacy from the relationships they developed with Buddhist monastic institutions and lamas, especially the Dalai Lamas.

The pervasiveness of Tibetan Buddhist conceptions within the Mongol worldview makes it difficult to separate the two worlds cleanly.[31] In addition, Tibetan polities that came under Mongol domination during the imperial reigns of the Great Khans from the mid-thirteenth to mid-fourteenth centuries to a degree became part of the Chinggisid world as well. Perhaps not as much in the civilizational sense and in terms of sources of legitimacy, for which rulers in Tibetan polities relied heavily on Tibetan Buddhism, but the legacy of the Mongol domination was felt in the systems of administration and the institutions Tibetans inherited from the Mongols. In particular, Khubilai Khan's enfeoffment of land and bonded subjects to every school of Tibetan Buddhism affected the social and economic structures and power relations of Tibetan society. Another enduring legacy was the connection between Tibetans and Mongols, which had political, strategic, military, and economic components but was always, at the core, Buddhist.

The partnerships between spiritual potentates and military rulers were consensual, flexible, and not exclusive. At any given time, relationships were in place between lamas from different schools of Tibetan Buddhism and various benefactors. Whereas the typical bond between Dalai Lamas and Mongol rulers provided the former with economic support in the form of offerings as well as political and military backing, this was not the only kind of relationship the Dalai Lamas entertained. Some were cast in terms of tribute relations, for example. Ladakh paid tribute to the Dalai Lama's court on the basis of the 1684 Tingmosgang Treaty ending the Tibet-Ladakh war (fought with the help of Mongol troops). Tibetan relations with Gorkha were marked by wars and the payment of an annual tribute by Tibet to the Gorkha rulers. Following the 1791 Tibet-Gorkha war it was to the Manchu court that both polities paid tribute. These tribute payments were not for the most part expressions of Tibetan Buddhist exchange relationships.

The Dalai Lamas differed from the rulers of other polities in Inner and East Asia in relying for military power mostly on relationships with protectors *outside* their own polity. Tibet did have an army of its own that fought some of its wars, with mixed results,[32] but it was usually to the Mongol benefactors and, in the eighteenth century, to Manchu emperors as well that the Dalai Lamas and other Tibetan political leaders turned for military assistance. It was Khoshot military power under Gushri Khan that enabled the Fifth Dalai Lama to consolidate political power in the first place. Successive Mongol khans and princes continued to exercise military power for extended periods in central Tibet and some other parts of the Tibetan Plateau. Mongol and Manchu benefactors also provided economic support; Mongol pilgrims were especially important for augmenting the domestic revenues that monastic institutions raised from their estates and the people tied to them. Thus, the military and economic resources needed to enable the realization of the Tibetan religiopolitical state and the role of monasticism in the Tibetan Buddhist world were obtained by supplementing Tibet's domestic capacity through relationships with benefactors and pilgrims. That military and economic power partly originated elsewhere does not mean that the Dalai Lamas were themselves powerless. These relationships were part of the exchange that endowed them with real power in the eyes of the Tibetan Buddhist world.

When we speak of the Dalai Lama in this context, it is to the institution as established during the reign of the Great Fifth that we refer rather than to the person. That institution headed the state, operated a government, and represented the authority of the Gelugpa institutions present through much of the Tibetan Buddhist world. Not all Dalai Lamas were effective in exercising their ruling power, and none was as powerful as the Fifth or the Thirteenth. Some exercised more spiritual than political authority, and a surprising number did not reach the age of majority, but the institution remained.

Although the Dalai Lama exercised considerable religious and political authority throughout the Tibetan Buddhist world, polities outside Tibet did not come under the Dalai Lama's worldly rule and could be linked to other centers of authority as well. Mongol polities had their own, mostly Chinggisid rulers, and Himalayan polities and those on the eastern part of the Tibetan Plateau in Kham and parts of Amdo were ruled by khans, kings, chieftains, or lamas. While all subscribed to the religiopolitical principles of the Tibetan Buddhist world, they gave shape to them in ways that were often distinctive. What sustained the Tibetan Buddhist world as a whole were the common overarching religiopolitical concepts, principles, and constructs already presented in this chapter. Together these constituted a normative legal order that shaped and made sense of authority and of relationships within and between polities.

In the rest of this chapter, we explore facets of the Tibetan Buddhist world and its legal order, from state structures and governance to economic, political, and religious relations, among Mongols, Tibetans, and Himalayan peoples as well as in relation to the Manchu court. Unlike the Chinggisid and Sinic worlds, the Tibetan Buddhist world did not have its own Great State in the period we cover in this book. It was not a territorial, much less a military, empire whose rise and decline we can narrate in linear fashion. Instead, we present short studies that provide insight into the significance of the normative order of the Tibetan Buddhist world and reveal how this world was perceived and utilized from a variety of vantage points. Given the importance, as we have indicated, of the seventeenth century in fashioning this Tibetan Buddhist world, it is primarily on that and the following century that we focus here.

The interdependence of spiritual and worldly domains that shaped so much of the Tibetan Buddhist world and its legal order permeates Tibetan Buddhist historical writing and is reflected in the nature of the writing itself. Among the contemporary sources available to us, life writings of Tibetan hierarchs, in particular the Dalai Lamas and their top officials and counselors, as well as the leading religious and political figures of other Tibetan Buddhist polities, dominate the field of historical writing.

Although couched primarily in religious terms, these provide considerable insight into the nature of those polities and their relations with others and reveal how people, events, and relationships were perceived and given a place within the paradigms and constructs of the Tibetan Buddhist world. Rather than attempt to disentangle the religious from the secular and political elements of the stories they tell, we choose to leave these strands combined so as to not interfere with our understanding of how political and religious actors as well as writers viewed the world they lived in. What we can add is a sense of the contexts, including the economic context, within which events took place so as to bring forward the political significance of what these writings recount.

MONGOL PILGRIMAGES AND THE TRANSFER OF WEALTH TO TIBET

· Dalizhabu ·

Studying Mongol pilgrimages to Tibet after the second Mongol conversion to Buddhism from the early sixteenth through the nineteenth century provides a useful avenue for understanding the nature of the enduring connection between Tibetans and Mongols. References to pilgrimages in the biographies of Dalai Lamas as well as in Mongol and Manchu sources[33] reveal in particular an enormous transfer of wealth from Mongols to Tibet. This wealth was significant for sustaining the Tibetan state and monastic institutions and pointed to the importance of keeping the main pilgrimage route open. The practice of Mongol pilgrimages also sheds light on the nature of the relations that the Dalai Lamas and the Gelugpa establishment maintained with the Mongols.

Mongol pilgrimages to Tibet began in earnest after Altan Khan, ruler of the Tümed Mongols, invited the Gelugpa leader, Sonam Gyatso, to his court. They met in 1578 in Amdo, on the northeastern part of the Tibetan Plateau known as Kokonor to the Mongols (Qinghai in Chinese) after the large lake that dominates the region.[34] There, the two leaders established a *chö-yön* relationship modeled after that of Phagpa and Khubilai Khan and exchanged honorific titles. The khan gave the lama the title Dorjechang Dalai Lama, a title subsequently used for all of Sonam Gyatso's successive incarnations and, retroactively, for two prior incarnations, so that Sonam Gyatso came to be known as the Third Dalai Lama.[35] The lama gave his benefactor the title of Brahma, king of the Dharma. During these meetings the two men decided to send Asing Lama, a lama from Amdo responsible for Altan Khan's conversion to Buddhism, to lead a pilgrimage to Tibet, bearing offerings for the famous three large Gelugpa monasteries of Lhasa: Drepung, Sera, and Ganden.[36]

Altan Khan died in 1582 and the Third Dalai Lama passed away six years later, after another visit to the Tümed at the invitation of Altan Khan's son, Sengge Dügüreng Khan. A year later, Sonam Gyatso was declared to have reincarnated as the great-grandson of Altan Khan. The Fourth Dalai Lama was therefore not only a Mongol and direct descendant of Altan Khan but also a descendant of Chinggis Khan. This cemented Mongol support for successive Dalai Lamas and the Gelugpa, which was expressed in acts of devotion, including the making of valuable offerings, and in the form of political and military backing. A sizable military escort accompanied the Fourth Dalai Lama to Tibet in 1603,[37] and many pilgrims, especially of the Tümed, Ordos, and Kharchin Mongols, belonging to the so-called right-wing *tümens*, journeyed to Tibet to present offerings.[38] When this Dalai Lama passed away in 1616, Tümed and Khalkha princes escorted by Mongol troops and accompanied by a large number of pilgrims went to Tibet and offered thousands of taels (a tael was equivalent to 1.3 ounces, or 37 grams) of silver, satin, gold, and jewelry and built a pagoda to house his relics.[39]

Mongol khans and nobles sent and often led missions of pilgrims to Tibet until the late nineteenth century. The pilgrims worshiped mostly the Dalai and Panchen Lamas (or Panchen Khutukhtu, as the latter were known to Mongols and Manchus) and requested Buddhist teachings and blessings from them and from other senior lamas, as well as the performance of religious services and rituals. They also requested the Dalai Lama to provide names for each new temple or monastery they built at home. Some nobles, Oirats in particular, requested the coveted title of khan and a seal from the Dalai Lama,[40] a title normally acquired in accordance with Chinggisid rules. The pilgrims made offerings of money and goods to the major monasteries and their monks. The offerings to the Dalai Lama, the Panchen Lama, and other senior lamas included gold, silver, silk, satin, jewelry, gold and silver utensils, decorated saddles, and tea. All these gifts contributed to the living expenses of monks and helped to finance the construction and maintenance of monasteries, temples, pagodas, and sacred statues. But they had a wider impact, since these hierarchs passed on part of their fortune to the population in recurrent wealth distribution rituals that played an important socioeconomic role in much of the Tibetan Buddhist world. Because Tibetans drank considerable amounts of butter-tea as part of their diet, the pilgrims always provided tea and food for the monks in the temples and monasteries they visited. As a result, these pilgrimages became known in Mongolian as *mangja činaqu* and in Tibetan as *mang-ja,* meaning "distributing tea among the many," and in Chinese as *aocha*, "boiling tea."[41]

The reincarnation of the Fourth Dalai Lama was discovered at a time of conflict in central Tibet between the king of Tsang, who patronized the Karma-Kagyu school, and Gelugpa hierarchs and monasteries supported by Mongol troops. As a result, the enthronement of the Fifth Dalai Lama was delayed until 1642. Many Tümed pilgrims, escorted by their own troops, went to Lhasa to profess their support for the Dalai Lama and to present thousands of gifts to him, including silk, satin, gold, silver, musical instruments, porcelain, pearl-decorated trees, and a variety of Chinese goods.[42] The monks who had come with them prepared tea for the Gelugpa monks of the Lhasa region multiple times a day for some forty days and also gave them bricks of tea, food, *khatas* (ceremonial silk scarves), as well as silver and refined silk. These offerings are described in the Fifth Dalai Lama's autobiography, as are the crowds of Tibetans awestruck at seeing "what seemed to them the treasure-house of Jambhala," the deity who bestows wealth and personifies abundance.[43]

During the life of the Fifth Dalai Lama the number of pilgrims and the value of gifts presented peaked. His autobiography records that every year several thousand Mongol pilgrims came to Tibet. Their missions, which varied from hundreds to more than a thousand persons, were organized and led by eminent lamas and Mongol nobles, accompanied by their own military escorts. These missions carried large quantities of offerings, including gold and silver as well as utensils made in these precious metals and saddles decorated with them. Silk, satin, tea, and horses also usually formed part of the offerings.

The full value of the offerings presented by Mongol pilgrims is difficult to determine. Descriptions of these distributions of wealth to the Dalai Lamas, the Panchen Lamas, and other senior religious figures can be found in the biographies and autobiographies of successive Dalai Lamas and Panchen Lamas, corroborated in part in the biography of the famous Khoshot scholar Lama Zaya Pandita (1599–1662).[44] These and other sources attest to the vast quantity and value of the gifts presented and also reveal that it was not only the Mongol nobles who made such prodigious offerings. Thousands of ordinary pilgrims who accompanied them, as well as wealthy Tibetan families and the Manchu court, did the same.[45]

We get a sense of the magnitude of the offerings made from accounts of specific pilgrimages. Thus, for example, we are told that in the winter of 1625, Tuba Tayiji, the son of the *jinong* (viceroy) of the Ordos Mongols, came to Tibet to present offerings for his father's good reincarnation and that he donated money to repair the chanting room of Drepung Monastery.[46] He gathered the lamas and monks of Drepung and Sera Monasteries, both near Lhasa, and donated some ten thousand Chinese and Mongolian goods, including silk, satin, gold, and silver. His relatives all gave large numbers of presents as well, all of them making offerings five or six times a day.[47]

In 1651 Zaya Pandita came to Tibet with 110,000 taels of silver, part of which was an offering he carried from Ochirtu Tayiji,[48] as well as prized Mongolian horses, each having a market value of 8–10 taels.[49] According to Zaya Pandita's biography, he gave 50,000 taels of silver to the Dalai Lama's administration, half of which was used to build a Buddha statue; the other half, to finance the crafting of golden roofs for Drepung Monastery. A further 50,000 taels of silver was offered to the Dalai Lama and to monks for the recitation or chanting of Buddhist scriptures. Zaya Pandita not only offered tea and gave donations to large and small Gelugpa monasteries during his pilgrimage but also gave a quantity of offerings to Sakyapa, Kagyupa, and Nyingmapa institutions. A year later he likewise brought large offerings to the Panchen Lama's monastery, Tashilhunpo.[50]

Between 1723 and 1795, the pilgrim missions were mostly from the Khalkhas and the Oirats of Kokonor, though Oirats further west (Zunghars) and Kalmyk pilgrims from the Volga region also sent important missions. In 1729 Khalkha leaders accompanied by thousands of pilgrims traveled to Lhasa, where they donated more than 300,000 taels of silver to the Dalai Lama, the Panchen Lama, and Gelugpa monasteries in connection with the choosing of the reincarnation of Jetsundhamba, the most important Khalkha lama.[51] Despite the crushing defeat the Zunghar khan Galdan Tsering suffered at the hands of Qing armies in 1732, he was granted permission by the Qianlong emperor several years later to send pilgrims through Kokonor to Tibet to make offerings for his deceased father. Although Galdan Tsering could not himself go on the pilgrimage for reasons of his personal safety, two Zunghar missions reached Tibet, one in 1743 and the other, after his death, in 1747. The first of these missions presented offerings to the Dalai Lama and Panchen Lama as well as to the monks of Ganden, Sera, Drepung, and Tashilhunpo Monasteries, consisting of 436 taels of gold, 175,506 taels of silver, and large quantities of silk, satin, cloth, leather, gold and silver utensils, and religious articles.[52] The second mission presented about 422 taels of gold and 19,448 taels of silver as well as other precious gifts.[53]

The Manchu court understood the economic significance of these gifts, as an order the Qianlong emperor issued to General Fukangan indicates. Fukangan had led the imperial army that helped Tibetans repel the Gorkha invaders in 1792. In a memorial reporting on the state of affairs in

Tibet and proposing security measures to safeguard Manchu interests, the general advised the emperor to prohibit foreigners, including Mongols, from going to Tibet. The emperor disagreed, reasoning, "There are few products in Tibet, the Potala *shangshang* [i.e., the Dalai Lama's administration] spends much on the maintenance of lamas and on Tibetan troops' rations, so it is unable to make ends meet. Tibet has always depended on Mongol and Tibetan pilgrims' donations to cover its expenses. Therefore, the Mongol and Tibetan pilgrimages and 'boiling tea' [should] all be permitted."[54] Fukangan himself noted in his memorial that the Dalai Lama's administration's annual revenue from taxes was 127,000 taels of silver and that of the Panchen Lama was 66,000 taels, whereas the annual expenditures of these hierarchs were estimated at 142,000 and 74,600 taels of silver respectively, suggesting a sizable deficit.[55]

The transfer of wealth in the form of offerings by Mongol pilgrims to Tibetan lamas and religious institutions and the trade that this engendered were of such importance to all concerned that it became vital to ensure that the main pilgrim route remain open and safe. The Northern Path through Kokonor was the preferred route because, unlike the Southern Path through Sichuan, it did not require travel through China with the risk of contracting smallpox there. The Fifth Dalai Lama referred to the Kokonor route as the Golden Bridge in recognition of the wealth transported over it,[56] and the route acquired great strategic significance.

To secure safe passage for pilgrims to Tibet, Altan Khan and the Third Dalai Lama had earlier decided to settle parts of Kokonor with relatives and allies of the khan and their subjects. These Tümeds, together with some Ordos who were stationed east of Kokonor, subjugated local Tibetan tribes that had been under Ming control, securing for themselves a dominant position that enabled them to ensure passage for pilgrims and to provide support, including military support, to the Gelug order. The Ming court understood the importance of the Kokonor region, which lay just beyond its northwesternmost outpost, and at first encouraged Altan Khan, in part because it hoped that the conversion of Mongols to Buddhism would reduce nomad attacks on Ming border regions. The Wanli emperor even allowed passage through the Great Wall to provide a shortcut for the khan and his people to reach Kokonor.[57] Many Mongol pilgrims used that shortcut. The enormous number of worshipers—some ten thousand, according to the biographies of the Fourth and Fifth Dalai Lamas—who did so to escort the Third Dalai Lama's ashes to Tibet following his death in 1588 alarmed the Ming court, however, prompting it not only to prohibit travel through Ming territory but also to attempt, unsuccessfully, to drive the Mongols out of Kokonor.[58]

When Chokhtu Tayiji of the Khalkha Mongols—who at the time patron-ized the Sakyapa—occupied Kokonor after defeating the Tümed there in 1632, the Fifth Dalai Lama complained that he obstructed the Golden Bridge, preventing the flow of offerings from eminent Mongol monks and wealthy benefactors from reaching Tibet. Both he and the Panchen Lama appealed to the Oirat Mongols to dispatch troops to Kokonor to restore order and make it safe for pilgrims. Responding to the call, Gushri Khan of the Khoshot Oirats and Bakhatar Kong Tayiji of the Jegünkhar Oirats attacked and defeated Chokhtu Tayiji. Following this, Gushri Khan and his armies remained in Kokonor and secured safe passage for the pilgrims. The Dalai Lama subsequently mediated internal conflicts among the Khoshots in efforts to ensure stability in the Amdo region.[59] It was from his position in Kokonor that Gushri Khan expanded his authority and that of the Dalai Lama across the plateau through the 1640s.

Once the Manchus had overrun Ming territory, they looked toward Ko-konor, understanding that whoever controlled it could influence political and religious developments in Tibet as well as the movement of Mongols in the region.[60] It was not until 1688, however, that the Qing managed to establish control over a section of the Kokonor pilgrim route. Galdan Khan, who had been a Gelugpa monk in Lhasa, had taken the leadership of the powerful Zunghar khanate in 1677 after uniting the Oirats and was awarded the supreme title, Boshokhtu Khagan, by the Fifth Dalai Lama shortly thereafter. In 1688, when he pursued Tüsiyetü Khan of the Khalkha into territory under Manchu authority, Qing imperial troops and Alasai Khoshot soldiers forced him to retreat, leaving the Qing in control of a nar-row passage on the Kokonor pilgrim route and of a garrison in Xining.[61] The Qing troops subsequently blocked passage through this route. For a time, only those Mongols who had settled in the Kokonor region and Kalmyk pilgrims from the Kalmyk khanate in the Russian Volga River basin—who were permitted passage—could visit Lhasa and other centers in Tibet. By 1723, when the Qing dynasty had consolidated its control of Kokonor and established a foothold in Lhasa, the flow of pilgrims had resumed.

For most of the period of Ming and Qing rule in China, Mongol pilgrim-ages were of economic importance not only to the Gelugpa and therefore the Tibetans but also to the Chinese and the Manchus. In order for the Mon-gols to make the kinds of offerings they did to Tibetan lamas and monas-teries, they needed to trade horses, other stock, and animal hides with the Ming and Qing in exchange for tea, gold, silver, jewels, silk, and the other goods used as offerings. This trade was important for all trading partners.[62] The Tümed, Ordos, and Kharchin Mongols established trade relations with the Ming in 1571, mostly navigating the rules the Ming had established for trading under the somewhat-artificial rubric of tribute-trade. As a result, for a time, most other Mongol leaders were required to trade indirectly with the Ming through their mediation.[63] Chinese-language sources, such as the court diary of the Qing, however, contain only records of tribute, ignoring other forms of trade with the Mongols. To find out about them, one needs to look at Tibetan, Mongolian, and Manchu sources. The biography of Zaya Pandita, for example, gives details of the trade that the Oirats from the Tarim Basin carried out with the Qing at least in part outside the tribute system. It describes how the silver and other precious goods Zaya Pandita offered in Tibet had been obtained by trading horses. When Zaya Pandita personally sent envoys to trade in Beijing with the Qing in 1647, the emperor would not have accepted many horses as tribute, since that would have required giving a large number of highly valuable gifts in exchange. So the bulk of the trade in Mongolian horses occurred outside the tribute system. In the same year Khoshot Oirat leader Ochirtu Tayiji ordered all the *otoγ* (princely domains) under his control to collect ten thousand horses and trade them in Beijing. He also ordered the Köke Hota border market to obtain the silver and other precious gifts that Zaya Pandita would present as offerings in Tibet.[64] These were not isolated cases, as Manchu sources tell us that the Qing established markets in the first half of the eighteenth century in Gansu and Kokonor in order to facilitate trade for Mongol pilgrims.[65]

Mongol military and political support played an important role in the rise of the Gelugpa and their hierarchs' governance of Tibet. So too did Mongol donations, for they raised the prestige of the Gelugpa and stimulated both religious and economic development in Tibet. By trading stock and animal hides for gold, silver, jewelry, silk, and other precious items as well as tea with the Ming and Qing, by donating these goods to lamas and institutions in Tibet, and by taking primarily religious goods back to Mongolia from Tibet, Mongol pilgrims were important agents of economic and cultural interaction among Mongols, Tibetans, Chinese, and Manchus. Mongol and Qing dependence on trade and Tibetan dependence on pilgrimage encouraged the maintenance of peace in the region, as all parties were conscious that disruption of these interactions was harmful to them.

STATE BUILDING IN THE HIMALAYAS

· John Ardussi ·

The nature of polities to the south of Tibet, in the Himalayan region, was very different from that of the Mongol polities. So too were the relations they maintained with Tibetan hierarchs and political leaders. The religio-political structure and philosophy of these polities and societies as well as the genesis and forms of statecraft or governance they developed tied them intimately to the Tibetan Buddhist world. But unlike most Mongol khans and nobles, who in the sixteenth century became devout supporters of the Gelug order, Bhutan, Sikkim, and Ladakh were, like many of the polities on the eastern portions of the Tibetan Plateau, strongholds of other schools and subschools of Tibetan Buddhism. Rivalry among these Buddhist orders at times expressed itself in political tensions and even violent conflict between the polities who supported them.

Proselytizing led to competition among Tibetan Buddhist schools to establish branch monasteries, often in far-flung locations well outside central Tibet. The Drukpa Kagyu school, which came to dominate in western Bhutan and Ladakh, exemplifies how a Tibetan Buddhist school might establish branch monasteries in order to enlarge its political impact. Beginning in the thirteenth century, tours by the order's hierarchs from Tibet were instrumental in bringing students from the leading families of western Bhutan to the Drukpa home monastery of Ralung. The people of Bhutan thus became integrated into the religious life of Tibet through the institutions of the monastic establishment and teaching lineage several centuries before the Bhutanese state was formally founded. Typically, frontier monasteries were small family or village structures, nothing like the massive monastic centers of Tibet. Until its unification in the seventeenth century, Bhutan remained a land of small, self-governing valley communities. The *chö-si* system—the interconnection of spiritual and temporal realms—arose in several of these communities, mirroring the political model of Tibet, but the system was basically local, or Bhutan-centric, in the sense that the monks and ruling elites were Bhutanese. Similar social movements took place in Sikkim (a smaller polity with a more complex ethnic structure), albeit on a lesser scale than in Bhutan. For both polities, the beginnings of their statehood emerged from among the local families who patronized these branch establishments of Tibetan monasteries.

When one looks closely at the unfolding historical relationships between Tibet and its southern neighbors, Sikkim and Bhutan, it is clear that the *perception* each had of the other played an important role. There was a gradual evolution in how Tibet perceived the territories on its south, beginning centuries before formal polities even existed there, from naively mythical ideas into more realistic appraisals.[66] Long centuries passed during which the fog of *misperception* benefited all parties. Tibetans feared the tropical climates of the south, its wild animals, and what they perceived as primitive peoples. They left the southerners largely alone, no doubt to the relief of southern societies.[67]

The Mongol penetration of Tibet forced a shift in the old perceptions, which would have an enormous impact on the southern Himalayan political communities. The fear of Mongol cavalry and social turmoil in central Tibet stimulated a revivalist movement there that included a focus on what Tibetans now called the Southlands. The movement engendered a new form of prophetic religious literature, Buddhist in inspiration but based on a body of "treasure texts" purportedly buried during the imperial era in anticipation of a future time when Buddhism would be threatened with extinction in Tibet by vaguely identified Mongol or Turkic invaders. As Mongol influence in Tibet persisted, the thirteenth to fifteenth centuries saw a powerful elaboration of this movement. Monks from throughout Tibet reported in their biographies visions identifying themselves as the "treasure finder" foretold to rediscover these sacred texts, often from "hidden lands" in the Southlands. The hidden lands, it was further elaborated in this exotic literature, must surely be pristine and peaceful, unlike Tibet. The inhabitants of the Southlands, though lowly, were therein portrayed as tranquil and virtuous guardians of the treasure texts and ripe for conversion to Buddhism. Treasure biographies describing the exploits in the Southlands of the semilegendary eighth-century Indian guru Padmasambhava, who Tibetan histories say had once worked miracles before the Tibetan emperor Tri Songdetsen (r. 755–797), were "revealed" during this period. To summarize, during this second phase of the Tibetan perception of the Southlands, the pejorative attitudes and military imagery stemming from Tibet's imperial era gave way to a spiritualized, idealistic presentation. Primitivism became an asset, a mark of spiritual innocence.

The Bhutanese responded to the increasing influx of pilgrims and refugee monks fleeing sectarian strife in Tibet in ways that maximized the value of these developments to the inhabitants of Bhutan while minimizing any implication of subordination to Tibet. For example, of the many small monasteries established in Bhutan as branches of Tibetan schools, almost none appear to have ever been incorporated politically into the parent Tibetan systems in ways that might affect their autonomy. Bhutanese largely accepted or participated in the initiatives that promoted their local cultural properties (e.g., the treasure text and hidden land theories) but exploited them in a distinctly Bhutan-centric way.

Perhaps the best illustration of this is the life story of one of Bhutan's most famous religious personages from the pre-Zhabdrung period, the treasure finder Pema Lingpa (1450–1521).[68] Pema Lingpa was born into a family of ancient Tibetan extraction in the Bumthang valley of central Bhutan, one of the Bhutanese districts culturally most linked to Tibet. According to his autobiography,[69] early in his youth miraculous visions guided him to uncover several troves of hidden texts from the inaccessible depths of a river, from cliffside caves, and so forth. His collected works and treasure discoveries number more than twenty volumes. He became so famous in his own region that he attracted the attention of Tibetan patrons from across the border in the Lhokha district. He went on to found numerous monasteries in Bumthang and acquired disciples and benefactors throughout the southern region of Tibet. After Pema Lingpa's death, his son and grandson continued his mission. Each gave rise to a lineage of reincarnate lamas that continues to this day. Some even attained exceptional reputations within Tibet. The Fifth Dalai Lama and his regent, although at war with the Drukpa state of western Bhutan throughout the seventeenth century, nevertheless welcomed one of the Pema Lingpa reincarnate lamas at the Potala in Lhasa, receiving teachings from him and bestowing on him a monastery in southern Tibet across the border from Bumthang. Even today, many of the elite families of central and eastern Bhutan claim descent from or marital ties to Pema Lingpa, including the line of Druk Gyalpos, who came to rule after 1907.

The phenomenon of Pema Lingpa simply would not have happened absent the treasure text movement, and the course of Bhutanese history would have been dramatically altered. His quixotic persona was a Bhutanese interpretation that adapted and yet transformed a Tibetan movement to the needs of Bhutan. Those unfamiliar with the unique dynamics of Himalayan polities may question the serious political relevance of traditions such as treasure texts and treasure finders, yet these phenomena are very much at the heart of what still shapes the sociopolitical consciousness of Sikkim and Bhutan today. For example, every government building in Bhutan, including the great fortress monasteries founded in the seventeenth century by the Zhabdrung Rinpoché,[70] contains a shrine devoted to the three historical founders, Zhabdrung Ngawang Namgyal (the Zhabdrung Rinpoché), Pema Lingpa, and Padmasambhava.

The founding of the distinct polities of Bhutan in 1625 and Sikkim around 1642, as well as the creation of the new Tibetan Ganden Phodrang government by the Fifth Dalai Lama in 1642, took place in an era of great sectarian strife, which ultimately boiled down to competition for political power. In the peculiar system of chö-si, politics could be expressed in both the civil arena and in that of "reincarnation politics." It was in this context, in 1616, that the young Tibetan hierarch of the Drukpa school, Zhabdrung Ngawang Namgyal (1594–1651), sought refuge among his followers in western Bhutan after political opponents in Tibet challenged his reincarnate status. The king of Tsang, who ruled central Tibet from Shigatse, supported the Zhabdrung Rinpoché's opponents and launched a war in the Southlands against him and his followers but was defeated. In the winter of 1625, the Zhabdrung Rinpoché proclaimed the formation of a new state based on the *chö-si* principle. He appointed a regent, or *desi*, in charge of civil affairs and an informal group of advisers. For the next twenty-six years the Zhabdrung Rinpoché consolidated his position in this new state, Bhutan, holding off repeated threats and actual invasions from Tibet, including several launched by the Fifth Dalai Lama.

Like the Fifth Dalai Lama, the founder of Bhutan was a spiritual hierarch, an incarnate lama with a forceful personality.[71] The persona that he and his followers cultivated for him included mastery over Buddhist and autochthonous protective deities, especially the raven-headed Mahakala, the wrathful aspect of Avalokitesvara. Mahakala is depicted on murals in the innermost temples of Bhutanese monasteries dedicated to the country's protective deities. In the Zhabdrung Rinpoché's elaborate biography, Mahakala in the form of a raven is said to have safeguarded his journey to Bhutan in fulfillment of a collection of prophecies found in the treasure literature attributed to Padmasambhava. The ceremonial headdress of the ruling kings of Bhutan since 1907 also displays the raven-headed Mahakala, symbolically empowering the monarch to defeat foreign enemies of the state.[72]

The violent struggle between the Gelugpa and the Bhutanese branch of the Drukpa and their respective Tibetan allies continued throughout the seventeenth century and into the eighteenth. Critical to the survival of the new Bhutanese state was the three-centuries-long history of Drukpa ties between the leading families of western Bhutan and the home monastery of Ralung in Tibet. Of equal importance was the Zhabdrung Rinpoché's construction between 1629 and 1651 of a series of enormous monastery-fortresses, called *dzong*, from which his Drukpa-based government ruled and repelled opposing armies.

The state of Sikkim was founded under a different version of the *chö-si* principle. The first monarch, or *Chogyal* (Dharma-king), Phuntsho Namgyal, was a layman from a Tibetan family. Sikkimese histories, all written by later Buddhist monks, contain an elaborate set of foundation legends tying his arrival in Sikkim to prophecies found in treasure text literature similar to those from Bhutan. In fact, prophecies from a Bhutanese treasure text discovered by Pema Lingpa were cited as foretelling the Sikkim monarchy. In these legends, Phuntsho Namgyal's lineage is traced to an eastern Tibetan branch of the early Tibetan monarchy. Arriving in Sikkim in conformance with the prophecies, he was enthroned in about 1642 by three Tibetan monks who themselves left Tibet to perform this act in accord with prophetic visions described in their biographies.[73]

From the outset the multiethnic makeup of Sikkim (including Lepcha, Bhutia, Monpa, and Tibetan communities) required a more open system of governance than the Zhabdrung Rinpoché had established in Bhutan. The Nyingma school of Tibetan Buddhism that prevailed in Sikkim was also more eclectic than the Gelugpa and Drukpa, and probably more acceptable to a mixed citizenry that included Hindus and animists. Thus, the Sikkimese Chogyals worked through a council of ministers representing the leading families and ethnic communities, whereas the mechanisms of state governance established in seventeenth-century Bhutan were completely tied to the Drukpa establishment and its lay patron families. Unlike Bhutan also, the Namgyal dynasty of Sikkim always had close ties to the Dalai Lamas of Tibet. In particular, the Fifth Dalai Lama and the first Chogyal shared spiritual teachers, and several subsequent Chogyals were invited to Lhasa, where they were cordially treated by the Tibetan authorities. Although sectarian tensions did exist between the Nyingmapa of Sikkim and the Gelugpa of Tibet, they never rose to the level of ferocity that existed with the Drukpa.

Following the Zhabdrung Rinpoché's death in 1651, and owing in great measure to the concealment of his death for many decades, the governing principle of Bhutan underwent a long evolutionary drift away from the primacy of reincarnate religious hierarchs to a situation where real governance rested in the hands of the various district governors and the *desi*, or civil regents. Few reincarnations of the Zhabdrung Rinpoché achieved a level of managerial competence or endured long in their roles, even though they were the rightful bearers of the title Dharmaraja (Dharma-king). For more than two centuries, between 1696 and 1907, powerful regional families competed for primacy of position, even while nominally acknowledging their subordination to the heads of the Drukpa religious structure.

During the mid-eighteenth century, competition between two factions in western Bhutan provided an opportunity for a Tibetan military expedition sent by Polhané (Polhanas) Sonam Tobgyal, the head of the Kashag (council of ministers) and de facto ruler of Tibet from 1727 to 1747. For a short interval, from 1735 to 1737, Tibet was able to exercise authority over Bhutan. But as Tibet increasingly came under Manchu dominance, it was to the latter's capital that monks representing the two Bhutanese factions were required to go to present letters of apology before the throne of Emperor Yongzheng.[74] Whatever Bhutanese officials may have known about the Qing Great State and its relationship to Tibet prior to this, it is clear that in the aftermath they took great precautions to avoid future conflicts with Tibet and hence with the Qing emperor. Almost immediately, Tibet and Bhutan began to patch up their long sectarian feud.

Because of Sikkim's cordial association with Tibet, when both Nepal and Bhutan attempted to encroach on Sikkimese lands during the late seventeenth and early eighteenth centuries, the Sikkim Chogyal appealed to the Dalai Lama for support. Lacking a true army of its own, however, Tibet was never able to provide effective military assistance except in relatively small ways. In the mid-eighteenth century, for example, Tibet appointed a temporary regent to settle an internal civil war in Sikkim and help reorganize the government.[75] Unlike Bhutan's mountainous frontier with Tibet, Sikkim's western and eastern borders presented no real obstacle to encroachments from Nepalese and Bhutanese settlers or raiding parties. The state had only a small agricultural tax base, and unlike Bhutan, the local communities appear to have had no tradition of organized village militias that could have been conscripted to join in a common defense. Even the palace of the Chogyal was not as fortified as the *dzongs* of Bhutan. Under pressure from Nepalese incursions it had to be shifted eastward several times. The Sikkim state was relatively weak from the outset. As the modern world encroached, it fell under the political domination of Tibet until the rise of British power in India after 1757 provided a counterbalance.

TIBETAN-MANCHU RELATIONS

The rise of the Manchu Qing empire in the Asian northeast and its expansion into Inner Asia and China affected Tibet profoundly. The Manchu court's earliest connection with Tibetans was recorded on a stone pillar erected in Mukden, the Manchu capital, by Nurhaci for his spiritual teacher, a lama from central Tibet.[76] Nurhaci's son and successor, Hong Taiji, invited the Fifth Dalai Lama to Mukden in 1639. Although the Dalai Lama declined the invitation, he sent a representative in his stead, which led to the establishment of a *chö-yön* relationship between the lama and the Manchu khan that would remain the ideological construct for relations between them and their respective successors for more than two and a half centuries.

Not until Hong Taiji's successor, Fulin, was on the throne as Emperor Shunzhi did a Manchu ruler meet the Fifth Dalai Lama. This meeting, which took place in Beijing in 1653, was of considerable significance and benefit to both rulers' status and ambitions. The latter had recently come to rule a largely unified Tibet and represented the Gelug order, which now

dominated the Tibetan Buddhist world, and the former had recently conquered China and exercised increasing authority in Inner Asia over Mongol khanates allied with or subjugated by him and his predecessors. The
details of this encounter have been extensively discussed and need not be
reproduced here except to note that the protocol observed emphasized
the mutual respect the two rulers displayed.[77] They went out of their way
to demonstrate their esteem for the high office of the other in ways that
maintained the subtle balance of worldly and spiritual authority present in
both their positions and the nature of the *chö-yön* relationship that existed
between them. In scenes described in the Dalai Lama's autobiography and
preserved to this day on the walls of the Potala, the Manchu emperor is
depicted as venturing outside his palace to receive the Dalai Lama, a sign
of respect rarely displayed for any other visitor to the court,[78] and the two
sovereigns exchanged exalted titles.[79]

Despite the importance of the meeting for both leaders, in practice it
did not alter the Tibet-Manchu relationship on the ground other than to
confirm it. Mongol khans, especially of the Khoshots, continued to be the
principal benefactors and protectors of the Dalai Lamas and the Gelugpa.
This changed at the beginning of the eighteenth century, when the Manchu court became increasingly concerned about Zunghar ties to Tibetan
leaders. Repeated costly military campaigns had failed to extinguish the
Zunghar khanate's formidable challenge to Manchu ambitions in Inner
Asia,[80] and it became important to prevent an expansion of Zunghar influence in Tibet. In 1705 the Manchu emperor encouraged Lhazang Khan—
the grandson of Gushri Khan who had seized power among the Khoshot
five years earlier and had claimed his grandfather's title of *gyalpo* (king) of
Tibet—to invade Lhasa and exercise authority there. Lhazang Khan exiled
the Sixth Dalai Lama and, when the latter died en route, put his own son
"on the throne." The Gelugpa authorities had already identified a reincarnation in the eastern Tibetan region of Kham, and they turned to the Zunghars for help in ousting the unpopular Lhazang Khan, which they succeeded in doing in 1717. The Zunghar leader Tsewang Rabten was unable
to fulfill his promise to bring the Seventh Dalai Lama to Lhasa, however.
The atrocities perpetrated by his armies, moreover, which included the
persecution and killing of monks and the ransacking of temples and monasteries, galvanized Tibetan resistance to the Zunghars, which the Qing
court fully supported. As the Manchus had the Dalai Lama in their custody in Kokonor, Tibetan leaders turned to the emperor for help. Emperor
Kangxi gladly asserted his role as the Dalai Lama's protector and ordered
his troops to help drive out the Zunghar forces and escort the Seventh
Dalai Lama to Lhasa, where he was enthroned in 1720. This marked the be-

ginning of a new era in Manchu-Tibet relations.[81] From then on, successive Manchu Qing emperors, revered by Tibetans as incarnations of the bodhisattva Manjusri, replaced Mongol khans in the role of principal benefactors and protectors of the Dalai Lama and Panchen Lama and therefore of the Gelugpa and the Tibetan state.

Though based on the *chö-yön* model, and thus couched in terms of the symbiotic relationship of worldly and spiritual domains and rule, the political aspect of the relationship took on an imperial character as well. The Qing court was determined to crush its Zunghar challengers in Inner Asia. To strengthen its ability to protect Tibet's new regime, the emperor endorsed governmental change. The Ganden Phodrang system created by the Fifth Dalai Lama was modified by transferring much of the *desi's* power to a council of ministers appointed from the Tibetan nobility, a change the Manchus thought would induce greater stability.[82] An imperial representative, known by the Manchu title *amban*, meaning "high official," was posted in Lhasa. At first a Mongol prince appointed to this position acted as a kind of resident ambassador, but after a number of incidents revealing the incompetence of successive holders of the office and continuing political instability in Lhasa, the *amban's* position was enhanced and he was expected by the emperor to play an active role in overseeing Tibet's foreign relations and preventing instability.[83]

In practice, the amount of influence exercised by the Manchu court over Tibetan affairs varied. It reached its peak following the 1792 imperial intervention, at the request of the Tibetan government, to help drive out Gorkha invaders. The *amban's* status was raised and Manchu involvement in Tibetan affairs became intrusive for a brief time. Although by early in the nineteenth century the Qing's position in Tibet and the *amban's* role there were, in practice, much reduced, the imperial court continued to claim authority to act on Tibet's behalf in external affairs, especially in regard to British expressions of interest in gaining access to Tibet. While the court listed Tibet among its foreign dependencies (*fanbang* and *fanshu* in Chinese, meaning "foreign polity" and "foreign dependency"), it was unable to enforce its own treaty obligations there and no longer defended Tibet against external attack.[84]

The imperial interventions in Tibet in the eighteenth century marked a change in the nature of the Qing court's relations with Tibet and with successive Dalai Lamas. The very beginning of this change is reflected in Tibetan historiography, a singular example of which is Changkya Rölpé Dorjé's biography of the Seventh Dalai Lama. Because Changkya Rölpé Dorjé places the spiritual and monastic life and role of the Seventh Dalai Lama as well as the religious nature of the events and personages surrounding him at the center of the story, the political and strategic motivations of the Qing court and of Tibetan political figures can be discerned only between the lines of his writings. This is not the approach of only this writer or of other writers of this historiographical genre, for even the formal communications of the Qing emperor to the Dalai Lama followed the diplomatic conventions and sensitivities of the Tibetan Buddhist *chö-si* and *chö-yön* paradigms.

IMPERIAL DIRECTIVES IN THE LANGUAGE OF *CHÖ-YÖN*

· Matthew Kapstein ·

The second quarter of the eighteenth century is when Tibet became in some sense a Manchu "protectorate," a term which must be used with caution and for which there is no equivalent in Tibetan sources. This is the period of the adult life of the Seventh Dalai Lama, which spanned the end of the Qing's Kangxi era to the beginning of Emperor Qianlong's rule.[85] We select a number of key events surrounding the Dalai Lama's exile to Litang and then Gartar on the Sichuan-Kham borderland (1727–1735) to shed light on these changing relations.

A key text among Tibetan-language sources for reconstructing these developments is Changkya Rölpé Dorjé's biography of the Seventh Dalai Lama. One peculiarity of this text and other sources from this period, which must be borne in mind throughout the discussion that follows, is that they adopt a uniformly philo-Manchu perspective. Discord must have surely been felt. This was, after all, a period of enforced exile of the Dalai Lama from his lawful capital at the center of the Tibetan Buddhist world. Whatever discord there was, however, Tibetan-language authors in this period chose systematically to downplay it in these writings.

Reading Changkya's biography of the Dalai Lama requires special care. It is an official document and not, for the most part, the product of independent biographical research. The author explicitly interjects his own perspective only when narrating events at which he was himself present, though even then he tends to refer to himself in the third person. To begin, we must ask just who was this Changkya, and why he, and not some suitably positioned member of the Dalai Lama's circle in Lhasa, was invited to author the official biography. Indeed, the questions surrounding how we situate Changkya already highlight some pertinent aspects of Tibetan relations with and perceptions of the Qing. Hence, before turning to Changkya's biography of the Dalai Lama, we must consider some facets of Chang-kya's own life and career.[86]

Changkya Rölpé Dorjé (1717–1786) was not an ethnic Tibetan. Like several among the Tibetan Buddhist clergy who rose to prominence under the Qing, he hailed from the Monguor community of eastern Kokonor on the Gansu frontier. As a child, he was identified as the reincarnation of one of the Kangxi emperor's Tibetan Buddhist chaplains, the Monguor lama Changkya Ngawang Chöden (1642–1714), who had been a protégé of the Fifth Dalai Lama. Following Kangxi's death in 1722, as his successor Yong-zheng was just consolidating his authority, the Khoshot Mongols of Kokonor, the Monguor, and some of the Tibetan population in that region rose against the Qing. When the imperial forces regained control, the main Monguor monastery, Gönlung Jampaling, which had been a center of the uprising, was sacked and the six-year-old Changkya Rölpé Dorjé was spirited into hiding.

As Qing armies and smallpox ravaged the countryside, there was no safety to be found anywhere. Military leaders were under strict orders to protect the Changkya incarnation, whose predecessor had been the previous emperor's preceptor, so terms were negotiated for the boy's surrender. His biographer Tukwan tells us that the Manchu officers involved were profoundly impressed by the child's composure and brilliance. Changkya was promptly sent to Beijing, where he was treated as a magnificent bird in a gilded cage, in effect a prisoner of the court. What is astonishing in Chang-kya's story, and what must be recalled in any consideration of Manchu–Tibetan Buddhist affairs throughout much of the eighteenth century (until 1792), is that the Qing did not just educate a lama of their own, as it were, but succeeded so well that he emerged as a respected religious figure in central Tibet as well.

Changkya was sent to study with the Seventh Dalai Lama during the period of the latter's return to Lhasa from exile at Gartar in 1735. He therefore was regarded in some sense as accompanying the reinstallation of the Dalai Lama in Lhasa. He received his own ordination from the Second Pan-chen Lama, Lozang Yeshé (1663–1737), who had also been the Dalai Lama's tutor. His subsequent close relationship with Lozang Yeshé's successor, the Panchen Lama Pelden Yeshé (1738–1780), was a major factor in his continuing authority within the Tibetan clergy.

Following the Seventh Dalai Lama's death in 1757, with Pelden Yeshé's and the Manchu court's encouragement, Changkya returned to Tibet from Beijing to undertake what became a highly successful teaching tour. His emergence in his own right as a teacher of the central Tibetan hierarchy decisively confirmed his status. It was while residing in Lhasa that he received the formal request on the part of a roster of clergymen and aristocrats, which reads like a virtual Who's Who of mid-eighteenth-century central Tibet, to serve as the late Dalai Lama's official biographer. His personal relations with the Seventh Dalai Lama, as with the Panchen Lamas, combined with the fame he now enjoyed as a leading teacher, were no doubt important factors here, but the motivations behind the selection of Changkya for the task are by no means transparent in the extant record. His imperial connections must have been of utmost importance. The Tibetan leadership wished to ensure that the official biography would be perceived as enjoying a universal consensus. Changkya may have been chosen by the Tibetan elite to write the biography precisely because of his close relationship to the Qing emperor. His writing might therefore reflect an effort to present Tibetan relations with the emperors in this new phase in *chö-yön* relations, not just from a Tibetan perspective, but from a position sensitive to, even reflecting, Qing imperial perceptions and interests.

Changkya worked from documents produced by the Dalai Lama's personal secretaries and transmitted to him to facilitate his work. The resulting text was primarily Changkya's edited version of documentation prepared by the Dalai Lama's own court, which he then organized and gave literary flourishes with occasional interventions concerning matters with which he was personally familiar. There is no reason to imagine that he had much to do with the informational content of the work. Still, form and style were important, particularly when these touched on the representation of the emperor and imperial actions.[87]

Changkya's biography records well over a hundred Manchu interventions in the life of the Seventh Dalai Lama.[88] These range from simple messages of felicitation to robust involvements in Tibetan affairs, such as the Dalai Lama's installation, under military escort, in Lhasa in 1720 following the expulsion of the Zunghars from central Tibet. Though the Manchu agencies directly involved were usually the civil or military officials on the ground, the biography is keen to accentuate throughout that the prime mover in matters concerning the Dalai Lama was always the Qing emperor. This is a point of some importance. We may note that right down to the Thirteenth Dalai Lama's trouble-ridden journey to Beijing in 1908,[89] when the Qing court was determined to impress upon him the rule that communications on Tibetan affairs were to pass through the *amban* (as had been the court's policy, in principle, since the 1750s), Tibetans nevertheless insisted upon a privileged and direct relation between the Dalai Lama and the emperor. Tibetan writers in the sources with which we are familiar emphasize the eminently personal tie between emperor and Dalai Lama and never suggest that a legal or political tie to abstract entities such as "the Manchu empire," much less "China," was what mattered. The Thirteenth Dalai Lama's famed declaration of Tibet's independence in 1913, therefore, in essence amounted to a declaration that, with the end of imperial rule as embodied in the person of the Manchu emperor, ties between Tibet and its eastern neighbor had ended, rather like a contract that terminates at the deaths of the parties to it. There was, simply, no contract with "China" that the Tibetans ever acknowledged. Hence, one further task here is to clarify the diction used by Tibetan writers to describe the relationship. And in this respect it must be underscored that, in emphasizing Changkya's work, we have before us the Tibetophone expression of the Qing emperor's own agent.

The role of the imperial court in relation to the Seventh Dalai Lama's exile deserves careful attention, as this preceded the administrative reforms that consolidated the Manchu "protectorate" in the 1750s. The exile of the Dalai Lama had been due to his family's association with the faction within the Tibetan ruling council that had assassinated the council's leader, Khangchenné, in 1727 and sought to assert their own rule. Another member of the council, Polhané, raised forces to put down the insurgency and allied himself with the Manchus in so doing. Thus began Polhané's two decades of rule as the virtual "king of Tibet" (by which title he was known to early-eighteenth-century Europeans), during the first years of which his insistence on preventing the Dalai Lama's father from meddling in state affairs required exiling the Dalai Lama as well. Here is the key entry during the year 1728 concerning the Dalai Lama's acceptance of his need to leave Lhasa:

> Then, there was very great disorder in Ü-tsang [central Tibet], and because people were possessed by the evil spirit of the dark side, they engaged in internecine struggle. Because the causes were gathering for collective ruin, there was concern that the Venerable [Dalai] Lama himself was becoming depressed. The Great Manjusri Emperor [Yongzheng], from the eastern quarter, then specially dispatched a great envoy and, providing all the requisite provisions, ordered that it would be necessary [for the Dalai Lama] to travel to Litang [in the eastern region of Kham, where he was born]. In general, it was the emperor's intention that, because during a time of strife in Tibet the Venerable Lama should be out of harm's way and content in spirit, he should be invited to Domé [Amdo and Kham]. Despite this, thinking that it would be best for the Teaching and for beings in general if the Lotus Feet [of the Dalai Lama] did not venture outside Tibet [Ü-tsang], the

Panchen Rinpoché, the Ganden Tri Rinpoché, and other lamas and reincarnations, together with the clergy and laity in general, earnestly
asked him to postpone. However, this Great Being [the Dalai Lama],
whose commitment to the well-being of creatures is altogether un-
wavering, . . . possessed an unerringly timely gnostic vision. It was
for this reason that, knowing the time had come to benefit vastly the
Teaching and beings in Domé, he joyfully accepted to accomplish
what the emperor had commanded.[90]

Changkya's words are wonderfully crafted. He understands that Tibetan
ecclesiastical protocols will not permit him to say that the Dalai Lama
was constrained by circumstances and acting under imperial orders because of his family's alliance with the losing side in recent Tibetan civil
disputes. Rather, based on the happy convergence of the intentions of the
great bodhisattvas Manjusri (the emperor) and Avalokitesvara (the Dalai
Lama), the imperial command coincided with the Dalai Lama's profound
spiritual intention to enhance the teaching in the eastern regions of Amdo
(Kokonor) and Kham.

A year after arriving in Litang, it was decided that the Dalai Lama
should move to a monastery newly constructed for him at Gartar, in far
eastern Kham. Here is how Changkya reports the presentation of this plan
to the Dalai Lama:

Master Ngawang Namka of Gomang, who had gone to honor the emperor, arrived. [The Dalai Lama] received [from him] the golden missive conferred by the Great Emperor [Yongzheng]. It contained even
greater praises than those previous, [noting] the excellent manner in
which the journey to Litang had been accomplished, and that owing
to fears of smallpox in China, [the emperor] could not invite [the
Dalai Lama to Beijing], but that, accepting to meet at some time when
the emperor would journey to the frontier, he had decided to construct a new monastic residence [for the Dalai Lama] in a place close
to Litang. At a later date, when it was acceptable [for the Dalai Lama]
to return to the great Potala Palace, he would offer further counsel.
These and other injunctions were very fine. Together with the golden
missive were varied gifts even more lavish than those previous, including crystals and porcelains, amounting to four chests.[91]

It is quite clear that the emperor did not wish for the Dalai Lama to come to
the imperial capital. That smallpox was current was likely a pretext here,

for shortly after this we find the Dalai Lama's father traveling to Beijing to meet the emperor and to some extent act as an intermediary, without any apparent concern for the disease. The promise of an imperial tour of the frontier seems also to have been intended just to sweeten the move to Gartar, an out-of-the-way place whose proximity to Litang was in fact a journey of nearly two weeks ("proximate" by the standards of premodern travel). The biography, in short, is bent on presenting the imperial decision not to meet the Dalai Lama in the Qing capital as the kindly fulfillment of the Dalai Lama's wishes rather than as the imperious will of the emperor.[92]

In 1734 came the decision to permit the Dalai Lama's return to Lhasa. Changkya narrates this moment as follows:

At this time the Great Manjusri Emperor [Yongzheng], thinking that the happiness of all Tibet and Kham as well as the increase of the Conqueror's [Buddha's] Teaching depend entirely on the Venerable One [Dalai Lama], and given that the disturbances in the region of Tibet had subsided, ordained that it was permitted for the Venerable One to proceed to the Land of Snows [Tibet]. This was conveyed to the noble father [of the Dalai Lama] via the [Dalai Lama's] attendant Rapjampa Lozang Peljor, who met with the Chinese officials permanently posted [at Gartar]. The noble father arrived to convey this report while [the Dalai Lama] was engaged in religious teaching. As he arrived just as the words "to the extent of space" were spoken, this was taken as an omen that, on returning to Tibet, [the Dalai Lama's] religious activity on behalf of the Conqueror's Teaching would equal the extent of space. The next day Chinese notables announced that a missive had come from the chancellery stating that the Great Emperor had ordered provisions be made to facilitate the Venerable One's return to Tibet, and that, as representatives of the emperor, the seventeenth prince [Yunli] and the national preceptor Changkya Hutukhtu [Rölpé Dorjé] would arrive.[93]

The formal nature of the relationship between the emperor and the Dalai Lama—understood as grounded in a common spiritual purpose—is conveyed by Changkya's record of the Dalai Lama's first meeting with Prince Yunli:

The great prince said, "According to the emperor's order, when the Dalai Lama returns to the Land of Snows, Tibet, may he make bright as the sun the teaching of the Omniscient Conqueror [Buddha] in general and that of the venerable [Tsongkhapa] Lozang Drakpa in particular, and may he ensure to the fullest extent that all the subjects of Tibet are established in the glories of happiness."

In response to this royal command, the supreme and venerable lama said,

"Though it is beyond my power to accomplish all that, impelled by the compassion of the Three Jewels I shall make all efforts, insofar as I am capable, for teaching, debating, and composing, and listening, pondering, and contemplating, and so forth, so as to ensure the increase of the Conqueror's Teaching in general and in particular and to ensure that all creatures of the central districts and the frontiers enjoy happiness."[94]

Both leaders understood the roles they had to play. Precise adherence to the required formalities was all-important, for only through such adherence was the lawfulness of their relationship established and broadcast. Whatever the underlying realpolitik may have been, the Tibetan official position would forever assert the formal character to be the substance of the relationship. What is clear is that both the ruling authority in the Qing state—the Manchu imperial family—and the Tibetan court of the Dalai Lama were content to endorse the mutually satisfying construct that obscured the underlying power imbalance. The Manchus, for their part, wishing to accentuate the spiritual underpinnings of their rule, systematically downplayed the role of sheer might in the equation, while the Tibetans, for theirs, modestly accepted the charge to reach beyond their very limited powers in order to benefit all by means of the Buddha's compassionate teaching. This courtly ceremonial, however, could no longer be sustained once the Qing dynasty lost its hegemony and the fundamental structural weaknesses of the Tibetan system were exposed. As both nations entered the twentieth century, these postures were by stages abandoned, though their legacies continue today.

CHAPTER FIVE

THE MANCHU
GREAT STATE

The Manchus, originally known as Jurchens, created and ruled one of Asia's largest and last Great States or empires. Its founder, Nurhaci, first extended his authority from his own Aisin Gioro clan to other Jurchen communities to create an expanding Jurchen state through victory on the battlefield combined with the application of ingenious legitimation strategies drawn from Inner Asian traditions and the securing of external endorsement. This ambitious project eventually became the Qing Great State, extending from the Pacific to the Inner Asian steppe. How could the rulers of a polity that was neither Chinese nor Mongol assert claims of legitimacy powerful enough to extend their rule over the Mongols and the Chinese and maintain their authority and influence over so vast a portion of Asia for almost three centuries? In this chapter we examine the rise to power of the Manchus—the ethnonym selected in 1635 to designate the Jurchen people by Hong Taiji, the son and successor of the founder of the empire—and consider how the Manchus understood and operated within each of the three civilizational worlds described in the previous chapters, and how they were able to situate themselves within each of them and at their pinnacles.

The sources of legitimacy that Manchu rulers drew on differed for each of the worlds they related to. Facing the Mongols, they claimed the position of Great Khan by variously allying with or defeating Mongol khans and adding legitimacy by patronizing Tibetan Buddhism. Hong Taiji successfully averred the right to inherit the Mongol Great State by purportedly receiving the famous jade seal and statue of Mahakala, Khubilai Khan's protector deity, following his victory over the last of the Chinggisid Great Khans, Ligdan, in 1632. Four years later, in 1636, he announced the founding of the Qing Great State, claiming Heaven's mandate and assuming the Chinese title of *huangdi*, "emperor." As *huangdi* and Son of Heaven, the Manchu emperor would occupy the pinnacle of the Confucian civilizational world and could present the Qing dynasty as the rightful successor to the Ming. Within the Tibetan Buddhist world the emperor took on the role of benefactor and protector of the Dalai Lama and Tibetan Buddhism. This, together with his recognition by the Dalai Lama and Panchen Lama as the incarnation of the bodhisattva Manjusri, provided legitimacy to successive Manchu emperors throughout the Tibetan Buddhist world, including, very significantly, among the Mongols.[1]

The empire was not uniformly ruled or administered but was managed through the particular relationships that the Manchu emperors developed and maintained with the ruling elite in each of those worlds and by utilizing mostly their own respective administrative structures to do so. As Great Khans of the Mongols, the Manchu rulers gave an elevated place to the Chinggisid and other Mongol khans and lords who had allied themselves with the Aisin Gioro (or who had been coerced into doing so). They bestowed princely titles upon them, allotted land, and provided generous stipends for the maintenance of their entourage and kin. They brought a number of them into the powerful Manchu military structure, the Eight Banners, where they received a place second only to the Manchus themselves. Instead of imposing an alien system to control Mongol polities, the Manchu Great Khan adopted the Mongols' own administrative system, the league and banner system described below, so that those polities were largely self-ruling.

The Manchu rulers' relationship with the Chinese part of the empire was different. It was one of conqueror and conquered and was ruled directly by the emperor. Having defeated the Ming with the help not only of Mongol armies but also of Chinese troops integrated into the Eight Banners, the Manchus occupied and maintained control over this heavily populated region by means of a network of military garrisons manned and headed by Manchu bannermen. In their capacity as *huangdi*, Qing emperors ruled over Zhongguo ("China") by means of the traditional Chinese system of territorial administration, using the vast bureaucracy taken over from the Ming. At the same time, as *tianzi*, Sons of Heaven, they extended benevolence to all peoples. The Mongols and Chinese were thus ruled separately, through discrete systems of administration, on the basis of different principles and using different logics, languages, rituals, and symbols and entirely distinct constructs of legitimacy.

The relationship that the Manchu emperors developed with leaders of the Tibetan Buddhist civilizational world was again entirely different. As discussed in the preceding chapter, a *chö-yön* relationship was established early on by Hong Taiji and the Fifth Dalai Lama, shaping successive Manchu emperors' relations with the Gelugpa hierarchs and rulers of Tibet. The emperors accepted the conferral by the latter of recognition as incarnations of Manjusri, a bodhisattva highly revered throughout the Tibetan Buddhist world.[2] Unlike the Manchu relationships with the Chinese and Mongol elites, this was not a relationship established by conquest or military alliance. Tibetans were never involved in the military, administrative, or political rulership of the empire, as the Mongols and Chinese were. Instead, the relationship was a complex consensual religiopolitical one that changed over time as the interests of the Manchu court evolved and conditions in Tibet changed—without, however, losing sight of the Tibetan Buddhist principles and construct on which it was built.

Manchu relations with the rulers of Chosŏn, Dai Viet (renamed Vietnam in 1804), and other polities within the Sinic zone were conducted according to Confucian logic and rituals consonant with the emperor's position as *tianzi*, but these rituals bore little connection to the true nature of those relations. Ming loyalists in China and in Chosŏn questioned whether "foreigners" such as the Manchus could claim to have received Heaven's mandate. Manchu rulers could assert that claim initially only by using military force to overcome resistance and compel submission, as they did both in Chosŏn and in Ming China.

The remarkable ingenuity with which the Manchus exercised authority and forged relationships based on the diverse legitimacy constructs indigenous to the polities and leaders with whom they interacted was an important reason for their success. It was displayed from the very beginning of their imperial project, when Hong Taiji's father, Nurhaci, set out, like Chinggis Khan some four centuries earlier, to assert his sovereignty over the expanding polity he created.[3]

STATE FORMATION AND LEGITIMATION

· *Nicola Di Cosmo* ·

Nurhaci began his rise to power in the late sixteenth century from within one of the many Jurchen communities in existence at the time.[4] The Jurchen people were incorporated within the Ming frontier defense administration as garrisons (*wei*) and posts (*suo*).[5] These retained a degree of internal political and territorial coherence consistent with the overall structure of the Ming tribute system. In practice, the various Jurchen leaders owed their power to a dual process: an internal process of acquisition of political authority on the basis of aristocratic lineages and personal qualities, and external recognition by the Ming, who granted them special titles that made them officials in the tribute system. That recognition in turn created obligations of loyalty and tribute payment to the Ming dynasty but also provided economic advantages, such as permits to trade at the frontier markets. While Jurchen aristocratic families exercised political authority within their community, their relationship of subordination to the Ming certainly made their position less than fully autonomous.

It would be somewhat difficult and artificial to consider the many Jurchen polities (*gurun* in Manchu) as a coherent political community in the sense of a political entity that might be regarded as self-contained and exclusive of others. The formation of a coherent Jurchen political community, or state, over which Nurhaci could establish his sovereignty was in essence the first phase of Nurhaci's rise to power. It culminated in 1616 with the establishment of what could reasonably be called a *jušen gurun*, a Jurchen state, that was no longer tied and subordinated to Ming China. In Manchu the term *gurun* was used to denote communities of various kinds and, not unlike the Mongol term *ulus*, has various distinct meanings in English, including "nation," "state," and the more generic "polity" or "political community." It can also signify an ethnic group, a people, or a dynastic entity. The meaning is therefore best understood from the context in which the term is used. In this section we use *gurun* unless a specific English term is called for. The first mention of the term *jušen gurun* in Manchu records seems to appear in 1613 with specific reference to Nurhaci's fledgling state.[6]

Tracing the evolution of the term used in Manchu to indicate Nurhaci's own state is not easy because later sources, such as the *Veritable Records of the Qing* (*Qing shilu*), anachronistically speak of *manju gurun*, when the original Manchu and Chinese sources might have used other terms.[7] While all the *gurun* that Nurhaci attacked and subjugated, such as the Hoifa, Hada, and Ula, were considered to be Jurchen, the only *jušen gurun* was the one Nurhaci created. We can therefore infer that the early political project set into motion by Nurhaci was the creation of a unified Jurchen state (a larger and more comprehensive *gurun*) out of the many smaller Jurchen *gurun* that corresponded by and large to the Ming administrative structure of garrisons and posts and whose leaders had been, like Nurhaci himself, legitimated in their role by Ming approval.

The idea of a unified Jurchen state was a remarkable political step: it allowed Nurhaci to envisage himself as the ruler of a political community that potentially included all Jurchens, not just his own *gurun* based in the Jianzhou region of Manchuria. Once the political space for that project was created, the forcible subjugation and annexation of recalcitrant Jurchens could proceed not as an act of conquest but rather as the logical expansion of a concept of a Jurchen state that necessarily included all Jurchen people. The ethnic dimension of Nurhaci's strategy was important and fully instrumental to the realization of his political project. Invoking a common ethnic identity for the Jurchens (later the Manchus) as a people was also meant to erase political or ethnic divisions between the various Jurchen *gurun* no matter how deep and intractable.

The several Jurchen *gurun* (Hada, Ula, Hoifa, etc.) that Nurhaci set out to conquer were recast from autonomous entities that had been living by and large in peaceful proximity under the political umbrella of the Ming tribute system into a medley of chaotic and litigious forces in need of being pacified under a new political order. The unification of the separate Jurchen *gurun* into a *jušen gurun* could therefore be presented in ways aimed to provide a basis for the legitimate rule over the whole Jurchen political community. Military annexation was presented on a rhetorical level as rightful retribution in reaction to an attack suffered by Nurhaci early on, while on another level it was justified as a necessary action meant to bring order to a critical and chaotic state of affairs. Success in war would clinch Nurhaci's claim by purportedly showing Heaven's support. In this respect Nurhaci's strategy was fully consistent with Inner Asian politics, since rightful retribution, bringing order to a situation of chaos, and evidence of divine support were the three traditional ways in which Inner Asian leaders justified their wars of conquest and their political ambitions.

But Nurhaci's strategy was more elaborate than that. Most important in the early period of Nurhaci's ascent was the creation of an *ideal* future body politic over which Nurhaci could *eventually* exercise sovereign power. It required that he make a claim for himself as the legitimate ruler over a political community much larger than his own. In other words, the theoretical reach of his authority had to extend over *gurun* that were until then by no means subject to him but ruled by aristocratic families that were in every respect the equal of Nurhaci's. Obtaining recognition as the legitimate ruler of a *jušen gurun* and avoiding political sanctions from the Ming or other powers (for instance, those Mongols who had already joined anti-Nurhaci coalitions) was extremely difficult, because it could not be based on a simple declaration by Nurhaci himself, no matter how elaborate his justifications. Nurhaci's redoubtable enemy, the Yehes, had long seen through his scheme and refused to acquiesce to his attempt to dissolve and annex separate Jurchen polities in the name of a new, expanded Jurchen state. Nor could Nurhaci establish a new regime solely by military means lest he provoke a reaction from the Ming state. For his claim to be credible, it had to arise from external endorsements. Only after Nurhaci had acquired a level of recognition and support that allowed him to cast his shadow beyond his original power base could he move toward the annexation of other Jurchen *gurun*. Note here the concurrence of two strategies of legitimation: one that arises from traditional patterns of Inner Asian politics, described above, and the other, new, based on the acquisition of outside support that confirmed Nurhaci's position as he proceeded with his military and political expansion.

The endorsements that Nurhaci obtained in the late sixteenth and early seventeenth centuries from the Ming and from the Mongol Khalkha aristocrats should be read in this light: that is, as a tool that Nurhaci could use to propel himself above other Jurchen aristocrats and claim the position of leader of all Jurchens. His first wars were conducted against his own relatives for full control over the Jianzhou Jurchen and established him as a loyal Ming subject who could keep order among the frontier Jurchens. Nurhaci's good relations with the Ming did not prevent Jurchen aristocrats from forming a coalition and mounting a military expedition against him. He defeated them at the battle of Mount Gure in 1593 in what became the first of several military victories that strengthened his position and increased his standing with the Ming. Nurhaci developed a complex expansionist strategy comprising military interventions, diplomatic maneuvering, and tactical shifts, and the means he used to claim, establish, and proclaim sovereignty were integral to this strategy.[8] In 1595 the Ming regaled him with the coveted title of "Tiger and Dragon General." Only after he had consolidated his relationship with the Ming did he begin his campaigns against other Jurchen *gurun*. In a diplomatic exchange with the Yehes, who in 1591 had warned him that occupation of their lands would not be tolerated, Nurhaci stressed the excellent relationship he had with the Ming as well as the titles he had been given, thus using Ming support to suggest that his authority could well extend beyond his territory.[9] In 1599 Nurhaci embarked on a campaign against the Hada people and, despite being reprimanded and stopped by the Ming, he resumed the campaign and pursued it to success in 1601.

A second external recognition of political legitimacy came from the Mongol delegation that in 1606 referred to Nurhaci as *kündülen qayan* (Enlightened Khan).[10] This was followed by a new wave of military operations undertaken by Nurhaci against his Jurchen foes. The recognitions received from Ming and Mongol rulers strengthened not just his political standing but also his particular claim to sovereignty, first over the Jianzhou aristocratic elite and later over the other polities. As a preliminary observation, therefore, we can say that the gap between the actual political community over which Nurhaci had political authority at any given point and the community of which he aspired to become the sovereign—a constantly moving bar—was filled with the appearance of external recognition and diplomatic support that Chinese and Mongol titles conveyed.

If external endorsements allowed Nurhaci to appear not as someone engaging in a policy of naked aggression—and therefore as a usurper—but as someone who was ordering the realm, the confirmation of the rightfulness of his actions, and therefore of the legitimacy of his position, came from victory on the battlefield, which was always presented as Heaven's grace. Nurhaci's rise was not based purely on rhetoric and propaganda, and victory in battle was essential to consolidate his power, though trumpeting such victories in a light that provided legitimacy was an essential component of Nurhaci's strategy.

This strategy could work only as long as the opposition remained divided and the Ming neutral. The Ming refrained from fully endorsing Nurhaci's notion of a sphere of sovereignty inclusive of the whole Jurchen people. One of the Jurchen *gurun*, the Yehes, remained under Ming protection and, with Ming support, resisted Nurhaci's expansion, preventing him from completing the annexation of all Jurchen *gurun* until he had defeated the Ming in 1619. In 1616 Nurhaci's affirmation of Jurchen sovereignty reached a point at which further expansion became incompatible with the political recognition from a greater power that Nurhaci was still theoretically obligated to serve as a tributary subject. If external recognition helped Nurhaci extend the political community he aspired to rule to almost all Jurchens, the withdrawal of Ming support in defense of the Yehes forced him to raise the stakes by aiming even higher. He cast off his tributary status, rebelled against the Ming, and, as an independent ruler, announced a new dynasty proclaiming sovereignty not only over the Jurchens but potentially over other peoples as well.

The frequent historical references to the Jin dynasty (*aisin gurun* in Manchu) attest to this ambition. The Jin state, comprising a significant portion of northeast Asia, was ruled by the Jurchens from 1115 until the Mongol conquest in 1234. With Nurhaci's founding of the Later Jin (*amaga aisin*) dynasty in 1616, a new pattern emerged.[11] The new political vision encapsulated in the notion of an *aisin* state foreshadowed a type of supreme sovereignty whose reach, like the Jin dynasty of the twelfth century, might go much further and include at least part of China. The concept of *aisin*, like so many Manchu political concepts, includes multiple references. The two obvious ones are the Jin dynasty, known as *aisin* ("gold," equivalent to Chinese *jin*) in Manchu, and Nurhaci's own clan name, Aisin Gioro (surname), which could be rendered as "golden clan." It also contained a clear reference to Mongol politics in that the Chinggisid royal line was referred to as *altan urugh*, or "golden lineage." The frequent references, even before 1616, to Nurhaci's having inherited the sovereignty of the Jin dynasty were meant to project a new goal foreshadowing a new political community. Potentially this included, in addition to the Jurchen people, Chinese, Mongols, and others. It is important to note that ethnic boundaries were often uncertain among frontier communities such as in the Liaodong peninsula. The very concept of New Manchus (*ice manju*), which was used during the Qing dynasty to endow Manchu ethnicity on certain frontier peoples in the northeast, is indicative of the instability between ethnic categories.[12]

The transition from *jusen gurun* to *aisin gurun* was a significant turn in Nurhaci's definition of sovereignty. At the battle of Mount Sarhū (1619), where Nurhaci defeated a large Ming army that was sent to crush him once and for all, he claimed the Mandate of Heaven (*abkai fulingga*) as part of his title.[13] Victory granted by Heaven was used to intimate that Nurhaci's sovereignty might reach beyond the Jurchens' domains. The transition from a definition of sovereignty tied to a political community, identified first with the Jianzhou Jurchen and later with the wider Jurchen community, to one supported by a divine mandate and graced by a dynastic name with overt historical references to the Jin dynasty moved the bar of Nurhaci's ambition upward once again toward a sovereignty limited neither to the Jurchen people nor to a specific territory.

The argument for a sovereignty that might compete with that of the Ming was embedded in a complex document known as the "Seven Great Grievances," issued in 1618. This document is the key manifesto of Nurhaci's political program and was meant to achieve at least three goals. First, and most obviously, it served to justify the war against the Ming. Second, it attempted to claim Nurhaci's preexisting sovereignty over the Jurchens as a fully independent ruler, thus retroactively transforming his earlier relationship with the Ming from tributary (and subordinate) to equal status. Several of the "grievances" refer to treaties and agreements between his state and the Ming state that had supposedly been violated by the Ming, as if Ming involvement in Jurchen politics was not (as the Ming would see it) dictated by the need to bring under control recalcitrant subjects but rather was undue interference into his own internal affairs. What the Ming saw as punitive expeditions against a rebellious subject, Nurhaci turned into acts of aggression in violation of a mutually binding treaty. Third, and most important, Nurhaci presented the argument that Heaven favors virtuous leaders and that virtue is what defines a worthy ruler. The seventh grievance refers explicitly to a theory of a mandate of Heaven with clearly universalistic overtones, suggesting that the throne of the Chinese empire could be lost by the Ming (and gained by him) in the general competition over virtuous rule. If in this document Nurhaci asserts his expression of sovereignty by justifying his war against the Ming in terms of defense of territorial frontiers demarcating the Jurchen political community, such an assertion was accompanied by claims meant to extend that sovereignty to an even wider community. Naming his regime *aisin* rather than *jušen* already changed the terms of the game and prefigured a multiethnic political community, inclusive of a variety of subject peoples, even before it was realized. The transitions from Jianzhou to *jušen* and from *jušen* to *aisin* illustrate clearly the logic and strategy that informed Nurhaci's politics.

The processes of state and empire building set into motion by Nurhaci and his son Hong Taiji underscore the central place of the notion of and quest for legitimacy of rule. If we reflect on the actual Manchu terms deployed to signify the two concepts that have been central to our discussion, namely, political community and sovereignty, *gurun* and *doro*, the impression that emerges is that we cannot speak of "state" in any sense that approximates a European Westphalian concept when discussing state building by the early Manchus. Nurhaci's state appears to be always divided into two components that are placed in dialectical relationship to one another: the *gurun* and the *doro*, that is, the political community and the sovereign power or, to use different expressions, the body politic and the legitimate authority of the ruler. Unless we see the state as resulting from a combination of these two elements, we will not be able to fully appreciate the mechanisms underlying Manchu state-building strategies.[14]

Doro in this period indicates, above all, a transcendental quality of rulership applicable to the creation of an all-encompassing and transformational political project. The concept of *doro* is most often linked in Manchu texts to the Mongol and Jurchen empires and, therefore, to an imperial tradition that transcended single political communities. Its semantic range came to include other meanings, such as "rule," "doctrine," "ceremony," *dao* (the Chinese principle of "the Way"), and was also related to other concepts that had to do with morality, propriety, and ritual.

In Manchu sources the question of *doro* arises in relation to the Jin dynasty and the holding of its *doro* by Nurhaci, as in the statement "abkai kesi de sure kundulen han amba gurun de isabufi, aisin doro be jafafi banjire de." This could be literally translated as "at the point when by Heaven's favor the wise and honored emperor had collected a great nation and wielded the sovereign power [*doro*] of the Jin."[15] Here *gurun* and *doro* are joined to indicate that a large political community had been gathered and that sovereignty had been established on the basis of the *amba gurun* (great state) of the Jurchen Jin dynasty. The document in which this statement appears precedes the establishment of the Later Jin dynasty by Nurhaci in 1616 and prefigures it. The painstaking diplomatic activity carried out by Nurhaci with treaties and marriage alliances was constantly accompanied by propaganda in which Nurhaci and, later, Hong Taiji stressed historical precedents for the transmission of the *doro*—the principle of authority or sovereignty—to show its transferability (a sort of *translatio imperii*) across separate political communities. In this respect Nurhaci's reference to the transfer of sovereignty from the Jin dynasty to the Mongols four centuries earlier is key. It is not by chance that the thirteenth-century Mongol conquest of the Jin dynasty is presented in several documents as a process that wrested the *doro* away from the Jin dynasty rulers and passed it to the Mongol khan.

If the Mongols could obtain the right to rule an empire by virtue of the mandate of Heaven, there was no reason why the Manchus could not claim the same for themselves. Nurhaci's notion of sovereignty was universalistic, unconstrained either by Mongol doctrines that wanted the imperial mantle to be donned only by Chinggisids or by Chinese doctrines that treated the mandate of Heaven as a Confucian principle. The Manchus missed no chance to stress that their military victories were indeed evidence of Heaven's support. The connection established with the glorious Mongol past in various ways (such as recovering the Yuan imperial seal) illustrated how the long strands of Mongol and Manchu history were braided into a common destiny and that sovereign rule was transferable and fungible. Nurhaci's emphasis on the transfer of the imperium between different political agents was the product of a series of moves that, at every step, redrafted legitimacy on the basis of the political reality and the objectives that were set for the long-term empire-building project.

RELATIONS WITH THE MONGOLS

The history of Manchu (and, later, Qing) relations with the Mongols does not lend itself to a simple narrative. The processes for establishing Manchu authority over Mongol leaders and polities were diverse, often delicate, and at times brutally forceful. The structures, institutions, and mechanisms used to maintain and administer that authority were specifically designed to reflect and give substance to the kind of relations the Manchu emperor established with the Mongols. When we refer to "Mongols" in this period, we mean primarily the ruling Chinggisids (i.e., the direct descendants of Chinggis Khan) and their subjects, known also as the Borjigid clan. Its leaders formed numerous polities in Inner Asia, loosely recognizing an affiliation to the Great Khan—a position that at the time of the formation of the Jurchen state was held by Ligdan Khan. We also include the Oirats, the western Mongols whose leaders were not part of the ruling Chinggisid clan (despite their descent from Chinggis Khan) but who played no less important roles.

A number of Mongol leaders allied themselves with Nurhaci and Hong Taiji. Others opposed them and were either defeated in battle and forcefully incorporated into the new imperial project or threatened that project for years. Before the Manchu conquest of Ming China in 1644, Nurhaci and Hong Taiji actively pursued alliances with the southern Mongol leaders. Already from 1635, many of those relationships were transformed into protection or tutelage relationships that progressively turned those Mongol leaders into vassals.[16] Once established, the Manchus continued to wage war and expend considerable resources in maintaining and extending Qing authority over Mongol polities, including the northern Mongols and the Oirats further west. The Khalkhas eventually accepted Qing suzerainty in 1691. The powerful Zunghar khanate of the Oirats, which had united the western Mongols under its authority early in the seventeenth century, was finally defeated by the Manchus only in 1757.

The early Manchus created the Eight Banners as a military organization that became the "engine of expansion."[17] Following the 1644 conquest of Ming China, this was retained as a central institution of Manchu imperial rule. Membership was closed, for it was hereditary and limited to the descendants of the preconquest warrior populations who made up the early Manchu polity. This martial caste, who were the subjects of the emperor and the Aisin Gioro princes, included Manchus and Mongols as well as the descendants of Chinese and Koreans from the Liaodong frontier regions who had been co-opted or coerced into joining the Manchu enterprise.[18] As much as the Eight Banners was a uniquely Manchu creation, the fundamental institutions and mechanisms for the administration of the Mongols were not. Indeed, the adoption of Mongol systems of governance and administration by the Manchu court, as we shall see, was an early manifestation of the simultaneous existence of multiple forms of rule that, as Pamela Crossley has persuasively argued,[19] was a characteristic of Qing emperorship. In addition to helping to explain the Manchu success in administering the Mongols, the use of the Mongol system, albeit with some modifications introduced by the Manchu court, testifies to the Inner Asian nature of Manchu relations with the Mongols.

EXTENSION OF CONTROL OVER THE MONGOLS

· Hiroki Oka ·

The Manchus are commonly believed to have adopted a preferential appeasement policy toward Mongol khans and lords and to have established a rigorous administrative structure at every level of Mongol society in order to assert control over them. Although the systems they deployed are often credited to the Manchu emperors' ingenuity, they should in fact be understood as constituting a successor regime of the Mongols' own structure of rule and administration, one that predated Manchu hegemony. This body of measures and structures is generally described using Chinese terms of provincial governance and therefore commonly known as the *waifan* system. *Waifan* means "outer regions or realms" but is usually translated into English as "outer dependencies," and it was used in Chinese-language sources to refer to the Mongols and their ruling clans' realms. Significantly, the Mongols used the term γadaγadu Mongγul (outer Mongol) without reference to dependency.

The Manchu ruling system always put the emperor or Great Khan in the center.[20] The sphere closest to the emperor was called "inner" and the farther one, "outer." China proper was called in Manchu *dorgi ba*, the "inner realm," not because it was the center of Chinese civilization but because it referred to those subjects under the direct rule of the emperor. The same designation was used for the Eight Banners because the bannermen were also ruled directly by the emperor and his royal clan. The Mongol nobility and their realms were collectively referred to as *tulergi golo* in Manchu, γadaγadu Mongγul in Mongolian, and *waifan Menggu* or simply *waifan* in Chinese, in every case identifying these realms as "outer" and, as we shall see, as distinct from the "inner" realm.[21]

The *waifan* system consisted of two components, the "princely system" and the "league and banner system." Mongol leaders who surrendered or submitted to the Manchu emperor were granted the princely titles of *wang-gung* (*wanggong* in Chinese) or *tayiji*, with *wanggung* ranked higher than *tayiji*. This ennoblement was followed by a generous stipend from the emperor. These Mongol nobles were invited to imperial banquets and entertained at the imperial court. Mongol *wanggung* married into Manchu noble families and flaunted their high status.

Mongol polities were under the rule of Borjigid khans, princes, and lords who, as the descendants of Dayan Khagan and the younger brothers of Chinggis Khan, constituted the Mongol nobility. The authority of the Borjigid clan was well established long before the Manchu emperors began to extend their authority over the Mongol realms in the first half of the seventeenth century. Similarly, among the Manchus, only members of the Aisin Gioro clan, to which Nurhaci and Hong Taiji[22] belonged, constituted the nobility. As the Manchu Great Khan or emperor expanded his authority, he granted leading members of both clans *wanggung* titles. Aisin Gioro nobles were granted the titles of "*wanggung* of the imperial clan" and "inner *wanggung*," while the Borjigid nobles became "outer *wanggung*," and their realms were consequently also identified as "outer." Exceptionally, in 1635 Hong Taiji transferred the Borjigid princes of the Kharchin and Tümed Mongols to the Manchu Eight Banners and elevated their non-Borjigid chieftains to the princely status of *wanggung*, making them equal to the Borjigid nobility.[23]

The Mongols were ruled and administered by means of a hierarchical system consisting of leagues or assemblies (*ciγulγan*) and banners (*qosiγu*). The banner (not to be confused with the Manchu Eight Banners) was the basic unit of administration. Each banner was headed by a *jasaq* who was appointed from among the *wanggung* and *tayiji* nobility by the emperor. The noble members of the banner were granted personal retainers according to their rank. Most of the banner population was organized into units of 150 soldiers called *sumus*, headed by an official called the *sumun janggi*. The banners were under the supervision of an upper-level administrative body, the *ciγulγan*, which although generally translated as "league" in English, originally meant "assembly," which is the term we will use here. Ten assemblies were established among the Mongol polities, four of them among the Khalkhas. Each was headed by an assembly chief. These assemblies were supervised by an imperial ministry of the outer regions or dependencies first established in 1636 as the central Manchu administrative organ in charge of Mongol affairs. Ministers and generals were dispatched by the emperor himself and stationed at strategic points to implement the orders of the emperor and the ministry in the assemblies and the banners.

Before the Manchu emperors started appointing *jasaqs*, they were chosen from among the Mongol princes by the assemblies to which they belonged. They worked under the headship of a Mongol khan, participating in their assemblies' deliberations and taking part in the promulgation of codes.[24] The *jasaqs* were not rulers but executors of the codes and were in charge of punishing acts that violated the decisions of the assembly. The Manchu emperors later modified this role through the adoption of the Qing Code, ordaining that each *jasaq* was in charge of the affairs of his banner, which also became his jurisdictional parameter. As a result, we have come to believe that the *jasaqs* were the chiefs of the banners and that their populations were under their jurisdiction and rule. This was in fact a new element introduced by the Manchus, though the nature of the jurisdiction the *jasaqs* exercised under the Qing Code still needs investigation.

Translations and interpretations of the name of the Qing ministry in charge of Mongol affairs as well as of the Chinese term *waifan* have caused some confusion regarding the nature of the Qing administration of the Mongols. When the ministry was originally established in 1636, it was called Monggo jurgan in Manchu. Its Chinese equivalent was Menggu yamen. Both literally meant Office of Mongol Affairs. Two years later the name was changed to Tulergi golo be dasara jurgan in Manchu and Lifan-yuan in Chinese. Its meaning thus changed to Ministry (or Board) for Administering the Affairs of the Outer Regions, or simply the Ministry for Outer Regions.[25] The Mongolian name of the ministry, Yadaγadu Mongγul-un törü-yi jasaqu yabudal-un yamu, maintained its original meaning of ministry for administering the outer Mongol polities, signifying the Borji-gid and other Mongol ruling princes together with their subjects. The Mongolian name therefore did not contain the equivalent of the Chinese word *fan* that has contributed to its misinterpretation as a territorial, geographical, or ethnic designation.

Waifan has often been understood as indicating Qing territory outside the Great Wall, including Mongolia, Tibet, and Xinjiang,[26] but it actually meant "outer regions," "outer realms," or, as it has more often been translated, "outer dependencies," that is, the realms of outer vassals. Although *fan* literally means "fence" or "fenced area," it actually did not have a spatial connotation. The misunderstanding may have resulted from Chinese geographical writings on the Qing realm, especially Zhang Mu's *Menggu youmu ji* (On the nomads of Mongolia) and the official Qing compilation of the realm's geography, *Da Qing yitongzhi* (Unification gazetteer of the Qing Great State), both of which have been widely used in modern historiography. In reality, the term *waifan* was neither a geographical nor an ethnic concept but a relational one, as becomes evident when the Qing court's own usage of the term is analyzed.

The outer and inner realms of the empire were kept strictly separate. Thus, no Chinese or Manchu bureaucrats were ever appointed by the emperor to posts in the outer realms of the Mongols. Similarly, no Mongol princes or officials were appointed to posts such as that of governor in the inner realm. This ruling principle was rigorously applied to the very end of the Qing empire.

Contrary to what is sometimes suggested, this system for the control, and later for the administration, of the Mongols was not a creation of the

Manchus. Rather, they adopted the Mongols' own dual system of organization that was in existence prior to the establishment of Manchu overlordship. The Mongol system comprised the *otoγ*, the princely domains consisting of subjects and livestock inherited by the Borjigid nobility from generation to generation,[27] and the banners (*qosiγu*), the units created to ensure fulfillment of military duties, enforce codes, and maintain order.[28] The Manchu emperors also adopted the Mongol assembly (*ciγulγan*), which had managed relations between the princedoms and lordships since the late sixteenth century. Even the granting of the *wanggung* title reflected a continuation of the Mongol political reality in existence before the advent of the Qing.

Historians have generally assumed that the Manchus eliminated the princely domains (*otoγ*) and replaced them by the banners. But recent study reveals that the princely domains continued to exist and function in some form under the banner administration after the Mongol submission to the Manchus and in some cases continued to be referred to as *otoγ*.[29] These domains were social units connected to the ruling clan by patrilineal inheritance. Subjects and livestock were divided among the sons as part of the appanage (*qubi*) of the clan leaders. Upon inheriting a designated portion of his father's subjects, each son left the household and formed an independent unit that became his own new domain. The status of these ruling princes was inherited from pre-Qing Mongol society and was not newly authorized by the Qing Code. The introduction by the Qing of the *sumu* units within the banners for the military mobilization of the Mongols was also less significant than this might seem, since the princely domains existed side by side with them.[30] Since the *wanggung*'s and *tayiji*'s ruling authority was maintained in their domains and not undermined by the introduction of the *sumu* within the banners, the original dualistic organization of Mongol society was in fact preserved.

The assembly (*ciγulγan*) also predated the Qing, and the early Manchu rulers used it to address disunity and intersegmental tensions among the Mongols as well as to exert a measure of control over them. This was particularly important since the ruling structure of the Mongols, whereby princely heirs established their own independent domains, tended to encourage fragmentation.[31] In early Manchu documents we find records of assemblies, referred to as *ciγulγan*, actually hosted by the Manchu emperors. Not only the name indicates continuity with the earlier Mongol assemblies; its procedures and the issues it could address were also strikingly similar. The earliest such record concerns an assembly hosted by Hong Taiji in the second year of his reign (1628) at Huhen River, at which his expedition against the Chakhar Mongols was discussed and codes on military action against them and the Ming were issued.[32]

As the number of southern Mongol rulers who submitted to Hong Taiji grew, the Manchus organized the assemblies into three groups. The first was the assembly of the non-Khorchin princes; the second, of the Chakhar, the southern Khalkha, and the Aru; and the third, of the Kharchin and the Tümed.[33] During the reign of the Shunzhi emperor and the early years of Kangxi, the number of assemblies was increased to seven. They were not permanent administrative institutions, however, but continuations of the decision-making assemblies held by the Mongol ruling nobility before their submission to the Manchus. Hong Taiji's successors continued to encounter disunity among the northern Khalkha princes in the latter half of the seventeenth century. For example, when those princes sent official letters to the emperor, so many names were listed that it was impossible to identify their supreme leader or representative. Eventually, the Shunzhi emperor appointed eight *jasaqs* among them to head groupings of nobles, a number that was increased to thirty-four in 1691 when the Khalkha surrendered to the Qing, after which the Khalkha nobility gathered in three assemblies. What this shows is that the Manchu emperors utilized preexisting Mongol institutions of princely domains, banners, and assemblies as well as the office of the *jasaq* to oversee the Mongol princes' rule and their administration of their own domains. They carefully kept the "outer realm," managed under the so-called *waifan* or *γadaγadu Mongγul* system, separate from the "inner" parts of the empire.

The Manchu emperors gradually bureaucratized the *waifan* system to strengthen their control over the Mongols, and in due course the roles of Mongol institutions were modified. The *sumu* was added to the governance structure, *jasaqs* became administrators who implemented the emperor's edicts, and the banners' administrative roles were strengthened. The permanent appointment of assembly chiefs and vice chiefs by the emperors beginning in the first half of the eighteenth century, combined with the introduction of new forms of administration of these assemblies, contributed to the latter's transformation into de facto permanent institutions.[34] But none of these changes relieved the Mongol princes of the responsibility to rule their own subjects. Indeed, the essential features of the Mongol ruling system at the banner level inherited from the late Northern Yuan were for the most part retained by the Manchus, albeit in modified forms, up to the end of the Qing empire. So much is this so that one can regard the Qing *waifan* or *γadaγadu Mongγul* system as a successor scheme of the Mongols' own ruling structures as they existed under the late Northern

Yuan, even if the processes of bureaucratization and semisedentarization to which many of the Mongol polities were subjected eventually transformed some of their institutions.

RELATIONS WITH TIBET

The relations between the Manchu emperors and the Tibetan Buddhist hierarchs, especially the Dalai Lamas, were complex, having both religious and political facets. As we shall see, the emperor not only carefully separated his dealings with Tibet and Tibetan Buddhist leaders from the administration of the "inner" realm but also intentionally kept the nature of those relations largely hidden from his Chinese subjects, for fear that their departure from Confucian norms and the hierarchy those norms imposed might prejudice his legitimacy in their eyes.

The relationship that Hong Taiji established with the Fifth Dalai Lama in 1639 was embedded in the Tibetan Buddhist *chö-yön* concept discussed in the previous chapter. The emperor took on the role of the *yöndag*, the benefactor, which bound him to support and protect the Dalai Lama and the Tibetan Buddhist faith, in particular the Gelugpa institutions. This patronage and the Dalai Lama's recognition of the emperor as the incarnation of the bodhisattva Manjusri were politically important in that they provided the Manchu ruler with legitimacy in the Tibetan Buddhist world, which included the Mongols. This interpretation is not to ignore or belittle the importance of Buddhism to the emperors, several of whom were devout Tibetan Buddhist practitioners. Given the Fifth Dalai Lama's considerable authority and influence among the Mongols, including the Oirats and their powerful Zunghar empire, however, this relationship was particularly important to Qing emperors engaged in efforts to bring Mongol rulers under their control. As Johan Elverskog has observed, "Tibetan hierarchs, the Great Fifth Dalai Lama in particular, were an independent and international source of legitimate power within the Oirat and Mongol realms as well as within that of the Manchu emperor. None of the recognized relations of Buddhist imperial legitimacy created a single hierarchy wherein any one of those realms was incorporated by any of the others." Elverskog offers the analogy of "the Roman Catholic Church's endowment of emergent European nations with a theory of sovereignty and bestowal of legitimacy without at the same time obliging them to achieve a universalizing empire." Under such an arrangement, "the Mongol, Oirat, and Manchu leaders were fundamentally equal in being recognized as the rulers of their respective nations within a Buddhist discourse based exclusively on the ritualized authority of Tibet." He concludes that "Buddhist patronage gave the Manchus no inherent authority on an international level, still less on a local level. If the Dalai Lama recognized the Manchu emperor as a Cakravartin or an incarnation of Manjusri, he received no more authority than Galdan of the Oirats received as the Boshugtu Khan, the incarnation of the first Tibetan Buddhist emperor Songsten Gampo."[35]

With the Manchu intervention in 1720, this delicate balance was compromised. The Kangxi emperor was certainly acting in his role as the protector of Tibetan Buddhism when he sent imperial armies to Lhasa to escort the Seventh Dalai Lama to his seat in 1720. But he also reversed the Zunghar invasion by doing so, thereby establishing himself as the principal benefactor and protector of the Dalai Lama and Tibetan Buddhism, superior in power to any Mongol patron. These achievements came in the course of acquitting his duties as a patron, but their real-world effects included the advancement of Manchu interests at the cost of Mongol ones.

ETIQUETTE AND THE COMMUNICATION OF POWER RELATIONS

· Nobuaki Murakami ·

Following a brief civil war in Tibet, Kangxi's son, the Yongzheng emperor, sent the first *amban*, or imperial envoy, to represent him in Lhasa in 1728.[36] This senior official's role was primarily to negotiate with the Tibetan government on matters of concern to the Qing.[37] When unrest broke out again in Tibet in 1751, however, Yongzheng's successor, the Qianlong emperor, instructed the *amban* to play a more significant role in important political matters and to do so together with the Dalai Lama.[38] Most important, the task of the *amban*, as envoy of the emperor-benefactor, was to implement measures for the support and protection of the Dalai Lama and his administration.[39]

A revealing indication of how the emperor viewed his relationship with the Dalai Lama and other high lamas, such as the Panchen Lama, was the etiquette his imperial officials observed when meeting them. Until the end of the eighteenth century, *ambans* had to kowtow, present a *khata* (a ceremonial scarf given as a sign of respect), and show Buddhist reverence to them. This is evident from memorials to the emperor written in Manchu by his envoys in this period. *Amban* Kinglin for example reported in 1785 that he "kowtowed, presented a *khata*, and received a blessing from the Hubilgan (incarnate being)" when he met the Fourth Panchen Lama at Tashilhunpo Monastery in central Tibet.[40] Two years later *amban* Yamantai similarly memorialized that he "kowtowed and presented a *khata* in accordance with the etiquette for meeting the Dalai Lama" when he visited the Eighth Dalai Lama in the Potala Palace at Lhasa.[41]

Qing officials kowtowed to Tibetan Buddhist leaders outside Tibet as well. They did so, for example, when the Third Panchen Lama visited Jehol and Beijing for the Qianlong emperor's seventieth birthday in 1780.[42] In fact, a visiting Korean who was in Jehol at the time recorded that the Grand Minister in the Council of State told him that the emperor had ordered all retainers as well as diplomatic envoys to kowtow when meeting the Panchen Lama.[43] A hundred years later *ambans* were still following this etiquette when meeting high lamas, at least in Mongolia, according to Alexei Pozdneyev, who reported in 1878 from Urga that the *amban* there was for the first time considering changing this protocol in regard to the Jebtsundamba Khutuktu, the leading incarnate lama of Khalkha.[44]

Until recently, scholars were unaware that Qing officials followed this etiquette, as the Manchu court kept no official records of its Buddhist activities or of the communications of emperors and their officials indicating reverence for Tibetan Buddhist values and hierarchs, particularly in Chinese. If records were kept at all, they could only be private in character. This is clear from a communication of the Qianlong emperor to his viceroy Lerkin, reprimanding him for reporting officially on the etiquette he and other officials followed upon receiving the Panchen Lama on his way to Jehol in 1779, which included performance of the kowtow ritual (*koujian*). The emperor complained specifically about Lerkin's reporting that he "performed a *koujian*" upon greeting the Panchen Lama:

> These words are very much in error. This year I twice gave Lerkin an audience and had him discuss everything with the Grand Minister in the Council of State and others. We also admonished the viceroy in charge [of receiving the Panchen Lama] in detail in a face-to-face meeting. When the Panchen Erdeni crosses the border, he should not receive kowtow from governors-general or governors of circuits or provinces; neither should any lower officers or officials kneel before him. If such a man should believe in revering the lama, he shall not be forbidden to visit the temporary residence of the lama and kneel or kowtow in private; we shall pay this no heed. All governors-general have been instructed that all should comply and pay this matter careful heed when in audience. The explanation passed down is exceedingly clear. Why does Lerkin not yet clearly understand? Why does he again use the term *koujian*? It is foolish indeed for this to appear in a report to the emperor.[45]

At a first glance, this edict appears to be reprimanding Lerkin for kowtowing to the Panchen Lama and to be mandating that government officials receiving him should not do so. But a closer analysis reveals that the emperor was in fact censuring Lerkin for using the term *koujian* in an official memorial to him. If officials were truly forbidden to kowtow, it would be unnecessary for the emperor to state that officials may kneel in obeisance in private. Indeed, kowtowing when meeting the Panchen Lama was an act required of Qing officials by the Manchu emperor in his capacity as patron and protector of Tibetan Buddhism. Qianlong would not forbid this.

The emperor wanted no official record of the practice of kowtowing to high Tibetan lamas, and he endeavored to keep as few people as possible in the know. The passage above suggests instructions in this respect were given verbally only. As long as such behavior was not officially recorded, it could be explained away as having been done in private. In his role in the Tibetan Buddhist world, the emperor required that his envoys and officials honor the proper etiquette for paying respect to the high lamas in Tibet and Mongolia, even when they encountered them in the "inner" realm. But in his role as emperor of China and Son of Heaven to the Sinic world founded on Confucian values, and from the perspective of the *hua/yi* (Chinese/foreign) order this entailed, he could not afford to reveal that his officials were kowtowing to a *yi* priest. Not surprisingly, therefore, very few accounts of such performances can be found in official memorials to the Qing throne, especially in Chinese. And so the true nature of the relationship between the Qing court and Tibetan Buddhist leaders (and to some extent the Tibetan polity), mostly based on Tibetan Buddhist norms and protocols, was kept unofficial and largely invisible by the Qing court, especially to the Chinese-speaking world.[46]

The nature of this relationship changed late in the Qianlong reign as a result of the Gorkha invasions of Tibet of 1788 and 1791. Following each invasion, officials of the Dalai Lama's government rather than the emperor's *ambans* negotiated the agreements with the Gorkhas to end the war. The Qianlong emperor expressed displeasure that his envoys had ignored the dangerous situation in Tibet that had occasioned those wars and that they had not effectively participated in the negotiations to end them. Following the first invasion he instructed the newly appointed *amban* Šuliyan that, while he should not disrespect the Dalai Lama in any way, he should not compromise his position by being inappropriately fervent in his reverence.[47] When the emperor learned that his envoy was again left out of the initial negotiations to end the second invasion (in which the commander of the Manchu forces sent by the emperor eventually did take charge) and, moreover, that he had no actual power or influence over Tibetan governmental affairs, Qianlong decreed that the *kalons* (Tibetan cabinet ministers) should in future take orders from the *amban*, who would now outrank them.[48] In a clearly political and somewhat-exceptional decision, he also instructed his *ambans* no longer to kowtow to the Dalai Lama and other lamas in central Tibet, although they were to continue to do so when meeting the lamas elsewhere. At the same time, Qianlong's edict and the *amban*'s response to it show that the emperor expected his envoys to continue to hold the Tibetan lamas in reverence and that he had no intention of undermining the religious authority of the Gelugpa or of fundamentally changing the nature of his relationship with the Dalai Lama. Thus, Qianlong praised the *amban* Heliyan, appointed in Lhasa after the Manchu intervention to end the Gorkha war, for no longer kowtowing to the Dalai Lama and for asserting his authority. He noted with approval that, except for the most senior lamas, "everyone else, from lama to *kalons*, kneels while speaking to him." But the emperor also cautioned that "if *ambans* were to conduct themselves with such hubris anywhere else, we would not allow it."[49] His envoy, Heliyan's successor Sungyun, replied: "I your servant shall carefully obey your reasoning. In Tsang [Ü-tsang, central Tibet], like Heliyan, I shall not kowtow to the Dalai Lama; neither shall I behave in such a way as to disrespect him. I shall be led and inspired by good as I have always done; I shall bring good to the Gelugpa; I want for everyone to obey [the will of the emperor] in their hearts." The emperor responded: "This is exactly right. Understood."[50]

In 1796 the Qianlong emperor yielded the throne to his fifth son, who became the Jiaqing emperor, though Qianlong continued to hold power until his death in 1799. Some argue that the Jiaqing emperor wished to continue his father's policies with respect to Tibetan Buddhism and the Dalai Lama, but evidence suggests that his attitude was very different from his father's.[51] In a letter to the emperor, the Ninth Dalai Lama protested that whereas in the past *ambans* sat in an inferior position to his side and on a lesser number of rugs when meeting with him, Fengšen, who became *amban* in 1812, seated himself on an equal level.[52] In an oblique reference to the negotiations with the Gorkhas that had precipitated earlier imperial intervention, he warned, "If this continues, the Gorkhas may start neglecting the Dalai Lama."[53]

On being informed of the Dalai Lama's complaint, which was not the only one he had received, the Jiaqing emperor ordered an investigation.[54] This revealed the modifications that had been made to the original protocol after the Tibet-Gorkha war, including Qianlong's instruction that *ambans* no longer kowtow to the Dalai Lama in central Tibet. In response to the emperor's inquiry, former *ambans* Sungyun and Hening, who had served in Lhasa between 1794 and 1803, described these changes in some detail.[55] According to Hening:

> *Ambans* meeting the Dalai Lama used to perform Buddhist obeisance rituals in accordance with traditional customs, and the Dalai Lama never came down from his throne. In the fifty-eighth year of the Qian-long reign [1793] the emperor advised that *ambans*, as imperial envoys, were equal to the Dalai Lama and did not have to perform obeisance rituals and could be treated according to the guest ritual. . . . When your servants [i.e., *ambans*] met with the Dalai Lama at the Potala Palace on official business [in 1794], the Dalai Lama came down from his throne and met us at the tower gate. After we exchanged *khatas*, the Dalai Lama ascended his platform once more. Your servants' seats were both to the west of the Dalai Lama's platform, in a row facing south. At the end of the audience, the Dalai Lama saw [us] to the tower gate.[56]

After the Eighth Dalai Lama passed away, the Tibetan administration (probably led by Demo Khutukhtu) used the ceremony for the enthronement of the Ninth in 1808 as an opportunity to reinstate the earlier etiquette, placing the seats of the *ambans* to the side of the Dalai Lama and facing toward him in accordance with traditional protocol. There is actually no evidence that the seating arrangement described by Hening was ever prescribed by imperial regulation. Instead, it appears to have been an exceptional treatment first accorded by the Eighth Dalai Lama in 1792, immediately following the Gorkha war, in appreciation of the emperor's support in ending it. Contemporary records, including testimony given for the investigation, indicate that it was the Dalai Lama who made a change to the seating arrangement and who politely stopped the *amban* from kowtowing to him in worship on that occasion. The Qianlong emperor's instruction to his envoys no longer to kowtow, referred to by Hening, was issued a year later.[57]

It would seem that Fengšen, who was appointed *amban* in 1812, looked into the protocol after meeting with the Ninth Dalai Lama, realized that the etiquette observed since the latter's enthronement differed from that observed in the 1790s, and demanded that the Tibetan administration revert to the post-Gorkha-war etiquette more favorable to the *ambans*. Fengšen also parted with traditional etiquette by not offering alms at the monastery or accepting a customary gift from the Dalai Lama, and he immediately returned a Buddhist statue the Dalai Lama had given to him personally, all of which Tibetans perceived as marks of disrespect.[58]

The Jiaqing emperor clearly understood what was going on, to judge from a comment he inserted in Hening's memorial: "To sum up, the lama often fights for a just cause!" Yet in his response to the investigation, which also covered other senior officials' complaints about Fengšen's behavior, he appears to belittle those complaints and advised that "all matters of stipulation should simply be handled by consulting old regulations."[59] It would seem that the emperor preferred to ignore the disrespect shown to the Dalai Lama and to pretend that no dispute existed concerning etiquette. This can be explained only if we accept that his attitude to Tibetan Buddhism and the Dalai Lama, and therefore to his own role as *yöndag*, differed from his father's. Even when it had been politically necessary to enhance the prestige and influence of his envoys, the Qianlong emperor instructed them to continue to show respect for the Dalai Lama and other lamas. So while on the surface there was no significant change in official policy, Qing attitudes toward the Dalai Lama and Tibetan Buddhism appear to have shifted under Jiaqing's rule.

The new attitude, and Tibetan reactions to it, did not go unnoticed by the British traveler Thomas Manning, who was in Tibet in 1811–1812. He put the situation more simply in terms of the Qing sending *ambans* "of bad character" to Tibet, but he registered the consequences:

> It no doubt displeases the Grand Lama and Tibetans in general, and tends to prevent their affections from settling in favour of the Chinese government. I cannot help thinking, from what I have seen and heard, that they would view the Chinese influence in Tibet overthrown without many emotions of regret; especially if the rulers under the new influence were to treat the Grand Lama with respect, for this is a point in which these haughty mandarins are somewhat deficient, to the no small dissatisfaction of the good people of Lhasa. I myself have heard Lhasa men inveigh against them for their disrespectful deportment before him.[60]

The change in deportment indicates a larger shift in the authority of the three centers of political legitimation in Inner and East Asia. In the seventeenth and eighteenth centuries, the Qing court was part of a Tibetan Buddhist world founded on the logic and values of Tibetan Buddhism, which it shared with Tibet and the Mongols. The Qianlong emperor was a devout follower of Tibetan Buddhism, revered his spiritual mentor, Changkya Rölpé Dorjé (whom we met in the preceding chapter as the biographer of the Seventh Dalai Lama), and was profoundly aware of his own role as bodhisattva-king and *yöndag* responsible for supporting and protecting the world of Tibetan Buddhism. The Jiaqing emperor did not have a Tibetan Buddhist mentor with whom he was particularly close and may not have had a deep understanding of the shared concepts of sovereignty and legitimacy at the core of the Manchu-Tibetan relationship. When Jiaqing came to power, moreover, the Manchu emperor had already replaced the Khoshot khan as the principal benefactor and protector of Tibetan Buddhism and the Dalai Lama, and with the defeat of the Zunghars, the most serious challenge to the Qing in Inner Asia had been overcome. The political reasons for pleasing the Dalai Lama and his government had thus begun to wane, and the nature of relations in the late Qing was never quite the same as it had been before the Tibet-Gorkha wars.[61]

MANCHU POSITIONING IN RELATION TO THE CHINESE CIVILIZATIONAL WORLD

The Manchu rulers' roles as Chinggisid Great Khans and protectors of Tibetan Buddhism did not place them at the pinnacle of the Chinese civilizational world. To occupy that position, they had to be *huangdi*, August Emperors, and *tianzi*, Sons of Heaven, embodying the Confucian rule of benevolence to all peoples near and far. Only by embodying this logic could the Qing present itself as the legitimate successor dynasty of a long line of dynasties that had ruled China, most recently the Ming. In 1627, a year after succeeding as Great Khan on the death of his father, Nurhaci, Hong Taiji made clear to the Ming military command that their dynasty could no longer claim a monopoly on Heaven's grace. The conflict between Ming and Qing, he explained, arose because of the contempt shown by Ming officials in the northeast, who "considered their emperor to be as high as heaven itself, and themselves as those who live in Heaven, and the khan of another nation merely the creation of Heaven and unworthy of any degree of independent standing." The Manchus had "taken our case to Heaven," and Heaven had found them to be in the right. "Heaven heeds not the magnitude of the nations," Hong Taiji warned the Ming, "but only the righteousness of the issue." The Ming being unrighteous, the Manchus had the right to succeed to Heaven's mandate.[62]

Once the Manchus captured Beijing in 1644, they moved their court there from Manchuria, establishing it as the capital of their Great State, just as Khubilai Khan had done before them. By putting their Great Khan on the throne there, the Manchus strengthened their bid for his legitimacy as *huangdi* to their Chinese subjects and as *tianzi* to the greater Chinese civilizational world. But neither Chinese nor those beyond China were entirely convinced. The Manchu identity of the dynasty and the Inner Asian character of the empire as a conquest regime remained obstacles to legitimacy. Those obstacles continued right to the end of the dynasty and proved the Manchus' Achilles' heel when Chinese revolutionaries called for its overthrow.

The Qing court conceived of its relations with its Chinese subjects in stark terms as their rulers. Accordingly, the Manchus were never truly absorbed into the civilization of the conquered people.[63] But the study of the Chinese classics and the mastery of all aspects of Chinese culture were incorporated into the emperor's persona as the supreme ruler of the Chinese civilizational world. Thus, it was with the logic of the Chinese classics that a century after the establishment of the Qing dynasty and some eighty-five years after its overthrow of the Ming, the Yongzheng emperor (r. 1722–1735) responded to the persistence of Chinese reservations regarding the legitimacy of the Manchu rule. Citing the Confucian philosopher Mencius in his 1730 treatise *Dayi juemi lu* (Awakening to supreme justice), the emperor argued:

Seditious rebels make the suggestion that we were the sovereign of Manchuria and later entered the Central State to become its ruler. Their prejudices about the territorial division between this land and that land have led to hateful lies and fabrications. What they have failed to understand is that Manchuria is to the Manchus what *jiguan* [birthplace or ancestral place] is to the people of the Central State. Shun was a man of the eastern *yi* and King Wen was a man of the western *yi*. Did that diminish their sagely virtue?[64]

Thus, virtue rather than the place of origin must be the criterion by which the legitimacy and fitness to rule of the emperor were to be judged. Three years later, in a criticism of the self-censorship of some literati in the use of the character *yi* (foreign), he reportedly stated:

The distinction between the *zhong* [central] and the *wai* [outer] is a line drawn on the Earth, but the distinction between the *shang* [high] and the *xia* [low] was made in Heaven. Our dynasty originated from the shore of the eastern ocean and has since unified the various states. The sovereign rules all under Heaven. The tradition that has been inherited [by this dynasty] is that of *zhongwai yijia* [center and outer as one family] which goes back to the times of King Yao and King Shun. The talents We employ, be they literary or military, join this universal family of the Center and the Outer. Our administrative policies, rituals, and military conquests are all made for this universal family of the Center and the Outer. Our subjects, from the Capital Region (Zhili) and the other interior provinces to Mongolia and the remote tribes, and even those living on the edge of the oceans and in mountain valleys, as well as tribute-bearers who travel hither by land or by sea from foreign places, all without exception show their respect toward their parents and deference toward Our sovereign rule. To trace the beginnings of Our empire to its original place and regard Us as the outer *yi* is merely to draw a territorial line between the center and the outer. We call it outrageous treachery, no matter how you avoid the words between the lines, for the only distinction in Heaven is that of the high and low.[65]

The geographic region in which the dynasty originated had nothing to do with their lawful right to rule. Qing imperial ideology as it related to the Chinese civilizational world in this period portrayed a universal family in which the Manchu nobility, the bannermen, the Han and other peoples, as well as tributaries and other polities, were all organized into a hierarchical order of universal kinship.[66]

This model of a universal Son of Heaven was derived, of course, from a Chinese precedent going back to the Zhou dynasty, an age in which the pyramid of hierarchical distinctions was not nearly as high as the Qing constructed it. Zhou rituals for acknowledging the Son of Heaven evolved in the imperial era into rituals for envoys bearing tribute to and prostrating before him. Their gestures created the impression that China exercised cultural and political hegemony over a variety of other nations, but the notion that Qing foreign relations constituted a coherent world order based on China, *pace* Fairbank, is neither an adequate nor a complete description, except perhaps at the level of Qing state ideology.[67] And the popular notion that the empire was Chinese because the Qing emperors took on the roles and position of *huangdi* and *tianzi* to the Chinese world and ruled from Beijing is not in keeping with the Manchu court's own outlook.

GUEST RITUAL AND QING
INTERNATIONAL RELATIONS

· Pamela Crossley ·

The Yongzheng emperor captured the Manchu dynastic perspective in the expression "Our dynasty considers itself Manchu, yet China is our place of residence."[68] Some scholars have taken the term *zhongguo*, the "central state"—*dulimba-i gurun* in Manchu—to suggest that the Qing considered its empire to be Chinese or at least congruent with China.[69] Whereas the court used the term in Manchu as an occasional way of referring to the empire, particularly in communications with Russia during treaty negotiations in the eighteenth century, it is probably unwise to leap to a conclusion that this can be globally glossed as "China," or that international relations were understood to mean relations of China with outside entities. Earlier northeastern empires before the Qing used "central state" to refer to themselves or their empires when they were clearly distinct from and even hostile to China.[70] In the 1689 Treaty of Nerchinsk, a focal document for scholars speculating on the meaning of *dulimba-i gurun*, Jesuits sent by the Qing to negotiate with Russian representatives designated Qing using the term *Sinarum imperatoris*, "emperor of/over/in China." The Manchu text is exactly parallel: *Dulimba-i gurun-i enduringge hūwangdi*. This sense of distinctness from, but possession of, was what Yongzheng meant when he wrote, "China is our place of residence." *Dulimba-i gurun* is also repeatedly used in the Qing catalog of peoples submitting tribute to the emperor, where it meant the continuing space, culture, and history of China. Past empires are specified by name: *Han-i gurun, Tang-i gurun, Ming-i gurun*, and so on, but there is no *Qing-i gurun* tagging along in their wake.[71] Context suggests, therefore, that the Manchu court considered itself to be based in a historical China that was central to its empire, but not that the empire itself was Chinese.

Under the Qing, as was the case in much earlier imperial times, envoys from foreign states subscribing to the international ethos of the *tianzi* presented themselves at the imperial capital. Although the relationships they maintained with the court were diverse, they performed the same rituals with the same literal meanings, at times even in ironic contrast to the nature of those relationships. The notion of Qing foreign relations amounting to a comprehensive world order to which all states subscribed is not persuasive to historians researching it. From Han times forward the Board (or Ministry) of Rites in the capital kept a list of polities sending envoys, organized their visits (including translators and guides), and trained the envoys in guest ritual and other aspects of court etiquette. There was no aspect of the guest ritual that compelled parties on either side into specific economic or strategic relationships, and two of the most significant foreign relationships for the Qing—with Russia and Japan—fell outside the jurisdiction of the Board of Rites. If the concept of a Chinese world order overseen from the Board of Rites is not persuasive, it is because the Qing emperors themselves did not feel the need to stretch the guest ritual to fit every kind of foreign relation. They created another institution, the Lifan-yuan, to deal not only with outer realms under indirect rule but also with independent Mongol federations, Tibetan Buddhist hierarchs, and Russia and conducted these relations outside the framework of the guest ritual and without involving the Board of Rites. So although the presentation of the emperor as the traditional Confucian Son of Heaven receiving tribute from the world's nations was intended to be universal, the Qing list of embassy states performing the guest ritual was in fact not that extensive, including only about a third of the states that had been on the Ming list. Moreover, despite the uniformity of the archly classical guest ritual, relationships between the Qing court and embassy states differed radically from one another. The careful scripting of the guest ritual related inversely to the variety and contingency of Qing international relations, as the examples of Dai Viet and Chosŏn Korea will demonstrate.

The Qing insisted that rank among its embassy states correspond to the frequency of visits by their envoys to the imperial capital. Dai Viet stood high on that list. Viet envoys were expected at the Qing court about every three years, registering a little under ninety such visits over the course of the dynasty. At the time of the Manchu defeat of the Ming and the relocation of the Qing capital to Beijing in 1644, Dai Viet was in the middle of a tumultuous political transition. Despite its ongoing state of turmoil and the reduction of the Lê emperors of Dai Viet to figureheads, the latter's communications with the Qing court and their tribute embassies remained undisturbed, as it was in neither side's interest to change that arrangement.

The conflict in Dai Viet between the Trinh and Nguyen factions divided the country. The Trinh were staunch supporters of the trappings of historically Chinese-style government, Confucian court ceremony, and the legitimating function of the guest ritual. So as long as the Trinh held their own in the ongoing civil war, it was hardly in their interest to alert the Qing court to the continuing struggle with the Nguyen faction. The Qing court, for its part, had no interest in intervening in Dai Viet. During the 1670s, as the Trinh were overwhelming their rivals, the Manchu emperors were fighting a war against their own agents in south China and Ming loyalists on Taiwan. Had the Trinh pleaded for help it would have been awkward for the Son of Heaven to ignore it, so it was far better, from his point of view, that the Viet embassies should confine their communications to guest ritual and other pleasantries and not stray into complexities of political and strategic matters. The embassy or tribute system under the Qing was not a means of managing foreign relations so much as a device for protecting ritual protocol.

When the general strategic condition of the empire did demand a focus on Dai Viet or Siam, relations were managed independently of guest ritual. Thus, during the five years of border tensions between the Qing empire and Dai Viet (1723–1728), when the Yongzheng emperor threatened war over a strip of historically unruly borderland occupied by Dai Viet that included some silver mines, the triennial guest ritual reception of Viet ambassadors at the imperial court remained undisturbed. In the end, the Qing court abandoned its war plans. Upon receiving a special envoy of the Lê emperor, Yongzheng announced a settlement entirely consistent with Dai Viet's territorial claim. The apparent lack of connection between realities on the ground and the guest ritual was not for lack of information on the part of the Qing court. The Qing court was not reliant upon tribute-bearing ambassadors for their information but had a serviceable intelligence network of their own based on merchants and officials of Chinese descent throughout Southeast Asia, who were able to communicate with border governors and in some cases with the imperial court, which ran an elaborate secret intelligence system of its own.[72]

The war in the southern part of Dai Viet in the latter half of the eighteenth century also had no apparent impact on the continuation of guest ritual. This war involved Siam and led to the massive rebellion by Tay-Son in 1769, the ousting of the Lê emperor, and the establishment in the south of the Nguyen's own dynasty. It pitted the Nguyen and the Trinh and the Tay-Son rebels against each other. Guangxi Province became a refuge for the deposed Lê emperor and also for the Trinh, all without reference to guest ritual. Although the network of Chinese merchants kept the Qing court apprised of developments on the ground, these events, which even included massacres of Chinese residents of Phú Xuân, did not incite a response. Eventually, in light of several ongoing Qing campaigns in southwest China and the enthusiasm of Qing officials for perpetual warfare, the court decided to intervene against the Tay-Son rebels. Qing troops made a grand entrance into the Dai Viet capital but suffered defeat when trying to extend control. Without delay the Board of Rites arranged for ambassadors of the Tay-Son rebel emperor—who is on record as inspiring his troops with a litany of China's long history of aggression against the Viet—to participate in the guest ritual. As it happened, Tay-Son rule over Dai Viet was not stable. In 1802 a Nguyen pretender—his progress, again, well known to the Qing through its informants—dealt the Tay-Son regime a decisive military defeat. Once again, the victor's representatives were briskly welcomed to the guest ritual, this time as ambassadors of Vietnam, as the state under Nguyen rule was now known.[73]

If the case of Dai Viet demonstrates near-total detachment of the guest ritual from political and strategic realities, the case of Chosŏn Korea attests to the ways in which the hypothesized ethics of the *tianzi* relationship could be reconstructed with a meaning nearly inverse to the Confucian posture of benevolent intercession. Dai Viet ranked high among the embassy states, but Chosŏn ranked higher. On the Qing envoy lists, it was the most frequent visitor, appearing almost seasonally and racking up nearly 440 visits during the Qing dynastic period, completely eclipsing the second-ranked visitor, Ryukyu (150 delegations), and the third, Dai Viet. Chosŏn had also ranked first on the Ming lists, visiting annually. But the steep increase in Chosŏn performance of the guest ritual under the Qing was hardly the result of a closer relationship that the illusory guest ritual was designed to communicate. Quite the contrary, it resulted from the coercive nature of their relations.

These differences rested on the fact that Chosŏn was the only state that had to be forced to venerate the Manchu emperor as the Confucian *tianzi*. During the early wars between the pre-Manchu Jurchen khanate and the Ming, Chosŏn had cleaved tightly to the Ming's side and provided safe harbor to Chinese resisters after the khanate conquered Liaodong Province. Shortly after succeeding to the khanate in late 1626, Hong Taiji invaded Chosŏn to punish it for aiding the Ming and extracted a promise of neutrality. When Chosŏn continued to aid the Ming, Hong Taiji mounted a massive campaign against Chosŏn immediately after he proclaimed the founding of the Qing empire in 1636, devastating croplands and seizing the capital. Under the gaze of his assembled officials, the Chosŏn king Injo was bound and forced to prostrate himself before Hong Taiji.

Korean elites had interpreted their country's relation to the Ming and their participation in guest ritual through the ideals of *sadae* (service to the greater) and *mohwa* (veneration of civilization), whereas they considered the enforced submission to Manchu domination at odds with both. In fact, they continued to hope for a Ming victory. Even after the latter's defeat in 1644, the Chosŏn court continued to aid Ming loyalists and other resisters to the Manchus. While some Chosŏn officials feared another punitive expedition, others plotted King Injo's overthrow because he was inclined to enforce the Manchu emperor's demands. In defiance of Qing threats, many Korean landowners, scholars, and officials continued to venerate the Ming. They perpetuated Ming period names and gave Ming dynastic descendants special status in Chosŏn, where they were permitted to erect temples and monuments in honor of the Ming. Academicians, who taught that barbarians never attained even a century of good fortune, optimistically predicted the early fall of the Qing empire and the resurgence of those loyal to the values of the Ming and civilization.

Qing coercion of Chosŏn had a real impact on the population. Perhaps as many as half a million Koreans were deported to Manchu slave farms during and following the 1627 and 1637 wars, precipitating the rebellions of the 1640s.[74] Manchu destruction of roads and farmlands aggravated the people's suffering from the famine in 1670, which may have claimed a million lives, while farmers faced tax increases to cover the tribute payments to the Qing emperor. These payments were not, as in the case of some other embassy states, a fiction balanced or surpassed by imperial payments and gifts to the ritual partners. Exactly how much the unprecedentedly frequent embassy missions and payments cost the Chosŏn court and the farming population underwriting them is unclear. It has been estimated that for every silver ounce given to the Chosŏn court by the emperor, ten were expended on embassy costs and tribute. This was a significant transfer of wealth and was probably not recouped through private trade.

The transfer of the management of the coercive Qing-Chosŏn relationship to the Board of Rites in 1644 and its subsequent draping in the rhetoric of the guest ritual not only ironically alluded to harmonious Ming-Chosŏn relations but also transformed some Board of Rites functions in relation to Chosŏn to resemble those of the Lifanyuan toward the Mongols.[75] The Qing changed the rules for Koreans of registered Chinese descent conducting trade by bringing this trade under the purview of the Board of Rites in the capital,[76] and financial obstacles to trade accumulated. Serious troubles arose when the Yongzheng emperor ordered the Board of Rites to create maps defining a boundary between Chosŏn Korea and the Great Qing state. Though roughly contemporary with the Qing border dispute with Dai Viet, which was amicably resolved in the latter's favor outside the purview of the Board of Rites, the substance and pursuit of this inquiry were radically different. The Board of Rites quickly encountered a morass of legal, financial, and military complications when Chosŏn officials repeatedly subverted its mapping expeditions. Unable to complete his task under these circumstances, the imperial official in charge simply constructed a border monument at a spot of his choosing, an act the Board of Rites sanctioned while rejecting Chosŏn court protests.[77]

Shortly thereafter, the Yongzheng emperor commissioned a project displaying in blunt detail the true nature of relations between the Qing and its highest-ranking embassy state[78] and highlighting his envoy's humiliation of the new Chosŏn king, Yeongjo, on the occasion of his accession to the throne in 1724. In a private ceremony distinct from the investiture, King Yeongjo reenacted—with the emperor's representative Akdun standing in for Hong Taiji—the humiliating prostration of Injo before the Manchu khan almost a century earlier, once again in full view of the Chosŏn court. This humiliating scene was depicted in detail in a series of poems and paintings collated for the private enjoyment of the imperial lineage and their circle.[79] While these depictions represented the true history of the coercive relationship, the idealized language and performance of the guest ritual remained in place without any connection to that history, other than punishing Chosŏn by demanding costly embassy missions at unprecedented frequency. Standard accounts of Qing-Chosŏn relations re-gard Chosŏn's position among Qing vassals as normative, accepting the Qing claim that it was simply continuing the preferential traditions of the Ming. Chosŏn's high frequency of appearances at Beijing has been taken as a sign of rank and favor, which is how Qing guest ritual rhetoric por-trayed it, even though it was understood that their punitive and financially onerous character crippled Chosŏn's ability to finance military and trade independence.[80]

If before the nineteenth century, Qing guest ritual and *tianzi* status bore little relationship to the substance of the court's foreign relationships and failed to represent a system of unified expectations of trade, politics, or strategic behavior, in its demise it did reflect some significant interna-tional developments. Thus, when tributaries such as Laos, Nepal, Sikkim, and Sulu came under the dominance or possession of European colonial powers, these polities simply disappeared from the guest ritual schedule. Chosŏn and Vietnam were eventually prevented by foreign powers from participating in the ritual as the diplomatic and international legal frame-works within which the Qing had operated were replaced from the outside by other protocols and by a system of international law that had origi-nated in Europe. In this new era, the multiple international legal systems corresponding to diverse civilizational worlds of Inner and East Asia and the forms of diplomatic engagement and relationships they engendered would be replaced by a new system, the international law of the Euro-pean powers. Just as the Manchus' remarkable ability to function simulta-neously in different civilizational environments had contributed to their dynasty's success and longevity, so their adoption of modern forms of statehood and international legal norms insensitive to that diversity con-tributed to the empire's demise.

CHAPTER SIX

TRANSITIONS TO THE MODERN STATE SYSTEM

The rules and expectations governing relations in Inner and East Asia changed hugely in the nineteenth and early twentieth centuries. The Asian order as it had been built since the thirteenth century was reconfigured, some would say abandoned, under pressures coming from outside continental Asia—most conspicuously from Europe but increasingly also from the United States and Japan. The new order of state sovereignty and international relations modeled on European constructs and practices weakened and then largely replaced the norms preexisting its arrival, a mostly painful process that entailed threat and coercion. The violence of nineteenth- and early twentieth-century imperialism was often unleashed around issues of trade and economic access, as foreign powers competed for advantage throughout Asia. The resort to violence was justified by utilizing self-serving doctrines of European international law, a body of norms and rules of conduct associated with the Peace of Westphalia but which had since much evolved to remove restraints on European ambitions across the world. Asian states that refused what the European powers regarded as rightful claims were branded as illegitimate under that law and subject to its sanctions.[1]

When Europeans first arrived in Asian waters in the sixteenth and seventeenth centuries, the situation was different. At that time they came principally as merchants seeking opportunities for trade. Small colonies sprang up at key ports around the Indian Ocean and South China Sea, mostly to support this trade rather than assert a political presence on behalf of their home states. The notable exception was Spain's direct colonization of the Philippines, carried out against small sultanates and tribes that lacked the political or military resources to block what Spain regarded as simply an extension of its colonies in the Americas. Other European states made inroads elsewhere, as did the Dutch in Java and the British in India, but full-blown colonial regimes were not in place until the eighteenth century. European imperialism in those days was largely run through negotiations and treaties with local partners. Only as European military and economic power rose on the wave of industrialization at the end of the eighteenth century did the European states impose their authority over numerous Asian states by the establishment of colonial governments and various other forms of indirect as well as direct rule.

Even then, most of Inner and East Asia remained beyond the control of European imperialism. The complex hierarchical systems of layered and shared sovereignties and of interpolity relations regulated by multiple legal orders of Inner and East Asia remained intact. When Lord Macartney arrived at the Qing court as Britain's first credentialed representative in 1793, his proposal for a restructuring of relations between the two states, including the signing of treaties and the establishment of permanent diplomatic missions, fell on deaf ears. It was not that the Manchus misunderstood what Macartney wanted; they understood clearly, and just as clearly did not see the need to abandon the hierarchical order over which they presided.[2] It would take "gunboat diplomacy," to use the oxymoronic phrase that captures the violent arrival of the new international order in the nineteenth century, to change this perception.[3] Suddenly, states in East Asia found themselves up against the demands of well-armed foreigners. They could no longer deal with them according to the established foreign relations protocols. Unable to bar their doors against this assault, Asian rulers found themselves having to negotiate and accept what came to be called "unequal treaties." These negotiations, often at gunpoint, led to the reorganization of, first, the practices of interpolity relations and, then, the institutions through which these relations were conducted. The transition from the existing norms and protocols to those of the new system was difficult and unpredictable. Some states, notably Japan, proved adept at weathering the onslaught and turning the arrival of the new rules and practices to their benefit. Others did not. Regardless, most governments that had ruled the states of Asia at the beginning of the nineteenth century were gone by the beginning of the twentieth, with the partial exceptions of Thailand, Mongolia, Tibet, and some Himalayan states. In most other states not under colonial rule, new political elites formed and took power. As colonized peoples asserted their independence, they too abandoned the preexisting forms of government in favor of constitutional monarchies and republics modeled on Western political institutions. Eventually, the rulership of khans, emperors, hierarchs, and kings largely gave way to a regime of presidents, party leaders, constitutional monarchs, and national assemblies.

This passage was far from uniform. It proceeded everywhere differently depending on internal movements for change and external pressures not just from the European powers but equally, and in some places primarily, from forces within or from neighboring state leaders asserting new roles to secure a place in the new international order. In every case, interpolity relations underwent a complete conceptual and organizational transformation.

THE NEW PARADIGM OF
INTERNATIONAL RELATIONS

Interpolity relations were reorganized globally in relation to the new European paradigm of "international relations," which imagined the world as existing in a state of "anarchy" as opposed to "hierarchy."[4] This reorganization had effects along two different axes; or rather, it split what had been one axis into two. The categorical distinction of polities as being domestic or foreign from another state's perspective, that is, whether it was to be considered as existing within or without its borders, required major adjustments, given the entanglements of Inner and East Asian polities with one another, and in particular with the larger empires. There could no longer be ambiguous or middle statuses, nor could there be different simultaneous interpretations of sovereign status. The rules had changed. The nation-state around which modern international law was built up in the nineteenth century was defined in terms of exclusive territorial sovereignty with hard borders. This required an entirely different understanding of sovereignty, entailing exclusivity of authority and of "ownership" of territorial space. According to the new system, in principle states were entirely independent, not subject to any outside authority; if not, they were to be considered as "part of" another state regarded as the sovereign entity.[5] In practice, as we shall see, the exit from the old legal orders was not as complete as has been claimed, nor was the entry into the new order as legal, unambiguous, or consistent with its own principles as many have insisted.

Lest we forget, many European states, including those from which the Westphalian model emanated, did not fit neatly into the normative and legal system associated with that model. Many retained features from earlier state forms or were themselves empires. They maintained relations with other states and asserted forms of authority over some of them that should have had no place in the nation-state paradigm they purported to represent. Their system of international law may have been based on principles of sovereign equality and rejection of hierarchy, but it was also crafted and manipulated to enable the fulfillment of their ambitions throughout the world, as a result of which it was inherently contradictory.

The passage to the new order also included a transition to new criteria by which to determine whether a ruler or state was legitimate. What the new system demanded was the application of a uniform and much narrower range of legitimizing mechanisms. The distinctive Tibetan Buddhist, Chinggisid, and Confucian legitimation ideologies were deauthorized and replaced by the new "universal" Euro-American construct. This transformation did not happen overnight and in some cases, it can be argued, has not fully occurred yet. The new ideology was constructed mostly on the idea—grounded in European Enlightenment thinking—that sovereignty was vested in the people, whose will could be expressed to determine the form and manner of rule as well as the identity of rulers. But it was also partly built on the popular nineteenth-century European discourse of civilization, which regarded European Christian civilization as the standard and argued in circular fashion that "uncivilized" nations had no right to exist, and "uncivilized" rulers, no right to rule. The people may have been installed as the authority from which legitimacy in some of these Asian states by the turn of the twentieth century was said to derive, but the ambiguity as to how their will should be determined and interpreted was vast, plunging many into struggles for power and in some cases revolution.[6] In some states the earlier sources of legitimacy continued—some even to this day—to command considerable authority, whether officially acknowledged or not. This chapter does not deal with these internal transformations as much as with the external manifestations of those states' coming to terms with the realities of the new international order as it arrived in Inner and East Asia.

The application of the new system of international relations and international law in Inner and East Asia was a complex and destabilizing experience, which changed existing power relationships, subtle balances, and functioning conventions. European-based international law and diplomacy, as well as the management of international order by force, were at times baffling, especially as they regularly failed to deliver what the new system promised: the inviolability of sovereign states as embodiments of the free will of nations. This destabilization is not simply something the new states had to "get over" in order to emerge from their different Asian past. It is the missing element in every equation that seeks to explain international relations in this part of Asia. Without being able to acknowledge, or even be aware of, the premises on which many Asian actors constructed their ideas of state legitimacy and interpolity justice in the wake of the transformation wrought by the new international system, we cannot hope to make sense of the crises that have beset the region or establish the grounds on which to negotiate conditions for alleviating them today.

The passage to the new international system of relations occurred throughout Asia, but it was not uniform. Some states proactively claimed their place in the new order by instituting Western-style reforms domestically and behaving like the Western imperialist powers to earn their place among the select "family of nations." Others reluctantly adapted to the new environment, though attempting to retain the privileged position they enjoyed in the otherwise-disappearing Asian system of relations. And some did not complete the transition in time to engage fully as nation-states in the international system, leaving them vulnerable to expansionist ambitions of others. Tracing the histories of the many complex transitions that took place in this period would require an entire book. In this chapter we bring to light only some episodes that, by way of example, help us appreciate the variety, complexity, and impact of this tumultuous period on relations among Inner and East Asian states. We look at Japan's assertion of big-power status that transformed its relations with other polities in Asia, in particular the Qing state, Korea, Ryukyu, and Taiwan; we consider the ambiguous transitional status of Korea under the machinations of the United States, the Qing, and Japan; and we observe the encounter of Tibetan Buddhist states, in particular Tibet, with British Indian imperial frontier policy as those states were reluctantly drawn into the modern international system. The Qing empire cast its shadow over all three cases as it moved to secure its interests on different fronts.

JAPAN'S QUEST FOR A PLACE IN THE NEW WORLD ORDER

· *Shogo Suzuki* ·

European diplomacy projected an ideology of orderly relations between equal sovereign states, but it also professed the legality of imperialism, which included abrogating the sovereignty of Asian states when circumstances warranted that recourse. A discourse of enlightenment argued that Europeans had an ethical obligation to introduce European civilization to the "savage" and "uncivilized" peoples they encountered as they enlarged their empires, placing non-European peoples under their tutelage rather than protecting the sovereignty of their polities. The European international order was therefore Janus-faced for the non-European world. On the one hand, the mode of interaction that applied to "civilized" European polities supported (at least in theory) the coexistence of multiple sovereign equals and, therefore, protected their sovereignty. On the other hand, the mode of interaction that applied to "savage" entities was a coercive one that suspended the sovereignty of non-European states and treated its peoples as children who were incapable of governing their own lives. They were to be placed under the guidance of the European powers—by force, if need be—until they could meet the standards of civilization, which included conformity to international law, diplomatic customs, and civilized behavior, all as defined by Europeans, as well as adoption of European domestic political institutions and legal codes and protection of foreign life and property. Failure of a state to conform to these standards made it unworthy of equal treatment by European states.

It was in this context that East Asian states such as the Qing and Japan were incorporated into the European international order. Like many other of their "uncivilized" counterparts, they were forced to open their doors to the European states against their will. Furthermore, their lowly status within the new international social hierarchy was confirmed through unequal treaties, robbing them of the sovereign prerogatives enjoyed by European states. As both the Qing and Japanese elites began to develop an awareness of the stigma attached to the "uncivilized" label, they sought to attain an equal social footing with the Europeans. Both initially believed that attaining equal military might would secure a change of status, and thus they began adopting European technology. As the leadership of Meiji Japan came to understand the Europeans' strong sense of universalism, however, they realized that the latter would interpret such efforts as merely superficial mimicking. They consequently embarked on a thorough program of "Westernization" that entailed adopting political institutions and social practices based on European models.

However, there was another facet to Japan's attempt to attain "civilized" status in the new international order: its goal of becoming an imperialist state. While Japanese desire to be an imperialist power has frequently been seen as motivated by geostrategic considerations, it was partly a result of Japan's wish to overthrow the Asian international order and, in so doing, to establish itself as the only European-style sovereign state in the region. Both European and Asian international orders were inherently hierarchical in practice: Japan's program was to achieve equality with the Western powers in the new order by raising its position in Asia. In succeeding, it established a difficult legacy for its later relations with China.

The domestic political reforms the Meiji leadership undertook to make Japan a "civilized state" have been covered in considerable detail elsewhere and need not be repeated here. This process has usually been depicted according to modernization theory as a success story, through which "modernization" lifted Japan out of the straitjacket of feudalism. In that narrative, developed in opposition to Marxist interpretations of Japanese history, the darker aspects of the process—Japan's transformation into an imperialist power—is "reduced to a product of 'strategic interests' or treated as an aberration of modernization whose roots could be traced back to Japanese society."[7] The fact that the imperialism of the Western powers may have inspired Japan's own aggressive expansion has consequently been downplayed.[8]

Crucially, these perspectives obscure the fact that Japan (and the Qing, for that matter) was socialized into a dualistic international order, in which the "civilized" were entitled to spread the trappings of "civilization" to "savage" lands, by coercive means if necessary. Subsequently, imperialist expansion became a key component of Japan's drive to demonstrate its "civilized" status and attain equality with the European powers. Asia was increasingly portrayed as Japan's other, an entity that functioned to illuminate Japan's "civilized" identity by being cast as inherently "savage" or "uncivilized" and therefore fundamentally different from Japan.[9] In this sense, the East Asian international order and its diplomatic norms—simplistically characterized by hierarchical tribute relations between the "Middle Kingdom" and its vassals—came to symbolize the "uncivilized" and anachronistic Asian world that Japan was so desperate to escape. Consequently, the undermining of the East Asian international order was to become a key component of Japan's attempts to attain "civilized" status in the European international order.

Even European-based international law, which Asian states could use to protect their interests from the Western powers, became a handmaiden of Japanese imperialism. Japanese encounters with it began through the Chinese translation of Henry Wheaton's *Elements of International Law*, which was influenced by the concept of natural law and therefore emphasized its universalistic aspects.[10] However, as their interactions with the Western powers deepened, Japanese became aware of the concept of positive international law. The reaction of Nishi Amane, who studied under Simon Vissering at Leiden University, was to regard international law as "Western international law," a body of law applicable to certain countries and not as universalistic as it was purported to be. Crucially, Nishi noted that while sovereign states did enjoy rights under that system, what rights they could enjoy depended on how powerful they were. States were "classified as primary countries, secondary countries, and third-rate countries"; "third-rate" countries could not enjoy the right to autonomy to the same degree the "primary countries" could, he concluded.[11] Japanese thus began to use modern international law dualistically. They justified an aggressive, expansionary diplomacy in terms of international law, arguing that their conduct was inherently "civilized," while at the same time showing little regard for the sovereignty of other polities they considered "uncivilized," since those did not qualify for protection under this law.

Japan's application of this new body of law entailed the gradual but relentless dismantling of any vestiges of tributary relations in its international diplomacy. The first casualty of this change was Ryukyu. The island kingdom, which had traditionally submitted tribute to the ruling dynasties in both China and Japan, had been under the control of the Satsuma fiefdom in Kyushu since the turn of the seventeenth century. Nevertheless, Ryukyuan leaders maintained their tribute relations with both throughout, thereby ensuring their kingdom's survival as a political entity in its own right.[12] However, such multiple relationships—which were not particularly idiosyncratic in the normative structures of the East Asian international order—could not be tolerated in a Westphalian order in which the sole legitimate international actors were sovereign states as conceptualized in that system.

Ryukyu's dual status as a vassal state of both regional powers created confusion. The Meiji government and its predecessors initially regarded the kingdom as a part of Japan's sphere of influence, not as a state to be inevitably or naturally incorporated. But in April 1871 Inoue Kaoru, Meiji oligarch and future foreign minister, submitted a memorial arguing for the first time that the kingdom's status should be amended to come fully under Japanese control. There was resistance among the Japanese elite. One legislative organ of the government protested that "the Ryukyu king was a Ryukyuan and should not be confused as a person of Japan," and that the kingdom should be allowed to come under both Chinese and Japanese sovereign authority.[13] The Meiji government, however, was keen to prevent foreign powers from taking advantage of the kingdom's indeterminate status, and it regarded vestiges of the East Asian international order as anathema to its pursuit of a "civilized" identity on Western terms. Thus, when Ryukyuan emissaries arrived in Tokyo in 1872 to congratulate the Meiji emperor on his assuming the throne, Meiji leaders quickly made the ruler of Ryukyu a member of the Japanese nobility and designated the kingdom a "fief." The Meiji government also took steps to ensure that Japan was seen as the sovereign authority over Ryukyu externally. It sent officials from the Finance and Foreign Ministries to administer the islands, although doing so did, in the words of British diplomat Ernest Satow, inadvertently show "that the islands were not yet regarded as an integral part of the Japanese Empire."[14] The government also declared that all "treaty and diplomatic matters concerning the Ryukyu fief were hereafter to be handled by the Japanese Ministry of Foreign Affairs."[15] Ryukyu continued to send tribute missions to the Qing in 1872 and 1874, to which Japan responded by dispatching Home Ministry official Matsuda Michiyuki to the kingdom and ordering the king to terminate his tributary relations with the Qing. These orders were justified in terms of modern international law and demonstrated the Meiji government's determination to conduct diplomacy along "civilized" Western lines. The Ryukyuans, however, did not identify with the European international order and thus did not use its legal language. Instead, they pleaded with Japan to allow them to maintain relations with both their "mother and father countries" in accordance with the hierarchical and familial East Asian interpolity relations they were accustomed to.[16] Given the Meiji government's ability to impose its will by force, Ryukyuan unwillingness to comply was of little importance. Japan's invocation of modern international law as an "identity marker" demonstrated its seriousness in seeking membership in the European "family of nations."

The Qing court responded with concern. As part of its so-called Tongzhi Restoration, which aimed at strengthening the empire by adopting Western military technology, the Qing also began using modern international law and tentatively adopted some Western practices of diplomacy in their interactions with Western powers. Yet the court continued to operate in accordance with the normative structures of the East Asian international order in regions where Europeans had no vested interests and were less likely to interfere. When Ryukyuan elites sent a secret mission to the Qing in 1877 to request help in resisting Japanese pressure, the court's diplomatic envoy to Japan, He Ruzhang, reported in a letter to Li Hongzhang: "The Japanese have neither mercy nor reason. They are like crazy dogs, bullying others as they please. We could rely on the Sino-Japanese peace; however, not only will they prevent Ryukyu from sending tribute, but they will also certainly try to eliminate the kingdom. Furthermore, they will attempt to cause trouble in Korea, and if they do not do so, they will make unreasonable demands on us. If we listen to them, we will lose our dignity; if we refuse them, war will be unavoidable."[17] Li Hongzhang agreed but was pessimistic about his government's ability to do anything to stop the Japanese. He was soon proven right. Qing protests to the Japanese were rebuffed in 1878 on the grounds that the Qing did not have effective rule of the territory at issue, again an argument based on European international law. Japan's foreign minister, Terashima Munenori, told He Ruzhang that China's relation with Ryukyu was like papal recognition of European sovereigns: it was merely ceremonial. What actually mattered was effective governance of territory.[18] When Ryukyu turned to the United States, France, and the Netherlands for help, Japan obliged the king of Ryukyu to reside as a diplomatic hostage in Tokyo. A week later, on 4 April 1878, Japan announced that the Ryukyu "fief" had been abolished and would henceforth be governed directly by the central government in Tokyo as Okinawa Prefecture, thereby terminating the existence of a member of the East Asian international order.

Japan's efforts to become part of the "civilized" European world were not just confined to dismantling the East Asian international order. Japan's exposure to the coercive side of the European international order bred an awareness that "civilized" polities had the prerogative of introducing higher "civilization," by force if necessary. The lesson that colonial expansionism was dependent upon a state's claim to a civilized identity in the European international order was not lost on the Meiji leadership. "Mimesis of Western imperialism," as Robert Eskildsen has noted, "went hand in hand with mimesis of Western civilization."[19] Japan's first opportunity to demonstrate a claim to superiority vis-à-vis the rest of Asia and to assert equality with the Europeans came in 1871, when some Ryukyu fishermen were murdered by Taiwanese aborigines. Based on the assertion that the Ryukyu Islands were Japanese territory and their inhabitants Japanese nationals, Japanese politicians called for a punitive expedition. The arrival of Charles W. Le Gendre, an American national, in 1872 boosted their cause. As US consul in Amoy between 1866 and 1872, Le Gendre had unsuccessfully demanded compensation from the Qing government for the murder of American citizens in Taiwan. Once in Japan, he piqued Foreign Minister Soejima Taneomi's interest by mentioning Taiwan's natural resource riches. Moreover, he emphasized that the Qing had failed to establish effective governance over the island, rendering Taiwan *terra nullius*. Japan could therefore quite legitimately take over the island in accordance with international law. Le Gendre subsequently submitted to Soejima a series of memoranda detailing propositions for the colonization of Taiwan's east coast that were peppered by references to the need to civilize savage lands. Le Gendre claimed that Japan could justify sending its military to Taiwan because, "in accordance with international law," a Great Power could take over the sovereignty of "savage lands," provided it introduced the trappings of "civilization."[20]

Given Qing claims to the island, Japan could not simply seize the island by force; it would have to engage in diplomacy. When Soejima traveled to

Beijing in March 1873 to ratify the 1871 Sino-Japanese Friendship Treaty, he used this mission to assert Japan's claims over Ryukyu and to demand clarification of the Qing position on Taiwan. To assert Japan's civilized status to the Qing, Soejima arrived in a Western gunboat and rejected the lodging his hosts had prepared for the embassy "in favor of a Western-style house with Western furniture" to show that he "deliberately sought to accentuate the modernity of his country and to draw a contrast between Japan's progress and China's stolid traditionalism."[21] When the negotiations over Taiwan commenced on 21 June of that year, the Japanese negotiators demanded to know how the Qing intended to deal with the Taiwanese aboriginals. Their counterparts from the Zongli Yamen, the Qing office in charge of foreign relations, responded that Taiwan's "ripe savages" had come under Qing rule but that its "wild savages" could not be controlled by them. Ignoring this traditional Chinese distinction, Soejima reported back to Tokyo that the Qing ministers admitted that "the savages and their land" were beyond their state's influence."[22] Using Le Gendre's arguments that "under international law a civilized country is permitted to bring the uncivilized aborigines up to a civilized level," and that Japan as a civilized country was now "taking over the task which had been neglected by the Chinese Government,"[23] Japan sent a "pacifying" military force to Taiwan. Landing in May 1874, this force overwhelmed aboriginal resistance in two months and executed their chief for the crimes against "Japanese" (Ryukyuan) fishermen. The Japanese commercial press and publishing industry printed images of Japanese soldiers in Western clothing pitted against Taiwanese aborigines in rags befitting their "savage" nature. By "exaggerating the savagery of the aborigines," Eskildsen notes, Japan was able to evacuate "the middle ground between civilization and savagery—semi-civilized status—that many Westerners believed Japan occupied at the time, so the exaggeration did more than simply foreclose the possibility of solidarity with the aborigines; it also implicitly challenged the Western view of Japan as semi-civilized."[24] Japan would complete the colonial process of civilizing Taiwan by taking possession of the island in 1895 under the terms of the Treaty of Shimonoseki at the end of the First Sino-Japanese War.

Japan thoroughly incorporated itself into the Janus-faced European international order. It pursued its *mission civilisatrice* not only in Taiwan but also, following World War I, in administering the League of Nations South Pacific Mandate, consisting of former German colonial territories in the Pacific, such as Palau, Northern Mariana Islands, Micronesia, and the Marshall Islands. Fulfilling this responsibility on behalf of the league "became an issue of honor as a 'first-class state' [*ittōkoku*], as it would demonstrate that Japan was a state on an equal footing with the Western civilized states."[25] Yet despite internalizing Western notions of civilization and superiority, many Japanese felt ambivalent about their status within the new international order, fearing that it was an order of, by, and for Europeans in which Japan could never attain full equality. It is perhaps no surprise, then, that Japan, fearful of its own survival as an empire, opted to invade China in 1931, justifying this move with the rhetoric of overthrowing Western dominance. But that overthrow was tied to Japan's aspiration to dominate the region. Despite calling for equality among Asian races during the war, Japan's superiority was never questioned. After the pernicious influence of European imperialism had been flushed out of the region, it was Japan that would guide Asian states to independence. In this sense, Japan remained unable to escape the intellectual framework of the European international order and remained the "civilized" country par excellence until its defeat in 1945 put an end to further illusions of imperial glory.

While we do not intend to diminish Asian agency in the transformation of Asian polities and their relations, the expansion of the European international order has had a profound, and not always positive, impact in Asia. It is certainly true that legal and normative concepts originating from the European international order have been internalized by many Asian polities, which may account for some of the more positive legacies of the global expansion of the Westphalian order. The Westphalian concept of sovereignty enabled many colonial states to bring European colonialism to an end, and together with the concept of national self-determination it was crucial for resisting Japanese imperialism in the 1930s. Furthermore, the notion of sovereign equality also meant that newly independent states could stand as equals—at least in theory—with states that had previously labeled them as "uncivilized," even "savage." Indeed, this new form of sovereignty achieved by many Asian states continues to be guarded with intense jealousy today. This is no reason, however, to be uncritical of the introduction and persistence of the European international order, which contributed to Japan's imperialist ventures in Ryukyu, Taiwan, and Korea and to the terrible price that the people in those states paid in the name of progress. Throughout Inner and East Asia, the turbulence, insecurity, and suffering provoked by the advent of the new international order need to be recognized, and their consequences understood, in order to appreciate the nature of the tensions and conflicts that currently exist there. They are part and parcel of the Westphalian package that the West delivered to Asia, and they have left many communities with little scope to shape alternatives to the nation-states that monopolize Asia today.

KOREA'S TRANSITIONS AND THE
HYPOCRISY OF MODERN LAW

· *Kirk Larsen* ·

The transformation of relations between the Qing empire and the kingdom of Chosŏn in the last quarter of the nineteenth century represents another element of this larger story.[26] Until recently, both states have been depicted as ignorant of, or resistant to, the modern international order, clinging to traditional assumptions and practices associated with the tribute system rather than interacting positively with the system of international law that was spreading from Europe. In fact, their responses were not as conservative as this portrait suggests. Foreign pressure did force them into accommodations with the new order, but they also took their own initiatives to adapt this order to their advantage, each side exploiting options and opportunities as these arose. Equally important was the unpredictability of the outcome of the process: the transformation was always a work in progress, and to some extent still is.

In this section we offer three reconsiderations of Qing-Chosŏn relations during this dynamic period. First, the Qing court, far from being an implacable opponent to Chosŏn's transformation from its tributary status to a member of the "family of nations,"[27] actually played an important and perhaps indispensable role in this transformation.[28] Second, in tension with its role in ushering Chosŏn into the new order, the Qing continued to assert a special relationship that clearly included elements of older practices—hierarchy and its ritual expression through tribute missions—while also introducing new elements. Third, and perhaps most surprising, foreign states, particularly Western ones, acquiesced to the continued Qing assertion of non-Westphalian suzerainty claims to Chosŏn. This acceptance highlights one of the most important aspects of the nineteenth-century transformation of international relations theory and practice: despite the appealing high-minded rhetoric of sovereign equality, the new international order that both the Qing and Chosŏn entered was not one in which treaties and legations secured Westphalian sovereignty. Rather, the "organized hypocrisy" (to borrow Stephen Krasner's evocative phrase) of the new order of international relations taking shape in East Asia in the late nineteenth century left it to rifles and gunboats to determine, assert, or protect sovereignty.[29] As Chosŏn lacked both, the treaties and diplomatic missions that ostensibly established and reinforced its independence turned out to be the very instruments that denied it the actual exercise of Westphalian sovereignty.

What would pry Korea from the tribute system was not a Western power but Meiji Japan. After engaging in gunboat diplomacy of its own—sending a survey ship to a sensitive area of the Chosŏn coast and claiming the resulting bombardment by Korean shore batteries as a provocation for war— Japan in 1876 gave the Chosŏn court the ultimatum to negotiate or fight. Chosŏn had fought in past encounters with foreigners (against France in 1866 and the United States in 1871) but agreed on this occasion to negotiate with Japan. This decision was the result of not only domestic political shifts but also behind-the-scenes advice from the high Qing official Li Hongzhang. Although the resulting Treaty of Kanghwa is often hailed as Korea's first modern treaty and a significant step into the new international order,[30] closer examination reveals this to be an overstatement. The Japanese negotiators chose to regard a key term in the first clause of the treaty, "autonomy" (Korean *chaju*; Chinese *zizhu*), as a marker of Korean sovereignty and independence. In Qing discourse, however, this term had long been in use to describe the status of Chosŏn as a self-governing tributary and by Chosŏn to describe their policy of self-reliance.[31] The first clause of the treaty could therefore also be understood as an expression of continuity, not a declaration of independence from the Qing. Both states' continued performance of the usual rituals and protocols associated with tributary diplomacy, such as Chosŏn's use of the Qing dynastic calendar and the Qing court's reception of tributary missions, indicates that this was their interpretation.

As for Chosŏn relations with Japan, Chosŏn neither expected nor welcomed a dramatic transformation in those relations. Two days after the treaty was ratified, King Kojong observed that the agreement was merely an important step to restoring traditional "neighborly relations" with Japan.[32] His officials subsequently persistently sought to limit Japan's presence in the country to its traditional site near the city of Pusan, denying its diplomats and merchants the access promised in the treaty. It took years of tireless effort on the part of Japanese diplomats to secure their access to the Chosŏn capital and to open two additional ports, Wŏnsan in 1880 and Inch'ŏn in 1883. Significantly, even after Japan opened a permanent legation in Hansŏng (present-day Seoul) in 1880, no corresponding Korean diplomatic presence was established in Tokyo. Chosŏn's relations with Japan were handled by Japanese diplomats in Korea, not by Chosŏn diplomats in Japan. Japan also resisted all Chosŏn attempts to establish a customs service or to otherwise monitor, regulate, or tax its trade with Japan. In short, the 1876 Treaty of Kanghwa did not usher in Chosŏn's independence or gain for it full membership in the family of nations.[33] In fact, Chosŏn did not sign treaties or enter into diplomatic relations with any other state until 1882. Even then, it continued to engage in tributary relations with the Qing empire.

Chosŏn began to extend its diplomatic relations in 1882, negotiating its first treaties with the United States, Great Britain, and Germany. While none of these treaties explicitly invoked any concept of Korean independence, they all implied the sovereign equality of the rulers and states on whose behalf the treaties were negotiated and signed by their duly accredited plenipotentiaries.[34] The conclusion of treaties with Russia and Italy in 1884, with France in 1886, and with others later would appear to be unequivocal evidence of Chosŏn's full sovereignty and participation in the modern family of nations. Yet Chosŏn's actual interactions with these states were fairly one-sided. Foreign powers established embassies and legations in the Korean capital, but reciprocity was much slower in coming. Furthermore, the Chosŏn government's range of free action in the arena of foreign relations was limited by most favored nation clauses in all its treaties, obliging Chosŏn to grant to all what it granted to one. Even more telling—and it is something to which the actual texts of the treaties make no reference—are the negotiation processes that resulted in the conclusion of the 1882 treaties. All three treaties were negotiated not in Korea but in the Chinese coastal city of Tianjin, and not by Chosŏn diplomats but by Qing officials led by Li Hongzhang. The Qing conducted these negotiations with the objective of preventing any one foreign power from emerging predominant in Korea. For their part, the foreign diplomats appear to have chosen to ignore whom they were negotiating with, while the Qing delegation seemed willing to maintain the fiction that it was with Chosŏn. Thus, whereas Li and his delegation insisted on conducting the negotiations, they exited the venue for the final signing.[35] The US delegation probably comforted itself with its success in excluding from the treaty text a clause explicitly declaring Korea to be a Qing vassal, which Li had demanded.[36]

The fact that the Qing mediated Chosŏn's first treaties with the outside world not only tells us that Chosŏn was not enjoying a role consonant with its apparent status as a sovereign state but shows as well that, far from being ignorant of or hostile to the European international law and system of international relations, Qing officials were willing to use treaties to their own advantage. Like any imperialist power, the Qing acted in its own interest. Li Hongzhang negotiated treaties that blocked any one state from gaining undue power in Korea by playing one power off against the other ("attack one poison with another poison," as he put it)[37] and ensured that benefits to Korea did not clash with Qing interests. At the same time, however, noting the inequality of the treaties the Qing itself had in the past been coerced into signing with the West, Li pushed for provisions that dampened such inequality in the treaties he negotiated for Chosŏn. He did so, for example, by stipulating an end to extraterritoriality and keeping tariff rates higher there than anywhere else in East Asia.[38]

Qing concern to buffer Korea from the unequal treaties under which the Qing state suffered should not blind us to the fact that the latter too was an imperialist power and would use whatever tools were necessary to protect and promote its interests in Chosŏn. Thus, soon after his representatives negotiated the treaties with the United States, Britain, and Germany, the emperor dispatched three thousand troops to Chosŏn to help put down a military mutiny in the capital, Hansông. After occupying the capital, the Qing stationed some of its commanders and troops there to play significant roles in the security and domestic affairs of the country in the years that followed. The Qing also immediately set out to negotiate its own agreements and treaties with Chosŏn. The two most significant were the "Regulations for Maritime and Overland Trade between Chinese and Korean Subjects" and the "Twenty-Four Rules for the Traffic on the Frontier between Liaotung and Corea," negotiated in 1882 and 1883.[39] Both included pointed declarations of continued Qing suzerainty over Chosŏn. They also formally asserted a variety of newer unequal privileges for Qing subjects in Chosŏn, including extraterritoriality, the right to establish and administer concessions in Korean treaty ports, and the provision of much lower tariff rates on Qing-Korean trade. The Qing had learned to use the new instrument of treaties to its advantage.

The governments in Washington, London, and Berlin studiously ignored the provisions declaring Qing suzerainty, despite the fact that they were a challenge to the treaties they had just concluded with Chosŏn and to the principle of sovereign equality generally. They did complain, however, that the special tariff provisions the Qing had negotiated for itself contravened those treaty terms.[40] The Japanese foreign minister protested that "China intended to assume great powers of control over Corea, and to secure exclusive commercial privileges in that country," and he demanded similar tariff rates for Japanese goods.[41] The foreign powers' insistence on the application of the most favored nation clauses in their treaties with Chosŏn resulted eventually in extending the same low tariff rates the Qing enjoyed to all of them: a victory for equal treatment but a loss for Qing claims of special privilege, not to mention Korean sovereignty. Interestingly, by invoking the 1882 and 1883 treaties, including those concluded between the Qing and Chosŏn, to push for lower tariff rates, foreign states not only recognized the legitimacy of all those treaties but also, at least implicitly, acknowledged the continuation of Qing suzerainty over its vassal, since that was reaffirmed in the Qing-Chosŏn treaties.

The solution for most foreign states was to ignore the issue and tolerate a state of affairs in which Korea was recognized to be a Qing vassal while at the same time being a sovereign state capable of negotiating treaties and maintaining diplomatic relations with Western powers. As long as foreign officials and merchants enjoyed their special access and privileges in Korea, most expressed little interest in supporting Western-style independence for it. As one official instruction to American diplomats unambiguously stated, "the agitation of the subject of Corea's complete independence of China, by representatives of the United States is neither desirable nor beneficial."[42] Not every foreigner agreed. Some, particularly advisers to the Chosŏn king, sought to promote Korean independence and reject Qing claims to suzerainty. For example, the American Owen Nickerson Denny, who served as an adviser to the Chosŏn court from 1886, urged Korea to push to establish permanent legations in Washington and other capitals as part of a general strategy to "prick the vassalage bubble" of Qing claims.[43] This view was acknowledged on a more general level. Secretary of State Thomas Francis Bayard wrote, "The reciprocal sending and receiving of diplomatic and consular officers is provided for in the treaty between the United States and Corea. No act of national sovereignty is more express and decided than this."[44]

The Qing did not firmly object to Korea's first legation abroad, established in Tokyo in 1887. Although its representative in Korea, Yuan Shikai, did protest when the intention of establishing a legation in Washington was announced, the objection was not absolute. So long as the Korean envoy agreed to be accompanied by the Qing minister to the United States upon his first official meeting with the US president, to consult with his Qing counterpart on matters of importance, and to accept a lower position than him at public functions, the Qing could approve the Korean venture. There is strong evidence that the Chosŏn envoy, Pak Chông-yang, was more than willing to abide by these "three protocols," as they were known. But Horace Allen, the American official tasked to advise and guide the Korean legation to Washington, steadfastly demanded that Pak reject the Qing demands, going so far as to threaten to abandon the Korean delegation if Pak did not ignore the three protocols. He also informed Pak that "the King would surely decapitate him" if he complied with the Qing demands.[45] Pak succumbed to Allen's pressure and refused to visit the Qing legation before calling on the US State Department and President Grover Cleveland.

The effort to establish a diplomatic legation in Washington raises interesting issues regarding the nature of the modern system of international relations of the time. First, the push for establishing a legation strongly suggests that treaties alone were not considered sufficient to establish and maintain a country's sovereignty in the face of contradictory positions on its status. Denny made this point in a dramatic fashion when he declared that the question of Korea's establishing legations abroad really was a "question as to whether or not the autonomy of this little kingdom, which is now struggling heroically to get a foot hold on the great plains of western civilization, shall be preserved or not."[46]

Second, the process by which a legation was established in Washington reveals the failure of Western participants to grasp the role of ritual in international relations. Many then and now dismiss ritual as inconsequential, part of the romance of Asian tradition and devoid of real significance for substantive relations. This dismissal of ritual allowed Western diplomats and observers to resolve the cognitive dissonance that arose when faced with Korea's continuing practice of both negotiating treaties with Western powers (and receiving Western diplomats) *and* sending tribute missions to the Qing court. Many Westerners simply dismissed the latter as inconsequential, as a form of Asian courtesy that had no bearing on the standards by which foreign relations were determined or judged. This dismissal allowed Westerners not only to ignore the implications of Chosŏn's continued practice of sending tribute to Beijing but also to do the same for Chosŏn's explicit statements acknowledging its status as a Qing tributary. Such was the case in 1882 when the Chosŏn court attached a separate letter to the text of its first treaties with the United States, Britain, and Germany expressly declaring this. Many dismissed the significance of the letter. As the American minister in Beijing, John Russell Young, wrote, "There would be no end of trouble if we ventured into the atmosphere of romance and hyperbole which surround these Oriental claims to sovereignty."[47]

But ritual did matter—to all the participants, not just the "Oriental" ones. At stake was clarifying not just Korea's international status but also whose rituals would take precedence. For Pak to visit President Cleveland without a Qing official was in fact a form of ritual that mattered as much to Americans as it did to the Qing. The historical record is silent on where Pak sat at banquets, but it does show that whatever the intentions of the Chosŏn government, the legation did little to help Chosŏn's international standing in the minds of the Americans. Whereas one story in the *New York Times* argued that the legation amounted to "a practical assertion of complete independence from China," another queried the significance of the report that King Kojong had "humbly begged" for permission from the Qing emperor before sending the legation.[48] But the number of media reports discussing Korea's international status was dwarfed by those concerned with the appearance, dress, accouterments, and behavior of Pak and his entourage and indicates that even properly conducted rituals were not sufficient to overcome American condescension, racism, and apathy. One article describing the all-important first visit to President Cleveland was more interested in what the Koreans were wearing—"in full dress, their silks richer, and more voluminous, their smiles more serene and their hats odder and taller than ever"—than in what they were doing.[49] Even stories that hailed the diplomatic significance of the legation often couched that significance in terms that made their praise of Korea backhanded at best, implying that Koreans had many more steps to take before being admitted to the ranks of the "advanced civilizations."[50] The American press's and public's perceptions aside, Chosŏn's international status remained ambiguous in the 1876–1894 period. It was simultaneously regarded as an autonomous, if not fully sovereign, member of the international community and as a tributary of the Qing.

The ambiguity of Korea's international status in general and of the Sino-Korean relationship in particular was shattered when Meiji Japan provoked war with the Qing empire in 1894 over who actually controlled Korea. Dramatic Japanese victories not only ended the Qing military presence in Korea but resulted in a series of treaties and proclamations that, taken together, spelled out Korea's status as an independent, sovereign nation. Within a week of King Kojong's being taken prisoner by Japanese troops, the Chosŏn government renounced its tributary status and repudiated all its treaties with the Qing.[51] Three weeks after the official declaration of war, Chosŏn announced an alliance with Japan aimed at expelling the Qing from Korea, using the term *tongnip* (Chinese *duli*), "independence," for the first time.[52] In the months that followed, King Kojong, under considerable Japanese pressure, continued to proclaim Korea's full independence and to reject any and all Chinese claims to suzerainty.[53] Tribute missions to Beijing as well as the use of the Qing calendar came to an end, and Korea's status of kingdom was elevated to empire. In 1897 King Kojong became Emperor Kwangmu of the Korean polity rechristened as the "Han Great State."[54] The 1895 Treaty of Shimonoseki between the Qing and Japan ended the First Sino-Japanese War, and subsequent Russian, British, and Korean treaties with Japan all emphasized Korea's independence.[55]

Both the ritual practices that animated the earlier Qing-Chosŏn relationship and the underlying assumptions of hierarchy that underpinned them were swept away. It is less clear whether what replaced the system of tribute relations actually amounted to Westphalian sovereignty and equality.

A range of proclamations, statements, and treaties projected Korea as a fully independent and sovereign nation, but the totality of those treaties also conveys that in reality Korea's independence was less than complete. This was the era of imposed or unequal treaties by which stronger powers secured one-sided privileges and prerogatives in Asia, as they did elsewhere, including extraterritoriality, self-governing concessions, and foreign control over tariffs, customs revenue, and even some of the finances of Asian governments. This is what happened in Korea. The very same treaties that established Korean sovereignty also abridged it, for the unequal privileges that the Qing had enjoyed as the suzerain in Korea were replaced by similar privileges of Western powers and Japan, prompting Denny, the adviser to the Korean court, to ask, "Would it not irresistibly follow that [Korea] would have as many suzerains as she has treaties?"[56]

In the years that followed, Japan set out to assert formal colonial rule over Korea. In the wake of its second major assault on the Asian mainland, the Russo-Japanese War (1904–1905), it proceeded to dismantle Korean sovereignty and ultimately the Korean state itself. The dramatic shift from guaranteeing the independence of Korea, written into the 1904 Japan-Korea protocol, to abrogating Korean independence by turning it into a Japanese protectorate in 1905 was accepted by every major power whose treaties with Korea had recognized its sovereignty. Most were quick to downgrade the status of their legations and withdraw their ambassadors despite Korea's pleas for support for its treaty-guaranteed independence. In 1907, when Emperor Kwangmu sent a delegation to the Hague Peace Conference to make the case for Korean independence, Japan's representatives called for its rejection, arguing that the peace conference could be attended only by representatives of independent nations.[57] World opinion conceded the point, and the Koreans were branded as "troublemakers" and shut out of the proceedings.[58] As Alexis Dudden has so pithily put it, "in the summer of 1907, the world declared Korea illegal."[59]

Korea's supposed entry into the family of nations was thus a process of replacing its old, "Asian" status as a Qing tributary with the new, "international" status of Japanese colony. Virtually every step of the treaty-making processes and the establishment of legations that would ostensibly secure Korea's independence was fraught with coercion and served other powers' interests, not those of Korea. In the age of imperialism, there as elsewhere, force rather than diplomacy drove the changes in international relations. As the influential Japanese thinker Fukuzawa Yukichi phrased it, "a hundred volumes of international law are no match for a few cannon. A handful of friendly treaties cannot compete with a little gunpowder. Cannons and gunpowder are machines that can make principles where there were none."[60]

FROM MANDALA TO MODERNITY: THE BREAKDOWN OF IMPERIAL ORDERS

· *Alex McKay* ·

Tibet had closed its frontiers to Europeans in 1793, refusing diplomatic dealings with British India and rejecting the application in Tibet of treaties the British had concluded with the Qing without its participation. The Ganden Phodrang government chose to close its frontiers to those outside the Buddhist world, as its legitimacy depended on fulfilling its role as defender of Buddhism. After more than a century of failed efforts to establish formal relations with Tibet, the British invaded Tibet in 1903, securing militarily what they had not achieved by diplomacy. The troops that the viceroy of India sent into Tibet under the command of Colonel Younghusband overcame Tibetan resistance and took Lhasa, where the British imposed a treaty establishing diplomatic and trading relations between Great Britain and the Ganden Phodrang government of Tibet.[61] When armed resistance failed, Tibetan isolationism had to give way to the Tibetan state's first sustained interaction with Western modernity.

The Qing court, through its imperial representative stationed in Lhasa to oversee the Tibetan government, had encouraged the policy of isolation for its own interests. Uncertain of the nature of the Qing position in Tibet, Britain had acknowledged its authority there but by the end of the nineteenth century found that in practice the Qing was unable to exercise any power over the Tibetan government or enforce its treaties there.[62] The idea, commonly held in China today, that the Younghusband mission was an invasion of "China" was not shared at the time. In reality, it was the absence of meaningful Qing authority in Lhasa that led the British to treat Tibet as a distinct polity and to deal with the Tibetan government directly. And the fear that Tibet might fall under the influence of Russia, which could pose a threat to British India, was Britain's justification for its "forward" policy on its imperial frontier.

Tibet's policy of diplomatic isolation from British India was a continuation of a long-standing policy that accorded with its perceived role in the Tibetan Buddhist world. Tibet had for centuries limited its formal relations to its immediate Buddhist neighbors and to states with significant Buddhist populations that looked to Tibetan centers of the faith such as

Lhasa, Shigatse, Sakya, and Ralung. Of particular importance to the north and east were the relations it maintained with Mongols/Mongolia and with Buddhist regions of the Russian empire, as well as with the Manchu court, also considered part of the Buddhist world. To the south, the connections between Lhasa and the governments of the Himalayan states, such as Ladakh, Bushahr, Nepal, Sikkim, and Bhutan, were maintained by regular diplomatic communications. In addition, individual Tibetan hierarchs maintained spiritual ties with significant authorities in India, as the Panchen Lama did with the maharaja of Benares. States with which Lhasa maintained regular communications, such as the Qing, Bhutan, and Nepal, kept resident diplomats in Lhasa, while others sent regular missions to the Tibetan capital, as did Ladakh. Rarely if ever did the Tibetan government communicate with states beyond the Tibetan Buddhist world. In one such rare relationship in the early twentieth century, Lhasa sent a trusted clerical agent of the Dalai Lama on missions as its ambassador to meet the czar of Russia in Saint Petersburg.[63]

Given the interweaving of secular and religious government, diplomatic contacts were also religious ones and at times doubled as pastoral missions by elite clerics to Tibetan Buddhist communities not under Lhasa's direct sway. Not until July 1942 did Tibet establish a Department of Foreign Affairs, which served as a conduit for relations with some states outside the Buddhist world, namely British India and the United States. Essentially, therefore, Tibet maintained layers of religious relationships that could be deployed as appropriate in foreign relations that were themselves shaped by its Buddhist worldview. Even for the critical negotiations with Younghusband, following the British invasion and the Thirteenth Dalai Lama's flight into exile, it was a highly respected spiritual figure, the abbot of Ganden Monastery, who was given the power to negotiate, not someone with any experience of secular diplomacy.

The Tibetan Buddhist worldview placed Lhasa at the center of a Buddhist world in which non-Buddhist states were beyond the boundaries of the so-called mandala of state. The mandala was simultaneously the realm of the bodhisattva Avalokitesvara (the patron deity of the land of Tibet, whose bodily manifestation was the Dalai Lama). The Tibetan view of their state's place in the world and of interpolity relations based on it starkly contrasted with the assumptions of the modern nation-state model. The differences became clear when Tibetans sought to present their country as a sovereign state early in the twentieth century. Tibet's political structure, like its culture, was shaped by its Buddhist ideology. In Buddhist cosmology, a state was defined by its center, not by its borders. Tibet's territory was defined by religion, not by secular forms of border-claiming. Its

sovereignty permeated outward from its center until it merged impercep-
tibly with the fringes of neighboring states.[64] Tibet had frontiers, but not
precisely demarcated borders in the sense of lines fixed on a map. Its frontiers marked zones of transition from one sphere of authority to another,
which is how spaces in a mandala work.[65] It is not surprising, then, that
there was no mention of Tibet's borders in the proclamation made by the
Thirteenth Dalai Lama in 1901, even though its intention was to define
Tibet to an external audience.[66] Similarly, the Dalai Lama's 1913 proclamation, which Tibetans regard as their declaration of independence, did
not define those borders although it implied that they were known.[67] Even
in the 1940s the Tibetan state had territorial anomalies inconsistent with
the modern international order, including overlapping sovereignties, some
claimed or theoretical, others real and negotiated.[68]

Borders in the modern sense did exist in some places, usually in the
form of a geographical marker such as a river or a pass, and there are
indications that certain mountains were understood as frontier markers.
More commonly, edges between sovereignties were border towns, such
as Dartsendo/Dajianlu, on the eastern border with the Chinese province
of Sichuan, and Phari, at the head of the Chumbi Valley bordering on
Bhutan.[69] Another such site, Lingtu, on the frontier with Sikkim, demonstrates the difficulties involved in a border that was not defined by international agreement with a European power. Tibetans considered Lingtu to be
within their territory, but the British, drawing their frontier on the understanding that the Himalayan watershed was the border, placed it within
the state of Sikkim, which they claimed as a British protectorate. Thus,
when Tibet stationed troops there to protect their frontier in 1888, British
forces were sent to expel them.

Tibetans had little understanding of British India outside the Buddhist
cosmological framework that placed them at the center of the mandala
and featured India only as the Buddhist Holy Land, the source of their
spiritual heritage and of the great teachers that brought the sacred scriptures to Tibet, and therefore as a place of pilgrimage. There were individual Tibetans who were interested in the non-Buddhist world and who
recorded their views of that world, but their understandings were also almost entirely shaped by Buddhist Abhidharmakośa cosmology rather than
geography.[70] "Facts" could not alter the cosmic reality.[71]

Tibet's relationship with the Manchu court was conceived in terms of
the *chö-yön* relationship discussed in detail in chapter 4. This relationship
was clearly located within a Tibetan Buddhist conceptual schema and did
not correspond to a territorial model of state sovereignty compatible with
the new international order emanating from Europe. Rather, it was—from

the Tibetan perspective—an affirmation that the Qing emperor should be responsible for the protection of the Dalai Lama and, by implication, the Ganden Phodrang government and state. That duty was breached when Qing troops invaded and briefly occupied Lhasa in 1909, driving the Dalai Lama into exile in India.[72]

When the Manchu court was forced out of power two years later by Chinese nationalists with a republican agenda, the chö-yön relationship definitively ended. Tibet made some moves to adopt the modern state model and to endow the state with responsibility for its citizens.[73] Soon after his return to Lhasa in 1913, the Thirteenth Dalai Lama instituted modernization measures. These included the founding of the Mentsi Khang, a free traditional-medicine hospital in Lhasa, which can be regarded as an early manifestation of the reimagining of the citizen-state compact, although such an initiative was also entirely in keeping with Buddhist principles. As the requirements of modernity increasingly bore on Tibet, the Ganden Phodrang government found it difficult to shape a national identity and state in the modern sense that was simultaneously Buddhist. Abandoning the Buddhist concept of the mandala state and the traditional relationships that that framework contained was seen as threatening to the fundamental legitimacy of the concept of a Buddhist state.

The British had little understanding of Tibet's Buddhist worldview and conceptualization of its relationship with the Manchu emperor within the chö-yön model, and so they regarded borders differently. As their power expanded northward from their eighteenth-century base in Bengal, their fundamental concern was the security of their Indian borders. They saw the Himalayan watershed as a natural northern boundary. Early on, toward the end of the eighteenth century, the security of those borders had been challenged by the rise of the Gorkha kingdom of Nepal, making conflict almost inevitable. As the Gorkha kingdom spread to the borders of Bhutan in the first decade of the nineteenth century, the British feared an alliance between Bhutan and greater Nepal. When its clash with Nepal came in 1815, British India allied with Sikkim, which had fallen to the Gorkhas, and the territory of which formed a wedge between Nepal and Bhutan. That alliance gave the British lasting influence over Sikkim. When they emerged victorious from the war with Nepal, they gained control not only over Nepal but also over Kumaon and Garwhal. Following the First Anglo-Burmese War of 1824–1826, Assam also became part of Britain's empire. Twenty years later, victory in the First Anglo-Sikh War gave the British authority over Kashmir and Ladakh as well. Bhutan lost territory in the plains of Cooch Behar to the British in the war of 1865, and when Sikkim turned out to be a problematic ally, the British eventually occupied it in

1888–1889. As a result, by the end of the nineteenth century, British India effectively shared more than two thousand miles of frontier with Tibet.

Although the British and Tibetans had little understanding of each other's worldviews and conceptual schemas, the Tibetan and the British Indian polities were not entirely dissimilar. Tibet was not simply a centralized state with a hierarchy of authority culminating in the Dalai Lama. Rather, it consisted of a complex web of vertical and horizontal, secular and religious, and regional and social-class layers, without precisely delineated boundaries. So too, British India was not a centralized polity in the sense that the viceroy could claim to occupy the apex of a pyramid of authority extending across the subcontinent. It was an empire consisting of a complex array of actors and circumstances dictating a variety of structures and processes of power. There were numerous layers of authority, and a series of checks and balances operated both horizontally and vertically. Additionally, the viceroy was under the control of the British government at Whitehall, yet that authority was not lineal, for rule over India was partly devolved through a ruling council under the secretary of state for India, who was a member of the British cabinet. Within India, British authority was further divided between an India under direct British rule and an India under the Princely or Residency system, by which local rulers enjoyed considerable local autonomy in return for acknowledging British control over foreign policy and defense. Even in areas under direct British rule there were further gradations of power. There were "non-regulation districts," for example, where local autonomy and culture were acknowledged and exemptions granted to the application of laws pertaining at the center. (Darjeeling and surrounds made up one such district in the British-ruled province of Bengal.) So the idea of a monolithic British empire in India is untenable. Power was fragmented and could be contested at every level.

Far from being centralized modern states with a pyramidal structure of law and government, therefore, both Tibet and British India were polities in which power was devolved and anomalies allowed. The British may have espoused a theoretical model of the nation-state very different from that of the Tibetan mandala of state, but in actuality they operated via similar arrangements of empire: a center whose authority was honored but not exclusive, a body of multiethnic subjects submitting nominally to a unified cultural-linguistic core, and a sovereignty whose boundaries were fluid and open to alteration—not unlike a Great State.[74] British theorists like Lord Curzon, viceroy of India, liked to stress that scientifically determined boundaries "sanctified in International Law" were "an agency of peace."[75] But in fact the British were willing to tolerate considerable delay in getting from an imperial model of soft frontiers to a modern nation-state model of hard boundaries when more flexible entities such as protectorates (such as Sikkim) or buffer states (such as Nepal) better separated them from other imperial adversaries. To quote Indian Foreign Secretary Alfred Lyall, "The true frontier of the British dominion in Asia . . . does not tally with the outer edge of . . . territory over which we exercise administrative jurisdiction." In his understanding, "The true frontier includes . . . large regions over which the English crown has established protectorates."[76] Britain did not consider the northern frontier states of British India to be nation-states in the sense dictated by modern international law; they were buffers between British and Russian imperial power. Tibet presents an even more complex case. Both British India and the Manchu Qing considered Tibet a buffer state, contesting control while at the same time remaining wary of a hypothetical Russian threat.

This British imperial model was not totally foreign to Inner and East Asian polities. Under the mandala state system, Sikkim, Mustang, and even Amdo as well as the kingdoms in Kham were beyond the direct administration of Tibet while in many ways serving as protectorates or buffer states for it. The Manchus similarly surrounded their empire with such buffer polities as Tibet, Mongolia, Xinjiang, and kingdoms in Yunnan. Both the Qing and the Tibetan polities resembled the British empire in India far more than they resembled modern nation-states. This commonality was something the British recognized and understood. Thus, while the nation-state was becoming the dominant model in much of the world, in this corner of Asia at least until the 1940s, British India, Tibet, and the Qing and then the Republic of China were still operating under the model of empire, not nation-state. That model had allowed for the distinct statehood of Tibet and for the Qing court's role as benefactor and protector of the Tibetan Buddhist system and state at the same time. The British did not try to impose nation-state status on Tibet: their concern was the security of their northern imperial border, best served by the system of protectorates (polities under direct influence or supervision of the empire) and buffer states (polities able to maintain a separate existence between powerful neighbors). They had no need for the installation of European-style independent states.

The variety of political formations that developed as part of these imperial models eventually needed to be made to fit into the modern state system, either as independent nation-states or as integral parts of such states. Nepal was allowed to exist as a buffer state and then to transform into an independent nation-state. So too was Bhutan, though it ceded its defense to Indian troops stationed on its territory. Sikkim, also effectively a British and then Indian protectorate, retained its autonomous status as a princely state until the mid-1970s, when it was incorporated as a state within a federal India. Kashmir, a princely state left largely to its own devices by the British, also became a state of India, while parts of its territory came under control of Pakistan and China. Broadly brushed, the modern status of the former Himalayan frontier states appears to have depended on their value to the British in protecting India. In Inner Asia, some buffer states, in particular Mongolia, became independent, but the rest were absorbed. Xinjiang reverted from the Russian empire (via its modern-day avatar as the USSR) to the People's Republic of China, while the buffer state Tibet, where the British held a dominating but not controlling influence from 1912 to 1947, was seized by the PRC soon after the latter's founding.

Although Tibetans did not entirely abandon the idea that a traditional teacher-benefactor relationship could be established with China, the intention that Tibet should establish itself as an independent state was clear.[77] The Kashag, Tibet's ministerial council, informed the viceroy of British India in October 1912 that, as the Manchu empire had disappeared, "we have decided to separate altogether from them."[78] Similar communications were sent to other governments as well. Although Tibet remained effectively independent from then until 1951, it did not sufficiently reformulate its polity to conform to the nation-state paradigm. Tibetans tentatively explored the steps necessary to join the community of modern nation-states. They investigated joining the League of Nations and the International Postal Union. They also created a flag and adopted a national anthem, using the tune of "God Save the King"![79] But interest in such symbols was not sustained, and Tibet instead sought to craft a unique status as "a purely religious country" within the international system,[80] arguing that "there is only one nation which is dedicated to the well-being of humanity in the world and that is the religious land of Tibet."[81] In this context, Tibetan neutrality in World War II can be seen not only as an assertion of independence from China but as an expression of its unique, even modernist, Buddhist identity.

If the British had taken on the role of benefactor and protector and created a status for Tibet akin to that of Bhutan, a status that the Ganden Phodrang government would probably have accepted,[82] things might have turned out differently. But Britain was unwilling to bear the costs of taking on that role or to encourage Tibet to seek formal independence. As the foreign secretary of the government of British India explained in 1935, "The large commercial interests of His Majesty's Government in China make it necessary to subordinate policy in Tibet to the general policy of the

British Government in China and to avoid incurring the hostility . . . of [its] government." But in view of the new Soviet threat, he cautioned, the "maintenance of an independent and autonomous Tibet" was preferable to "resumption of effective Chinese control in Tibet."[83] World War II, the subsequent British withdrawal from India, and the victory of the Communist forces in China put an end to this possibility.

Christiaan Klieger has argued that the system of a Tibetan Buddhist state could not exist without a patron.[84] Melvyn Goldstein has differently proposed that that system was headed for collapse owing to the declining availability of estates to support the growing nobility.[85] Yet there may be other grounds on which to imagine how a Buddhist state could maintain its existence on Buddhist terms in the modern world. Bhutan's concept of Gross National Happiness comes to mind as a suggestive possibility. This concept, developed by Bhutan's King Jigme Singye Wangchuck in the 1970s as an alternative to GNP, defines the state's policy in terms of holistic development and progress, giving equal importance to noneconomic aspects of well-being, such as psychological well-being, health, education, time use, cultural diversity and resilience, good governance, community vitality, ecological diversity and resilience, and living standards.[86] Despite the nationalist aspects of the concept, it has been taken up in a wider critique of Western civilization as part of a search for alternative models of development. Bhutan today finds a sympathetic hearing for its claim to a unique and spiritual status and prides itself on having remained a "Dharma kingdom"—an option, it can be argued, that is made possible by India's assumption of responsibility for that state's defense. Early last century, Tibet had also sought nation-state status on its own terms as a Buddhist nation. It did so without fully engaging with the international community, however, and to some extent such engagement was also prevented by Britain and China. Unlike Bhutan, when British imperial interest in Tibet ended upon their withdrawal from India, Tibet did not come under India's protection. Instead, it was left to defend its fragile independence in a fast-changing Asian landscape.

CHAPTER SEVEN

THE PRESENCE
OF THE PAST

This inquiry into the historical nature of polities and their relations in Inner and East Asia was conceived as a case study, first, to understand how states in this region were ruled and have interacted historically and, second, to develop a methodology to address the impact that incompatible perceptions of a shared past have on conflicts and on efforts to prevent and resolve them. Our most basic finding has been that meaningful analysis of historical and, to a certain extent also, current interpolity relations in Inner and East Asia requires that we use an entirely different lens than we are accustomed to. A prerequisite has been that we shed the political and legal baggage of modern concepts of statehood, sovereignty, independence, and the like and therefore not use those terms unqualifiedly. Doing so yields a different and more accurate picture of the past, which allows for a better-informed assessment of assertions made in support of claims to territory, authority, and related political projects in this part of the world. Moreover, although modern international law has deauthorized the norms and principles that once shaped polities and legitimized the multiple laws of nations that ordered their relations, we reckon that the assumptions and beliefs on which they were based continue to play a role and still motivate the conduct of states and of nonstate actors today. Some of the principles themselves continue to surface as shaping influences in the present, not least in the People's Republic of China, where some recent foreign policy postures appear to challenge the universality of the existing international order, which China may never have wholly considered its own. As the PRC is now the main regional power, its testing of the limits of playing by its own rules will have a major impact on shaping the future order in Asia and beyond, which may show some similarities to the Sinic legal order of the imperial past.

Looking through this different lens has not only yielded insights into the historical experience of Asia but furnished a broadened base from which to posit fresh suggestions for analyzing how history underpins competing claims in conflicts, the main subject of this chapter. Our purpose is to stimulate thinking in the fields of international relations and international legal history that might then provide new insights for resolving interstate and intrastate conflicts in Inner and East Asia.

To fully grasp the role history plays in conflicts and in efforts to resolve them requires an appreciation of the very different worlds that existed in this region between the thirteenth and early twentieth centuries, each with its distinct center of civilizational authority, its own worldview, and its own mostly sacred sources and ideologies of legitimacy of rulers that flowed from that worldview. Each produced a distinct set of principles, norms, and rules governing relations among polities, and the resulting international legal orders were completely different from the universal order that is assumed to govern interstate relations today. Although these worlds were very different from each other, they influenced one another and at times overlapped in some respects. We believe this framework is useful not just for analyzing historical Asian relations but also for recognizing how different historiographies developed and why there are today such different, and sometimes conflicting, interpretations of relations that existed among these polities in the past.

That actual historical experiences and the systems that shaped them differed is not surprising. But appreciating *how* they differed is essential for understanding how their invocation and reinterpretation in terms of the Westphalian principles embodied in modern international law produced, and continue to produce today, irreconcilable views on entitlements that cause serious tensions in the region and stand in the way of resolving some protracted conflicts. On a practical level, therefore, we hope that an awareness of the distinctiveness of the three legally ordered systems that governed rule, legitimacy, and interpolity relations, as well as of the scars left by the tumultuous events accompanying their conversion to the alien single construct of the modern territorial nation-state and interstate relations, will persuade policy- and decision-makers to appreciate the role these factors continue to play in the region.

CONFLICTS AND THE DEPLOYMENT OF HISTORY

In the extensive regions of Asia covered in this book, numerous states and their populations are affected by protracted conflicts and by tensions that can easily flare up and turn violent. In most cases, positions are taken on a certain reading of history, and history is invoked to demonstrate or deny the legitimacy of conflicting claims. Especially in conflicts centered on identity and territory, competing views of history constitute a formidable obstacle to their resolution. The issues at stake are in the present, but often the origins of the dispute and the emotions that feed it reside in the past. This is as much the case in relations between states as it is within states between the government and one or more distinct population groups or between such groups.

Political leaders of parties in conflict invoke history in a variety of ways as they address domestic as well as international audiences to garner support for their positions or engage in negotiations. Sometimes a specific historical event is made part of the agenda; sometimes wholesale acceptance of one party's historical narrative is demanded, exceptionally as a precondition to discussions on other matters. Even when history is not deployed overtly, deep-seated sentiments of victimization, righteousness, and entitlement rooted in historical perceptions and nourished by historical narratives often underlie parties' claims or are fanned to mobilize support for them. Some claims to sovereignty, borders, or the validity of past agreements are presented in terms of today's international law but are actually based on historical arguments. Others appear to be grounded in principles and assumptions that derive from earlier Asian legal orders, even though the language used to advance them is entirely modern. When claimants approach such disputes using different logics—for example, one based on today's legal system and the other on a premodern legal order—or when they use logics that are based on different premodern legal orders, this can produce irreconcilable outcomes. Our purpose in this book is not to delve deeply into the substance of current Asian conflicts and tensions but to illustrate, by way of some examples, the role that history plays. In doing so, we do not attempt to be comprehensive in describing the many actors and factors at play in these conflicts. Instead, we focus only on the manner in which history is deployed in them in order to reflect on the conditioning effects of the way in which history and historical narratives are produced, presented, and used.

A prime example is the conflict regarding sovereignty over the islands, territorial waters, and seabeds of the South China Sea. Vietnam, the PRC, and to some extent Taiwan base their claims on their respective historical narratives. This is true also of the international law claims they make, which they argue by means of evidence they derive from history. As the PRC asserts its perceived right to control this large navigable area, it openly challenges not just the countries on its rim, including Vietnam, the Philippines, and Brunei, but also the United States, which currently predominates in the western Pacific. As naval vessels are deployed and tensions rise, so has the danger of one or more parties using force in a way that could trigger armed conflict. Because of the natural resources the area contains and the strategic importance of its sea routes, all parties make claims to sovereignty over the islands.

Vietnam argues that its Nguyen dynasty controlled the Paracel and Spratly Islands already in the seventeenth century, and its government uses contemporary documents and maps to show that it regularly sent ships and men to some of the islands back then. Using such evidence, and also documentation from the eighteenth and nineteenth centuries, Vietnam further contends that it maintained its claim to the islands throughout, except under French colonial domination, when France administered its rights. Following French rule, South Vietnam and then a united Vietnam continued to assert sovereignty over the islands, even when the PRC occupied some of the Paracel Islands in 1956 and the entire archipelago in 1974.[1]

The PRC also grounds its claim in history but in addition appears to found its claim to modern sovereignty on the traditional Sinic concept of "all-under-heaven." Beijing claims China was first to discover and name the islands, in the Han dynasty, and argues that maps from the Song dynasty forward show the South China Sea islands as belonging to it.[2] It further claims that the voyages of Chinese mariners and their accounts, including Zheng He, referred to in chapter 3, demonstrate that this territory was subject to China. China's historical claim was first formulated in the early twentieth century and crafted "to produce a sense that the island groups were 'naturally' a part of China and always had been," as Bill Hayton has recently observed. Chinese officials at the time attempted "to present their 'all under heaven' sense of territorial entitlement within the rubric of 'international' attitudes towards sovereignty."[3] This continues to be the thrust of the PRC's argument, which has been given shape on its maps in the form of a maritime boundary, referred to as the "nine-dash line," dating back to 1936 and used a decade later to assert its claim. This U-shaped line runs along the coastlines of the Philippines, Brunei, Malaysia, and Vietnam. Hanging from China's southern shore and Taiwan like a fishing net, it holds more than 80 percent of the South China Sea and the islands, reefs, and shoals contained in it. In 2009 the PRC filed the map with the United Nations as evidence of its sovereignty, and since 2012 it is displayed on PRC passports.[4]

Similar elements appear in PRC arguments in favor of its claims to other territories on its borders. The PRC claims ninety thousand square kilometers of territory south of the Himalayan watershed in today's Arunachal Pradesh in northeast India, over which it waged an inconclusive war in 1962. This claim is an extension of its historical claim to Tibet. Tawang and parts of Arunachal Pradesh were Tibetan borderlands that became a part of India under the 1914 agreement between Tibet and Britain, which delimited the border between Tibet and British India. India confirmed the validity of this agreement when it achieved independence in 1947. The PRC, however, insists that Tibet did not have the authority to conclude treaties at the time, on the grounds that it was, and had for centuries been, part of China, a claim that appears to be mostly based on a reinterpretation of historical Inner and East Asian relations and on projections of modern notions of sovereignty and political geography onto the past.[5] Tensions flared in April 2017, as the Chinese government warned India of serious consequences for facilitating the Dalai Lama's visit to this predominantly Tibetan Buddhist region, which the PRC calls southern Tibet.[6] If India and the PRC go to war again, according to some security experts, it will be over this issue.[7]

The PRC has made the acceptance of its position on the historical status of Tibet a critical issue in the decades-old conflict over its rule of Tibet. It demands the Dalai Lama's recognition of its claim that Tibet has been a part of China since antiquity as a precondition to substantive talks with him.[8] The Dalai Lama has not been willing to meet this requirement because, in his view, it does not accord with the history of Tibet and its relations.

In yet other current conflicts—between Japan and China over the Senkaku Islands and between Cambodia and Thailand over Preah Vihear—the parties not only use historical arguments to bolster their case but also mobilize sentiments of victimization and entitlement arising from historical events. Let us briefly consider each of these in turn.

Japan's claim to sovereignty over the Senkaku Islands is based mostly on the application of modern international law, which it was already keen to apply in the late nineteenth century as part of its transformation into a Western-style "civilized nation." In contrast, the PRC relies on historical arguments similar to those used to validate its claim to South China Sea islands. Japan dates its sovereignty over the Senkaku Islands to 1884, when its government surveyed them and a year later erected a sovereignty marker there for the purpose. This was just five years after it annexed the Ryukyu kingdom, which was a de facto dependency of Kyushu but until then had paid tribute to both the Meiji and Qing emperors.[9] Those two island chains—the Senkakus and Ryukyus—form an almost continuous porous barrier, as it were, stretching from the main islands of Japan to Taiwan and separating the Chinese mainland from the Pacific Ocean, which makes control of them strategically important. The PRC claims that the Diaoyu Islands (its name for the Senkaku Islands) have belonged to China since ancient times, as the waters around them were used as fishing grounds administered from Taiwan. It contends that the islands should have been returned to China together with Taiwan when Japan was made to hand over Taiwan after World War II. But the conflict, which has recently seen an escalation and has prompted the United States to reconfirm its commitment to defend Japan's possession of the islands, is not just about territory, strategic advantage, or economic resources. It unleashes strong nationalist sentiments in both the PRC and Japan. Beijing appears to portray this conflict very much in terms of redressing the decades of humiliation the Chinese suffered at the hands of an expansionistic and, in its view, upstart imperial Japan intent on destroying the regional order of which China had been the undisputed center and pinnacle. The islands are especially symbolic in that respect, since Japan's incorporation of the Ryukyu kingdom and the cutting off of the latter's tribute relations with the Qing marked the beginning of Japan's drive for regional dominion at the expense of the Qing and then China.[10]

Regarding the second conflict, the Preah Vihear temple area was the focus of armed conflicts between Thailand and Cambodia in 1954 and again from 2008 to 2011. Although the rival claims to this border territory were argued on the basis of international law before the International Court of Justice in 1962 and again in 2011–2013, historical victimization narratives have played their part on the ground. The border was a product of territorial demarcation in 1907, in the colonial period. The French drew the boundary following survey activities by a Franco-Siamese commission. This was not entirely in accordance with the governing treaty on the matter, concluded between France and Siam (Thailand) in 1904, because it did not follow the Dangrek Mountains watershed line referred to in the agreement.[11] Nationalist fervor was stoked in both Cambodia and Thailand, using narratives of historical wrongs committed against each by the other. Past Thai invasions were depicted as having destroyed glorious Khmer empires and eventually rendered the country defenseless against French conquest. Narratives of Thailand's aggression and occupation of parts of Cambodia during World War II have also been used. Thai nationalists, for their part, portrayed *their* country as the victim of territorial theft.[12]

Profound historical consciousness resides at the core of these and other conflicts in which ethnic and national identities are inextricably intertwined with historical narratives that animate emotions of pride, injustice, victimization, loss, and righteousness. This is apparent, for example, in protracted conflicts in Myanmar between the Burman-dominated government and self-determination movements of the Shan, Karen, Mon, Karenni, and Kachin peoples. So too in Xinjiang, where Uighur movements challenge Beijing's rule; in Kashmir, where the issue is complicated by the dispute over ownership of the region by India and Pakistan; and in Northeast India, where successive Naga and other armed independence movements have engaged in decades of fighting with government forces. In processes to resolve such conflicts, perceptions of history affect both the substance and the dynamics of negotiations. Negotiators on one or both sides do not just employ historical narratives to underpin their respective claims; these narratives often touch the essence of their perception of their own identity. Challenging a historical narrative can be taken as challenging the legitimacy of who believes that narrative, either personally or as a group or nation. This has manifested in the India-Naga peace process yet to be concluded, as also in the Sino-Tibetan talks, which were discontinued in 2010. At the negotiation table, therefore, history must sometimes be understood not just as a debate about the past but equally as the negotiators' experience in the present.

The historical narratives that are propagated regarding a state's, a people's, or a minority's history and their relations with others, though often closely related to the historiographies they rely on, are composed by selecting events, episodes, and developments of the past and stringing them together to generate an explanation that serves a purpose in the present. They reveal the beliefs and perceptions of people about their history and are, at the same time, expressions of them that in turn have an impact on those beliefs and perceptions. In conflict situations and other instances when narratives are crafted to legitimize political projects, this selectiveness can be particularly pronounced. Apart from self-serving interpretations given to past events, those that are invoked are selected to support present-day objectives and are often presented in spatial and temporal isolation from circumstances that might shed a different light.

When facilitating negotiations to prevent or resolve conflicts in which parties invoke powerful, incompatible narratives to build their case, loosening the grip that such narratives have on the negotiators is a tall order. Exploring how these narratives have come about can be helpful. Placing historical events and developments upon which the parties draw to substantiate their claims in their broader context can bring to light the selectiveness that underlies their narratives. Bringing to bear a wide variety of contemporary sources to this examination can, moreover, uncover the diversity of understandings that existed at the time and help negotiators appreciate the relative nature and limitations of each narrative, thereby creating the mental and emotional space to receive new information. Placing historiographies on which the parties rely to build or validate their narratives in the context of their production generates awareness of who exactly wrote the histories, for what purposes, and on the basis of what type of information. After all, histories have not been written just to keep a record of what happened. More often than not they were commissioned by rulers to legitimize or aggrandize them, to justify wars, impose religions, and validate territorial expansion and other political projects.

Apart from looking at the production of historiography, we need to consider the circumstances in which the narratives themselves were produced. Today's narratives are created to address present conditions, including disputes for which parties seek to build a winning case. Significantly, the narratives currently in use in Inner and East Asia are to a large extent based on those that were generated to accompany the tumultuous events that took place as Asian polities transformed into nation-states, discussed in the previous chapter. They inform us about the needs they were intended to address at the time, and their persistent invocation testifies to the continuing relevance of the legacy of those events today.

Many of the narratives crafted to accompany the above-mentioned transformations contained seeds of conflict in them. Nineteenth- and early twentieth-century elites struggling to respond to internal pressures for reform and external demands for participation in the new world order needed to reinvent their states and endow them with histories that justified their existence as modern states. Once established, the latter served as vehicles for the fulfillment of national aspirations as well as for the imposition of authority over subject populations, old and new. As Prasenjit Duara has shown, these modernizing elites were keen to create "national histories" that projected current political configurations into the past in order to show that "this nation," "this state," or "this people" had always existed.[13] People could thus be conditioned to think of themselves as belonging not just to a new state but to one that embodied the same nation and the same people, even if known by different names, as had existed since the distant past on the same territory. Although important for building national cohesion, this kind of narrative tends to privilege dominant groups at the expense of less powerful ones, who are retroactively included in the history of the state as if they had always been part of it, albeit as a subnational category, or who are left out of the story altogether. Over time this may serve to solidify existing power relationships, but it has also provoked resistance, insurgency, and conflict.

To be sure, resolving conflicts requires more than a critical and empathetic assessment of the historical narratives in play. Conflicts take place in the present, in which power relations and strategic, economic, and other interests all play key roles. But when it comes to contested legitimacy to rule over a particular territory and population, evocative historical narratives that mobilize national sentiments cannot be left unaddressed. Addressing them requires understanding the assumptions that lie behind them, as well as exposing the distortions that result from projecting current political geographies, concepts, and terminologies onto the past. These common practices not only obscure and distort historical realities but can also produce irreconcilable understandings of aspects of history pertinent to the conflict.

THE GREAT REINTERPRETATION

Of all the concepts that are invoked in contests over authority, territory, and legitimacy, "sovereignty" is the most difficult and at the same time essential to address. It is politically highly charged and, when used unqualifiedly to describe the premodern past, in our case that of Asian rule and relations, can lead to serious distortions and irresoluble claims.

As we stated in the opening chapter, the modern term "sovereignty" is tied to the concept of defined territory and the right of states to exercise exclusive and supreme authority. In contrast, in historical Inner and East Asia, sovereignty was personal, hierarchical, and multiple. It was layered and could be shared. Sovereigns were not equal in power, stature, or status. Indeed, inequality was inherent in relations between rulers and hence in relations between polities. Although such relations may have entailed constraints on the exercise of authority by less powerful rulers, they did not imply an extinction of their sovereignty or the incorporation of their polities into another.

Bearing this in mind, we also found it necessary to revisit the implications of the use of the term "empire." Rather than assume that the European concept of empire necessarily applies to the forms of layered rule that existed in Inner and East Asia, we use the indigenous Asian term "Great State" (*yeke ulus, da guo, amban gurun*). The Great State concept has ancient roots but, as we have noted, was given particular meaning by Chinggis as the Yeke Mongqol ulus. This political formation, conceptualized as a form of rule over many and influence over more, became the concept that later rulers aspired to reproduce. It included direct rule, indirect rule, and vassalage. It could entail a variety of hierarchical relationships of the powerful—acting as Great Khan, Son of Heaven, or *chakravartin*—with lesser rulers, who may or may not have considered themselves as being "within" or "without" the Great State but who did recognize a closer or looser relationship with its ruler. Although the concepts of Great Khan, Son of Heaven, and *chakravartin* signified universal kingship, this did not exclude the existence of other overlords. In a sense, therefore, the universalism they represented was "finite," to borrow a term that Sugata Bose has used to describe the ancient Indian allowance for the simultaneous existence of numerous overlords "turning the wheel of *Dharma*."[14] Not unqualifiedly using "empire" encourages us to explore the nature of the polities and their relationships on their own merits and to withstand the temptation of categorizing polities in simplistic terms as being or not being "part of" or "within the borders of" a dominant polity such as the Great State.

With the European imperialist expansion in the nineteenth century, the Japanese imperial project, and the Asian decolonization struggles of the twentieth century came the greater territorial emphasis in European understandings of sovereignty and empire. This shift produced what Bose has called a "generalized cartographic anxiety over territorial possessions,"[15] requiring sharp definitions and demarcations of frontiers. Since the modern system of international law required all territory to be claimed by some state to the exclusion of others, conflicts over territory and the authority to rule inevitably ensued. Assertiveness was rewarded as some claimants expanded their territorial possessions while others could barely cope with the fundamental changes taking place around them. In regions that had been subject to overlapping spheres of authority of distant rulers and overlords or had been subject to none, attempts were now made to assert exclusive authority and demarcate borders, at times expansively. Where allegiances or loyalties of lesser rulers to greater ones and special relationships between overlords and religious leaders formed part of the fabric of interruler and interpolity relations, the new imperative drove some to claim and enforce the new concept of sovereignty over others.

The moves on the ground were accompanied by the new language of the nation-state and modern international law, intended to legitimize the transformed states and their territorial claims. Narratives were created in support of political projects, including territorial ones, invoking centuries of history, which was reinterpreted by means of this new language. Hierarchical relations and the rituals that had accompanied them were reinterpreted as evidence of past sovereignty over claimed territory, with all that this term implied in the new system. New Japanese discourses of nationalism helped shape new historical narratives throughout East Asia, as Duara has shown. Vietnamese revolutionaries, inspired by French Enlightenment thought and Marxist theories, cast their history in new ideological terms. So too Thai, Burmese, Lao, and Cambodian leaders presented their anticolonial struggles in nationalist terms and gave them corresponding histories. The new formulations were very much of the present, not the past. But while some elites were ready to participate in major intellectual and political shifts, conservative elites in Inner Asia, in particular Tibetan Buddhist clerics, feared change and resisted it, adapting only partially and grudgingly to the new circumstances. Mongols formulated nationalist discourses to animate political movements, but in Outer Mongolia and in Tibet it was primarily the forward policies of the Qing just before the demise of that state in 1911 that precipitated declarations of independent statehood and the narratives that accompanied them. Tibetans in particular held on to key elements of Tibetan Buddhist notions of governance and statehood, hoping to enter the new international order on their terms.

Narratives freshly crafted to explain the new nation-state and promote a sense of loyalty to it often drew on accounts of historical greatness as well as on modern political and philosophical discourses. As a result, the nation-state was mostly presented as the natural culmination and achievement of a long history of a people's evolutionary and civilizational development. Some were accompanied by "maps of loss" that depicted past glory, real or imagined, and included large areas outside the recognized boundaries of the state as belonging or having belonged to it. In *Siam Mapped*, Thongchai Winichakul shows how such maps created emotional effects and shaped memories, enabling the expropriation of the past in the service of present needs, including the support of claims to "recover lost territories." Winichakul examines a series of maps produced in Thailand in the 1930s and 1940s, some with evocative titles ("Demand for Return of Territories," "Map of the History of Thailand's Boundary"), that present a presupposed legitimate realm that is much larger than Thailand was at the time. Most of the losses depicted on the maps were to European powers. The purpose of their production was to inspire a sense of the greatness of the Thai people and to mobilize support for the return of lost territories. These maps conveyed the conception of a Thai nationhood and geo-body (territorial imagination) that "existed with the Thai since time immemorial," thus rejecting "any idea that nationhood was conceived only in the recent past as a result of the intercourse between the old Siam and the Western powers" and occluding the notion that the modern state was "the result of ruptures, not continuity." The *Historical Atlas of Thailand*, in which maps of this sort appeared, was distributed to schools and government offices to emphasize Thailand's ascendancy rather than fluctuations of authority, thereby conveying a sense of "the movement and growth of its body—thus nationhood—from the beginning to the present."[16]

The Qing Great State's encounter with the new international legal order in the nineteenth and early twentieth centuries was in many ways brutal, as it was for most other Asian states. But it was experienced as humiliating not only by the Qing's ruling Manchu elite but also by the Chinese elite. For the latter especially, the court's inability to safeguard the Sinic world order that placed the Son of Heaven at the top of its hierarchy and the Chinese elite at the center of its Confucian civilizational world was a particularly degrading experience. The modern international order did not acknowledge or accommodate this power structure, and its European proponents and Japan openly defied the Sinic legal order as they secured dominance in Asia under the new rules at the expense of the Qing. Following the initial allocation of blame to the Manchu court and elite for their failure to protect the empire and the Sinic order by succumbing to alien power at home and abroad, leading to Chinese calls for their ouster, revolutionary leaders of all persuasions claimed the victimization of the Qing as a humiliation for the Chinese people and nation. By identifying the Republic of China with the imperial dynastic state that they brought down, and at the same time denouncing that regime as having been incapable of defending the empire and its preeminent status, the new rulers claimed legitimacy within the Sinic order in much the same way as earlier dynasties had. The corollary was the narrative that presented the target and victim of European and Japanese imperialist attacks to have been a humiliated Chinese nation rather than the Qing imperial state. The habitual European reference to the latter as the Chinese empire and as China, an identification that was increasingly made by the regime itself in the last decades of its existence, moreover greatly facilitated the later identification by the Chinese republic with the Great States of Inner and East Asia, including the translation of the extensive reach of their emperors into territorial sovereignty claims.

The creation of the new Chinese state laid the basis for one of the most significant reorganizations of Inner and East Asia directly affecting the three worlds that have been our focus in this book. Once Chinese nationalists drove their Manchu rulers from the Qing capital to establish a republic of their own, they replaced this intent with a much more comprehensive one, expressed in their provisional constitution. They declared that the Chinese republic had succeeded to the Qing empire and inherited its imperial borders such that it comprised also the Mongolian, Tibetan, and Uighur regions of Inner Asia.[17] Tibet and Mongolia were invited to join the new republic; both rejected the proposition, considering themselves independent states.[18]

The Chinese republican government in its turn produced a map of loss in 1938, the "Map of China's Shame," which presents large areas as belonging to China and wrested from it by European and Japanese imperialists. The "lost territories" depicted on this map include, besides Mongolia, Tibet, and the rest of Inner Asia, much of Siberia, the Ryukyu Islands, Taiwan, the South China Sea, Korea, Vietnam, Cambodia, Laos, Thailand, the Malay Peninsula and Singapore, as well as the Andaman and Nicobar Islands in the Bay of Bengal and the waters around them, Myanmar, Nepal, Bhutan, and parts of India and Pakistan. Like the Thai maps, it was calculated to display China's past national greatness and to create a sense of unity in supporting the regime's mandate to restore its status and pride. This map is a powerful visual presentation of a narrative of past greatness, reinterpreted as territorial possession, in which the specificities of historical interpolity relations completely disappear into a delimited flat surface depicting an imagined reach of the nation's territorial sovereignty.[19] Narratives that accompanied and justified the new Chinese republic have had a lasting effect, for they formed the basis for the narratives the PRC has used to legitimize its borders and claims.

Other examples of narratives used today originated in this pivotal period as well. A Tibetan narrative emphasizing the end of Tibet's particular relationship with the Qing court with the emperor's abrogation of the teacher-benefactor bond, and the absence of any such relationship with the new Chinese republic, was deployed following the events of 1908–1912 and is still in use today. Just as China's current narrative of the "century of humiliation" originated in this period of transformation, so did the present official Chinese and Vietnamese narratives on sovereignty over the islands and reefs in the South China Sea. More such examples could be given. The point is that, to understand the narratives that are in use today, it is necessary to comprehend the profound impact of the events that shaped them in this turbulent period. At the same time, since these narratives invoke episodes from earlier centuries of history, it is equally essential to properly contextualize *those* on their own terms—that is, freed from the distorting lenses of the modern nation-state and interstate system and of a European understanding of empire.

But even when analyzing current Asian affairs, we need to remain mindful of the extent to which we are conditioned to think in those limiting terms and prevented from recognizing other realities. We noted in the opening of this chapter that the assumptions and principles underlying the ideologies and legal orders of the past are not entirely extinguished but live on to a certain degree and operate in the same political space as modern international law. We close this chapter, then, with two examples that reveal the continuing relevance of elements of the Tibetan Buddhist world order and the Sinic one in today's political reality and illustrate the deployment of historical events, evidence, and narratives to serve today's political ends. Our aim here is not to provide an analysis of current Asian affairs and relations. That we leave to the experts on the subject. We limit our intention to suggesting how these legacies continue to affect political behavior in Inner and East Asia today. The first example is the emerging dispute over the selection and appointment of the Dalai Lama's reincarnation, which vividly demonstrates how elements of the Tibetan Buddhist order are still in play in the traditionally Tibetan Buddhist regions of Inner Asia and are acknowledged and acted upon even by China's Communist leaders. The second concerns the PRC's growing assertion of power in Asia and beyond, which involves moves to establish its primacy and even hegemony in Asia and is arguably guided by the past and may signal a lingering nostalgia for the former Sinic world order.

HISTORY IN PLAY TODAY

There is more to the burgeoning dispute over the selection of the reincarnation of the Dalai Lama than meets the eye. One might ask what motivates the leaders of the Chinese Communist Party, who mandate that all party members be atheist, to put so much effort into persuading Tibetans and the international community that it is the PRC central government's right and responsibility to select and appoint the next incarnation of the Dalai Lama.[20] Given that the Fourteenth Dalai Lama is known internationally as one of the world's foremost *religious* rather than political leaders, Beijing's insistence on its prerogative to identify his reincarnation may seem archaic and irrelevant to twenty-first-century political realities. PRC leaders realize, however, that the vast majority of Tibetans accept only the Dalai Lama as their legitimate leader and that the institution of the Dalai Lama continues to exert influence in Tibetan Buddhist regions that goes beyond religion alone. A Dalai Lama willing to cooperate with the Chinese Communist Party would endow the PRC with more legitimacy to rule Tibet, provide the party and government with a tool to project soft power and influence in Tibetan Buddhist areas outside the PRC and to Buddhists worldwide, as well as help dissolve Tibetan resistance to Beijing's rule and silence international criticism of it. The Fourteenth Dalai Lama stands in the way of achieving these goals, hence Beijing's concerted efforts to discredit him and persuade world leaders not to meet with him. China appears determined to select and groom the next incarnation of the Dalai Lama to accomplish these purposes and to halt what it perceives to be India's influence over the Dalai Lama and its use of the Dalai Lama to project that country's soft power as the cradle and patron of Buddhism.[21]

Interestingly, Chinese leaders are not attempting to end the Dalai Lama institution as a way of overcoming the persistent obstacle they have encountered in past decades. Quite the contrary. In 2011 the Dalai Lama reverted to the solely religious institutional role of the Dalai Lamas that came before the Great Fifth, who assumed the political powers of the state in 1642, even suggesting that he might be the last Dalai Lama should Tibetans consider the institution no longer useful. Yet the Chinese government insists on discovering his reincarnation after he dies and on giving that incarnation a political role.[22] It is the institution of the Dalai Lama, with the legitimacy and authority that emanate from it at the center of the Tibetan Buddhist world, that Beijing appears to covet for its own ends.

The basis on which Beijing claims the right to select and appoint the next Dalai Lama brings us to the problematic identification of the PRC with the Qing Great State and the interpretation of historical relationships to fit present needs. We are concerned here, not with the casual reference to the Qing state as "China," but with the PRC's legal identification with the Manchu imperial state for present-day political ends. The PRC government bases its claim on the grounds that beginning late in the eighteenth century Qing emperors played a role in the process of selecting and appointing the Dalai Lama, citing in particular Emperor Qianlong's 1793 regulations for Tibet, referred to in chapter 4.[23] That document is invoked because one of its clauses provides for such a role through a ceremony involving the drawing of a name, by the *amban* on behalf of the emperor, from a "golden urn" after two or three candidates have been identified by the Tibetan clergy according to existing Tibetan Buddhist tradition. The use of urns for divination rituals was not new to Tibetans, but the role of the Manchu emperor in the selection of the Dalai Lama was. The procedure is thought to have been used only twice in the actual selection process.[24] Viewed with an awareness of the Tibetan Buddhist worldview, it quickly becomes apparent why invoking the 1793 regulations will not persuade Tibetans and other Tibetan Buddhists of Beijing's right to select the next reincarnation of the Dalai Lama. In part this is because their understanding of the relevant history comes largely from Tibetan-language sources in which the identification of Dalai Lamas is described as occurring according to well-established Buddhist processes, with little reference to Manchu influence. The Manchu emperor's role was as *yöndag*, protector and benefactor of the Dalai Lama, Buddhism, and the Tibetan state, and was independent of his role as *tianzi* or *huangdi* in the Sinic world. Finally, as the teacher-benefactor relationship came to an end before the fall of the Qing and was not reestablished with the Republic of China or with the PRC, the claim to this precedent is rendered moot.

The PRC invocation of a late eighteenth-century Manchu document to justify its claim exemplifies Beijing's reliance on historical arguments to legitimize current objectives and policies.[25] But the reasoning used in this case seems to be geared mostly toward the PRC's Chinese population, as it will be unacceptable to Tibetans and other Inner Asians. It presumes the identification of the PRC with the Manchus' Great State, and China's Communist leaders with its emperors. It furthermore presumes the existence of a religiously based relationship between the PRC's central government and the Dalai Lama. And it entails an acceptance of the continuing validity of Manchu policies in regard to Tibet. None of these presumptions are Tibetan Buddhists likely to accept.[26] It seems more plausible that Beijing's reference to the Qing regulations is directed at strengthening support from Chinese for its policies in Tibet. The issue is fundamentally one of legitimacy, in this case the legitimacy of the Chinese Communist Party to rule Tibet. Challenging that claim could bring into question the party's legitimacy to rule China as well. A Chinese audience might welcome the PRC's use of Qing precedents to reinforce its inheritance of the Qing empire, but Tibetans and other Inner Asians will not be persuaded.

Today, the PRC's rise and projection of power in Asia inevitably loom large in any analysis of the region's relations and conflicts. The Chinese government persistently deploys history and historical narratives in support of political projects and claims. It has promoted the notion of "China's peaceful rise" also by invoking narratives portraying China as a historically benevolent and peace-loving center of the Sinic world. This brings us to our second example, which concerns the PRC's projection of power in Asia, including Inner Asia and the western Pacific, for some observers discern an objective underlying Beijing's current political and economic projects, informed by past imperial history. They suggest that Chinese leaders may wish to reestablish aspects of the Sinic world order, albeit updated ones, that would "reinstate" China's preeminence at the center of a modified order designed to better serve the PRC's interests, including its security needs, and, importantly, to secure the continuance of the Chinese Communist Party in power.

This picture emerges from observing the broader scope of Beijing's foreign policies and actions. It has led Howard French to argue that the PRC's goal on the way to global-power status is to "restore a semblance of the region's old order, an updated kind of tributary system in which nations of Southeast Asia or even wealthy and customarily diffident Japan will have no choice but to hitch their fortunes to and bow to Beijing's authority."[27] French asserts that in its quest for supremacy the PRC is guided by the past, especially the notion of "all-under-heaven" placing the rulers of China at the apex of the region. He and other analysts of the PRC's growing assertiveness and its New Silk Roads initiative suggest the possible emergence of a new, modernized version of that order.[28]

These claims have economic as well as strategic significance. China is particularly concerned to project power in what might be called its "near abroad," to use the Russian concept. Of note in this respect is Beijing's exertion of critical and growing influence in Nepal and Mongolia at the expense of the long-standing Indian and Russian relationships with those states, respectively, and also in Pakistan and the Central Asian republics. In what the *Economist* described as a display of "imperial pomp, power and benevolence," on 15 May 2017 Xi Jinping laid out before the heads of state and representatives of some forty countries gathered in Beijing a blueprint of Chinese-led investment in infrastructure that would transform some sixty countries throughout Eurasia. Xi promised "Chinese guidance and more than \$100bn of Chinese money to create what he called 'A big family of harmonious coexistence.'"[29] The New Silk Roads project would connect virtually all of Eurasia to the PRC in a super–Marshall Plan, thereby potentially forging relationships of economic and political dependency with the recipients of its investments.[30]

To understand what motivates Beijing in these projects, Andrew Nathan and Andrew Scobell have drawn attention to the importance given by China's leaders to national security considerations. They point to the fact that the country is bordered by numerous states with some of the world's biggest populations and also largest armies, against many of which the PRC has fought wars in past decades. In addition, there is the history of dissent and resistance the PRC faces from peoples in strategic Inner Asian border regions.[31] As Wang Gungwu and Zheng Yongnian have pointed out, today's leaders are guided by their understanding of historical experience and long-standing Chinese political thinking, and consequently regard the state's security and its place in the international order to be intimately related to their capacity to maintain internal stability. Projecting power in the region and beyond is thus tied to their legitimacy at home. Economic performance is no longer sufficient to generate regime legitimacy: the PRC now asserts its stature in the region and the world, gesturing toward a restoration of past greatness.[32]

Although modern conceptions of statehood, popular legitimacy, and materialism have supplanted the sacredness of mandates that conferred legitimacy on rulers, not all that colored historical interpolity relations has been erased or forgotten. The presence of the past in policy-making, especially in conflict situations, is palpable in Asia. To restrict our analysis of what motivates state and nonstate actors to economic and strategic factors alone leaves us with an incomplete picture, for the richness and diversity of Asian pasts continue to matter for understanding the present and negotiating the future.

AUTHORS AND CONTRIBUTORS

Timothy Brook is Professor of Chinese History and the Republic of China Chair at the University of British Columbia in Vancouver, Canada. He is the author of, among other works, *The Troubled Empire: China in the Yuan and Ming Dynasties*.

Michael van Walt van Praag, formerly Visiting Professor of International Relations and International Law at the Institute for Advanced Study, Princeton, is currently Senior Fellow at the Institute for Social Sciences at the University of California at Davis and the executive president of Kreddha. His publications include *The Status of Tibet: History, Rights, and Prospects in International Law*.

Miek Boltjes is a mediator and facilitator with extensive experience in intrastate conflicts and peace processes in Asia, Africa, and the South Pacific. She is the Director of Dialogue Facilitation at Kreddha. Her publications include *Implementing Negotiated Agreements: The Real Challenge to Intrastate Peace*.

PARTICIPATING SCHOLARS

This volume arose from the series of roundtables on the theme of the nature of polities and political relations in Inner and East Asia from the thirteenth to the early twentieth century convened by Michael van Walt van Praag and Miek Boltjes from 2010 to 2012. Timothy Brook served as discussant at all five roundtables, and Scott Relyea and Stacey Van Vleet as rapporteurs. The participants listed below are identified by the titles they held and the institutions at which they worked at the time of each roundtable.

The first roundtable was convened at the University of British Columbia, Vancouver, in April 2010 and examined the nature of relations among Asian polities from the fourteenth to the eighteenth century, with special emphasis on Ming China:

Johan Elverskog, Associate Professor of Religious Studies, Southern Methodist University, Dallas

Victoria Tin-bor Hui, Assistant Professor, Department of Political Science, University of Notre Dame, South Bend

Liam Kelley, Associate Professor, Department of History, University of Hawai'i

Kirk Larsen, Associate Professor, Department of History, Brigham Young University

Ji-Young Lee, Visiting Assistant Professor of Politics and East Asian Studies, Oberlin College, Oberlin

Yoshiaki Nakajima, Associate Professor, Department of History, Kyushu University

Ratanaporn Sethakul, Associate Professor, History Department, Payap University

Tsering Shakya, Canada Research Chair in Religion and Contemporary Society in Asia, Institute for Asian Research, University of British Columbia, Vancouver

Geoffrey Wade, Visiting Senior Research Fellow, National University of Singapore

Siddiq Wahid, Vice Chancellor, Islamic University of Kashmir, Awantipora

Yuan-kang Wang, Assistant Professor, Department of Sociology and School of Public Affairs and Administration, Western Michigan University, Kalamazoo

Feng Zhang, Assistant Professor, Department of International Relations, Tsinghua University, Beijing

The second roundtable was convened at the Austrian Academy of Sciences, Vienna, in November 2010 and examined the Mongol empire and its legacy:

Christopher Atwood, Chair of Central Eurasian Studies Department and Director of the Center for Languages of the Central Asian Region, Indiana University

Dalizhabu, Director, Research Center of History and Geographical Studies of China's Frontier Regions and Nationalities, Minzu University, Beijing

Nicola Di Cosmo, Henry Luce Foundation Professor of East Asian Studies, The Institute for Advanced Study, Princeton

Yoshiyuki Funada, Assistant Professor, Faculty of Humanities, Kyushu University

Birgitt Hoffmann, Professor of Iranian Studies, Bamberg University

Hodong Kim, Director of the Center for Central Eurasian Studies, Seoul National University

Karénina Kollmar-Paulenz, Professor and Codirector, Institute for Religious Studies, University of Bern

Helmut Krasser, Director, Institute for the Cultural and Intellectual History of Asia, Austrian Academy of Sciences

Ik-Joo Lee, Professor, Department of Korean History, Seoul National University

Lhamsuren Munkh-Erdene, Lise Meitner Fellow, Austrian Academy of Sciences; and Professor, Department of Social and Cultural Anthropology, National University of Mongolia

Koichi Matsuda, Professor, Faculty of Letters, Osaka International University

Florian Schwarz, Director, Institute of Iranian Studies, Austrian Academy of Sciences

Weirong Shen, School of Chinese Classics, Renmin University of China, Beijing

Tatiana Skrynnikova, Principal Researcher, Department of Philosophy, Culture, and Religion Studies, Institute for Mongolian, Buddhist, and Tibetan Studies, Siberian Branch of the Russian Academy of Sciences

David Sneath, Reader in Anthropology, Department of Social Anthropology, University of Cambridge

Vladimir Uspenskiy, Chair of Mongolian and Tibetan Studies, Oriental Department, Saint Petersburg State University

Veronika Veit, Professor, Department of Mongolian and Tibetan Studies, University of Bonn

The third roundtable was convened at the Nalanda-Sriwijaya Centre, Institute of Southeast Asian Studies, National University of Singapore, in April 2011 and examined the changing nature of Asian relations from the eighteenth to the twentieth century:

John Ardussi, Senior Fellow, The Tibet Center, University of Virginia, Charlottesville

Christopher Beckwith, Professor, Central Eurasian Studies, University of Indiana, Bloomington

Uradyn Bulag, Reader, Selwyn College, Department of Social Anthropology, University of Cambridge

Prasenjit Duara, Director, Asia Research Institute, National University of Singapore

Konuralp Ercilasun, Associate Professor, Maltepe University, Istanbul

Yumiko Ishihama Fukudo, Professor of Asian History, Waseda University, Tokyo

Sergius Kuzmin, Institute of Ecology and Evolution, Russian Academy of Sciences, Moscow

Kirk Larsen, Associate Professor of History, Department of History, Brigham Young University

Tirtha Prasad Mishra, Head, Central Department of History, Tribhuvan University, Kathmandu

Jiang Qian, Centre of Asian Studies, University of Hong Kong, Hong Kong

Tansen Sen, Senior Fellow, Nalanda-Sriwijaya Centre, Institute of Southeast Asian Studies, Singapore; and Associate Professor of Asian History and Religion, Baruch College, City University of New York

Tsering Shakya, Canada Research Chair in Religion and Contemporary Society in Asia, Institute for Asian Research, University of British Columbia

Shogo Suzuki, Lecturer, Politics, School of Social Sciences, University of Manchester

Nikolay Tsyrempilov, Institute of Mongolian, Buddhist, and Tibetan Studies, Siberian Branch of the Russian Academy of Sciences, Ulan Ude

Geoffrey Wade, Senior Fellow, Nalanda-Sriwijaya Centre, Institute of Southeast Asian Studies, Singapore

Thongchai Winichakul, Professor of History, University of Wisconsin

R. Bin Wong, Director, The Asia Institute, and Professor of History, University of California at Los Angeles

Goh Geok Yian, School of Humanities and Social Sciences, Nanyang Technological University, Singapore

Lishuang Zhu, Postdoctoral Fellow, Department of History, Peking University, Beijing

The fourth roundtable was convened at the University of California at Los Angeles in May 2012 and examined the nature of historical political and spiritual relations among Asian polities and leaders within the Tibetan Buddhist world:

Agata Bareja-Starzynska, Mongolian and Tibetan Studies, Department of Turkish Studies and Inner Asian Peoples, University of Warsaw

Johan Elverskog, Fellow, Center for Advanced Study in Behavioral Sciences, Stanford University

Hsiao-ting Lin, Curator, Research Fellow, Hoover Institution, Stanford University

Dan Martin, Fellow, Institute for Advanced Studies, The Hebrew University of Jerusalem

Koichi Matsuda, Professor, Faculty of Business, Osaka International University

Alex McKay, Alumnus fellow, International Institute of Asian Studies, Leiden

Saul Mullard, Researcher, École pratique des hautes études, Université Sorbonne, Paris; and Visiting Researcher, Namgyal Institute of Tibetology, Gangtok, Sikkim

Thubten Phuntsok, Professor of Tibetology, Central Nationalities University, Beijing

Charles Ramble, Professor and Directeur d'études, École pratique des hautes études, Université Sorbonne, Paris

Kurtis Schaeffer, Professor of Tibetan and Buddhist Studies, University of Virginia, Charlottesville

Ron Sela, Associate Professor of Central Eurasian Studies, Indiana University, Bloomington

Tsering Wangyal Shawa, Head, Digital Map and Geospatial Information Center, Peter B. Lewis Library, Princeton University

Gray Tuttle, Assistant Professor of Modern Tibetan Studies, Department of East Asian Languages and Cultures, Columbia University, New York

R. Bin Wong, Director, The Asia Institute and Professor of History, University of California at Los Angeles

The fifth roundtable was convened at the Institute for Advanced Study, Princeton, in November 2012 and examined the nature of the Manchu Qing empire and its relations:

Zvi Ben-Dor Benite, Professor of History, Middle Eastern and Islamic Studies, New York University

Pamela Crossley, Collis Professor of History, Dartmouth College

Nicola Di Cosmo, Henry Luce Foundation Professor of East Asian Studies, The Institute for Advanced Study, Princeton

Yongling Jiang, Associate Professor, East Asian Languages and Cultures, Bryn Mawr College

Matthew Kapstein, Numata Visiting Professor of Buddhist Studies, Philosophy of Religions, and History of Religions, The Divinity School, University of Chicago; and faculty member, École pratique des hautes études, Université Sorbonne, Paris

Yochimichi Kusunoki, Professor of Asian History, University of Tsukuba

Tong Lam, Associate Professor of History, University of Toronto

Lhamsuren Munkh-Erdene, Professor of History, National University of Mongolia

Nobuaki Murakami, Associate Professor, Faculty of Literature, Soka University

Guanjie Niu, Associate Professor, Department of History, Renmin University of China, Beijing

Hiroki Oka, Professor, Center for Northeast Asian Studies, Tohoku University

Peter C. Perdue, Professor of History, Yale University

Ron Sela, Associate Professor of Central Asian History, Department of Central Eurasian Studies, Indiana University, Bloomington

Weirong Shen, Professor, Institute for China Studies, Renmin University, Beijing

Brantly Womack, Professor of Foreign Affairs and C. K. Yen Chair, Miller Center, University of Virginia

NOTES

CHAPTER ONE

1. Although some political scientists highlight the influence of history (one could cite Iain Johnston, Victoria Hui, Yan Xuetong, David Kang, Yuan-kang Wang, Qin Yanqing, and Brantly Womack), for the most part, as Womack himself points out, they are "looking for things Western in places Eastern." He notes that European and British international relations is more open to historical reflection than American international relations (e-mail to the editors, 8 October 2016).

2. The locus classicus of this argument may be found in Wong, *China Transformed*, pp. 1–7.

3. For China's most recent white paper stating its position, see State Council Information Office of the People's Republic of China, "China Adheres to the Position of Settling through Negotiation the Relevant Disputes between China and the Philippines in the South China Sea." The Ministry of Foreign Affairs of the Socialist Republic of Vietnam has published several white papers: *Vietnam's Sovereignty over the Hoang Sa and Truong Sa Archipelagos*; *The Hoang Sa and Truong Sa Archipelagoes: Vietnamese Territories*; and *The Hoang Sa and Truong Sa Archipelagoes and International Law*. Other claimants, including the Philippines and Malaysia, argue their case on the basis of the modern Law of the Sea, in particular the United Nations Convention on the Law of the Sea.

4. Walker, *Inside/Outside*, p. 179; also pp. 88–92.

5. Walker, *After the Globe, before the World*, p. 133.

6. Rune Svarverud usefully reviews the place of Westphalia in the creation of European international law, though he chooses to distinguish this mode of conceiving interstate relations from the social Darwinist mode of gunboat diplomacy; see his *International Law as World Order in Late Imperial China*, pp. 3–4, 32–41. This distinction may absolve European international law of more than it deserves.

7. Fairbank, *Chinese World Order*; the quotations that follow in this chapter are taken from his introduction, "A Preliminary Framework," pp. 1–3, 8–9, 12.

8. David Kang takes a more positive view, using a historical comparison with Europe to argue that China and its neighboring states "developed and maintained peaceful and long-lasting relations with each other" (*East Asia before the West*, p. 2). Kang attributes this "systemic stability" to the capacity of the tribute system to allow

China to dominate the region without seeking to annihilate its competitors. We revisit this claim in chapter 3.

9. E.g., David Kang argues that China provided "the core organizing principles of the system" and induced "all the political units in the system to play by the rules" (*East Asia before the West*, p. 8). Hamashita Takeshi offers a more ambitious reformulation of the East Asian system based on tribute submission by incorporating trade as an equally defining feature, although in this formulation too China remains at the center of the system; see his *Chōkō shisutemu to kindai Ajia*; also *China, East Asia and the Global Economy*, pp. 12–16. For a recent plea to recognize the complexity of the historical situation in Eurasia and attend to what the historical actors within the tribute system actually did rather than rely on the apparent rules of the system, see Koo, "Dai Shin teikoku no Chōsen ninshiki to Chōsen no isō."

10. Also referred to as Tibeto-Mongolian Buddhism, as this distinct form of Buddhism was adopted by Mongols as well.

11. The *Travels* of Marco Polo is a highly problematic text for which no original manuscript exists, as Frances Wood and others have pointed out; see, e.g., her *Did Marco Polo Go to China?*, esp. pp. 140–151. But the text is a font of valuable historical data, as Hans Ulrich Vogel has argued in *Marco Polo Was in China*.

12. Polo, *Travels*, pp. 44–45.

13. On the expectation of legal protection for state envoys in the ancient world, see Bederman, *International Law in Antiquity*, pp. 88–120.

14. Shaw, *International Law*, p. 1.

15. Ibid.

16. Polo, *Travels*, p. 118.

17. Ibid., p. 115.

18. David Bederman, *International Law in Antiquity*, p. 14, makes this point in his study of diplomacy in antiquity, observing that the connotations of "international law" in contemporary legal scholarship "may not consistently convey the sense of international relations in antiquity," but that this should not rule out the adaptation of these terms to other, nonmodern contexts.

19. On shifting the history of international law away from its modernist and Europeanist bases, see Lesaffer, "International Law and Its History."

20. Ruskola, *Legal Orientalism*, p. 23.

21. Quoted in Bederman, *International Law in Antiquity*, p. 5. As it happens, Preiser proposed 1300 as the onset of the emergence of such a law of nations in Europe, coinciding with the era just after Marco Polo.

22. Our model of the simultaneous operation of three bodies of international law may resonate with the findings of recent research on the existence of plural legal environments in parts of the Qing empire also at the local level; e.g., Heuschert-Laage, "Negotiating Modalities of Succession," identifies three distinct bodies of law operating under Qing authority among the Mongols: Qing imperial law, Mongol legal tradition, and Buddhist law.

23. Biersteker and Weber, *State Sovereignty as a Social Construct*, p. 2.

24. Cassese, *International Law*, p. 49.

25. It bears noting that even today, as Krasner argues in *Sovereignty: Organized Hypocrisy*, the sovereign equality of states is a legal fiction. Although most states enjoy formal recognition of their sovereignty, few actually fully exercise it.

26. The concept is discussed in Brook, "Great States."

27. It should be noted that although the signing of contracts was widely practiced in Asia as a way of confirming an agreement to take on the obligations specified in the contract, only commercial contracts were signed, never diplomatic agreements. Asian rulers came to agreements, but they did not sign them, nor did their subordinates on their behalf. Rulers did not enter into obligations as contracting parties; rather, they referred to a hierarchy of obligations deemed to be already established. When representatives of European states pressed officials in East and also Inner Asia to sign contracts binding their rulers to certain obligations, these officials were at a loss, fearing to commit what could easily be construed as lèse-majesté, or making decisions in place of their rulers rather than on their behalf. The Westphalian process tolerated this distinction; Asian relations did not. The Treaty of Nerchinsk (1689) between the Russian and Qing empires would seem to be the first exception, but it was signed with a European state and drawn up by European Jesuits working in the service of the Manchu emperor. Songgotu signed the document on behalf of the Kangxi emperor, and Fedor Golovin on behalf of the tsars Peter I and Ivan V.

28. Sun Daigang, "Last Pitch," pp. 79–81, argues that the significance of the signing of treaties at the end of the First Opium War (1839–1842) has been exaggerated. Qing negotiators regarded them as extending the Canton system, a state monopoly over foreign trade run seasonally out of Canton, rather than as the supplanting of tribute relations by treaty relations. Not until the Second Opium War (1856–1860), he argues, did treaties fatally disrupt the tribute system.

29. Zarrow, *After Empire*, pp. 92–95.

30. On China's protracted probation leading up to its acceptance into the family of nations, see Svarverud, *International Law as World Order in Late Imperial China*, pp. 54–67, 190–265.

31. Aside from asserting this in communications to China and a number of European powers, Tibet and Mongolia concluded a treaty in 1913 recognizing each other's independence; see Van Walt van Praag, "A Legal Examination of the 1913 Mongolia-Tibet Treaty of Friendship and Alliance." At the time, neither Tibet nor Mongolia actively sought formal recognition as independent states from the broader international community, creating sufficient ambiguity to enable China to assert its claim to these territories internationally without significant challenge except from Britain and Russia, in whose spheres of influence these states existed.

CHAPTER TWO

1. On the inception of Temüjin's use of the title Chinggis Khan, see de Rachewiltz, *Secret History of the Mongols*, vol. 1, pp. 457–460. The title was conferred on Temüjin by Mongol nobles before 1206 and was confirmed at his second coronation as khan of all Mongols in 1206. Contrary to the usual gloss on Chinggis Khan as meaning Uni-

versal Ruler, de Rachewiltz argues that the title means Fierce Ruler. Urgunge Onon, *Secret History of the Mongols*, p. 30, suggests that the title *chinggis* may have been derived from the shamanistic concept of the ruler on land, as distinct from *tenggeri*, he who rules above.

2. In romanizing Mongolian words we have generally followed the usages in Atwood, *Encyclopedia of Mongolia and the Mongol Empire*, rather than the transliterations that Mongolicists would consider technically more accurate—hence, *khan* rather than *qan*, and *khagan*. While we recognize that the distinction between khan and Great Khan—for which see Allsen, "Rise of the Mongolian Empire," pp. 332, 367; also Krader, "Qan-Qaγan and the Beginnings of Mongol Kingship"—is significant, in general we avoid using the Mongol term *khagan* in favor of Great Khan, simplified to khan when referring to the titles of particular Great Khans such as Khubilai Khan. On the retroactive application of the title of Great Khan to Chinggis, see de Rachewiltz, *Secret History of the Mongols*, vol. 1, pp. 222-223, 466-467.

3. On the concept of the Great State, see Brook, "Great States."

4. This was also the case for other fields, such as the arts, communications, and architecture; see Robinson, "The Ming Court and the Legacy of the Yuan Mongols."

5. The *Secret History of the Mongols* gives Chinggis Khan the speaking role in presenting the outlines of the system; de Rachewiltz, *Secret History of the Mongols*, vol. 1, pp. 152-155.

6. Fletcher, "The Mongols," pp. 24-26, 36-38.

7. Ratchnevsky, *Genghis Khan*, p. 140.

8. For a different interpretation of these events, see Beckwith, *Empires of the Silk Road*, pp. 192-193.

9. For a detailed discussion, see Hodong Kim, "Was 'Da Yuan' a Chinese Dynasty?" However, some Mongols who remained in China after the establishment of the Ming dynasty underwent acculturation, becoming a military caste serving that regime; see Serruys, "Mongols in China during the Hung-wu Period," pp. 158-76; also Serruys, "Mongols Ennobled during the Early Ming," p. 255.

10. Koryŏ, on the Korean peninsula, should also be considered part of the Mongol empire, but not of the Yuan dynasty as we use the term in this book; see Robinson, *Empire's Twilight*, pp. 8-9, 274-278. The similar status of Tibet in the Mongol empire is briefly discussed below.

11. Authoritative Chinese-language Yuan-era geographic references indicate that Tibet was not considered to be within the Yuan realm. Elliot Sperling points out that "the most telling indication of Tibet's status [at this time] is the fact that the Yuan dynasty's official history (the *Yuan shi*, compiled a year after the dynasty collapsed by the Ming), in detailing the geography of the Yuan realms, excludes Tibet from the relevant chapters" (Blondeau and Buffetrille, *Authenticating Tibet*, p. 13). In fact, the only reference to what appear to be Tibetan areas in the dynastic history is found in an editor's note stating that very little is known about them.

12. Quoted in Cleaves, "Sino-Mongolian Inscription of 1346," p. 83, adjusted and augmented by drawing on the parallel Chinese inscription on p. 33.

13. Munkh-Erdene, "Where Did the Mongol Empire Come From?" The Ong Khan was named Toghril.

14. Sneath, *Headless State*; also Barfield, *Perilous Frontier*, pp. 24–28.

15. These ideas predate the Chinggisid state and recur as resilient elements of pre-modern Inner Asian statecraft and political culture. Most of these institutions were already in place in the time of the Xiongnu, the earliest known Inner Asian empire. The Xiongnu term for Heaven, *chengli*, is a Chinese corruption of Inner Asian *tengri* or *tenggeri*, and the title of the Xiongnu leader, *chanyü*, is the equivalent of later *qan* or *qa'an* as heavenly mandated ruler. So too hereditary decimal divisions and the appanage system, as well as the divisions of offices into left and right, and a council of ministers and top commanders, all were elements of Xiongnu statecraft. *Tengri, törü* (*törö*), and *qa'an* (*xagan, kagan*) all are attested in the Orkhon inscriptions: see Di Cosmo, *Ancient China and Its Enemies*, pp. 171–177; Clauson, *Etymological Dictionary of Pre-Thirteenth-Century Turkish*, pp. 523–524, 531–532, 611. Hansgerd Göckenjan, "Zur Stammesstruktur und Heeresorganisation altaischer Völker," documents the continuous use of the decimal system by Xiongnu, Xianbei, T'ü-chüeh, Khitan Liao, Jurchen Jin, and Mongol and Timurid empires.

16. For a detailed discussion, see Munkh-Erdene, "Where Did the Mongol Empire Come From?" Rashīd al-Dīn defines the term *ulus* as a community of common "shape, form, vocabulary, dialect, customs and manners" (Thackston, *Rashiduddin Fazlullah's "Jami'u't-tawarikh,"* vol. 1, p. 44).

17. The author of the *Secret History of the Mongols*, while recounting the events that took place during the 1206 assembly that established the new Mongol state, denotes the body politic that came under Chinggis Khan's rule in three different ways: first as "felt-tent *ulus*" (*sisgei to'urqatu ulus*), denoting nomadic people of the Mongolian Plateau; then as "Mongolic *ulus*" (*mongqolijn ulus*), denoting the polity of the people of Mongolian language and custom; and finally as "Mongol *ulus*" (*mongqol ulus*), stretching the concept of "original Mongols" to include all those organized and administered under the state established in 1206; see de Rachewiltz, *Index to "The Secret History of the Mongols,"* pp. 113–114.

18. Because of the expansion of the designation of "Mongols" and "Mongol *ulus*," the original bearers of these designations distinguished themselves as the "original," or *dürlükin*, Mongols.

19. De Rachewiltz, *Index to "The Secret History of the Mongols,"* p. 114.

20. Ibid., pp. 60, 115, 141.

21. Boyle, *Genghis Khan*, pp. 42–43.

22. Ligeti, *Monuments préclassiques*, vol. 1, p. 20.

23. De Rachewiltz, *Index to "The Secret History of the Mongols,"* p. 98. This contains the only paragraph where the *Secret History* refers to the Mongols as *irgen*, and it applies to pre-1206 Mongols.

24. Allsen, *Culture and Conquest in Mongol Eurasia*, p. 18.

25. Another Song author pushed this usage in Chinese back by another decade to 1211, barely five years after the ascendancy of Chinggis Khan. It is not clear what

formal designation in Mongolian was then used, as the Stele of Yesüngge erected in 1224/1225 speaks of *qamuq mongqol ulus* rather than *yeke mongqol ulus*. See Munkuev, *Men-da bei-lu "Polnoe Opisanie Mongolo-Tartar,"* p. 249. Mongols initially considered "Menggu" somewhat derisive and not a term they wished to use, preferring to Sinicize their ethnonym as "Manhe'er"—which makes it even more difficult to read back from Chinese reports to actual Mongol usage.

26. Cleaves, "Sino-Mongolian Inscription of 1335," p. 105; Cleaves, "Sino-Mongolian Inscription of 1346," pp. 82–83; Cleaves, "Sino-Mongolian Inscription of 1362," pp. 94–95. What bears noting is that "Dai Ön" does not appear in Mongolian sources without "Yeke Mongqol ulus," whereas "Yeke Mongqol ulus" could stand without reference to "Dai Ön"; see Munkh-Erdene, "Where Did the Mongol Empire Come From?"

27. The biography of one of Tolui's servants helps us place his fief in this region; "Jiashi shide zhi bei" [Stele inscription of the achievements over generations of the Jia family], in Wang Yun, *Qiujian xiansheng wenji*, vol. 51. The official biography of a Chinese doctor, Xu Guozhen, helps determine that following his death his family resided in the Khangai range, not far from Karakorum; Song Lian, *Yuan shi*, p. 3962. For a discussion, see Matsuda, "Tolui-ke no hangai no yūbokuchi," pp. 286–297; Matsuda, "Furagu-ke no tōhōryō," p. 42.

28. Sugiyama, "Mongoru teikoku no genzō."

29. Matsuda, "Mongoru no kanchi tochi seido."

30. Boyle, *Successors of Genghis Khan*, pp. 163, 202.

31. Song Lian, *Yuan shi*, vol. 95; see also Jackson, *Mission of Friar William*, pp. 223–224.

32. The date of 5 May is given in the *Yuan shi*; in the *Jāmi al-tawārīkh* the enthronement is stated to have taken place between 11 June and 9 July.

33. Boyle, *Successors of Genghis Khan*, p. 312.

34. Hülegü's territory was located at Zhangde circuit, but his subjects lived in the capital. Rule in the Mongol empire was over people; territory played only a secondary role.

35. Song Lian, *Yuan shi*, vol. 85, in section on the Ministry of War, and vol. 95, in section on annual imperial gift-giving.

36. Matsuda, "Furagu-ke no tōhōryō," p. 55; Yokkaichi, *Mono kara mita kaiiki Ajia shi*, pp. 42–44.

37. This allotment was not recorded in the *Yuan shi*, vol. 95, but it is recorded in the biography of Hazhi Haxin (Ḥājjī Hāshim), in Xu, *Zhizheng ji*, vol. 53.

38. Matsuda, "Mongoru no kanchi tochi seido."

39. Makino, "Genchō chūshōshō no seiritu." The Central Secretariat was known as Zhongshusheng in Chinese.

40. The representatives, Hazhi Haxin (Ḥājjī Hāshim) and Gulishade, are named in Xu, *Zhizheng ji*, vol. 53.

41. Boyle, *Successors of Genghis Khan*, p. 165.

42. Matsuda, "Furagu-ke no tōhōryō," p. 55; Yokkaichi, *Mono kara mita kaiiki Ajia shi*, pp. 134–136.

43. Saguchi, "Jūyon seiki ni okeru Genchō dai Kān to seihoku san Ō-ke no rentai-sei ni tuite," p. 147.

44. These features are abstracted from the reports on Chinggisid demands in the chapters on Gaoli (Koryŏ) and Annan (Annam, i.e., Dai Viet) in the Yuan dynastic history: Song Lian, *Yuan shi*, pp. 4607–4653.

45. Tucci dated the Mongol invasion to 1239 in his *Tibetan Painted Scrolls* (1980), vol. 1, p. 9, and he referred to sources giving 1240 as the date of the arrival of Mongol troops on p. 251n16. Okada Hidehiro, "Mōko shiryō ni mieru shoki no Mō Zō kankei," citing Tucci, thought it occurred in 1239 or 1240. Inaba, "Gen no teishi ni kansuru kenkyū," pp. 94–96, concluded that it occurred in 1240. See also Petech, *Central Tibet and the Mongols*, p. 7.

46. Okada Mareo, *Shin'yaku kegonkyō ongi shiki wakunko*, p.1; Inaba, "Gen no teishi ni kansuru kenkyū," p. 96.

47. Inaba, "Gen no teishi ni kansuru kenkyū," pp. 94–96; Petech, *Central Tibet and the Mongols*, p. 8.

48. "Central Tibet" usually refers to the regions of Ü and Tsang and sometimes also to Ngari to the west and parts of Kham to the east. Until recently scholars based their understanding of the early submission of Tibetans on a letter allegedly written by the Sakya Pandita explaining to the Tibetan people the need and benefits of submission to Mongol supremacy. Recent scholarship, however, believes the document to be pseud-epigraphical, "written in the light of the circumstances that evolved after Sakya Pandita's passing" (Kapstein, *Tibetans*, p. 111). For earlier interpretations of the Pandita's letter, see Tucci, *Tibetan Painted Scrolls*, vol. 1, pp. 10–12; Wylie, "Khubilai Khan's First Viceroy of Tibet," p. 392.

49. Song Lian, *Yuan shi*, p. 45; Szerb, "Glosses on the Oeuvre of Bla-ma 'Phags-pa II," pp. 278–280.

50. Tucci, *Tibetan Painted Scrolls*, vol. 1, pp. 12–13; Satō, "Pagumotupa seiken shoki no Chibetto jōsei," pp. 90–93; Szerb, "Glosses on the Oeuvre of Bla-ma 'Phags-pa II," pp. 270–271; Petech, *Central Tibet and the Mongols*, pp. 50–68; Kawamoto, "Chūō Ajia no tumen naru chiiki kubun ni tsuite," pp. 52–54; Matsuda, "Chūgoku kōtsūshi," p. 142. Another census was carried out in 1268 during the reign of Khubilai, yet the Möngke census seems to be the basic data for the Mongol domination of Tibet.

51. Wylie, "First Mongol Conquest of Tibet Reinterpreted," p.108n15; Petech, *Central Tibet and the Mongols*, pp. 10–11.

52. Chen Qingying, *Yuan chao dishi Basiba*, pp. 48–55; Chen Dezhi, "Zailun Wusizang 'benqin,'" pp. 291–292.

53. Karl-Heinz Everding, "The Mongol States and Their Struggle for Dominance over Tibet," explains that Great Khan Möngke placed various Tibetan petty states under different Mongolian rulers: Sakya was placed under Köten, Tshalpa under Khubilai, Phaggru under Hülegü, Staglung under Ariq Böke, and Brigung was kept by Möngke himself. See also Sperling, "Hülegü and Tibet."

54. Song Lian, *Yuan shi*, pp. 2193–2194; Franke, "Tibetans in Yuan China," p. 311; Petech, *Central Tibet and the Mongols*, p. 33. The Zongzhi yuan (Bureau of General

Regulation) was changed in 1288 to Xuanzheng yuan, the Bureau for Propagating Administration, conventionally translated as the Bureau of Buddhist and Tibetan Affairs.

55. Fukuda and Ishihama, *Tukan "Issai shūgi" Mongoru no shō*, pp. 66–68; Petech, *Central Tibet and the Mongols*, pp. 17, 33–35.

56. Wylie, "Khubilai Khan's First Viceroy of Tibet," pp. 395–399; Chen Dezhi, "Zailun Wusizang 'benqin,'" p. 290.

57. Tucci, *Tibetan Painted Scrolls*, vol. 1, pp. 22–23; Otosaka, "Rigon-pa no ran to sakya-pa seiken," p. 72; Petech, *Central Tibet and the Mongols*, pp. 85–137.

58. Seventy thousand of this army's soldiers were troops from several Mongol armies, two of which were led by Khubilai's sons, the princes A'uruɣchi and Mangara. The Mongol armies were supplemented by conscript armies from the eastern Tibetan Plateau regions of Amdo and Kham.

59. These events appear to be linked to broader Central Asian opposition and rebellion against Khubilai, including that of the Mongol princes Shigiri, Qaidu, and Du'a. See Petech, *Central Tibet and the Mongols*, pp. 22–31, 197–198; Otosaka, "Rigon-pa no ran to sakya-pa seiken," pp. 59–65; Nakamura Jun, "Chibetto to Mongoru no kaikuo," pp. 124–129; Everding, "The Mongol States and Their Struggle for Dominance over Tibet."

60. Ishihama, "Pakupa no chōsaku ni miru Fubirai seiken saishoki no Enkei chiiki no jōkyō ni tsuite," p. 12; Ishihama, "The Image of Ch'ien-lung's Kingship as Seen from the World of Tibetan Buddhism," pp. 26–29.

61. Muraoka, "Gendai Mongoru hōzoku to Mongoru Bukkyō," pp. 86–94.

62. Hodong Kim, "Monggol jeguk kwa Dae Wǒn"; Hodong Kim, "Was 'Da Yuan' a Chinese Dynasty?," pp. 275–277, 280.

63. Rashīd al-Dīn completed his history after Ghazan's death and so presented it to Öljeitü Khan (r. 1304–1316). The new khan ordered that the book be named after his predecessor; thus, it was called *Tārīkh-i Mubārak-i Ghazānī*, or simply *Tārīkh-i Ghazānī*. Öljeitü then ordered Rashīd al-Dīn to compile an additional work in two parts, one on global history and the other on world geography. The part on global history contains the chronicle of Öljeitü's reign as well as the history of rulers of other nations, such as the Arabs, Iranians, Turks, Jews, Franks, Indians, and Chinese. The last part, on world geography, is now lost.

64. The most recent work on the part of Rashīd al-Dīn's history dealing with rulers other than the Mongols is by the Iranian scholar Muḥammad Rawshan, who between 2005 and 2010 published eight volumes in Tehran under the title *Jāmi' al-tavārīkh*. For general overviews, see Franke, "Some Sinological Remarks on Rashid ad-Din's History of China"; Karl Jahn, "Rashīd al-Dīn and Chinese Culture." No detailed analysis has been done of the section on China.

65. E.g., see Pelliot, *Notes on Marco Polo*, vol. 1, pp. 216–229; Jackson, *Mission of Friar William*, pp. 202–203; Gibb and Beckingham, *Travels of Ibn Baṭṭūṭa*, pp. 888, 905.

66. The early Buddhist monarchs of Dali adopted the name Gandhara or Kandahar for their territory.

67. Thackston, *Rashiduddin Fazlullah's "Jami'u't-Tawarikh,"* vol. 1, p. 18.

68. Cf. Karl Jahn, "Rashīd al-Dīn and Chinese Culture," pp. 144–146.

69. Karl Jahn and Herbert Franke, *Die Chinageschichte des Rašīd ad-Dīn* (hereafter Hazine 1653), 341b–342a.

70. Rashīd al-Dīn tells his readers that the authors were three Buddhist monks, whose names he spells out but whom he otherwise cannot identify. Scholars have since discovered that the contents of this book are quite similar to a Chinese history of Buddhism entitled *Fozu lidai tongzai* (Comprehensive account of Buddhist patriarchs throughout history); see Franke, "Some Sinological Remarks on Rashid ad-Din's History of China"; Miya, *Monggoru jidai no shuppan bunka*, pp. 106–112. Completed by a monk named Nianchang in 1341, it predates the "History of Khitay and Machin." Comparison shows that Rashīd al-Dīn did not simply translate *Fozu lidai tongzai* but adapted it so that it made better sense to him and his readers, in the course of which he produced subtle discrepancies.

71. This phrase is translated by Jahn as "die rechtmässige Dynastie" in Jahn and Franke, *Die Chinageschichte*, p. 13, though the Arabic word *aṣl* has little to do with political legitimacy; its meaning is closer to "origin" or "source."

72. Couland, "ṭabaqāt," in Bearman et al., *Encyclopaedia of Islam*, pp. 7–10.

73. Hazine 1653, 404b. The manuscript in the Khalili Collection does not use a different color of ink for those dynasties. Among the foreign dynasties, however, Rashīd al-Dīn singles out the Jurchen Jin by including illustrations of its founders, a device he otherwise restricts to dynasties listed as *ṭabaqa-yi aṣlī*. He explains this distinction by saying that he was following Khitay practice: "These emperors were extremely influential, important, powerful, and courageous. Because of the power and importance that they possessed the Khitayans drew their portraits just like the emperors of the original dynasties" (ibid., 409b).

74. Thackston, *Rashiduddin Fazlullah's "Jami'u't-tawarikh,"* vol. 1, p. 6.

75. Hazine 1653, 392b–393a.

76. Hazine 1653, 409a–409b.

77. On Zhongguo, see Dirlik, "Born in Translation"; Bol, "Middle-Period Discourse on the *Zhong guo*"; Lydia Liu, *Clash of Empires*.

78. E.g., Elvin, *Pattern of the Chinese Past*, p. 53.

79. Kern, *Stele Inscriptions of Ch'in Shih-huang*, pp. 13, 18, 39, 42, 44.

80. Pines, "Imagining the Empire?," pp. 85, 86.

81. Sima, *Shi ji*, p. 3.

82. Ibid., pp. 235–236.

83. Fan, *Hou Han shu*, pp. 16, 23. The phrase "lacked the means to rule all as one" (*wu suo tong yi*) comes from the Han dynastic history, where it is used at the end of the two chapters on the Western Regions to describe what the editors considered a failing on the part of Inner Asian rulers: "The countries of the Western Region have each their own ruler, their military forces are dispersed and weak, and they lack the means to rule all as one" (Ban, *Han shu, juan* 96, p. 3930).

84. Tuotuo, *Song shi*, pp. 50–51.

85. To track these changes, we have looked at two sources containing early documents on Mongol state institutions. One is the *Yuan dianzhang* (Yuan institutions), the official compilation of regulations that includes major ideological statements of the

regime, consulted in both the original Yuan edition reprinted by the Palace Museum and the early twentieth-century edition, *Da Yuan shengzheng guochao dianzhang*. The other is the *Yuan chao diangu biannian kao* (Chronology of "Institutions of the Yuan dynasty"), a selection of Yuan documents that Beijing historian Sun Chengze compiled in the mid-seventeenth century to narrate the history of the Mongols during the Yuan as a history of assimilation to Chinese political forms and values. Sun's book follows a chronological sequence that maps out a progressive history for the Mongols as rulers of China. It also appears to imply the steps that Chinese expected the Manchus to take in order to assemble a regime that they could tolerate. Anxiety on that score was misplaced, for the Manchus were quicker to adopt Chinese modes of government than the Mongols had been. Sun could not know that and was using his considerable skills as a historian in the hope of making the best out of the bad situation of being forced to return to Inner Asian rule.

86. Sun Chengze, *Yuan chao diangu biannian kao*, 1.3b, 9b, 10b. The latter two texts appear in *Yuan dianzhang*, 1.1a–1b.

87. Sun Chengze, *Yuan chao diangu biannian kao*, 1.14b–15a.

88. Sun Chengze, *Yuan chao diangu biannian kao*, 3.13b; *Yuan dianzhang*, 1.2b.

89. Sun Chengze, *Yuan chao diangu biannian kao*, 1.4a; *Yuan dianzhang*, 1.3a.

90. Tao Zongyi, *Nancun chuogeng lu*, pp. 16–17.

91. Sun Chengze, *Yuan chao diangu biannian kao*, 8.13b–19b. This text is also preserved in Tao Zongyi, *Nancun chuogeng lu*, pp. 32–38. Tao prefaces the text with an approving comment that Yang "at one stroke cleansed the disputations in the realm," even though the decision went against him.

92. Cleaves, "Sino-Mongolian Inscription of 1346," pp. 33, 82.

93. Brook, *Troubled Empire*, p. 28.

94. Some forty years later, in 1407, the Yongle emperor briefly occupied the northern part of Vietnam; the region remained under the Ming until 1427. Tibet was considered to be outside the geographies of both the Yuan and Ming states, according to their official dynastic histories.

95. Atwood, "National Questions and National Answers," p. 47.

96. Beckwith, *Empires of the Silk Road*, pp. 196–224.

97. Kapstein, *Tibetans*, pp. 116–123.

98. For a detailed discussion, see Elverskog, *Our Great Qing*, pp. 41–62. For the Mongols, actual military, political, and economic success constituted ipso facto evidence of Heaven's grace. A dual appeal to the will of Heaven and to Buddhism is constantly reenacted in Mongolian texts that recite the lineage of khans back to Chinggis. For example, the *Jewel Translucent Sutra*, a biography of Altan Khan written in 1607, declares Chinggis Khan's birth and rulership to have been fated by *degere tengri*, translated as "highest God" by Elverskog (*Our Great Qing*, p. 44) and as "Heaven-on-High" by de Rachewiltz (*Secret History of the Mongols*, vol. 1, p. 224). The Chinese official history of the Yuan, *Yuan shi*, gives both bases of legitimacy equal credit, praising Chinggis Khan as "the holy martial emperor for whom the Dharma and Heaven opened good fortune" (Song Lian, *Yuan shi*, p. 1).

99. Early on, Nurhaci appears to have patronized a Tibetan Buddhist monk of the

Gelug order and appointed him state preceptor. Known only as Oluk Darhan Nangso, the monk visited his court in 1621. Hong Taiji invited the Fifth Dalai Lama to his court in Mukden six years later. See Kam, "The dGe-lugs-pa Breakthrough"; also Grupper, "Manchu Patronage and Tibetan Buddhism," p. 51.

100. The Ming emperors, like the Manchus who replaced them, borrowed legitimacy conceptualizations that the Mongols took from Tibetan Buddhism; see Robinson, "The Ming Court and the Legacy of the Yuan Mongols"; also Kapstein, *Tibetans*, pp. 123–126.

CHAPTER THREE

1. These observations on Confucianism have been derived from the *Analects* of Confucius, particularly sections 2.4, 3.2, 9.5, 12.1, 16.18, 20.1. Translations have been adapted from Legge, *Confucian Classics*, vol. 1.

2. Jiang, *Great Ming Code*, p. 3.

3. *Analects*, 9.13 (restated at 13.19), 15.5.

4. Brook, "What Happens When Wang Yangming Crosses the Border?," p. 83.

5. Paying tribute was not unique to historical Asia, much less China. Polities in Europe, the Middle East, and elsewhere engaged in tribute-paying activities for much of their history. What distinguishes the Chinese tribute scheme from the rest was an elaborate set of rules, derived from Confucianism, including tributary institutions, protocols, and rituals to be complied with by those who wished to have diplomatic relations with China. We thank Yuan-kang Wang for pointing this out.

6. David Kang, *East Asia before the West*, pp. 8–10.

7. *Analects*, 15.1.

8. In Viet sources the polity was called Đại Việt (Viet Great State) from 1054 to 1804, except for a short interval from 1400 to 1407, when the name Dai Ngu was used, and during the Chinese occupation of the country from 1407 to 1427. Later polities referred to themselves as Nam Viet and Vietnam. Annam, "pacified south," is the Chinese name that Ming sources used to refer to the northern half of today's Vietnam. In this chapter we use Dai Viet, except when quoting Chinese sources, in which case we may use Annam.

9. Chin, *Savage Exchange*, chap. 1.

10. Koo, *"Imun" yŏkchu*, vol. 3, p. 39.

11. Ibid., vol. 1, p. 246.

12. *Ming Yingzong shilu*, 337.4b; our thanks to Geoff Wade for bringing this and the next reference to our attention.

13. *Ming Xiaozong shilu*, 159.6a.

14. Bielenstein, *Diplomacy and Trade in the Chinese World*, p. 673. In fairness to Bielenstein, the accusation was not an absurd assessment of Song tribute relations, which more often involved the Song paying tribute to other states than the other way round. His approach was to de-emphasize the rhetoric of tribute and investiture in favor of the language of diplomacy, recognition, and trade so as to de-Sinify the study of China's foreign relations (pp. 5–7).

15. Fairbank and Teng, "On the Ch'ing Tributary System," p. 141.

16. Fairbank, *Chinese World Order*, p. 12.

17. Hamashita, *China, East Asia and the Global Economy*, pp. 12–20; see also his *Chōkō shisutemu to kindai Ajia*. This position has received pushback from younger Japanese scholars, such as Yasufumi Toyooka, who feels that tribute is not a good enough rubric to capture the complexities and realities of interpolity relations, particularly in the Qing period; see his comments in "Shinchō to kyū Min rei kokusai kankei."

18. As it happened, a Javanese envoy to the Yuan court was in Fujian on his way home when the dynasty fell. Prevented from leaving the country, he was brought to Nanjing until the appropriate protocol for handling an ambassador to the previous dynasty had been worked out, which it was early in 1369 (*Ming Taizu shilu*, 39.3a).

19. Ibid., 37.23a.

20. Ibid., 38.11a, 39.1b.

21. Ibid., 39.2b. That day Hongwu also sent a calendar to Java via returning emissary Niezhimouding so that, as he tells the ruler of Java, "you will know where the legitimate calendar is kept."

22. Ibid., 43.3b.

23. Ibid., 39.2b. This and the majority of the following references to the *Veritable Records of the Ming* (*Ming shilu*) follow the translation in Wade, *Southeast Asia in the "Ming Shi-lu."*

24. *Ming Taizu shilu*, 47.4a.

25. Ibid., 47.5b–6a, 48.5a.

26. Ibid., 50.7a–b.

27. Ibid., 53.9b.

28. Zhang Tingyu, *Ming shi*, pp. 23–28, 34–35; see also the observations in Fuma, *Chūgoku higashi Ajia gaikō kōryūshi no kenkyū*, p. 319.

29. *Ming Taizu shilu*, 126.4b.

30. Zhang Tingyu, *Ming shi*, pp. 7906–7908.

31. The argument that follows runs the risk of falling into the sort of functionalist explanation for which James Hevia took John Fairbank to task in *Cherishing Men from Afar*, pp. 10–11. Hevia worried that Fairbank's interpretation of the tribute system as performing "the useful function of garnering to the court the prestige it needed to remain in power" implies an assumption of isolation and Sinocentrism that misses the dynamic of ritual exchange protocols. Yet as Hevia writes, "the submission of foreign princes to the emperor *functioned* [Hevia's emphasis] to legitimize the ruling house." This after all is what ritual does: it *functions*.

32. Zhang Tingyu, *Ming shi*, pp. 717–776.

33. *Ming Taizong shilu*, 12a.7a.

34. Ibid., 17.2a.

35. Ibid., 24.5b.

36. Ibid.

37. Ibid., 47.4a.

38. For the case of Japan, see Wang Zhenping, *Ambassadors from the Islands of Immortals*.

39. *Ming Taizong shilu*, 20a.2b, 22.3a. For a sensible account of the significance of the Zheng He expeditions, see Sen, "Impact of Zheng He's Expeditions on Indian Ocean Interactions." For a helpful corrective on the size of the so-called "star rafts" or "treasure ships," see Church, "Colossal Ships of Zheng He," pp. 160–162.

40. *Ming Taizong shilu*, 43.3b.

41. Song Lian, *Yuan shi*, chap. 210.

42. Huntington, *Clash of Civilizations and the Remaking of World Order*, pp. 234–238.

43. David Kang, "Getting Asia Wrong," p. 66; David Kang, *East Asia before the West*, p. 8.

44. Shambaugh, "China Engages Asia," p. 95.

45. Brzezinski, *Second Chance*, pp. 209, 206.

46. Rossabi, *China among Equals*, p. 1; Fairbank, "Tributary Trade and China's Relations with the West," p. 137.

47. The fifteen countries are Korea, Japan, Greater and Lesser Ryukyu Islands, Dai Viet, Champa, Cambodia, Samudra/Pasai (northern Sumatra), Java, Pahang, Srivijaya (central and southern Sumatra), Siam, Brunei, Coromandel, and Baihua. The identity of Baihua is uncertain: Mills, *Ma Huan, Ying-yai Sheng-lan*, p. 270, identified it as Pajajaran in western Java, but Paka on the Terengganu coast is an equally plausible candidate.

48. Rossabi, "The Ming and Inner Asia," p. 249.

49. On these five campaigns, see Zhongguo junshi shi bianxiezu, *Zhongguo junshi shi*, vol. 2, pp. 521–530; Chan, "Chien-Wen, Yung-Lo, Hung-Hsi, and Hsüan-Te Reigns," pp. 226–229.

50. Waldron, *Great Wall of China*, pp. 74–75.

51. On the limits placed on China's expansionist activities by logistical problems, see Hui, "China's Long March to the Periphery."

52. *Ming Xuanzong shilu*, 26.2a.

53. *Ming Taizong shilu*, 94.5a–b.

54. Zhang Tingyu, *Ming shi*, p. 7767; Zheng Hesheng and Zheng Yijun, *Zheng He xia Xiyang ziliao huibian*, p. 902; see also Dun Li, *Ageless Chinese*, p. 283.

55. Wade, "Zheng He Voyages."

56. *Ming Taizong shilu*, 71.6a–b.

57. Arab states were treated on a more equal footing, probably because "the Chinese were awed by the wealth and power of many of the Muslim potentates" (Swanson, *Eighth Voyage of the Dragon*, pp. 39–40).

58. Clark, "Sino-Korean Tributary Relations under the Ming."

59. Yun, "Rethinking the Tribute System," p. 184; Clark, "Sino-Korean Tributary Relations under the Ming."

60. Clark, "Sino-Korean Tributary Relations under the Ming," pp. 273–279; Yun, "Rethinking the Tribute System," pp. 182–196.

61. Zhang Tingyu, *Ming shi*, pp. 8341–8342; Dreyer, *Early Ming China*, p. 120.

62. Cohen, *East Asia at the Center*, pp. 170–171; Mote, *Imperial China*, p. 613.

63. Jing-shen Tao, *Two Sons of Heaven*, p. 4; Feng Zhang, "Rethinking the 'Tribute System'"; Wills, *Embassies and Illusions*, p. 4.

64. Rossabi, "The Ming and Inner Asia," p. 245. At this time Tibet consisted of several polities and was home to four principal schools of Tibetan Buddhism.

65. Yuan-kang Wang, *Harmony and War*.

66. Feng Zhang, "Rethinking the 'Tribute System,'" pp. 568–569.

67. On the concept of asymmetry in China's foreign relations, see Womack, *China and Vietnam*.

68. Jing-shen Tao, *Two Sons of Heaven*, 4, 8; Bielenstein, *Diplomacy and Trade in the Chinese World*, p. 675; Mancall, "Persistence of Tradition in Chinese Foreign Policy," p. 18; Ledyard, "Yin and Yang in the China-Manchuria-Korea Triangle."

69. Wang Gungwu, "Early Ming Relations with Southeast Asia," p. 60.

70. *Ming Taizong shilu*, 44.5b–6b.

71. *Ming Yingzong shilu*, 190.12b–13a.

72. *Ming Taizu shilu*, 244.2b–4a.

73. See Yuan-kang Wang, *Harmony and War*, pp. 151–154. Still the best overview of the Ming occupation is Woodside, "Early Ming Expansionism."

74. *Ming Taizong shilu*, 63.1a, 68.3b–7a.

75. Ibid., 80.3b–4a.

76. Ibid., 65.1b–2a.

77. *Ming Shizong shilu*, 248.1b–5a.

78. *Ming Xuanzong shilu*, 33.1a–b.

79. *Ming Yingzong shilu*, 43.2b.

80. *Ming Taizong shilu*, 72.1a–b.

81. *Ming Shizong shilu*, 268.3a–b.

82. *Ming Xianzong shilu*, 3.5b–6a.

83. *Ming Xiaozong shilu*, 105.6b–8a.

84. Examples abound; e.g., *Ming Taizong shilu*, 130.1b–2a: "*Man* and *yi* are just like birds and animals"; *Ming Shizong shilu*, 199.6b–7b: "The *man* and *di*, like the birds and the beasts, are without human morality"; *Ming Xuanzong shilu*, 64.4a–5b: "The *man* and *yi* are wily and deceitful"; *Ming Xiaozong shilu*, 273.2a: "the various *yi* of Yunnan are barbarous, rebellious, and perverse."

85. *Ming Taizong shilu*, 217.1a–b.

86. See, e.g., *Ming Yingzong shilu*, 81.5b–6a; *Ming Shenzong shilu*, 428.9b–10b, citing a supervising secretary as explaining that "the reason China is respected by the *yi* in the four directions is entirely because it enfeoffs with titles and issues seals."

87. *Ming Taizong shilu*, 116.2a–b; see also Yuan-kang Wang, "Myth of Chinese Exceptionalism," p. 61; Dreyer, *Zheng He*, pp. 70–73. After receiving the royal hostage at court, Yongle decided to free him and send him home on Zheng He's next voyage.

88. *Ming Xiaozong shilu*, 175.5b–6a. Ming princes (lateral kinsmen of the imperial line) were also regarded as providing a "screen" for the emperor; see Clunas, *Screen of Kings*, p. 9.

89. See *Ming Taizu shilu*, 244.2b–4a, which distinguishes China from "the foreigners and chieftains surrounding China on its borders" (3b) and places Yunnan within the pale ("Yunnan is already what we possess").

90. *Ming Taizong shilu*, 58.1a, 185.2a–b. Even though Dai Viet's "country" status was restored once China ended its occupation, it was again referred to as historically part of China soon after. See, e.g., *Ming Xianzong shilu*, 219.6a–7b, citing the Chenghua emperor stating in 1481 that "the two countries of Annam and Champa have been administrative divisions of China since the Qin and Han dynasties"; and *Ming Shizong shilu*, 248.1b–5a, where the Jiajing emperor claims in 1541 that "Annam has since ancient times belonged to China."

91. *Bang giao luc*, A.691, 1/25a.

92. Kelley, "Vietnam as a 'Domain of Manifest Civility.'"

93. On Zhao Tuo, see Burton Watson, *Records of the Grand Historian: Han Dynasty*, vol. 2, pp. 207–208. On Shi Xie, see Keith Taylor, *Birth of Vietnam*, pp. 70–80.

94. Ly, *Viet dien u linh tap luc toan bien*, p. 171. This is an early nineteenth-century edition of a work first published in the fourteenth century. The edition contains "appraisals" (*tiem binh*) by unidentified later scholars, one of which is quoted here.

95. For Sino-Vietnamese history in this period, see James Anderson, *Rebel Den of Nung Tri Cao*.

96. Ngo, *Daietsu shiki zensho*, p. 97. For an example of the equivalence argument, see Keith Taylor, *Birth of Vietnam*, p. 309.

97. Ngo, *Daietsu shiki zensho*, p. 98.

98. *Ming Wuzong shilu*, 4.11a–b; *Ming Shizong shilu*, 5.15b.

99. We are grateful to Yuan-kang Wang for contributing some of the insights in the final section of this chapter.

100. Quoted in Larsen, *Tradition, Treaties, and Trade*, p. 28, with minor changes.

101. Zhang Tingyu, *Ming shi*, p. 8281; Clark, "Sino-Korean Tributary Relations under the Ming," p. 272.

102. Clark, "Sino-Korean Tributary Relations under the Ming," p. 272.

CHAPTER FOUR

1. The emperors extended their power throughout the Tibetan Plateau, Ladakh, and other Himalayan regions as well as beyond what we now think of as the Tibetan cultural region, to encompass what is today Xinjiang (including Khotan) and Gansu (including Dunhuang). For a short while it even extended to the capital of Tang China, Chang'an. Though the empire ended in the ninth century, Tibetan Buddhism survived and spread as a potent force in Inner Asia. For an overview, see Van Schaik, *Tibet*, pp. 1–60.

2. Kapstein, *Tibetans*, p. 52.

3. For a discussion of the post-imperial period until the establishment of the Sakya hegemony, see Kapstein, *Tibetans*, pp. 84–110; also Van Schaik, *Tibet*, pp. 61–75.

4. Kapstein, *Tibetans*, p. 112.

5. Mullin, *Fourteen Dalai Lamas*, p. 7.

6. According to Buddhist belief, bodhisattvas can also incarnate in animal form and in the form of spirits of other, ethereal worlds.

7. On a deeper level of understanding, these bodhisattvas also symbolize aspects of our own consciousness, which we can develop to full enlightenment.

8. Ishihama, "On the Dissemination of the Belief in the Dalai Lama as a Manifestation of the Bodhisattva Avalokiteśvara," pp. 44–50, demonstrates that the emperor Songtsen Gampo was considered the manifestation of Avalokitesvara, who subsequently repeatedly manifested as the ruler of Tibet, in particular as Phagpa and the successive Dalai Lamas.

9. For a discussion of origin myths, see Kapstein, *Tibetans*, pp. 33–46. A popular myth referred to in the Fifth Dalai Lama's autobiography relates that Tibetans are the descendants of the union between a monkey and a rock-dwelling demoness, the monkey being a manifestation of Avalokitesvara.

10. The ninth-century *Old Tibetan Chronicles* already had reflected the belief in the sacred character of the early Tibetan dynastic rulers, but it was only much later that the *tsenpos* (heavenly monarchs) of Tibet's imperial past were portrayed as emanations of Avalokitesvara.

11. On terminology, see Ruegg, "Preceptor-Donor (*Yon Mchod*) Relation," p. 864.

12. Ardussi, "Formation of the State of Bhutan," pp. 14, 17.

13. Ishihama, "On the Dissemination of the Belief in the Dalai Lama as a Manifestation of the Bodhisattva Avalokiteśvara," pp. 46–48.

14. Mullin explains the basic concept thus: "Every action we do leaves an impression on the mind and acts as a propelling force in our unfoldment. . . . The emphasis is on self-responsibility, and on gaining control over all actions of body, speech and mind in order to attain personal liberation and nirvana" (*Fourteen Dalai Lamas*, p. 4).

15. Ibid., pp. 8–9.

16. The term *chö-si* is an abbreviation for *chos srid gnyis ldan* or its variant *chos srid zung 'brel*. For a discussion, see Ishihama, "Notion of 'Buddhist Government.'" It was a common idea among Tibetans, Mongols, and Manchus from the latter half of the sixteenth century to at least the end of the seventeenth. A seminal work on the topic is Dungkar Rinpoche, *Bod kyi chos srid zung 'brel skor bshad pa*, reprinted in his collected works, *gSung-rtsom Phyogs-bsgrigs*, and translated into English as *The Merging of Religious and Secular Rule in Tibet*. According to Sinha, "while in organizational sense *chos srid gnyis ldan* meant diarchy of clerical and lay elements, in ideological sense it meant synthesis" ("Chhos srid gnyis ldan," p. 13).

17. Ishihama, "Notion of 'Buddhist Government,'" pp. 15–21.

18. The translation of "Dharma" as "religion" is inadequate in denoting only one aspect of the multiple and varied content of this Sanskrit word and its Tibetan equivalent *chö* (Sinha, "Chhos srid gnyis ldan," pp. 13–14).

19. Ruegg, "Preceptor-Donor (*Yon Mchod*) Relation," p. 857; for a more detailed discussion, see his *Ordre spirituel et ordre temporel dans la pensée bouddhique de l'Inde et du Tibet*.

20. "Chogyal" combines the terms *chokyi* (religious) and *gyalpo* (king); see Kolås, "Tibetan Nationalism," p. 53.

21. Ruegg explains that *mchod gnas* "literally means worthy of honour / an honorarium, i.e. of the ritual present or fee . . . due the preceptor-officiant" (the lama) from his royal disciple. *Yon bdag* is an honorific appellation, according to Ruegg, applicable to rulers who are donors giving sustenance to a monk donee in the Buddhist structure of society ("Introductory Remarks on the Spiritual and Temporal Orders," p. 9).

22. The English word "patron," in its dictionary meaning of "a person who gives financial or other support to a person, organization, cause, or activity" (www.oxforddictionaries.com), used frequently in the context of the arts, comes close to the usage of *yöndag*. But it should not be confused with other meanings of "patron" as regular customer or client of a business or with its rare meaning of Roman slave master. Closely related is the word "benefactor": "a person who gives money or other help to a person or cause" (www.oxforddictionaries.com). Arguably, none of these characterizations provides a complete sense of the relationship; see Ruegg's critique of the use of the term "patron" in his "*Mchod Yon, Yon Mchod* and *Mchod Gnas / Yon Gnas*," pp. 443–447.

23. *Chöné* is perhaps most accurately translated as "officiant," a person who performs a religious service or ceremony, from the medieval Latin meaning "performing divine service."

24. Hierarchs of all schools of Tibetan Buddhism forged *chö-yön* relationships with powerful supporters. Tibetan lamas of the Kagyu order acted as state preceptors (head chaplains) to the rulers of the Tangut empire (also known as the Western Xia) already in the eleventh century.

25. The establishment of Mongol authority over Tibet occurred following the military campaign of Möngke Khan in 1252, and not in 1244 as was previously often assumed. See Kapstein, *Tibetans*, p. 111.

26. *Rgya-bod-yig-tsang* quoted and translated by Sinha, "Chhos srid gnyis ldan," p. 20.

27. Ganden Phodrang (or Gaden Phodrang) was the name of the Dalai Lama's residence in Drepung Monastery outside Lhasa. It came to designate the Tibetan government, in a similar way perhaps as the White House today refers to the executive branch of the US government, and L'Élysée the French. The Ganden Phodrang government exercised authority, at least over central Tibet (encompassing the region of Ü-Tsang and Ngari and the western Kham), until the mid-twentieth century.

28. Ruegg, "Introductory Remarks on the Spiritual and Temporal Orders," p. 10.

29. Ruegg, "*Mchod Yon, Yon Mchod* and *Mchod Gnas / Yon Gnas*," p. 451; Ishihama, "Notion of 'Buddhist Government,'" pp. 15–21.

30. Ruegg, "Introductory Remarks on the Spiritual and Temporal Orders," p. 10.

31. Ishihama, review of Elverskog, *Our Great Qing*, pp. 515–516.

32. Examples are the wars against Bhutan in the seventeenth century, Gorkha in 1789 and 1856, Nyarong in the nineteenth century, and the British in 1904.

33. Dalizhabu uses the Chinese translations of the biographies. Biographies of the

First to Twelfth Dalai Lamas were almost all translated into Chinese and published by China Tibetology Press. These include those of the First, Second, Third, Fourth, Fifth, Seventh, Eighth, Ninth, and Twelfth Dalai Lamas. The biography of the Fifth Dalai Lama is an autobiography, although the final three volumes (vols. 4–6), written by the *desi* (regent) Sanggyé Gyatso, cover the years after his death, which was concealed by the *desi*. The data used in this section concerning the Zunghar missions to Tibet in 1743 and 1747 are from Zhongguo diyi lishi dang'anguan, *Qingdai junjichu manwen aocha dang*.

34. Altan Khan sent envoys for this purpose in 1571 and again in 1576; Chen Qingying and Ma Lianlong, *Yishi-sishi Dalai Lama zhuan*, pp. 225–228.

35. Qiao, *Menggu fojiao shi Bei Yuan shiqi*, p. 60.

36. Chen Qingying and Ma Lianlong, *Yishi-sishi Dalai Lama zhuan*, p. 238.

37. Ibid., p. 279.

38. Ibid., pp. 307, 311–312, 315.

39. Ibid., p. 319; see also Chen Qingying and Ma Lianlong, *Wushi Dalai Lama zhuan*, vol. 1, pp. 57–58.

40. Bormanshinov, "Kalmyk Pilgrims to Tibet and Mongolia."

41. The Tibetan expression is a variation of *manggye* (*mang-'gyed*), meaning literally "to divide among the many" or "to distribute." For a discussion of this important socioeconomic wealth distribution ritual in Tibet and Bhutan, see Ardussi, "Wealth Distribution Rituals," pp. 127–135. The full Mongolian version is *burqan-dur mörgön mangja činaqu* (to brew tea bowing to Buddha); the Manchu equivalent is *dzang de manja fuifume genembi* (*manja fuifumbi* for short) and *jin zang ao cha* in Chinese, both meaning "to go to Tibet and brew/boil tea."

42. Chen Qingying and Ma Lianlong, *Wushi Dalai Lama zhuan*, vol. 1, p. 55.

43. Ibid., pp. 54–55.

44. Radnabahdara, *Zay-a Bandida zhuan*.

45. See Ardussi, "Wealth Distribution Rituals."

46. Wulan, *Menggu yuanliu yanjiu*, pp. 466–470, 714–718; Chen Qingying and Ma Lianlong, *Wushi Dalai Lama zhuan*, vol. 1, p. 64.

47. Chen Qingying and Ma Lianlong, *Wushi Dalai Lama zhuan*, vol. 1, pp. 57–58. We are told by the Fifth Dalai Lama that he received vast amounts of presents during that one and a half month period, including Chinese and Mongolian goods and money to repair temples.

48. Radnabahdara, *Zay-a Bandida zhuan*, pp. 65, 75–76, 80.

49. Perdue, "The Qing State and the Gansu Grain Market," p. 111.

50. Radnabahdara, *Zay-a Bandida zhuan*, pp. 92–93.

51. Zhongguo diyi lishi dang'anguan Zhongguo bianjiang diqu lishi yu dili yanjiu zhongxin, *Junjichu manwen Zhungaer shizhe dang*, vol. 2, pp. 1839–1840. They gave 10,000 taels of silver to the Dalai Lama and to a number of his disciples and 7 taels to each monk of the Gelugpa monasteries in the Lhasa area and half a tael of silver each to the monks of the monasteries of the other schools of Tibetan Buddhism; Duka, Wangjie, and Tang, *Poluonai zhuan*, p. 339.

52. They gave 5 taels of silver to the lamas of each monastery, and 450 monks selected to chant scriptures were each rewarded with 15 taels of silver and other gifts; Zhongguo diyi lishi dang'anguan Zhongguo bianjang diqu lishi yu dili yanjiu zhong-xin, *Junjichu manwen Zhungaer shizhe dang*, vol. 2, pp. 1827–1830. One memorial re-cords that a total of 156,167 taels of silver was dispersed (pp. 1822–1823).

53. Zhongguo diyi lishi dang'anguan, *Qingdai junjichu manwen aocha dang*, vol. 2, pp. 1853–1859.

54. *Qing Gaozong shilu*, vol. 1427, p. 83.

55. Chen Xiaoqiang, "Qingdai zhongyang zhengfu dui Xizang xingzheng guanli de caizheng zhichu."

56. Chen Qingying and Ma Lianlong, *Wushi Dalai Lama zhuan*, vol. 1, p. 101; see also Chen Qingying and Ma Lianlong, *Yishi-sishi Dalai Lama zhuan*, p. 241.

57. The Wanli emperor encouraged the khan to build Thegchen Chonkhor Monas-tery in Kokonor for the Third Dalai Lama; *Ming Shenzong shilu* [Veritable records of the Wanli reign], vol. 61, in *Chaoben Ming shilu*, p. 365.

58. Zhang Tingyu, *Ming shi*, pp. 5850–5853.

59. Chen Qingying and Ma Lianlong, *Wushi Dalai Lama zhuan*, vol. 1, pp. 313, 318, 390.

60. Cai, *Menggu jin Zang aocha qianyi*, p. 101.

61. *Qing Shengzu shilu*, p. 810.

62. This is demonstrated in the work of Henry Serruys, notably *Sino-Mongol Rela-tions during the Ming*, vol. 3. From Tibet, the Mongols brought back religious statues, books, and scroll paintings as well as medicine.

63. This was interrupted when Ligdan Khagan, of the Chakhars, conquered and subdued the Tümeds, Ordos, and Kharchins living in what is now Inner Mongolia in 1627 and took control of the trade route. Ligdan patronized the Sakya lamas, as Khubilai had, and prevented leaders of the Khalkhas and Oirats, who patronized the Gelugpa, from trading with the Ming to obtain the goods they needed to make offer-ings in Tibet. Although this did not affect those Tümeds and Khalkhas who were al-ready in the Kokonor region at the time, Khalkha and Oirat trade, and therefore also their pilgrimages to Tibet, fully resumed only after Ligdan died in 1634 and the Cha-khars submitted to the expanding Manchu empire together with the Tümeds, Ordos, and Kharchins.

64. Radnabahdara, *Zay-a Bandida zhuan*, pp. 65, 75–76, 80.

65. Cai, *Menggu jin Zang aocha qianyi*, p. 101; Ma, "Qianlong chunian Zhungaer shouling shouci ru Zang aocha shimo."

66. For simplicity, we use the names Sikkim and Bhutan to designate the territories that were to emerge as state polities in the seventeenth century.

67. Ardussi, "Sikkim and Bhutan in the Crosscurrents of Seventeenth and Eigh-teenth Century Tibetan History."

68. On Pema Lingpa, see Tshewang et al., *Treasure Revealer of Bhutan*.

69. The autobiography of Pema Lingpa, edited by his student Rgyal-ba Don-'grub, is reprinted in Pema, *Rediscovered Teachings of the Great Padma-gling-pa*, vol. 14.

70. The title Zhabdrung Rinpoché was an honorific style adopted by several reincarnate lamas during that period, translating roughly as "the reincarnation at whose feet one must submit."

71. For an evaluation of the Zhabdrung's personality and deeds, see Ardussi, "Formation of the State of Bhutan."

72. For images of the raven crown of the Druk Gyalpo, or king of Bhutan, see Aris, *Raven Crown*, p. 57.

73. Mullard, "Bkra dkar bkra shis sdings kyi sku 'bum," presents evidence for a somewhat later date for the coronation, arguing that the year 1642 was retrospectively adopted to conform to the foundation date of the Ganden Phodrang government.

74. The source for this discussion is Ardussi, "Rapprochement between Bhutan and Tibet."

75. In 1747, during the troubled times of the Fifth Chogyal Namgyal Phuntshog, the Tibetan government deputed an official named Rabten Sharpa to serve as a regent and assist in reestablishing firm governance under Sikkimese rulers; see Yeshe Dolma and Thutob Namgyal, "The History of Sikkim" (1908), an unpublished typescript manuscript currently being retranslated for publication by John Ardussi and Per Sørensen.

76. Nurhaci patronized Tibetan Buddhism as of 1621. Nurhaci's son and his successors maintained *chö-yön* relations with a number of Tibetan Buddhist hierarchs; see Rawski, *Last Emperors*, p. 251.

77. See Karmay, "Fifth Dalai Lama and His Reunification of Tibet," pp. 433–434; Schaeffer, Kapstein, and Tuttle, *Sources of Tibetan Tradition*, pp. 540–542; also Ahmad, *Sino-Tibetan Relations in the Seventeenth Century*, pp. 166–191; Rockhill, "Dalai Lamas of Lhasa and Their Relations with the Manchu Emperors of China," pp. 15–18; Tuttle, "Tibetan Buddhist Mission to the East."

78. It is clear from the correspondence between the Fifth Dalai Lama and Emperor Shunzhi that the latter had actually intended to travel beyond the Great Wall to Taika to await the Dalai Lama there; see Ahmad, *Sino-Tibetan Relations in the Seventeenth Century*, pp. 168–177. In fact, their meeting took place inside the Forbidden City.

79. The Dalai Lama received the title of "Very Virtuous, Bliss-Abiding Buddha of the Western Heaven, the One Securer of Buddha's Word for All Beings beneath the Sky, the Immutable Vajradhara Dalai Lama." The emperor received the title of "Great Master, Spiritual One, Emperor of the Heavens, Manjusri Incarnate"; Van Walt van Praag, *Status of Tibet*, p. 210n18.

80. For a detailed discussion, see Perdue, *China Marches West*, pp. 227–240.

81. For a succinct account of these events, see Brook, "Tibet and the Chinese World-Empire."

82. Scholars generally consider that the reforms were directed by the Manchu emperor. Petech, *China and Tibet in the Early XVIIIth Century*, pp. 78 ff.; Kapstein, *Tibetans*, p. 150. Mullin, *Fourteen Dalai Lamas*, p. 291, however, suggests that the decision was made by Tibetan leaders themselves.

83. The title used in Chinese-language Qing documents for the imperial representative was Grand Officer Stationed in Tibet (*zhuzang dachen*). *Dachen* was a term routinely used to denote ambassadors to a foreign country, including Qing ambassadors

to Britain and Japan, and foreign ambassadors stationed in China; see Lau, "Evidence from Chinese Archival and Historical Records," chap. 3.3.

84. Although the Qing emperor intervened against the Zunghars and in support of the Dalai Lama in 1720 and helped drive out Gorkha invaders in 1792, the Qing did not provide military support against the Dogra invasion from Jammu and Ladakh in 1841, nor against the second Gorkha invasion fifteen years later and the British military advance on Lhasa in 1904; see Van Walt van Praag, *Status of Tibet*, pp. 22–23, 33–35.

85. Kapstein, "Seventh Dalai Lama, Kalsang Gyatso," provides a summary of his life and times.

86. Though three biographies of him are known, our remarks here are based solely on the most extensive of them, the extraordinary *Lcang skya rol pa'i rdo rje'i rnam thar* by his disciple Tukwan, regarded as one of the great literary achievements in the Tibetan language. An ornate and intricate text, there is no way that we can do justice to its subtleties here.

87. Some attention must be given to Changkya's role in the recognition of the Eighth Dalai Lama, a role assigned to him by the Qianlong emperor and conducted in tandem with the Panchen Lama Pelden Yeshé, an arrangement that enabled the emperor to participate at a distance in the recognition process without arousing Tibetan animosity. This selection preceded, by some four decades, the Manchu court's introduction of the use of the "golden urn" to select incarnations by lottery, a requirement detested by Tibetans. During the search for the Eighth Dalai Lama, however, the Qianlong emperor was content to let the oracular procedures of the Tibetans run their course.

88. In selecting examples of these for citation here, I have relied on Bod rang skyong ljongs spyi tshogs tshan rig zhib 'jug khang and Krung dbyang mi rigs slob grwa'i bod rig pa'i zhib 'jug khang, eds., *Krung go'i bod sa gnas kyi lo rgyus yig tshang phyogs btus*. Comparison with the 1984 Dharamsala edition of the Seventh Dalai Lama's biography—*Rgyal dbang thams cad mkhyen pa bskal bzang rgya mtsho'i rnam thar*—in *'Phags pa 'jig rten dbang phyug gi rnam sprul rim byon gyi 'khrungs rabs deb ther nor bu'i 'phreng ba* reveals a precise correspondence.

89. See Jagou, "Thirteenth Dalai Lama's Visit to Beijing in 1908."

90. *Krung go'i bod sa gnas kyi lo rgyus yig tshang phyogs btus*, pp. 493–494.

91. Ibid., p. 495.

92. In a later passage detailing the architectural features of the newly constructed Gartar Monastery, it is noted that the cost of construction, amounting to 140,000 silver pieces, was covered from the imperial coffers; ibid., pp. 497–498.

93. Ibid., pp. 501–502. Perhaps Changkya refers to himself in the third person here because he was paraphrasing the announcement as it was made, for a few lines later he writes that "the seventeenth prince and I reached Gartar."

94. Ibid., p. 504.

CHAPTER FIVE

1. Portions of this chapter, notably the introductory paragraphs, draw on Crossley, *Translucent Mirror*; Crossley, *Wobbling Pivot*; Crossley, "Three Governments in One State and the Stability of the Qing Empire"; also Rowe, *China's Last Empire*; Rawski, *Last Emperors*; Elliott, *Manchu Way*.

2. The Dalai Lama and the Panchen Lama recognized Hong Taiji as an emanation of Manjusri in letters they wrote to him in 1640. This recognition was applied to Hong Taiji's successor Fulin, on whom the Dalai Lama bestowed the title of "Great Master, Spiritual One, Emperor of the Heavens, Manjusri Incarnate."

3. The following section by Nicola Di Cosmo is adapted from his "Nurhaci's Gambit: Sovereignty as Concept and Praxis in the Rise of the Manchus," from *The Scaffolding of Soveriegnty*, by Zvi Ben-Dor Benite, Stefanos Geroulanos, and Nicole Jerr, eds. Copyright © 2017 Columbia University Press. Reprinted with the permission of Columbia University Press.

4. The evolution of a notion of sovereignty in the different phases of the preconquest period, specifically in relation to the construction of a Jurchen state and, in the 1620s and 1630s, to the creation of an expanded multiethnic state, has been insufficiently analyzed. The notion of multiple "rulerships"—as distinct from sovereignty—has been discussed recently, particularly in relation to the Qianlong emperor; e.g., Crossley, "Rulerships of China." The construction of the Qing emperors' images and attributes belongs historically and conceptually to the postconquest Qing dynasty. Also, while representative, symbolic, and ideological facets have been studied, the establishment of "sovereignty" as a legitimate authority over a political community that was recognized externally, and the concepts deployed in this process, have not received equal attention.

5. Some of these communities were creations of Ming diplomacy, whereas others had existed during the Yuan dynasty; see Romeyn Taylor, "Yuan Origins of the Wei-so System."

6. *Manbun rōtō*, vol. 1, p. 36; *Jiu manzhou dang*, vol. 1, p. 80.

7. Exceptionally, we do find the term *niozi manju gurun*, or "Jurchen Manchu nation," in a very early source: *Jiu manzhou dang*, vol. 1, p. 81. For a history of the Jurchen during the first part of the Ming dynasty, see Kawachi, *Mindai nyoshinshi no kenkyū*.

8. Wada, "Some Problems concerning the Rise of T'ai-tsu."

9. Several scholars have stressed how Nurhaci's relations and rather aggressive stance with other Jurchen polities were colored by the protection that the Ming gave him (e.g., Diao, "Nuerhaci jueqi yu dongya hua-yi guanxi de bianhua").

10. For the titles Nurhaci acquired or by which he was known, see Di Cosmo, "Nurhaci's Names."

11. *Manbun rōtō*, vol. 1, p. 293.

12. Uray-Köhalmi, "Von woher kamen die Iče Manju?"

13. See Di Cosmo, "Nurhaci's Names," p. 270. The first time *abkai fulingga* appears as a reign name seems to be in 1625; see *Jiu manzhou dang*, vol. 4, p. 1953.

14. A conceptual history of *gurun* and *doro* has a parallel in the recent discussion of the Mongol terms *ulus* and *törö*; see, e.g., Elverskog, *Our Great Qing*, pp. 17–27. A comparative analysis of these concepts would require a thorough reconnaissance of Mongol sources and of the arguments that have been developed by other scholars. While the Mongol term *ulus* in the sense of political community is broadly coterminous with Manchu *gurun*, the term *törö*, in the meaning of "state," cannot be equivalent to *doro*, which in the Manchu usage does not support the notion that it is equivalent to a state, unless by state one means political authority, government, right to rule, or sovereignty.

15. This entry refers to the sixth month of the forty-first year of Wanli (1613): *Manbun rōtō*, vol. 1, p. 28; *Jiu manzhou dang*, vol. 1, p. 58.

16. See Di Cosmo, "From Alliance to Tutelage." "Southern Mongols" refers to Mongols inhabiting the regions south of the Gobi desert. They were called Inner Mongols during the Qing imperial era; as a result, the corresponding region is today known as Inner Mongolia. Similarly, broadly speaking, the region inhabited by Mongols north of the Gobi desert came to be identified as Outer Mongolia and today constitutes the independent state of Mongolia. Hiroki Oka, in a communication to the authors (8 June 2014), explains: "We first encounter the names Inner Mongolia and Outer Mongolia in the historical and geographical works of Chinese scholars of the Qing era, including Qi Yingshi's *Huangchao fanbu yaoliie*. His work divided the Mongols into three groupings including Inner Mongols (*Nei Menggu*), Outer Mongols, and Khalkha and Elute Mongols, meaning the western Mongols or Oirats. In the second decade of the twentieth century, the territory of independent Mongolia under the rule of Bogdo khaan of Khalkha was called Outer Mongolia; it included some Oirat Mongols living in Qobdo and separated from other Mongols under the rule of the Republic of China. After the establishment of the PRC, the geographical and administrative concept of Inner Mongolia included the six ciγulγans of present-day Inner Mongolia, Alasha and Ejine banners, which previously had been included in the Outer Jasaγs or Elute Mongols, as well as Hulunbuir and Chaqar Mongols, who had been part of the Qing's Eight Banners. Finally, in modern Chinese the Republic of Mongolia is still called *Wai Menggu* or Wai Meng, Outer Mongolia."

17. Elliott, *Manchu Way*, p. 40.

18. Ibid., p. 39. The Eight Banners was originally the home of the Manchu power elite, who retained important military functions for much of the imperial period. Although bannermen lost much of their political power beginning in the mid-eighteenth century, the Eight Banners remained a principal instrument for the maintenance of Manchu identity.

19. Crossley, *Translucent Mirror*, pp. 205–214, 311–327.

20. The Northern Yuan, the continuation of the Mongol imperial regime after the fall of the Yuan in China, used khagan or Great Khan. After Altan of Tümed was presented this title by the Great Khan Bodi Alaγ, it was used by a number of Mongol rulers and chieftains. The Manchus used the term for the first two Manchu rulers, Nurhaci and Hong Taiji. After the second enthronement of Hong Taiji in 1636, the Manchu rulers called themselves *enduringge han* in Manchu (*boγda qaγan* in Mongolian),

meaning "the holy khagan," and *huangdi* (emperor) in Chinese. In the middle of the Qing era, the title changed to *enduringge ejen* in Manchu (*boɣda ejen* in Mongolian), meaning "holy lord."

21. Qing administrative categorization further divided the *ɣadaɣadu mongɣol* (outer Mongols) into two categories, the inner *jasaqs* and the outer *jasaqs*. The former referred to the six *ciɣulɣans* (assemblies) located in present-day Inner Mongolia, and the latter referred to the other assemblies, including those of the Khalkhas, located in present-day Mongolia, Qinghai, and Xinjiang.

22. Hong Taiji's "name" is actually a title, the Mongolian *khong tayiji*, meaning "crown prince." Curiously, no sources survive from which we can derive his personal name.

23. These chieftains, or *tabunangs*, belonged to the Uriyankhai clan, who came under Borjigid rule in the sixteenth century. Later, princely status was also granted to the non-Borjigid Oirat chieftains, including those of the Coros clan of the Ögeled and the Dörbed, the Yeke mingɣan clan of the Qoyid, and the Kereyid clan of the Torgud.

24. The officials were called *jasaq bariɣsan tüsimed* (princes appointed to the rank of *jasaq*).

25. This term has been misleadingly translated into English as the Court of Colonial Affairs; see Fairbank, *Cambridge History of China*, vol. 10, p. 37.

26. Bao, "Qingdai 'fanbu' yici kaoshi."

27. On the *otoɣ* of the Northern Yuan, see Morikawa Tetsuo's articles, including "Chaharu hachi otoku to sono bunpū ni tsuite"; "Chūki Mongoru no tumen ni tsuite, tokuni urusu to no kankei wo tsūjite"; "Haruha tumen to sono seiritsu ni tsuite"; "Orudosu jūni otoku kō."

28. Vladimirtsov (*Obshchestvennyi stroi mongolov*) suggested that the *qosiɣu* was a military unit organized by the *otoɣ*, and this implies that the *qosiɣu* was not a permanent institution but a temporary organization that was formed in wartime. Actually the pre-Qing *qosiɣu* had been more or less as permanent as it was in Qing times. In fact, the Mongolian social organization had two sides—that is, *qosiɣu* and *otoɣ*—even in peacetime.

29. Oka, *Shindai Mongoru meiki seido no kenkyū*.

30. This is evident from the registration of soldiers in some banners such as the Central Last Banner of Sečen qan ayimaɣ of the Khalkhas, where the *sumu* personnel were also members of the corresponding princely domains. In his recent study of the Left-Wing Rear Banner of Tüsiyetü qan ayimaɣ, Nakamura Atsushi reveals that the *sumu* of this *qosiɣu* was organized and functioned independently from the *baɣs* of qan ayimaɣ; see his "Shinchō chika Mongoru shakai ni okeru Somu o megutte." Similar cases can be found in some *qosiɣus* in what is today Inner Mongolia; see Chaogeman-dula, "Shilun Qingdai Zhelimu meng shiqi nutuke."

31. From the very beginning of the Manchu effort to extend influence or control over Mongol rulers, they faced the problem of disunity among them. In 1619 Nurhaci entered into an alliance with the twenty-five Khalkha ruling princes and lords in a bid to overcome divisions among them. Although some bore the title of khan, none could

represent all the Khalkha rulers. The alliance was short-lived, however, so in 1626 Nurhaci tried to form a core group among his Khalkha supporters and urged one of them, Uuba Tayiji (a Khorchin Mongol lord and descendant of Küi Möngke Tasqara), to receive the prestigious title of Tüsiyetü khagan, literally "Great Khan with Supporters."

32. Laws prohibiting the crossing of pastureland borders were also issued at this assembly. The codes or laws issued at the end of an assembly were the product of deliberation rather than edicts prescribed unilaterally by the Manchu khan.

33. Besides the ministers dispatched by the emperor to report on the proceedings, Mongol officers of the Eight Banners appeared in the latter two assemblies. According to contemporary Mongol documents, their participation in assemblies continued at least through the reign of Hong Taiji. Because they had Mongolian names, we know they were Mongols incorporated into the Eight Banners as what were called *nuktere monggo* (migrating Mongols).

34. The Shunzhi and Kangxi emperors also changed the assembly procedures for dealing with criminal claims, which further affected the lines of authority, at least in these matters.

35. Elverskog, "Mongol Time Enters a Qing World," pp. 145–146.

36. The Tibetan nobleman Polhané had emerged victorious in a brief civil war and drew all political government power to himself. The Dalai Lama's authority as a Tibetan Buddhist leader was undiminished, but his political authority was in abeyance until he recovered temporal authority in 1751 after a renewed power struggle upon Pohlané's death, in which the *ambans* played a central role and for which they were killed.

37. Yu, "'Chūzō daijin' haken zenya ni okeru Shinchō no tai Chibetto seisaku."

38. Komatsubara, "Jūhachi seiki kōhanki no Chūzō daijin," p. 3.

39. Suzuki Chūsei, *Chibetto o meguru Chū In kankei shi*, p. 44.

40. Memorial of 13 April 1785, *Junjichu manwen lufu zouzhe* [Transcripts of palace memorials in Manchu in the Grand Council] (hereafter abbreviated as *JMLZ*), First Historical Archives of China, Beijing, 3065-16 (134-58): Manchu memorial of Kinglin, QL50.3.5.

41. Memorial of 12 July 1787, *JMLZ* 3166-3 (140-1141): Manchu memorial of Yamantai, QL52.6.7.

42. Murakami, "Panchen Rama sansei no nekka raihō to Shinchō kijin kanryō no taiō," pp. 133–134.

43. Ibid., pp. 130–131.

44. Pozdneyev wrote: "In 1878 Chih-kang arrived in Urga to assume the post of Manchu amban, and at the very first he thought of changing the customs whereby the ambans greeted the Jebtsun damba hutukhtu. According to the forms established since olden times, the ambans, when they met with the hutukhtu, would always bow to the ground before him three times, and then they would exchange khadaks" (*Mongolia and the Mongols*, p. 376). This process was also documented by Thomas Manning, who visited the Ninth Dalai Lama in December 1811: "I made the due obeisance, touching the ground three times with my head to the Grand Lama (Dalai Lama), and once to

the Ti-mu-fu. I presented my gifts, delivering the coin with a handsome silk scarf with my own hands into the hands of the Grand Lama and the Ti-mu-fu. . . . Having delivered the scarf to the Grand Lama, I took off my hat, and humbly gave him my clean-shaven head to lay his hands upon" (Markham, *Narratives of the Mission of George Bogle to Tibet*, p. 265).

45. Zhongguo diyi lishi dang'anguan, *Qianlong chao shangyu dang*, vol. 9, p. 859.

46. Yanagisawa, "Shinchō to Roshia," pp. 194-196, points to a similar practice with regard to Qing dealings with the Russian empire, whose relations on a basis of equality were also kept invisible to the Chinese-speaking world. In that case the invisibility was assured by using Manchu as the principal language of negotiations with Russians.

47. Komatsubara, "Jūhachi seiki kōhanki no Chūzō daijin," p. 12. In an edict in November 1788, the Qianlong emperor expresses displeasure regarding the *ambans*; they had very little influence on political affairs in Tibet, which allowed the Dalai Lama and the *kalons* to act on their own. The emperor points out that this was caused by the incompetence of the *ambans*, as well as the fact that the only thing they were concerned about was kowtowing to and revering the Dalai Lama and Panchen Lama. *Gongzhong manwen tingji* [Court letter in Manchu in the Imperial Palace], Document Category, First Historical Archives of China, Beijing, 63: Manchu imperial edict to Šuliyan, QL53.10.14.

48. Suzuki Chūsei, *Chibetto o meguru Chū In kankei shi*, pp. 42-53.

49. *Junjichu manwen jixin dang* [Court letter record book in Manchu in the Grand Council], Document Category, First Historical Archives of China, Beijing, 141-3: Manchu imperial edict to Sungyun, September 1794, QL59.8.11.

50. *Junjichu manwen jixin dang*, Document Category, First Historical Archives of China, Beijing, 159-1207: Manchu memorial of Sungyun, QL59.11.13.

51. Zhou, "Lun Jiaqingdi dui Xizang difang de zhili," pp. 310-312, comments that in his Tibetan policies, the Jiaqing emperor placated local nobility and priests while taking measures to prevent the expansion of their influence and strictly adhering to the regulations and systems set in place at the end of the Qianlong emperor's reign.

52. The letter was reported to the emperor by the minister of the Lifanyuan on 15 February 1814. Other complaints received by the emperor included one from the most senior Tibetan monk official, Demo Khutukhtu, in *JMLZ*, 3844-39 (184-2142); the Manchu petition in the Grand Council, JQ19.3, is presumed to be a Manchurian translation of Demo Khutukhtu's verbal message. For views on this incident, see Zhou, "Lun Jiaqingdi dui Xizang difang de zhili," p. 312; Xiao, *Qingdai zhu Zang dachen*, p. 143; Liu Limei, "Guanyu zhu Zang dachen yu Dalai Lama xiangjian liyi wenti," pp. 73-74.

53. Zhongguo diyi lishi dang'anguan, *Jiaqing chao shangyu dang* (hereafter abbreviated *JSD*), vol. 19, pp. 21-22: imperial edict to Hutuli and others, JQ19.1.26. See also *JMLZ*, 3844-39 (184-2142): Manchu petition in the Grand Council, JQ19.3.

54. *JSD*, vol. 19, pp. 21-22: imperial edict to Hutuli and others, JQ19.1.26.

55. *JSD*, vol. 19, pp. 111-112: imperial edict to Hening, JQ19.2.30; imperial edict to Sungyun, JQ19.2.30.

56. *Junjichu lufu zouzhe* [Transcripts of palace memorials in Chinese in the Grand Council] (hereafter abbreviated *JLZ*), Document Category (microfilms), First Histori-

cal Archives of China, Beijing, 165-8005-2: Chinese memorial of Hening, JQ19, intercalary 2.6.

57. See the autobiography of the Eighth Dalai Lama; the complaint of Demo Khutukhtu, *JMLZ*, 3844-39 (184-2142): Manchu petition in the Grand Council, JQ19.3; *JLZ*, 165-8005-5: the Chinese memorial of Sungyun, JQ19, intercalary 2.17; *JLZ*, 165-8005-2: Chinese memorial of Hening, JQ19, intercalary 2.6.; *JLZ*, 165-8005-1: Yu Wenfeng's testimony in the Chinese memorial of Cangming, JQ19.2.14.

58. *JLZ*, 165-8005-1: Yu Wenfeng's testimony in the Chinese memorial of Cangming, JQ19.2.14.

59. *JSD*, vol. 19, pp. 197–198: Chinese imperial edict to Hutuli and others, JQ19.3.7.

60. Markham, *Narratives of the Mission of George Bogle to Tibet*, p. 274.

61. It is worth noting that the Jiaqing emperor's reign was also marked by a growing assertion by the Chinese elite in the affairs of the empire, including imperial policies in Inner Asia; see Mosca, "The Literati Rewriting of China in the Qianlong-Jiaqing Transition."

62. Quoted in Crossley, *Translucent Mirror*, pp. 192–193.

63. In offering this perspective, we contradict earlier popular assumptions. In this regard, see Lydia Liu, *Clash of Empires*, p. 83; also Elliott, *Manchu Way*, pp. xiv–xv, 26–35.

64. Crossley discusses this text in "*Dayi juemi lu* and the Lost Yongzheng Philosophy of Identity." The passage is quoted in Lydia Liu, *Clash of Empires*, p. 84.

65. From the *Veritable Records of the Qing*, as cited in Lydia Liu, *Clash of Empires*, pp. 85–86.

66. Like dynasties that ruled China before them, the Qing represented its hegemony over all outsiders (*tulergi*) in an illustrated catalog of the peoples presenting tribute. Of the ten volumes of the Qing edition, the first deals with those nations that addressed the emperor in his role as *tianzi*. The remaining nine depict those tribute-bearing peoples who were under the rule or overlordship of the Qing emperor either as *huangdi*, khan, or Great Khan.

67. See, e.g., Fairbank, *Chinese World Order*, p. 3.

68. "Benchao zhi wei manzhou, you zhongguo zhi you jiguan"; for details, see Crossley, "*Dayi juemi lu* and the Lost Yongzheng Philosophy of Identity."

69. For an overview of Chinese scholarship asserting a direct equivalence between *zhongguo* and *dulimba-i gurun*, see Zhao, "Reinventing China," esp. pp. 6–10.

70. On the ambiguities and complexities of this usage for the Jurchen Jin and Khitan Liao states, see Kane, "Great Central Liao Kitan State."

71. See Walravens, "Das *Huang Ch'ing chih-kung t'u* als der Werk der mandjurischen Literatur."

72. For related background, see Dai, "To Nourish a Strong Military," p. 71; Mosca, *From Frontier Policy to Foreign Policy*, pp. 10–11; Mosca, "Empire and Circulation of Frontier Intelligence."

73. Wills, "Great Qing and Its Southern Neighbors"; Tana Li, *Nguyen Cochinchina*.

74. Jung-chul Lee, "Analysis of the Studies of Taedongpŏp from the Historical-Institutional Perspective."

75. Schmid, "Tributary Relations and the Qing-Chosŏn Frontier on Mount Paektu"; Chul-sung Lee, "Re-evaluation of the Chosŏn Dynasty's Trade Relationship with the Ch'ing Dynasty," esp. pp. 106–112.

76. In 1645 the Qing refused to allow Koreans of registered Chinese descent to conduct their trade through the Board of Rites branch office in Mukden, as they had done in Ming times. They were forced to petition to bring their trade regulations under the jurisdiction of the Board of Rites in Beijing. Slightly later, the Kangxi emperor approved their applications to have Beijing Board of Rites staff or contractors handle their lading, though the fees were to go directly to the coffers of the Qing imperial family.

77. Seon-min Kim, "Border and Border Trespassing between Qing China and Chosŏn Korea."

78. Crossley, "Coercion and the Inner History of Qing-Joseon Relations."

79. The imperial representative Akdun was accompanied on his mission by the distinguished painter Zheng Ma.

80. The closest comparison with the Chosŏn case might be Qing relations with Burma. Burma entered the guest ritual in the late eighteenth century after decades of military pressure from the Qing. But in its case, the Qing was unable to compel political subordination and failed in its claim over Burmese territory. When Burma invaded Thailand, which then suffered a series of violent coups d'état resulting in the elevation of Rama as the first Chakri king of Siam in 1782, the Qing took no action and made little inquiry.

CHAPTER SIX

1. On Chinese adaptations to this transformation, see Svarverud, *International Law as World Order in Late Imperial China*.

2. See Hevia, *Cherishing Men from Afar*, for the reversal of the once-standard account of the Chinese response to Macartney as one based on a Qing failure of understanding.

3. For a comprehensive overview of the changes that were wrought globally in the nineteenth century, we recommend Osterhammel, *Transformation of the World*.

4. Among the originators of this positive interpretation of the development of the European international order is A. H. L. Heeren, who in his opposition to Napoleon's invasions of European states exaggerated the "freedom" that the Westphalian order gave to sovereign states; see Heeren, *Manual of the History of the Political System of Europe and Its Colonies*, esp. pp. vii–viii. His influence on international relations theory is discussed in Keene, *Beyond the Anarchical Society*, pp. 21–22.

5. International law did and continues to recognize a limited number of relationships entailing reduced sovereignty. At the time, and especially in the colonial context, the concepts of protectorates and spheres of influence were particularly relevant in this regard.

6. It should be noted that in Europe and the United States the discrepancy between the ideology and practice was also considerable at the time, and the selection of rulers

was far from democratic by today's standards, especially considering the lack of universal suffrage and the vested privileges of the ruling classes.

7. Shogo Suzuki, *Civilization and Empire*, p. 8.

8. This point is discussed in Dower, "E. H. Norman, Japan and the Uses of History." A similar phenomenon can be seen in the literature of international relations theory; e.g., Gong, *Standard of "Civilization" in International Society*; Suganami, "Japan's Entry into International Society."

9. This is the argument of Tanaka, *Japan's Orient*.

10. For a more thorough discussion of Japanese perceptions of international law, see Shogo Suzuki, *Civilization and Empire*, pp. 81–85.

11. Cited in Yamamuro, *Shisō kadai to shite no Ajia*, p. 231.

12. Ryukyu's tribute relations with the Qing empire allowed the Satsuma fiefdom to engage in lucrative trade. Its tribute relations with Japan were regarded by the Tokugawa rulers as a valuable means of legitimizing their rule to Japanese, as the visits of Ryukyuan emissaries were interpreted as proof of the shogun's prestige beyond the shores of Japan; see Toby, *State and Diplomacy in Early-Modern Japan*.

13. Cited in Oguma, *"Nihonjin" no kyōkai*, p. 20.

14. Memorandum by Ernest Satow, 6 July 1879, in Nish, *British Documents on Foreign Affairs*, ser. E, vol. 2, p. 63.

15. Gaimushō chōsabu, "Ryūkyū han ni taishi waga hanzoku taisei no tettei o kisubeku shochi aritaku mune negaide no ken," in *Dai Nihon gaikō bunsho*, vol. 5, p. 392.

16. The Ryukyuan pleas are summarized in Nish, *British Documents on Foreign Affairs*, ser. E, vol. 2, pp. 63–64.

17. He Ruzhang, "He Zie lai han," in Li Hongzhang, *Li Hongzhang quanji*, vol. 7, p. 4369.

18. Oyama, "Ryūkyū kizoku to nisshin fungi," p. 98.

19. Eskildsen, "Of Civilization and Savages," p. 389.

20. Eskildsen, "Meiji nana nen Taiwan shuppei no shokuminchiteki sokumen," p. 71.

21. McWilliams, "East Meets East," p. 248.

22. "Soejima taishi tekishin gairyaku," in Meiji bunka kenkyūkai, *Meiji bunka zenshū*, vol. 11, p. 71; Mori, *Taiwan shuppei*, p. 57.

23. Yen, *Taiwan in China's Foreign Relations*, pp. 196, 202.

24. Eskildsen, "Of Civilization and Savages," p. 396.

25. Sakai, *Kindai Nihon gaikō to Ajia taiheiyō chitsujo*, p. 115.

26. The state actors in this story are the Qing empire and the kingdom of Chosŏn (Joseon). We at times will use "China" and "Korea" to stand in for these two entities without implying that either can be directly mapped onto its latter-day replacement.

27. Declarations that the Qing empire was interested primarily in maintaining traditional tributary relations with Chosŏn are myriad; see, e.g., Lin, "Li Hung-chang," pp. 205–206; Han Woo-keun, *History of Korea*, p. 387; Chay, *Diplomacy of Asymmetry*, p. 57; Kim Hakjoon, *Korea's Relations with Her Neighbors*, p. 584; Ki-baik Lee, *New History of Korea*, p. 274.

28. This interpretation sharply contrasts with the conventional wisdom that the Qing empire's attitudes toward and activities in Korea were anachronistic and in-

compatible with modern international relations; see, e.g., Jung, *Nation Building*, pp. 164–165: "China pursued an unrealistic obsession—through Yuan's often irrational and childish interference—to attach Korea to the disintegrating Middle Kingdom. The Ch'ing court's desperate attempts to gain an international recognition for its dominating influence in Korea were not that much different from its traditional preoccupation to dominate Korea. Even with thousands of years of intercourse, the Chinese had utterly failed to understand the Korean reality." For similar statements, see Woong Kang, *Korean Struggle*, p. 266; Yur-bok Lee, *West Goes East*, p. 172.

29. Krasner, "Organized Hypocrisy in Nineteenth-Century East Asia."

30. Statements to this effect in Korean survey history texts are legion: "Korea had entered into a modern diplomatic relationship, not one of the traditional Chinese type" (Han Woo-keun, *History of Korea*, p. 374). "The Treaty of Kanghwa was Korea's first modern treaty" (Eckert et al., *Korea, Old and New*, p. 200). "The Treaty of Kanghwa proved a turning point in Korean history. It ended its isolation, undermined the tributary system that had framed Korean foreign relations for centuries" (Seth, *Concise History of Modern Korea*, p. 13); and "it brought Korea for the first time out onto the international stage" (Ki-baik Lee, *New History of Korea*, p. 269). To be sure, some qualify the significance of the treaty and its influence, but few go so far as to thoroughly interrogate the underlying assumptions of the entire process, as does Bruce Cumings: "In one book after another, we find this phrase: it was Korea's first modern treaty. Surely it was, but what might 'modern' mean in this context? Fair? Equal? In accord with international law? Concluded by sovereign nations? A lawyer in a courtroom could get an affirmative verdict on all these points: the treaty was integral to the 'common law' of the Western imperial system" (*Korea's Place in the Sun*, 102).

31. For examples, see Zongli Yamen to Rutherford Alcock, 10 March 1868 (TZ 7.2.17), Zhongyang yanjiuyuan jindaishi yanjiusuo, ed., *Qingji Zhong-Ri-Han guanxi shiliao* (hereafter abbreviated ZRHGX), p. 96; Zongli Yamen to Frederick Low, 23 December 1871 (TZ 10.11.12), *ZRHGX*, pp. 243–244; Zongli Yamen memorial, 8 February 1879 (GX 5.1.18), *ZRHGX*, pp. 353–354.

32. Key-hiuk Kim, *Last Phase of the East Asian World Order*, p. 258. See also Kojong's retrospective explanation of his 1876 decision to approve the treaty in *Sŭngjŏngwŏn ilgi*, 16 September 1882 (KJ 19.8.5), as cited in Choi, "Dawning of a New World," pp. 113–114.

33. The Korean scholar Kim Chŏng-wŏn, "Cho-Chung sangmin suyuk muyôk changjông e daehayô," p. 123, has argued that Korea cannot be thought to have been "open" until at least 1882.

34. In their preambles, all three treaties contain very similar terminology to the effect that the negotiators had "reciprocally examined their respective full powers" and "found them to be in due form" and that there should be "peace and friendship" between, for example, "the President of the United States and the King of Chosen and the citizens and subjects of their respective governments."

35. On the negotiation and signing of the treaty with the United States, see Drake,

Empire of the Seas, pp. 297–298; Key-hiuk Kim, *Last Phase of the East Asian World Order*, pp. 303–313; Woong Kang, *Korean Struggle*, pp. 134–141.

36. Drake, *Empire of the Seas*, pp. 252, 255–256.

37. *Kojong sillok*, 26 August 1879 (KJ 16.7.9).

38. See Larsen, *Tradition, Treaties, and Trade*, pp. 76–79.

39. For texts of the treaties, see *Kojong sillok*, 27 November 1882 (KJ 19.10.17); *Kojong sillok*, 31 December 1883 (KJ 20.12.3).

40. See, e.g., Harry Parkes to Earl Granville, 12 January 1883, in Nish, *British Documents on Foreign Affairs*, ser. E, vol. 2, pp. 104, 112.

41. Harry Parkes to Earl Granville, 21 December 1882, Nish, *British Documents on Foreign Affairs*, ser. E, vol. 2, p. 104.

42. Swartout, *Mandarins, Gunboats, and Power Politics*, p. 93.

43. Denny to Mitchell, 6 February 1888, *Deni munsô*, p. 96. See also Swartout, *Mandarins, Gunboats, and Power Politics*, p. 90; Yur-bok Lee, "Establishment of a Korean Legation," p. 6; Harrington, *God, Mammon, and the Japanese*, p. 226; Conroy, *Japanese Seizure of Korea*, p. 188.

44. Yur-bok Lee, "Establishment of a Korean Legation," p. 13.

45. Harrington, *God, Mammon, and the Japanese*, pp. 236–237.

46. Owen Nickerson Denny to Everett Frazar, 14 November 1886, *Deni munsô*, pp. 87–88.

47. John Russell Young to Frederick Theodore Frelinghuysen, 28 January 1883, cited in Nelson, *Korea and the Old Orders in Eastern Asia*, p. 162.

48. "Ambassadors Sent to the United States," *New York Times*, 2 February 1888, 4.4; "Embassy to the United States Not Subject to China's Control," *New York Times*, 2 February 1888, 4.2. I am indebted for these references (and the discussion of American media depictions of the legation more generally) to Christine Tanner, "Failures and Legacies of the Print Media."

49. "The Corean Embassy: They Put on Their Best Robes and Call on the President," *Washington Evening Star*, 17 January 1888.

50. See Dudden, *Japan's Colonization of Korea*, p. 16.

51. *Kojong sillok*, 30 July 1894 (KJ 31.6.28).

52. *Kojong sillok*, 22 August 1894 (KJ 31.7.22). The 22 August declaration also used the recurring term "autonomy" along with "independence" to describe the putative goals of the Korean-Japanese alliance.

53. See Kojong's "14-point oath" of January 1895, in *Kojong sillok*, 7 January 1895 (KJ 31.12.12); see also *Kojong sillok*, 8 January 1895 (KJ 31.12.13).

54. The chief Qing diplomat in Korea, Tang Shaoyi, sought to discourage the step by engaging in some classic imperialist condescension: "in South America and Africa, there are still small countries of black savages, but the tribal rulers of these states all call themselves King of Kings, Emperor, and all sorts of names, but it is not an indication of these countries' greatness" (cited in Larsen, *Tradition, Treaties, and Trade*, 249). While Qing opposition to the move could be expected, some Korean reformers such as Independence Club member Yun Ch'i-ho dismissed the move as "humbuggery" and

queried, "has the title of emperor ever been so disgraced as this ever before in the history of the world?" (*Yun Ch'i-ho ilgi*, vol. 5, 82, 102).

55. The Treaty of Shimonoseki began with the declaration that the Qing recognized the complete and unrestricted independence and autonomy of Korea, and the 1898 Russo-Japanese agreement, the 1902 Anglo-Japanese Alliance, and the 1904 Korean-Japanese protocol affirmed Korea's independence also.

56. Denny, *China and Korea*, p. 17.

57. For Japan's efforts to bar the Korean delegation from entry, see Dudden, *Japan's Colonization of Korea*.

58. For the "troublemaker" designation, see Davis, *United States and the Second Hague Peace Conference*, p. 193.

59. Dudden, *Japan's Colonization of Korea*, p. 7.

60. Cited in Yong-ju Lee, "Path from a Theory of Civilization to Escape of Asia," p. 146.

61. The Ganden Phodrang government was instituted by the Fifth Dalai Lama (1617–1682). It was closely aligned with the Gelugpa.

62. That became clear in the aftermath of the 1890 Anglo-Chinese Convention and associated 1893 Trade Regulations, agreements on Tibet made between Britain and China but successfully resisted by the Tibetans.

63. The Thirteenth Dalai Lama sent Agvaan Dorjiev, a high-ranking monastic official in Lhasa of Buriat origin, on missions to Saint Petersburgh. In 1913 he also dispatched him to Mongolia to negotiate a bilateral treaty with the new Mongolian government.

64. Carole McGranahan, "Empire and the Status of Tibet," p. 268, has identified five differences between the Ganden Phodrang model of statehood and the modern European system: boundaries were locally determined; sovereignty and boundary were not coterminous; there were overlapping zones between polities; there was no imperative for external ratification of rules; and there was a privileging of power relationships between territory and center over territorial integrity.

65. For a discussion of frontiers in the context of center-periphery relations in the Himalayas, see Todd Lewis, "Himalayan Religions in Comparative Perspective."

66. Chodak, "1901 Proclamation of HH Dalai Lama XIII."

67. This declaration is reprinted in Shakabpa, *Tibet*, pp. 246–48.

68. Examples include Missar and Darchen in Ngari, which were under Ladakhi and Bhutanese authority, respectively, and paid tax to those states. See Bray, "Ladakhi and Bhutanese Enclaves in Tibet." The people of Nilang, near the headwaters of the Jadh Ganga River, paid taxes to the authorities in Tibet and to the raja of Bashahr as well as to the Garwhal raja. See Hodgson, "Journal of a Survey to Heads of the Rivers, Ganges and Jumna," p. 91.

69. Phuntsho, *History of Bhutan*, chap. 3.

70. Aris, "India and the British according to a Tibetan Text of the Later Eighteenth Century"; Lamb, *Bhutan and Tibet*, vol. 1, p. 379; Huber, *Holy Land Reborn*.

71. When Frank Ludlow began teaching geography at the English school in Gyantse in 1924, his pupils still believed the earth was flat, a belief that persisted well into the

1940s; Ludlow diary entry, 2 September 1924, Oriental and India Office Collection and Records (hereafter abbreviated as OIOC), MSS Eur D979. This persisting attachment to earlier conceptions was consistent with Tibetan understandings of other elements of modernity such as biomedicine, which was fully accepted only by a generation educated in the scientific worldview; see McKay, *Their Footprints Remain*.

72. The Thirteenth Dalai Lama declared the *chö-yön* relationship at an end in 1909, when the empress dowager first dispatched troops to take control of Tibet and denounced the Dalai Lama, on the grounds that these actions violated the very fundament of that relationship.

73. On the state's taking responsibility for its citizens within defined borders, see Robb, "Colonial State and Constructions of Indian Identity." We are reminded of Benedict Anderson's observation that nationalism fills a gap left by the decline of sacrally based empires, although Anderson argues that more factors, such as print, are required for nationalism to develop; *Imagined Communities*, pp. 5–7, 114–16.

74. McKay, "'Tracing Lines upon the Unknown Areas of the Earth.'"

75. Curzon, *Frontiers*, p. 48.

76. Lyall, *Rise and Expansion of the British Dominion in India*, pp. 334–335.

77. The idea of establishing a *chö-yön* relationship is suggested in a British India document of 1917, which notes the "desire of the Dalai Lama to send a number of Abbots to the Tibetan monastery in Peking"; National Archive of India, File Index, 1917, Sec-E Nov 27–35.

78. Tibetan Chief Ministers to Viceroy of India, 14 October 1912, OIOC, L/P&S/11/38/4515.

79. Ford, *Captured in Tibet*, p.81.

80. Bernard, *Penthouse of the Gods*, p. 120, quoting a telegram from the Kashag.

81. Goldstein, *History of Modern Tibet*, p. 542, quoting correspondence from the National Assembly to Chiang Kaishek in 1946.

82. This was reported to the Government of India on a number of occasions by British frontier officers in Tibet. E.g., Political Officer Charles Bell to Government of India, 17 July 1910, OIOC, L/P&S/10/147–995; Viceroy to Secretary of State, 10 August 1932, copying Political Officer J. L. R. Weir to Government of India, 10 August 1932, OIOC, L/P&S/12/4174; also see the entry dated 3 May 1912 in Charles Bell's *Tibet Notebook*, vol. 1 (held by the British Museum), quoting the Mahajar Kumar of Sikkim stating that the Tibetans wanted to be a British protectorate like Bhutan.

83. Foreign Secretary, Government of India, to India Office, 28 June 1935, OIOC, L/P&S/12/187–4682; see also McKay, *Tibet and the British Raj*, for a discussion of British policy toward Tibet in this period.

84. Klieger, *Tibetan Nationalism*.

85. Goldstein, "Circulation of Estates in Tibet."

86. Center of Bhutan Studies, grossnationalhapiness.com, accessed 25 April 2016.

CHAPTER SEVEN

1. Pedrozo, "China versus Vietnam," pp. 37–40, 57 ff. See also n. 3, chap. 1, above.

2. Shen, "China's Sovereignty over the South China Sea Islands"; Han Zhenhua, Lin Jinzhi, and Hu Fengbin, *Woguo nanhai shiliao huibian*. We thank Bill Hayton for this reference.

3. Hayton, "Lines in the Sea," pp. 1, 9.

4. Hayton, *South China Sea*, pp. 56, 249–250.

5. The Republic of China formally accepted the credentials of the Tibetan plenipotentiary to the tripartite Simla negotiations between Tibet, China, and Britain. Its government rejected the resulting Simla Convention because of disagreement over the border between Inner and Outer Tibet only, not on the grounds that Tibet lacked the capacity to conclude treaties or for reasons connected with the Indo-Tibetan border. The Anglo-Tibetan border treaty was concluded bilaterally immediately after the Chinese rejection of the more comprehensive Simla Convention, which Britain and Tibet did sign. Van Walt van Praag, "Simla Agreements in International Law." See also Anand, "Tibet as an International Actor during the Simla Convention and Its Disappearance."

6. Narayanan, "Cross Signals across the Himalayas,"; "Dalai Lama's Arunachal Pradesh Visit Asserts India's Territorial Claim, a Provocation: China," WIO News, 12 April 2017, accessed 26 May 2017, https://www.wionews.com/south-asia/dalai-lamas -arunachal-pradesh-visit-asserts-indias-territorial-claim-a-provocation-china-14450.

7. Sarah Watson and John Chen, "Sino-Indian Border Talks Not Enough to Defuse Tensions."

8. State Council Information Office of the People's Republic of China, *Tibet's Path of Development Is Driven by an Irresistible Historical Tide*, p. 67.

9. Ministry of Foreign Affairs of Japan website, http://www.mofa.go.jp/region/asia -paci/senkaku/qa_1010.html.

10. French, *Everything under the Heavens*, pp. 10, 40–53.

11. International Court of Justice, *Request for Interpretation of the Judgment of 15 June 1962 in the Case concerning the Temple of Preah Vihear (Cambodia v. Thailand)*.

12. See Sothirak, "Cambodia's Border Conflict with Thailand," pp. 87–100.

13. Duara, *Rescuing History from the Nation*.

14. Bose, *A Hundred Horizons*, p. 70.

15. Ibid., p. 56.

16. Winichakul, *Siam Mapped*, pp. 150–156.

17. "Provisional Constitution of the Republic of China" (1912), chap. 1: General Provisions.

18. Van Walt van Praag, *Status of Tibet*, pp. 49–52, 136; Belov, *Rossiya i Mongoliya*, pp. 60, 102–103.

19. See Wade, "China's Six Wars in the Next 50 Years"; French, *Everything under the Heavens*, p. 72.

20. "China to Choose Next Dalai Lama by Draw of Lots," *Hindustan Times*, 11 April 2017, quoting the PRC Ministry of Foreign Affairs; "China Sticks to Right to Decide

Reincarnation of the Dalai Lama," 30 November 2015, accessed 29 May 2017, www
.reuters.com/article/us-china-tibet-idUSKBN0TJ0LN20151130.

21. Renade, "Buddhism."

22. Dalai Lama, "Reincarnation"; also Barnett, "Note on the Statement by the Dalai
Lama concerning His Successor"; Powers, *Buddha Party*, pp. 128–129.

23. State Council Information Office of the People's Republic of China, *Tibet's Path
of Development Is Driven by an Irresistible Historical Tide*, p. 58.

24. Dalai Lama, "Reincarnation." Qianlong proposed the regulations primarily to
disrupt the practice of selecting reincarnate lamas from among the Tibetan nobility
and to prevent the Gelugpa leadership from exerting influence over the selection of
Mongol incarnate lamas. The golden urn was used various times to select other reincarnate high lamas in the nineteenth century; see Schwieger, *Dalai Lama and Emperor of China*, pp. 182–208.

25. The PRC passed its own regulation for the selection and recognition of all reincarnate lamas: see Order No. 5 issued by the State Administration of Religious Affairs in August 2007, accessed 29 May 2017, http://english.peopledaily.com.cn/90001
/90776/6231524.html. See also Powers, *Buddha Party*, pp. 95–119; Schwieger, *Dalai
Lama and Emperor of China*, p. 216.

26. Beijing's efforts to gain acceptance in Tibet for the incarnation of the Panchen
Lama it selected in 1995, in opposition to the candidate recognized by the Dalai Lama,
may provide indications of the difficulties it may encounter with respect to selecting
the Dalai Lama; Powers, *Buddha Party*, pp. 116–125.

27. French, *Everything under the Heavens*, p.11.

28. For various perspectives, see Miller, *China's Asian Dream*; Pan and Lo, "Re-
conceptualizing China's Rise as a Global Power"; Yong Wang, "Offensive for Defensive."

29. "Xi Jinping Is Enjoying a 'Belt-and-Road Glow,'" *Economist*, 18 May 2017. Xi's
appeal to family unity discursively echoes the language of steles celebrating Qin unification in 221 BCE, which praised the First Emperor for having "unified all-under-
heaven under one family," which was meant explicitly to say the one family of the
ruler himself, not some abstract family of all the people; for the text, see Kern, *Stele
Inscriptions of Ch'in Shih-huang*, p. 13.

30. Critics include India; see, e.g., "India Slams China's One Belt One Road Initiative," *Times of India*, 14 May 2017. For an opposing view from the Chinese government,
see "World Loves Belt and Braces Approach," *China Daily*, 15 May 2017.

31. Nathan and Scobell, *China's Search for Security*, pp. 3–36, 195–212.

32. Brown, *Critical Transition*, pp. 6–8. Wang Gungwu and Zheng Yongnian, *China
and the New International Order*, p. 5.

BIBLIOGRAPHY

Ahmad, Zahiruddin. *Sino-Tibetan Relations in the Seventeenth Century.* Serie Orientale Roma, vol. 40. Roma: Istituto italiano per il Medio ed Estremo Oriente, 1970.

al-Dīn, Rashīd. *Dzhami at-tavarikh.* Moscow: Nauka, 1980.

Allsen, Thomas T. *Commodity and Exchange in the Mongol Empire: A Cultural History of Islamic Textiles.* Cambridge: Cambridge University Press, 1997.

———. *Culture and Conquest in Mongol Eurasia.* Cambridge: Cambridge University Press, 2001.

———. "The Rise of the Mongolian Empire and Mongolian Rule in North China." In *The Cambridge History of China,* vol. 6, *Alien Regimes and Border States, 907–1368,* edited by Herbert Franke and Denis Twitchett. Cambridge: Cambridge University Press, 1995.

Anand, Dibyesh. "Tibet as an International Actor during the Simla Convention and Its Disappearance." *Tibet Policy Journal* 1 (2014): 68–81.

Anderson, Benedict. *Imagined Communities.* London: Verso, 1992. First published 1981.

Anderson, James. *The Rebel Den of Nung Tri Cao: Loyalty and Identity along the Sino-Vietnamese Frontier.* Seattle: University of Washington Press, 2007.

Anon. "India-China Border Dispute." *Global Security,* accessed 8 August 2016, http://www.globalsecurity.org/military/world/war/india-china_conflicts.htm.

Ardussi, John. "Formation of the State of Bhutan ('*Brug gzhung*) in the 17th Century and Its Tibetan Antecedent." *Journal of Bhutan Studies* 11, no. 2 (2004): 10–32.

———. "The Rapprochement between Bhutan and Tibet under the Enlightened Rule of sDe-srid XIII Shes-rab-dbang-phyug (r. 1744–1763)." *Journal of Bhutan Studies* 1, no. 1 (1999): 64–83.

———. "Sikkim and Bhutan in the Crosscurrents of Seventeenth and Eighteenth Century Tibetan History." In *Buddhist Himalaya: Studies in Religion, History and Culture,* vol. 2, edited by Anna Balicki-Denjongpa and Alex McKay. Gangtok: Namgyal Institute of Tibetology, 2008.

———. "Wealth Distribution Rituals in the Political Economy of Traditional Tibet and Bhutan." In *Tibet and Her Neighbours: A History,* edited by Alex McKay. London: Edition Hansjong Meyer, 2003.

Aris, Michael. "India and the British according to a Tibetan Text of the Later Eighteenth Century." In *Tibetan Studies: Proceedings of the 6th International Seminar of the International Association for Tibetan Studies*, edited by Per Kvaerne, vol. 1. Oslo: Institute for Comparative Research in Human Culture, 1992.

———. *The Raven Crown: The Origins of the Buddhist Monarchy in Bhutan*. London: Serindia, 1994.

Atwood, Christopher P. *Encyclopedia of Mongolia and the Mongol Empire*. New York: Facts on File, 2004.

———. "National Questions and National Answers; or, How Do You Say *Minzu* in Mongolian?" *Indiana East Asian Working Paper Series on Language and Politics in Modern China* 5 (July 1994): 36–73.

Ban Gu, ed. *Han shu* [History of the Han dynasty]. Beijing: Zhonghua shuju, 1962.

Bao Wenhan. "Qingdai 'fanbu' yici kaoshi" [Notes on the term *fanbu* in the Qing dynasty]. *Qingshi yanjiu*, no. 4 (2000): 98–105.

Barfield, Thomas J. *The Perilous Frontier: Nomadic Empires and China*. Cambridge: Blackwell, 1989.

Barnett, Robbie. "Note on the Statement by the Dalai Lama concerning His Successor," 26 September 2011, accessed 29 May 2017. http://lawprofessors.typepad .com/files/note-on-the-statement-by-hhdl-concerning-his-successor-4.pdf.

Bearman, P. J., et al., eds. *The Encyclopaedia of Islam*. New ed. Leiden: Brill, 2000.

Beckwith, Christopher I. *Empires of the Silk Road: A History of Central Eurasia from the Bronze Age to the Present*. Princeton, NJ: Princeton University Press, 2009.

Bederman, David. *International Law in Antiquity*. Cambridge: Cambridge University Press, 2001.

Bell, Charles A. *Portrait of a Dalai Lama: The Life and Times of the Great Thirteenth*. 1946. Reprint, London: Wisdom, 1987.

———. *Tibet: Past and Present*. Oxford: Clarendon Press, 1924.

Belov, E. A. *Rossiya i Mongoliya, 1911–1919*. Moscow: Vostochnaya Literatura, 1999.

Bernard, Theos. *Penthouse of the Gods: A Pilgrimage into the Heart of Tibet and the Sacred City of Lhasa*. New York: Scribner, 1939.

Bielenstein, Hans. *Diplomacy and Trade in the Chinese World, 589–1276*. Leiden: Brill, 2005.

Biersteker, Thomas J., and Cynthia Weber, eds. *State Sovereignty as a Social Construct*. Cambridge: Cambridge University Press, 1996.

Biran, Michal. "The Mongol Transformation: From the Steppe to Eurasian Empire." *Medieval Encounters* 10, nos. 1–3 (2004): 339–361.

Blondeau, Anne-Marie, and Katia Buffetrille, eds. *Authenticating Tibet: Answers to China's 100 Questions*. Berkeley: University of California Press, 2008.

Bod rang skyong ljongs spyi tshogs tshan rig zhib 'jug khang and Krung dbyang mi rigs slob grwa'i bod rig pa'i zhib 'jug khang, eds. *Krung go'i bod sa gnas kyi lo rgyus yig tshang phyogs btus* [Biography of the Seventh Dalai Lama]. Lhasa: Bod ljongs mi dmangs dpe skrun khang, 1986.

Bol, Peter. "Middle-Period Discourse on the *Zhong guo*—the Central Country." *Hua-xue yanjiu*, 2009, pp. 1–30.

Bormanshinov, Arash. "Kalmyk Pilgrims to Tibet and Mongolia." *Central Asiatic Journal* 42, no. 1 (1998): 1–22.

Bose, Sugata. *A Hundred Horizons: The Indian Ocean in the Age of Global Empire.* Cambridge, MA: Harvard University Press, 2006.

Bosson, James. *A Treasury of Aphoristic Jewels: The Subhāṣitaratnanidhi of Sa Skya Paṇḍita in Tibetan and Mongolian.* Indiana University Uralic and Altaic Series, vol. 92. Bloomington: Indiana University, 1969.

Boyle, John A., trans. *Genghis Khan: The History of the World-Conqueror by Ata-Malik Juvaini.* Manchester: Manchester University Press, UNESCO Publishing, 1997.

———, trans. *The Successors of Genghis Khan.* New York: Columbia University Press, 1971.

Bray, John. "Ladakhi and Bhutanese Enclaves in Tibet." In *Recent Researches in Ladakh 7: Proceedings of the 7th Colloquium of the International Association for Ladakh Studies,* edited by Thierry Dodin and Hans Räther. Ulm: Ulmer Kulturanthropologische Schriften, 1997.

Brown, Kerry, ed. *The Critical Transition: China's Priorities for 2021.* Chatham House Research Paper. London: Royal Institute for International Affairs, 2017.

Brook, Timothy. "Great States." *Journal of Asian Studies* 75, no. 4 (November 2016): 957–972.

———. "Tibet and the Chinese World-Empire." In *Empires and Autonomy: Moments in the History of Globalization,* edited by Stephen Streeter, John Weaver, and William Coleman. Vancouver: University of British Columbia Press, 2009.

———. *The Troubled Empire: China in the Yuan and Ming Dynasties.* Cambridge, MA: Harvard University Press, 2010.

———. "What Happens When Wang Yangming Crosses the Border?" In *The Chinese State at the Borders,* edited by Diana Lary. Vancouver: University of British Columbia Press, 2007.

Brzezinski, Zbigniew. *Second Chance: Three Presidents and the Crisis of American Superpower.* New York: Basic Books, 2007.

Buell, Paul D. "Tribe, Qan and Ulus in Early Mongol China: Some Prolegomena to Yuan History." PhD diss., University of Washington, 1997.

Cai Jiayi. *Menggu jin Zang aocha qianyi* [A brief comment on Mongols going to Tibet to boil tea]. *Xibei shidi,* 1988.

Cassese, Antonio. *International Law.* 2nd ed. Oxford: Oxford University Press, 2005.

Chan, Hok-Lam. "The Chien-Wen, Yung-Lo, Hung-Hsi, and Hsüan-Te Reigns, 1399–1435." In *The Cambridge History of China,* vol. 7, *The Ming Dynasty, 1368–1644,* pt. 1, edited by Frederick W. Mote and Denis Twitchett. Cambridge: Cambridge University Press, 1988.

Chaoben Ming shilu [Manuscript copy of the Ming Veritable Records]. Beijing: Xianhuang shuju, 2005.

Chaogemandula. "Shilun Qingdai Zhelimu meng shiqi nutuke" [Tentative discussion on the *nutuɣ* of the tenth banner of the Zhelimu confederacy in the Qing dynasty]. *Heilongjiang minzu conggan,* no. 6 [89] (2005): 85–89.

Chay Jongsuk. *Diplomacy of Asymmetry: Korean-American Relations to 1910.* Honolulu: University of Hawai'i Press, 1990.

Chen Dezhi. "Zailun Wusizang 'benqin'" [Further considerations on Ü-tsang's *benqin*]. In *Meng Yuan shi yanjiu congkao* [Collected research essays on the history of the Mongol Yuan dynasty]. Beijing: Renmin chubanshe, 2005.

Chen Qingying. *Yuanchao dishi Basiba* [Yuan imperial preceptor Phagpa]. Beijing: Zhongguo zangxue chubanshe, 1992.

Chen Qingying and Ma Lianlong, trans. *Wushi Dalai Lama zhuan* [Biography of the Fifth Dalai Lama]. Beijing: Zhongguo zangxue chubanshe, 2006.

———, trans. *Yishi-sishi Dalai Lama zhuan* [Biographies of the First to Fourth Dalai Lamas]. Beijing: Zhongguo zangxue chubanshe, 2006.

Chen Xiaoqiang. "Qingdai zhongyang zhengfu dui Xizang xingzheng guanli de caizheng zhichu" [Disbursements of the Qing central government for the administration of Tibet]. *Xibei minzu yanjiu*, no. 3 (2001): 150–164.

Ch'en Yüan. *Western and Central Asians in China under the Mongols.* Monumenta Serica Monograph 15. Los Angeles: Monumenta Serica at the University of California, 1966.

Chin, Tamara T. *Savage Exchange: Han Imperialism, Chinese Literary Style, and the Economic Imagination.* Cambridge, MA: Harvard University Asia Center, 2014.

Chodak, Tenzing. "The 1901 Proclamation of HH Dalai Lama XIII." *Tibet Journal* 3, no. 1 (1978): 30–38.

Choi Deok Soo [Choi Tŏk-su]. "The Dawning of a New World: Korea and the West, Korea and Changing Asia in 1882." Paper presented at Koryŏ University, 14 July 2005.

Church, Sally. "The Colossal Ships of Zheng He: Image or Reality?" In *Zheng He: Images and Perceptions*, edited by Roderich Ptak and Claudine Salmon. Wiesbaden: Harrassowitz, 2005.

Clark, Donald N. "Sino-Korean Tributary Relations under the Ming." In *The Cambridge History of China*, vol. 7, *The Ming Dynasty, 1368–1644*, pt. 1, edited by Frederick W. Mote and Denis Twitchett. Cambridge: Cambridge University Press, 1988.

Clauson, Gerard. *An Etymological Dictionary of Pre-Thirteenth-Century Turkish.* Oxford: Clarendon Press, 1972.

Cleaves, Francis W. "The Bodistw-a Čara-a Awatar-un tayilbur of 1312 by Čosgi Odsir." *Harvard Journal of Asiatic Studies* 17 (1954): 1–129.

———. "The Sino-Mongolian Inscription of 1335 in Memory of Chang Ying-jui." *Harvard Journal of Asiatic Studies* 13 (1950): 1–153.

———. "The Sino-Mongolian Inscription of 1338 in Memory of Jigüntei." *Harvard Journal of Asiatic Studies* 14 (1951): 1–104.

———. "The Sino-Mongolian Inscription of 1346." *Harvard Journal of Asiatic Studies* 15, nos. 1–2 (June 1952): 1–123.

———. "The Sino-Mongolian Inscription of 1362 in Memory of Prince Hindu." *Harvard Journal of Asiatic Studies* 12 (1949): 1–133.

Clunas, Craig. *Screen of Kings: Royal Art and Power in Ming China.* London: Reaktion, 2013.

Cohen, Warren I. *East Asia at the Center: Four Thousand Years of Engagement with the World.* New York: Columbia University Press, 2000.

Conroy, Hilary. *The Japanese Seizure of Korea, 1868–1910: A Study of Realism and Idealism in International Relations.* Philadelphia: University of Pennsylvania Press, 1960.

Crossley, Pamela. "Coercion and the Inner History of Qing-Joseon Relations." Forthcoming.

———. *"Dayi juemi lu* and the Lost Yongzheng Philosophy of Identity." *Crossroads: Studies on the History of Exchange Relations in the East Asian World* 5 (April 2012): 63–80.

———. "The Rulerships of China: A Review Essay." *American Historical Review* 97, no. 5 (December 1992): 1468–1483.

———. "Three Governments in One State and the Stability of the Qing Empire." In *World History of Empire,* edited by Christopher Bayly et al., vol. 2. Oxford: Oxford University Press, 2014.

———. *A Translucent Mirror: History and Identity in Qing Imperial Ideology.* Berkeley: University of California Press, 1999.

———. *The Wobbling Pivot: China since 1800, an Interpretive History.* Malden, MA: Wiley-Blackwell, 2010.

Cumings, Bruce. *Korea's Place in the Sun: A Modern History.* New York: Norton, 2005.

Cüppers, C. "A Letter Written by the Fifth Dalai Lama to the King of Bhaktapur." *Journal of the Nepal Research Center* 12 (2001): 39–42.

Curzon, George. *Frontiers: The Romanes Lecture.* Oxford: Clarendon Press, 1907.

Da Yuan shengzheng guochao dianzhang [Regulations of the sagely administration of the Yuan Great State]. Ca. 1322. Reprint of 1908 ed., Taipei: Gugong bowuyuan, 1972.

Dai, Yingcong. "To Nourish a Strong Military: Kangxi's Preferential Treatment of His Military Officials." *War and Society* 18, no. 2 (October 2000): 71–91.

The Dalai Lama (H.H. the Fourteenth Dalai Lama of Tibet). "Reincarnation," 24 September 2011, accessed 29 May 2017. https://www.dalailama.com/messages/retirement-and-reincarnation/reincarnation.

Davis, Calvin. *The United States and the Second Hague Peace Conference: American Diplomacy and International Organization, 1899–1914.* Durham, NC: Duke University Press, 1975.

Dawson, Christopher. *Mission to Asia.* Toronto: University of Toronto Press, 1980.

de Rachewiltz, Igor. *Index to "The Secret History of the Mongols."* Bloomington: Indiana University, 1972.

———. *Prester John and Europe's Discovery of East Asia.* New York: New Directions, 1972.

———, trans. *The Secret History of the Mongols: A Mongolian Epic Chronicle of the Thirteenth Century.* 2 vols. Leiden: Brill, 2004.

Denny, Oliver N. *China and Korea.* Kenny and Walsh, 1888.

Di Cosmo, Nicola. *Ancient China and Its Enemies: The Rise of Nomadic Power in East Asia History.* New York: Cambridge University Press, 2004.

———. "From Alliance to Tutelage: A Historical Analysis of Manchu-Mongol Relations before the Qing Conquest." *Frontiers of History in China* 7, no. 2 (2012): 175–197.

———. "Nurhaci's Gambit: Sovereignty as Concept and Praxis in the Rise of the Manchus." In *The Scaffolding of Sovereignty*, edited by Zvi Ben-Dor Benite, Stefanos Geroulanos, and Nicole Jerr. New York: Columbia University Press, 2017.

———. "Nurhaci's Names." In *Representing Power in Ancient Inner Asia: Legitimacy, Transmission, and the Sacred*, edited by Isabelle Charleux et al. Bellingham: Western Washington University, 2010.

———. "State Formation and Periodization in Inner Asian History." *Journal of World History* 10 (1999): 1–40.

Diao Shuren. "Nuerhaci jueqi yu Dongya hua-yi guanxi de bianhua" [The rise of Nurhaci and the change in Chinese-barbarian relations in East Asia]. *Zhongguo bianjiang shidi yanjiu / China's Borderland History and Geography Studies* 22, no. 3 (2012): 70–82.

Dirlik, Arif. "Born in Translation." Paper presented at the Kreddha seminar "The Nature of Inner- and East Asian Polities and Relations from the 13th to the early 18th Century: Perspectives of Contemporary Sources," University of California at Davis, 22–24 September 2016.

Dower, John W. "E. H. Norman, Japan and the Uses of History." In *Origins of the Modern Japanese State: Selected Writings of E. H. Norman*, edited by John W. Dower. New York: Pantheon Books, 1975.

Drake, Frederick C. *The Empire of the Seas: A Biography of Rear Admiral Robert Wilson Shufeldt*. Honolulu: University of Hawai'i Press, 1984.

Dreyer, Edward L. *Early Ming China: A Political History, 1355–1435*. Stanford, CA: Stanford University Press, 1982.

———. *Zheng He: China and the Oceans in the Early Ming Dynasty, 1405–1433*. New York: Pearson Longman, 2007.

Duara, Prasenjit. *Rescuing History from the Nation*. Chicago: University of Chicago Press, 1995.

Dudden, Alexis. *Japan's Colonization of Korea: Discourse and Power*. Honolulu: University of Hawai'i Press, 2004.

Duka Ceren, Wangjie Zhu, and Tang Anchi Yi. *Poluonai zhuan* [Biography of Polhané Sonam Tobgyal (Pho-lha-nas bSod-nams stobs-rgyal)]. Lhasa: Xizang renmin chubanshe, 2002.

Dungkar Rinpoche [Dung-dkar Blo-bzang 'Phrin-las]. *Bod kyi chos srid zung 'brel skor bshad pa* [The merging of religious and secular rule in Tibet]. Dharamsala: Library of Tibetan Works and Archives, 1982.

———. *gSung-rtsom Phyogs-bsgrigs* [Collected works]. Qinghai: Krung go'i bod kyi shes rig dpe skrun khang, 1997.

———. *The Merging of Religious and Secular Rule in Tibet*. Beijing: Foreign Languages Press, 1991.

Eckert, Carter, et al. *Korea, Old and New: A History*. Cambridge, MA: Korea Institute, Harvard University, 1990.

Elliott, Mark C. *The Manchu Way: The Eight Banners and Ethnic Identity in Late Imperial China.* Stanford, CA: Stanford University Press, 2001.

Elverskog, Johan. "Mongol Time Enters a Qing World." In *Time, Temporality, and Imperial Transition: East Asia from Ming to Qing,* edited by Lynn Struve. Honolulu: University of Hawai'i Press, 2005.

———. *Our Great Qing: The Mongols, Buddhism, and the State in Late Imperial China.* Honolulu: University of Hawai'i Press, 2006.

Elvin, Mark. *The Pattern of the Chinese Past.* Stanford, CA: Stanford University Press, 1973.

Eskildsen, Robert. "Meiji nana nen Taiwan shuppei no shokuminchiteki sokumen" [Colonial aspects of the military intervention in Taiwan in 1874]. In *Meiji ishin to Ajia* [The Meiji Restoration and Asia], edited by Meiji ishinshi gakkai. Tokyo: Yoshikawa kobunkan, 2001.

———. "Of Civilization and Savages: The Mimetic Imperialism of Japan's 1874 Expedition to Taiwan." *American Historical Review* 107, no. 2 (2002): 388–418.

Everding, Karl-Heinz. "The Mongol States and Their Struggle for Dominance over Tibet in the 13th Century." In *Tibet, Past and Present (PIATS 2000),* edited by H. Blezer. Leiden: Brill, 2002). Reprinted in S. Mullard, ed., *Critical Readings on the History of Tibetan Foreign Relations,* vol. 1 (Leiden: Brill, 2002).

Fairbank, John K., ed. *The Cambridge History of China.* Vol. 10, *Late Ch'ing.* Cambridge: Cambridge University Press, 1978.

———, ed. *The Chinese World Order: Traditional China's Foreign Relations.* Cambridge, MA: Harvard University Press, 1968.

———. *Trade and Diplomacy on the China Coast: The Opening of the Treaty Ports, 1842–1854.* Cambridge, MA: Harvard University Press, 1953.

———. "Tributary Trade and China's Relations with the West." *Far Eastern Quarterly* 1, no. 2 (February 1942): 129–149.

Fairbank, John K., and S. Y. Teng. "On the Ch'ing Tributary System." *Harvard Journal of Asiatic Studies* 6, no. 2 (1941): 135–246.

Fan Ye. *Hou Han shu* [History of the Latter Han dynasty]. Beijing: Zhonghua shuju, 1965.

Fletcher, Joseph F. "The Mongols: Ecological and Social Perspectives." *Harvard Journal of Asiatic Studies* 46, no. 1 (June 1986): 11–50.

———. "China and Central Asia, 1368–1884." In *The Chinese World Order: Traditional China's Foreign Relations,* edited by John Fairbank. Cambridge, MA: Harvard University Press.

———. "Turco-Mongolian Monarchic Tradition in the Ottoman Empire." *Harvard Ukrainian Studies* 3/4, no. 1 (1979–1980): 236–251.

Ford, Robert. *Captured in Tibet.* London: Harrap, 1957. Reprint, Oxford: Oxford University Press, 1990.

Franke, Herbert. "Some Sinological Remarks on Rashid ad-Din's History of China." *Oriens* 4, no. 1 (1951): 21–26.

———. "Tibetans in Yuan China." In *China under Mongol Rule,* edited by John Langlois. Princeton, NJ: Princeton University Press, 1981.

French, Howard. *Everything under the Heavens: How the Past Helps Shape China's Push for Global Power*. New York: Alfred H. Knopf, 2017.

Fu Fanwei. "Cong 'Yu zhongyuan xi' de chuanchao kan Mingdai huayi zhengtong guan de zhuanbian" [Changing perspectives on barbarians and dynastic legitimacy in the Ming dynasty: A case study of the "Edict to the Central Plains"]. *Mingdai yanjiu* 22 (2014): 51–76.

Fukuda Yōichi and Ishihama Yumiko. *Tukan "Issai shūgi" Mongoru no shō* [The Mongolian text of *Yiqie zongyi*]. Chibettyo Bukkyō shūgi kenkyū 4. Tokyo: Tōyō bunko, 1986.

Fuma Susumu, ed. *Chūgoku higashi Ajia gaikō kōryūshi no kenkyū* [Studies on the history of China's foreign relations and foreign exchanges in East Asia]. Kyoto: Kyōtō daigaku gakujutsu shuppankai, 2007.

Gaimushō chōsabu [Research Department, Ministry of Foreign Affairs], ed. *Dai Nihon gaikō bunsho* [Diplomatic documents of the Japan Great State]. Vol. 5. Tokyo: Nippon kokusai kyōkai, 1939.

Gibb, H. A. R., and C. F. Beckingham, trans. *The Travels of Ibn Baṭṭūṭa, A.D. 1325–1354*. London: Hakluyt Society, 1994.

Gilpin, Robert. *War and Change in World Politics*. New York: Cambridge University Press, 1981.

Göckenjan, Hansgerd. "Zur Stammesstruktur und Heeresorganisation altaischer Völker: Das Dezimalsystem." In *Europa Slavica—Europa Orientalis: Festschrift für Herbert Ludat zum 70. Geburtstag*, ed. Klaus-Detlev Grothusen and Klaus Zernack. Berlin: Duncker und Humblot, 1980.

Golden, Peter. "The Headless State: Aristocratic Orders, Kinship Society, and Misrepresentations of Nomadic Inner Asia." *Journal of Asian Studies* 68, no. 1 (February 2009): 293–296.

———. "Imperial Ideology and the Sources of Political Unity amongst the Pre-Chinggisid Nomads of Western Eurasia." *Archivum Eurasiae Medii Aevi* 2 (1982): 37–77.

———. "Nomads and Their Sedentary Neighbors in Pre-Chinggisid Eurasia." *Archivum Eurasiae Medii Aevi* 7 (1987–1991): 41–81.

Goldstein, Melvyn. "The Circulation of Estates in Tibet: Reincarnation, Land, and Politics." *Journal of Asian Studies* 32, no. 3 (1973): 445–455.

———. *A History of Modern Tibet, 1913–1951: The Demise of the Lamaist State*. Berkeley: University of California Press, 1989.

Gong, Gerrit W. *The Standard of "Civilization" in International Society*. Oxford: Clarendon Press, 1984.

Grupper, Samuel M. "Manchu Patronage and Tibetan Buddhism during the First Half of the Ch'ing Dynasty." *Journal of the Tibet Society* 4 (1984): 47–74.

Hamashita Takeshi. *China, East Asia and the Global Economy: Regional and Historical Perspectives*. Edited by Linda Grove and Mark Selden. London: Routledge, 2008.

———. *Chōkō shisutemu to kindai Ajia* [The tribute system and modern Asia]. Tokyo: Iwanami shoten, 1997.

Han Woo-keun. *The History of Korea*. Translated by Lee Kyung-shik. Edited by Graften K. Mintz. Seoul: Eul-Yoo, 1970.

Han Zhenhua, Lin Jinzhi, and Hu Fengbin, eds. *Woguo nanhai shiliao huibian* [Compilation of historical documents concerning our country's South China Sea]. Beijing: Dongfang chubanshe, 1988.

Harrington, Fred. *God, Mammon, and the Japanese: Dr. Horace N. Allen and Korean-American Relations, 1884–1905*. Madison: University of Wisconsin Press, 1944.

Hayton, Bill. "Lines in the Sea: The Construction of China's Maritime Geobody." Paper presented at the Kreddha seminar "The Nature of Inner- and East Asian Polities and Relations from the 13th to the early 18th Century: Perspectives of Contemporary Sources," University of California at Davis, 23 September 2016.

———. *The South China Sea: The Struggle for Power in Asia*. New Haven, CT: Yale University Press, 2014.

Hazine 1653. *See* Jahn, Karl, and Herbert Franke, eds., *Die Chinageschichte des Rašīd ad-Dīn*.

Heeren, A. H. L. *A Manual of the History of the Political System of Europe and Its Colonies*. London: Henry G. Bohn, 1846.

Heuschert-Laage, Dorothea. "Negotiating Modalities of Succession: The Interplay between Different Legal Spheres in Eighteenth-Century Mongolia." *Buddhism, Law and Society* 1 (2015–2016): 165–194.

Hevia, James. *Cherishing Men from Afar: Qing Guest Ritual and the Macartney Embassy of 1793*. Durham, NC: Duke University Press, 1995.

Hodgson, J. A. "Journal of a Survey to Heads of the Rivers, Ganges and Jumna." *Asiatic Researches* 14 (1822): 60–152.

Huber, Toni. *The Holy Land Reborn: Pilgrimage and the Tibetan Reinvention of Buddhist India*. Chicago: University of Chicago Press, 2008.

Hui, Victoria Tin-bor. "China's Long March to the Periphery: How Peripheral Regions Became Parts of China." Paper presented at the "Roundtable on the Nature of Political and Spiritual Relations among Asian Leaders and Polities," University of British Columbia, 19–21 April 2010.

Huntington, Samuel P. *The Clash of Civilizations and the Remaking of World Order*. New York: Simon and Schuster, 1996.

Inaba Shōjū. "Gen no teishi ni kansuru kenkyū: Keitō to nenji o chūshin to shite" [A study concerning the imperial preceptor in the Yuan, focusing on genealogy and chronology]. *Otani daigaku kenkyū nenpō* 17 (1965): 81–155.

International Court of Justice. *Request for Interpretation of the Judgment of 15 June 1962 in the Case concerning the Temple of Preah Vihear (Cambodia v. Thailand)*. Reports of Judgments, Advisory Opinions and Orders, Judgment of 11 November 2013.

Ishihama Yumiko. "Chibetto bunsho no kōzō kara mita jūshichi seiki no Chibetto, Mongoru, Shin kankei no ichi tanmen" [An aspect of the Tibet, Mongol, and Qing relationship in the seventeenth century from the vantage point of the Tibetan letter format]. *Ajia Afurika gengo bunka kenkyū* 55 (1998): 165–190.

———. "The Image of Ch'ien-lung's Kingship as Seen from the World of Tibetan

Buddhism." *Nihon seizō gakkai kaihō* 40 (1996): 35–44. Reprinted in Ishihama Yumiko, *Chibetto Bukkyō sekai no rekishiteki kenkyū* [Historical studies of the world of Tibetan Buddhism] (Tokyo: Tōhō shoten, 2001). Page citations refer to the Tōhō shoten edition.

———. "The Notion of 'Buddhist Governnment' (*chos srid*) Shared by Tibet, Mongol and Manchu in the Early 17th Century." In *The Relationship between Religion and State* (chos srid zung 'brel) *in Traditional Tibet*, edited by Christoph Cüppers. Lumbini: Lumbini International Research Institute, 2004.

———. "On the Dissemination of the Belief in the Dalai Lama as a Manifestation of the Bodhisattva Avalokiteśvara." *Acta Asiatica* 64 (1993): 38–56. Reprinted in Alex McKay, ed., *The History of Tibet*, vol. 2 (London: Routledge Curzon, 2003). Page citations refer to the *Acta Asiatica* article.

———. "Pags pa no chōsaku ni miru Hubilai seiken saishoki no Enkei chiiki no jōkyō ni tsuite" [On the situation in the Beijing region during the earliest period of Khubilai's regime as seen in Phagpa's writings]. *Shiteki* 25 (2002): 226–249.

———. Review of *Our Great Qing: The Mongols, Buddhism, and the State in Late Imperial China*, by Johan Elverskog. *Journal of Chinese Studies* 48 (2008): 511–516.

Jackson, Peter. "From Ulus to Khanate: The Making of the Mongol States, c. 1220–c. 1290." In *The Mongol Empire and Its Legacy*, edited by Reuven Amitai-Preiss and David Morgan. Leiden: Brill, 1999.

———, ed. *The Mission of Friar William of Rubruck*. London: Hakluyt Society, 1990.

Jagou, Fabienne. "The Thirteenth Dalai Lama's Visit to Beijing in 1908: In Search of a New Kind of Chaplain-Donor Relationship." In *Buddhism between Tibet and China*, edited by Matthew Kapstein. Boston: Wisdom, 2009.

Jahn, Beate. *Cultural Construction of International Relations: The Invention of the State of Nature*. New York: Palgrave, 2000.

Jahn, Karl. "Rashīd al-Dīn and Chinese Culture." *Central Asiatic Journal* 14, nos. 1–3 (1970): 134–147.

Jahn, Karl, and Herbert Franke, eds. *Die Chinageschichte des Rašīd ad-Dīn*. (Persian version from the Topkapi Library: Hazine, no. 1653.) Vienna: Böhlau, 1971.

Janhunen, Juha. *Manchuria: An Ethnic History*. Helsinki: Fino-Ugrian Society, 1996.

Janis, Mark W., and Carolyn Evans, eds. *Religion and International Law*. The Hague: Martinus Nijhoff / Kluwer Law International, 1999.

Jiang, Yonglin, trans. *The Great Ming Code / Da Ming lü*. Seattle: University of Washington Press, 2005.

Jin Yufu. "*Da Yuan da yitong zhi* kaozheng" [Bibliographic notes on the *Great unitary succession gazetteer of the Great Yuan*]. In *Liaohai congshu* (1934), reprinted 1985.

Jiu manzhou dang [Old Manchu documents]. Taipei: Guoli gugong bowuyuan, 1969.

Jung, Walter. *Nation Building: The Geopolitical History of Korea*. Lanham, MD: University Press of America, 1998.

Kam, Tak-Sing. "The dGe-lugs-pa Breakthrough: The Uluk Darxan Nangsu Lama's Mission to the Manchus." *Central Asiatic Journal* 44, no. 2 (2000): 161–176.

Kane, Daniel. "The Great Central Liao Kitan State." *Crossroads*, forthcoming.

Kang, David C. *East Asia before the West: Five Centuries of Trade and Tribute.* New York: Columbia University Press, 2010.

———. "Getting Asia Wrong: The Need for New Analytical Frameworks." *International Security* 27, no. 4 (Spring 2003): 57–85.

Kang, Woong Joe. *The Korean Struggle for International Identity in the Foreground of the Shufeldt Negotiation, 1866–1882.* Lanham, MD: University Press of America, 2005.

Kapstein, Matthew. "The Seventh Dalai Lama, Kalsang Gyatso." In *The Dalai Lamas: A Visual History,* edited by Martin Brauen (Chicago: Serindia, 2005).

———. *The Tibetans.* Malden: Blackwell, 2006.

Karmay, Samten G. "The Fifth Dalai Lama and His Reunification of Tibet." In *Lhasa in the Seventeenth Century,* edited by F. Pommaret. Leiden: Brill, 2003. Reprinted in Saul Mullard, ed., *Critical Readings on the History of Tibetan Foreign Relations* (Brill: Leiden 2013). Page citations refer to the reprint edition.

Kawachi, Yoshihiro. *Mindai nyoshinshi no kenkyū* [Studies on the Jurchens of the Ming dynasty]. Kyoto: Dōhōsha, 1992.

Kawamoto Masatomo. "Chūō Ajia no tumen naru chiiki kubun ni tsuite" [On the division of territory into *tümen* in Central Asia]. *Seinan Ajia kenkyū* 53 (2000): 24–60.

Keene, Edward. *Beyond the Anarchical Society: Grotius, Colonialism and Order in World Politics.* Cambridge: Cambridge University Press, 2002.

Kelley, Liam C. "Vietnam as a 'Domain of Manifest Civility' (*Van Hien chi Bang*)." *Journal of Southeast Asian Studies* 34, no. 1 (2003): 63–76.

Kern, Martin. *The Stele Inscriptions of Ch'in Shih-huang: Text and Ritual in Early Chinese Imperial Representation.* New Haven, CT: American Oriental Society, 2000.

Kim Chông-wôn. "Cho-Chung sangmin suyuk muyôk changjông e daehayô" [Regarding the regulations for maritime and overland trade between Chinese and Korean subjects]. *Yŏksa hakbo* 32 (1966): 120–69.

Kim Hakjoon. *Korea's Relations with Her Neighbors in a Changing World.* Elizabeth, NJ: Hollym, 1993.

Kim, Hodong. "The Early History of the Moghul Nomads: The Legacy of the Chaghatai Khanate." In *The Mongol Empire and Its Legacy,* edited by Reuven Amitai-Preiss and David Morgan. Leiden: Brill, 1999.

———. "Monggol jeguk kwa Dae Wŏn" [The Mongol empire and the Great Yuan]. *Yeoksa hakbo* 192 (2006): 221–251.

———. "Was 'Da Yuan' a Chinese Dynasty?" *Journal of Song-Yuan Studies* 45 (2015): 259–285.

Kim, Key-hiuk. *The Last Phase of the East Asian World Order: Korea, Japan, and the Chinese Empire, 1860–1882.* Berkeley: University of California Press, 1980.

Kim, Seon-min. "Border and Border Trespassing between Qing China and Chosŏn Korea." *Late Imperial China* 28, no. 1 (June 2007): 33–61.

Klieger, P. Christiaan. *Tibetan Nationalism: The Role of Patronage in the Accomplishment of a National Identity.* Berkeley: Folklore Institute, 1992.

Kolås, Åshild. "Tibetan Nationalism: The Politics of Religion." *Journal of Peace Research* 33, no. 1 (1996): 51–66.

Kolbas, Judith, *Mongols in Iran: Chingiz Khan to Uljaytu, 1220–1309*. New York: Routledge, 2006.

Komatsubara Yuri. "Jūhachi seiki kōhanki no Chūzō daijin: Darairama seiken ni taisuru Chūzō daijin no dōkō to yakuwari" [The *ambans* in Tibet in the latter half of the eighteenth century: Their motives and roles with regard to the Dalai Lama government]. *Sundai shigaku* 128 (2006): 1–19.

Koo Bum-jin. "Chao-Min shixing wanglai he Chao-Qing shixing wanglai de bijiao" [Comparison of the exchange of Chosŏn-Ming and Chosŏn-Qing envoys]. *Fudan daxue wenshi yanjiuyuan xueshu tongxun*, no. 42 (2014): 27–28.

———. "Dai Shin teikoku no Chōsen ninshiki to Chōsen no isō" [Phases in east Eurasian international relations: Chŏson Korea from the Qing perspective]. *Chūgoku shigaku* 22 (2010): 91–113.

———, ed. *"Imun" yŏkchu* [An annotated translation of *Imun*]. Seoul: Sech'ang ch'ulp'ansa, 2012.

Krader, Lawrence. "Qan-Qayan and the Beginnings of Mongol Kingship." *Central Asiatic Journal* 1, no. 1 (1955): 17–35.

Krasner, Stephen. "Organized Hypocrisy in Nineteenth-Century East Asia." *International Relations of the Asia-Pacific* 1 (2001): 173–197.

———. *Sovereignty: Organized Hypocrisy*. Princeton, NJ: Princeton University Press, 1999.

Laird, Thomas. *The Story of Tibet: Conversations with the Dalai Lama*. New York: Grove, 2006.

Lamb, Alastair, ed. *Bhutan and Tibet: The Travels of George Bogle and Alexander Hamilton, 1774–1777*. Vol. 1. Hertingfordbury: Roxford Books, 2002.

Langlois, John, ed. *China under Mongol Rule*. Princeton, NJ: Princeton University Press, 1981.

Larsen, Kirk W. *Tradition, Treaties, and Trade: Qing Imperialism and Chosŏn Korea, 1850–1910*. Cambridge, MA: Harvard University Asia Center, 2008.

Lau, Hon-shiang. "Evidence from Chinese Archival and Historical Records." Unpublished manuscript.

Ledyard, Gary. "Yin and Yang in the China-Manchuria-Korea Triangle." In *China among Equals: The Middle Kingdom and Its Neighbors, 10th–14th Centuries*, edited by Morris Rossabi. Berkeley: University of California Press, 1983.

Lee, Chul-sung. "Re-evaluation of the Chosŏn Dynasty's Trade Relationship with the Ch'ing Dynasty." *International Journal of Korean History* 3 (2002): 95–122.

Lee, Jung-chul. "Analysis of the Studies of Taedongpŏp from the Historical-Institutional Perspective." *International Journal of Korean History* 6 (December 2004): 161–187.

Lee, Ki-baik. *A New History of Korea*. Translated by Edward W. Wagner. Cambridge, MA: Harvard University Press, 1984.

Lee, Yong-ju. "The Path from a Theory of Civilization to Escape of Asia: Yukichi

Fukuzawa's Perception of Asia and the 'Mission to Civilize.'" *Sungkyun Journal of East Asian Studies* 3, no. 2 (2003): 123–152.

Lee, Yur-bok. "Establishment of a Korean Legation in the United States, 1887–1890: A Study of the Conflict between the Confucian World Order and Modern International Relations." Center for Asian Studies, University of Illinois, 1983.

———. *West Goes East: Paul Georg von Möllendorff and Great Power Imperialism in Late Yi Korea.* Honolulu: University of Hawai'i Press, 1988.

Legge, James, trans. *The Confucian Classics.* Vol. 1, *"Confucian Analects," "The Great Learning," "The Doctrine of the Mean."* 2nd ed. Oxford: Clarendon Press, 1893.

Lesaffer, Randall. "International Law and Its History: The Story of an Unrequited Love." In *Time, History and International Law,* edited by Matthew Craven et al. Leiden: Nijhoff, 2007.

Lewis, Mark Edward. *The Early Chinese Empires: Qin and Han.* Cambridge, MA: Harvard University Press, 2007.

Lewis, Todd T. "Himalayan Religions in Comparative Perspective: Considerations regarding Buddhism and Hinduism across Their Indic Frontiers." *Himalayan Research Bulletin* 14, nos. 1–2 (1994): 25–46.

Li, Dun J. *The Ageless Chinese: A History.* 3rd ed. New York: Scribner's, 1978.

Li Hongzhang. *Li Hongzhang quanji* [Complete works of Li Hongzhang]. Changchun: Shidai wenyi chubanshe, 1998.

Li, Tana. *Nguyen Cochinchina: Southern Vietnam in the Seventeenth and Eighteenth Centuries.* Ithaca, NY: Cornell Southeast Asia Program Publications, 1998.

Lieberman, Victor. *Strange Parallels: Southeast Asia in Global Context, c. 800–1830.* 2 vols. Cambridge: Cambridge University Press, 2003–2010.

Ligeti, Louis [Lajos]. *Monuments préclassiques.* Vol. 1, *XIIIe et XIVe sieclès.* 2 parts. Monumenta Linguae Mongolicae Collecta, 2. Budapest: Akadémiai Kiadó, 1972.

Lin, T. C. "Li Hung-chang: His Korea Policies, 1870–1885." *Chinese Social and Political Science Review* 19, no. 2 (1935): 202–233.

Lindner, Rudi P. "What Was a Nomadic Tribe?" *Comparative Studies in Society and History* 24, no. 4 (1982): 689–711.

Liu Limei. "Guanyu zhu Zang dachen yu Dalai Lama xiangjian liyi wenti" [The problem of the greeting etiquette between the amban and the Dalai Lama]. *Zhongguo zangxue* 9, no. 1 (1997).

Liu, Lydia. *Clash of Empires: The Invention of China in Modern World Making.* Cambridge, MA: Harvard University Press, 2004.

Ly Te Xuyen. "Viet dien u linh tap luc toan bien" [Complete compilation of the collected records of the Viet realm's spirits of the departed]. In *Yuenan Hanwen xiaoshuo congkan* [Collection of novels and fables from Vietnam written in Chinese], edited by Chan Hing-ho, Cheng A-tsai, and Tran Nghia, series 2, vol. 2. Paris: École française d'Extrême-Orient; Taipei: Student Book Company, 1992.

Lyall, Alfred. *The Rise and Expansion of the British Dominion in India.* 1891. Reprint, Delhi: Manohar, 1973.

Ma Lin. "Qianlong chunian Zhungaer shouling shouci ru Zang aocha shimo" [The

Zunghar leader's first journey to Tibet to boil tea in the initial year of Qianlong]. *Xizang yanjiu*, no. 1 (1988): 62–69.

Makino Shūji. "Genchō chūshōshō no seiritu" [The formation of the Central Secretariat in the Yuan dynasty]. *Tōyōshi kenkyū* 25, no. 3 (1966): 60–84.

Manbun rōtō: Tongki fuka sindaha hergen i dangse [Archives of old Manchu documents]. Tokyo: Tōyō bunko, 1955.

Mancall, Marc. "The Persistence of Tradition in Chinese Foreign Policy." *Annals of the American Academy of Political and Social Science* 349 (September 1963): 14–26.

Markham, Clements R., ed. *Narratives of the Mission of George Bogle to Tibet and of the Journey of Thomas Manning to Lhasa.* 1876. Reprint, New Delhi: Manjusri Publishing House, 1971.

Matsuda Koichi. "Chūgoku kōtsūshi: Gen jidai no kōtsū to nanboku butsuryū" [History of transportation in China: Yuan-era transportation and commodity circulation between south and north]. In *Chugoku keizaishi no shomondai* [Questions in Chinese economic history], edited by Matsuda Koichi. Kyoto: Aunsha, 2001.

———. "Furagu-ke no tōhōryō" [Eastern domain of the house of Hülegü]. *Tōyōshi kenkyū* 39, no. 1 (1980): 35–62.

———. "Mongoru no kanchi tochi seido: Bunchi bunmin seido o chūshin toshite" [The Mongol land allotment system, focusing on the system of distribution of land and labor]. *Machikaneyama ronsō (shigaku hen)* 11 (1978): 33–54.

———. "Tolui-ke no hangai no yūbokuchi" [The *hangai* grazing lands of Tolui's family]. *Ritsumeikan bungaku* 537 (1944): 285–304.

McGranahan, Carole. "Empire and the Status of Tibet: British, Chinese, and Tibetan Negotiations, 1913–1934." In *The History of Tibet*, edited by Alex McKay, vol. 3. London: Routledge Curzon, 2003.

McKay, Alex, ed. *The History of Tibet*. 3 vols. London: Routledge Curzon, 2003.

———. *Their Footprints Remain: Biomedicine across the Indo-Tibetan Frontier*. Amsterdam: University of Amsterdam Press, 2007.

———. *Tibet and the British Raj: The Frontier Cadre, 1904–1947*. Richmond, Surrey: Curzon Press, 1997.

———. "'Tracing Lines upon the Unknown Areas of the Earth': Reflections on the Indo-Tibetan Frontier." In *Fringes of Empire: Peoples, Places and Spaces at the Margins of British Colonial India*, edited by Sameetah Agha and Elizabeth Kolsky. Delhi: Oxford University Press, 2009.

McWilliams, Wayne C. "East Meets East: The Soejima Mission to China, 1873." *Monumenta Nipponica* 30, no. 3 (1975): 237–275.

Meiji bunka kenkyūkai [Meiji culture research group], ed. *Meiji bunka zenshū* [Collection on Meiji culture]. Tokyo: Nippon hyōronsha, 1978.

Miller, Tom. *China's Asian Dream: Empire Building along the New Silk Road*. London: Zed Books, 2017.

Mills, J. V. G. *Ma Huan, Ying-yai Sheng-lan, "The Overall Survey of the Ocean's Shores" (1433)*. Cambridge: Cambridge University Press, 1970.

Ming shilu [Veritable records of the Ming]: *Ming Taizu shilu* [Veritable records of Emperor Taizu (Hongwu, 1368–1398)]; *Ming Taizong shilu* [Veritable records of Emperor Taizong (Yongle, 1403–1424)]; *Ming Xuanzong shilu* [Veritable records of Emperor Xuanzong (Xuande, 1426–1435)]; *Ming Yingzong shilu* [Veritable records of Emperor Yingzong (Zhengtong, Jingtai, Tianshun, 1436–1464)]; *Ming Xianzong shilu* [Veritable records of Emperor Xianzong (Chenghua, 1465–1487)]; *Ming Xiaozong shilu* [Veritable records of Emperor Xiaozong (Hongzhi, 1488–1505)]; *Ming Wuzong shilu* [Veritable records of Emperor Wuzong (Zhengde, 1506–1521)]; *Ming Shizong shilu* [Veritable records of Emperor Shizong (Jiajing, 1522–1566)]; *Ming Shenzong shilu* [Veritable records of Emperor Shenzong (Wanli, 1573–1620)]. Reprint, Taipei: Zhongyang yanjiuyuan lishi yuyan yanjiusuo, 1962.

Ministry of Foreign Affairs of the Socialist Republic of Vietnam. *The Hoang Sa and Truong Sa Archipelagoes and International Law.* Hanoi, 1988.

———. *The Hoang Sa and Truong Sa Archipelagoes: Vietnamese Territories.* Hanoi, 1982. Reprinted as "Vietnamese White Book: Claim to Paracel and Spratly Island," in British Broadcasting Corporation, Summary of World Broadcasts, pt. 3, Far East, no. 6932: A3/10.

———. *Vietnam's Sovereignty over the Hoang Sa and Truong Sa Archipelagos.* Hanoi, 1979.

Miya Noriko. *Monggoru jidai no shuppan bunka* [Publishing culture in the Mongol era]. Nagoya: Nagoya daigaku shuppankai, 2006.

Morgan, David. *The Mongols.* 2nd ed. Cambridge: Blackwell, 2007.

Mori Toshihiko. *Taiwan shuppei* [Military intervention in Taiwan]. Tokyo: Chūō kōronsha, 1996.

Morikawa Tetsuo. "Chaharu hachi otoku to sono bunpū ni tsuite" [On the granting of the eighth *otoɣ* of Chahar]. *Tōyō gakuhō* 58, nos. 1–2 (1976): 127–162.

———. "Chūki Mongoru no tumen ni tsuite, tokuni urusu to no kankei wo tsūjite" [On *tümen* in the middle Mongol period, especially its relationship to *ulus*]. *Shigaku zasshi* 81, no. 1 (1972): 32–54.

———. "Haruha tumen to sono seiritsu ni tsuite" [On the establishment of the Khalkha *tümen*]. *Tōyō gakuhō* 55, no. 2 (1972): 32–63.

———. "Orudosu jūni otoku kō" [On the twelfth *otoɣ* of the Ordos]. *Tōyōshi kenkyū* 32, no. 3 (1973): 32–60.

Mosca, Matthew. "Empire and Circulation of Frontier Intelligence: Qing Conceptions of the Ottomans." *Harvard Journal of Asiatic Studies* 70, no. 1 (2010): 147–207.

———. *From Frontier Policy to Foreign Policy: The Question of India and the Transformation of Geopolitics in Qing China.* Stanford, CA: Stanford University Press, 2013.

———. "The Literati Rewriting of China in the Qianlong-Jiaqing Transition." *Late Imperial China* 32, no. 2 (December 2011): 89–132.

Mostaert, Antoine. *Le matériel mongol Du Houa i i iu de Houng-ou (1389).* Vol. 1. Brussels: Institut belge des hautes études chinoises, 1977.

Mostaert, Antoine, and Francis Cleaves. "Trois documents mongols des Archives secrètes vaticane." *Harvard Journal of Asiatic Studies* 15, nos. 3–4 (December 1952): 419–506.

Mote, Frederick. *Imperial China, 900–1800.* Cambridge, MA: Harvard University Press, 1999.

Mullard, S. "Bkra dkar bkra shis sdings kyi sku 'bum: The Text, the Author, the Stupa, and Its Importance in the Formation of Religious Politics in Sikkim." *Bulletin of Tibetology* 39, no. 1 (2003): 13–24.

Müller, Claudius. *Dschingis Khan und Seine Erben: Das Weltreich der Mongole.* Schallaburg: Hirmer Verlag, 2005.

Mullin, Glenn H. *The Fourteen Dalai Lamas: A Sacred Legacy of Reincarnation.* Santa Fe, NM: Clear Light Books, 2001.

Munkh-Erdene, Lhamsuren. "The 1640 Great Code: An Inner Asian Parallel to the Treaty of Westphalia." *Central Asian Survey* 29, no. 3 (September 2010): 269–288.

———. "Where Did the Mongol Empire Come From? Mongol Ideas of People, State and Empire." *Inner Asia* 13 (2011): 211–237.

Munkuev, N. T. *Men-da bei-lu "Polnoe Opisanie Mongolo-Tartar"* [Detailed account of the Mongol-Tatars]. Moscow: Nauka, 1975.

Murakami Nobuaki. "Panchen Rama sansei no nekka raihō to Shinchō kijin kanryō no taiō: Jūhachi seiki kōhan no Shinchō Chibetto kankei no ichisokumen" [The visit of the Third Panchen Lama to Rehe and his reception by bannermen and officials of the Qing dynasty: A view of the Qing-Tibet relationship in the latter half of the eighteenth century]. *Chūgoku shakai to bunka* 20 (2006): 125–141.

Muraoka Hitoshi. "Gendai Mongoru hōzoku to Mongoru Bukkyō—Seizō Temuru no shinkō o Chūshin ni shite" [The Mongol imperial family and Mongolian Buddhism in the Yuan dynasty, based on the beliefs of Chengzong Emperor Temür]. *Bukkyō shigaku kenkyū* 39, no. 1 (1996): 79–97.

Nakamura Atsushi. "Shinchō chika Mongoru shakai ni okeru Somu o megutte: Haruha Toshēto han bu sayoku kōki o jirei to shite" [On the *sumu* in Mongol society under Qing rule, using the case of the Left Wing Rear Banner of *Tüsiyetii qan ayimaγ*]. *Tōyō gakuhō* 93, no. 3 (2011): 1–25.

Nakamura Jun. "Chibetto to Mongoru no kaikuo: Harukanaru kōsei heno mebae" [The relationship of Tibet and the Mongols]. In *Iwanami kōza sekaishi*, vol. 11, *Chūō Yūrashia no tōgō* [Iwanami world history lectures: Survey of central Eurasia]. Tokyo: Iwanami shoten, 1997.

Narayanan, M. K. "Cross Signals across the Himalayas." *The Hindu*, 17 April 2017.

Nathan, Andrew J., and Andrew Scobell. *China's Search for Security.* New York: Columbia University Press, 2014.

Nelson, M. Frederick, *Korea and the Old Orders in Eastern Asia.* Baton Rouge: Louisiana State University Press, 1945.

Ngawang Losang Gyatso [Fifth Dalai Lama]. *Ngag dbang blo bzang rgya mtsho* [Autobiography of Ngawang Losang Gyatso].

Ngo Si Lien. *Daietsu shiki zensho: Kōgōbon* [Collated edition of the "Complete book of the historical records of the Viet Great State"]. Edited by Chen Jinghe. Tokyo: Tōyō bunka kenkyūjo, 1984. Modern edition of Ngo Si Lien, *Dai Viet su ky toan thu* [Complete book of the historical records of the Viet Great State]. Compiled 1479.

Nish, Ian, ed. *British Documents on Foreign Affairs: Reports and Papers from the For-*

eign Office Confidential Print. Series E, vol. 2, *Korea, the Ryukyu Islands, and North-East Asia, 1875–1888*. Frederick, MD: University Publications of America, 1989.

Oguma Eiji. *"Nihonjin" no kyōkai: Okinawa, Ainu, Taiwan, Chōsen, shokuminchi shihai kara fukki undō made* [The boundaries of the "Japanese": Okinawa, the Ainu, Taiwan, and Korea from colonial control to the movement for their return]. Tokyo: Shin'yōsha, 1998.

Oka Hiroki. *Shindai Mongoru meiki seido no kenkyū*. [Studies of Mongol league and banner systems in the Qing dynasty]. Tokyo: Tōhō shoten, 2007.

Okada Hidehiro. "Mōko shiliao ni mieru shoki no Mō Zō kankei" [Early Mongol-Tibet relations as seen in Mongol sources]. *Tōhō gaku* 23 (1962): 95–108.

Okada Mareo. *Shin'yaku kegonkyō ongi shiki wakunko*. Kyoto: Kyoto daigaku kokubun gakkai, 1962.

Onon, Urgunge. *The Secret History of the Mongols: The Life and Times of Chinggis Khan*. Abingdon: Routledge, 2001. Taylor and Francis e-Library, 2005.

Osterhammel, Jürgen. *The Transformation of the World: A Global History of the Nineteenth Century*. Princeton, NJ: Princeton University Press, 2013.

Otosaka Tomoko. "Rigon-pa no ran to sakya-pa seiken: Gendai Chibetto kankeishi no ichi tammen" [The Drigung-pa rebellion and the Sakya-pa administration: One phase of relations between China proper and Tibet in the Yuan). *Bukkyō shigaku kenkyū* 29, no. 2 (1986): 59–82.

Oyama Azusa. "Ryūkyū kizoku to nisshin fungi" [Reversion of Ryukyu and Japan-Qing disputes]. *Seikei ronsō* 38, nos. 1–2 (May 1970): 76–126.

Pan, Su-Yan, and Joe Tin-Yau Lo. "Re-conceptualizing China's Rise as a Global Power: A Neo-tributary Perspective." *Pacific Review* 30, no. 1 (20 August 2015).

Pedrozo, Raul (Pete). "China versus Vietnam: An Analysis of the Competing Claims in the South China Sea." CNA Occasional Paper. Arlington, VA: CNA, 2014.

Pelliot, Paul. *Notes on Marco Polo*. Vol. 1. Paris: Librairie Adriend-Maisonneuve, 1959.

Pema Lingpa. *The Rediscovered Teachings of the Great Padma-gling-pa*. Thimphu: Kunsang Topgay, 1976.

Perdue, Peter. *China Marches West: The Qing Conquest of Central Eurasia*. Cambridge, MA: Harvard University Press, 2005.

———. "Embracing Victory, Effacing Defeat: Rewriting the Qing Frontier Campaigns." In *The Chinese State at the Borders*, edited by Diana Lary. Vancouver: University of British Columbia Press, 2007.

———. "The Qing State and the Gansu Grain Market, 1739–1846." In *Chinese History in Economic Perspective*, edited by Thomas Rawski and Lillian Li. Berkeley: University of California Press, 1992.

Petech, Luciano. *Central Tibet and the Mongols: The Yüan Sa-skya Period of Tibetan History*. Rome: Instituto italiano per il Medio ed Estremo Oriente, Instituto Universitario orientale, 1990.

———. *China and Tibet in the Early XVIIIth Century: History of the Establishment of a Chinese Protectorate in Tibet*. 2nd ed. Leiden: Brill, 1972.

Phuntsho, Karma. *The History of Bhutan*. New Delhi: Random House India, 2013.

Pines, Yuri. "Imagining the Empire? Concepts of 'Primeval Unity' in Pre-imperial Historiographic Tradition." In *Conceiving Empire: China and Rome Compared*, edited by Fritz-Heiner Mutschler and Achim Mittag. Oxford: Oxford University Press, 2008.

Polo, Marco. *The Travels*. Translated by Ronald Latham. Harmondsworth: Penguin, 1986.

Poppe, Nicolas. *The Twelve Deeds of Buddha: A Mongolian Version of the Lalitavistara*. Wiesbaden: Harrassowitz, 1967.

Powers, John. *The Buddha Party: How the People's Republic of China Works to Define and Control Tibetan Buddhism*. Oxford: Oxford University Press, 2017.

Pozdneyev, A. M. *Mongolia and the Mongols*. Translated by John Roger Shaw and Dale Plank. Edited by John R. Kueger. Bloomington: Indiana University, 1971.

"Provisional Constitution of the Republic of China." *American Journal of International Law* 6 (1912): 149–154.

Qiao Ji. *Menggu fojiao shi Bei Yuan shiqi* [History of Mongol Buddhism in the Northern Yuan (1368–1634)]. Qökeqota: Nei Menggu renmin chubanshe, 2008.

Qing shilu [Veritable records of the Qing]: *Qing Shengzu shilu* [Veritable records of Emperor Shengzu (Kangxi, 1662–1722)]; *Qing Gaozong shilu* [Veritable records of Emperor Gaozong (Qianlong, 1736–1795)]. Reprint, Beijing: Zhonghua shuju, 1985.

Radnabahdara. *Zay-a Bandida zhuan* [Biography of Zaya Pandita]. Qökeqota: Öbür Mongol-un arad-un keblal-un qoriy-a, 1999.

Ratchnevsky, Paul. *Genghis Khan: His Life and Legacy*. Oxford: Blackwell, 1992.

Rawski, Evelyn. *The Last Emperors: A Social History of Qing Imperial Institutions*. Berkeley: University of California Press, 1998.

Reid, Anthony. *Southeast Asia in the Age of Commerce, 1450–1680*. 2 vols. New Haven, CT: Yale University Press, 1988–1993.

Renade, Jayadeva. "Buddhism: A New Frontier in the India-China Rivalry." *Carnegie India*, 17 March 2017.

Reynolds, Susan. *Kingdoms and Communities in Western Europe, 900–1300*. 2nd ed. Oxford: Clarendon Press, 1997.

Robb, Peter. "The Colonial State and Constructions of Indian Identity: An Example on the Northeast Frontier in the 1880s." *Modern Asian Studies* 31, no. 2 (1997): 245–283.

Robinson, David. *Empire's Twilight: Northeast Asia under the Mongols*. Cambridge, MA: Harvard University Press, 2009.

———. "The Ming Court and the Legacy of the Yuan Mongols." In *Culture, Courtiers, and Competition: The Ming Court (1368–1644)*, edited by David Robinson. Cambridge, MA: Harvard University Asia Center, 2008.

Rockhill, W. W. "The Dalai Lamas of Lhasa and Their Relations with the Manchu Emperors of China, 1644–1908." *T'oung Pao* 11 (1910).

Rossabi, Morris, ed. *China among Equals: The Middle Kingdom and Its Neighbors, 10th–14th Centuries*. Berkeley: University of California Press, 1983.

———. *Khubilai Khan: His Life and Times*. Berkeley: University of California Press, 1988.

———. "The Ming and Inner Asia." In *The Cambridge History of China*, vol. 8, *The Ming Dynasty, 1368–1644*, pt. 2, edited by Denis Twitchett and Frederick W. Mote. Cambridge: Cambridge University Press, 1998.

Rowe, William. *China's Last Empire: The Great Qing*. Cambridge, MA: Harvard University Press, 2009.

Ruegg, David Seyfort. "Introductory Remarks on the Spiritual and Temporal Orders." In *The Relationship between Religion and State* (Chos srid zung 'brel) *in Traditional Tibet*, edited by Christoph Cüppers. Lumbini: Lumbini International Research Institute, 2004.

———. "*Mchod Yon, Yon Mchod* and *Mchod Gnas / Yon Gnas*: On the Historiography and Semantics of a Tibetan Religio-social and Religio-political Concept." In *Tibetan History and Language*, edited by E. Steinkellner. Vienna: Arbeitskreis für tibetische und buddhistische Studien, Universität Wien, 1991.

———. *Ordre spirituel et ordre temporel dans la pensée bouddhique de l'Inde et du Tibet: Quatre conférences au Collège de France*. Publications de l'Institut de civilisation indienne, fasc. 64. Paris: Édition-Diffusion de Boccard, 1995.

———. "The Preceptor-Donor (*Yon Mchod*) Relation in Thirteenth Century Tibetan Society and Polity: Its Inner Asian Precursors and Indian Models." In *Tibetan Studies: Proceedings of the 7th Seminar of the International Association for Tibetan Studies*, vol. 2, edited by E. Steinkellner. Vienna: Verlag der Österreichischen Akademie der Wissenschaften, 1997.

Ruskola, Teemu. *Legal Orientalism: China, the United States, and Modern Law*. Cambridge, MA: Harvard University Press, 2013.

Saguchi Tōru. "Jūyon seiki ni okeru Genchō dai Kān to seihoku san Ō-ke no rentaisei ni tuite" [The connections between the Great Khan and the three princely families in the northwest in the fourteenth century]. *Kita Ajia gakuhō* 1 (1942): 151–214.

Sakai Kazuomi. *Kindai Nihon gaikō to Ajia taiheiyō chitsujo* [Modern Japan's situation and the Asia-Pacific order]. Kyoto: Shōwadō, 2009.

Satō Hisashi. "Pagumotupa seiken shoki no Chibetto jōsei" [The situation in Tibet in the early Pakmodrupa regime]. In *Chūsei Chibetto shi kenkyū* [Studies on the medieval history of Tibet], edited by Satō Hisashi. Kyoto: Dōbōsha, 1986.

Schaeffer, Kurtis, Matthew Kapstein, and Gray Tuttle, eds. *Sources of Tibetan Tradition*. New York: Columbia University Press, 2013.

Schmid, Andre. "Tributary Relations and the Qing-Chosŏn Frontier on Mount Paektu." In *The Chinese State at the Borders*, edited by Diana Lary. Vancouver: University of British Columbia Press, 2007.

Schwieger, Peter. *The Dalai Lama and the Emperor of China*. New York: Columbia University Press, 2015.

Scott, James. *Seeing like a State: How Certain Schemes to Improve the Human Condition Have Failed*. New Haven, CT: Yale University Press, 1998.

Sen, Tansen. "The Impact of Zheng He's Expeditions on Indian Ocean Interactions." *Bulletin of the School of Oriental and African Studies* 79, no. 3 (2016): 609–636.

Serruys, Henry. "The Dates of the Mongolian Documents in the *Hua-i i-yu*." *Harvard Journal of Asiatic Studies* 17, nos. 3–4 (1954): 419–427.

———. "Mongols Ennobled during the Early Ming." *Harvard Journal of Asiatic Studies* 22 (December 1959): 209–260.

———. "The Mongols in China during the Hung-wu Period (1369–1398)." Diss., 1956–1959.

———. *Sino-Mongol Relations during the Ming*. Vol. 2, *The Tribute System and Diplomatic Missions (1400–1600)*. Brussels: Institut belge des hautes études chinoises, 1967.

———. *Sino-Mongol Relations during the Ming*. Vol. 3, *Trade Relations: The Horse Fairs (1400–1600)*. Brussels: Institut belge des hautes études chinoises, 1975.

Seth, Michael. *A Concise History of Modern Korea: From the Late Nineteenth Century to the Present*. Lanham, MD: Rowman and Littlefield, 2010.

Shakabpa, Tsepon W. D. *Tibet: A Political History*. New York: Potala, 1984.

Shambaugh, David. "China Engages Asia: Reshaping the Regional Order." *International Security* 29, no.3 (Winter 2004/2005): 64–99.

Shaw, Malcolm N. *International Law*. 5th ed. Cambridge: Cambridge University Press, 2003.

Shen, Jianming. "China's Sovereignty over the South China Sea Islands: A Historical Perspective." *Chinese Journal of International Law* 1, no. 1 (2002): 94–157.

Sima Qian. *Shi ji* [Records of the historian]. Beijing: Zhonghua shuju, 1973.

Sin Pong-nyong and Kim Un-gyŏng, eds. *Deni munsŏ* [The writings of Oliver Denny]. Seoul: Pyŏngminsa, 1987.

Sinha, Nirmal C. "Chhos srid gnyis ldan." *Bulletin of Tibetology* 5, no. 3 (1968): 13–27.

Skrynnikova, Tatyana. "Concept *Törö* as Supreme Law of the Universe in the Political Culture of Both Mongol Ulus and Yuan Empire." Paper presented at the "Roundtable on the Mongol Empire and Its Legacy," Austrian Academy of Sciences, Vienna, 4 November 2010.

———. "Mongolian Nomadic Society of the Empire Period." In *Alternatives of Social Evolution*, edited by N. N. Kradin, A. V. Korotayev, D. M. Bondarenko, V. de Munck, and P. K. Wason. Vladivostok: Far Eastern Branch of the Russian Academy of Social Sciences, 2000.

Sneath, David. *The Headless State: Aristocratic Orders, Kinship Society, and Misrepresentations of Nomadic Inner Asia*. New York: Columbia University Press, 2007.

Song Lian, ed. *Yuan shi* [History of the Yuan dynasty]. Reprint, Beijing: Zhonghua shuju, 1979.

Sothirak, Pou. "Cambodia's Border Conflict with Thailand." *Southeast Asian Affairs*, 2013, pp. 87–100.

Sperling, Elliot. "Hülegü and Tibet." *Acta Orientalia Academiae Scientiarum Hungaricae* 44, nos. 1–2 (1990): 147–157.

———. "rTsa-mi lo-tsa-ba Sangs-rgyas grags-pa and the Tangut Background to Early Mongol-Tibetan Relations." In *Tibetan Studies: Proceedings of the 6th Seminar of the*

International Association for Tibetan Studies, Fagernes 1992, vol. 2, edited by Per Kvaerne. Oslo: Institute for Comparative Research in Human Culture, 1994.

State Council Information Office of the People's Republic of China. "China Adheres to the Position of Settling through Negotiation the Relevant Disputes between China and the Philippines in the South China Sea." White paper, published 13 July 2016.

———. *Tibet's Path of Development Is Driven by an Irresistible Historical Tide*. Beijing: Foreign Language Press, 2015.

Suganami, Hidemi. "Japan's Entry into International Society." In *The Expansion of International Society*, edited by Hedley Bull and Adam Watson. Oxford: Clarendon Press, 1984.

Sugiyama Masaaki. "Mongoru teikoku no genzō: Chingisukan ichizoku bunpō o megutte" [The Mongol empire's original form: Concerning the enfeoffment of Chinggis Khan's relatives]. *Tōyōshi kenkyū* 37, no. 1 (1978): 1–34.

Sun Chengze, ed. *Yuan chao diangu biannian kao* [Chronology of "Institutions of the Yuan dynasty"]. Reprint, Taipei: Taiwan shangwu yinshuguan, 1971.

Sun Daigang. "The Last Pitch: A Critical Study of the Supplementary Treaty of the Nanking Treaty." MA diss., University of Toronto, 1996.

Suzuki Chūsei. *Chibetto o meguru Chū In kankei shi: Jūhachi seiki nakagoro kara jūkyū seiki nakagoro made* [Tibet and the history of international relations between China and India: From the mid-eighteenth to the mid-nineteenth century]. Tokyo: Hitotsubashi Shobō, 1962.

Suzuki, Shogo. *Civilization and Empire: China and Japan's Encounter with European International Society*. London: Routledge, 2009.

Svarverud, Rune. *International Law as World Order in Late Imperial China: Translation, Reception and Discourse, 1847–1911*. Leiden: Brill, 2007.

Swanson, Bruce. *Eighth Voyage of the Dragon: A History of China's Quest for Seapower*. Annapolis, MD: Naval Institute Press, 1982.

Swartout, Robert. *Mandarins, Gunboats, and Power Politics: Owen Nickerson Denny and the International Rivalries in Korea*. Honolulu: Asian Studies Program, University of Hawai'i, 1980.

Szerb, Jânos. "Glosses on the Oeuvre of Bla-ma 'Phags-pa II: Some Notes on the Events of the Years 1251–1254." Acta Orientalia Academiae Scientiarum Hungaricae 34 (1980): 263–285.

Tanaka, Stefan. *Japan's Orient: Rendering Pasts into History*. Berkeley: University of California Press, 1993.

Tanner, Christine. "Failures and Legacies of the Print Media: Korea's First Legation in Washington, DC (1888)." Unpublished manuscript.

Tao, Jing-shen. *Two Sons of Heaven: Studies in Sung-Liao Relations*. Tucson: University of Arizona Press, 1988.

Tao Zongyi. *Nancun chuogeng lu* [Notes after the plowing was done]. Completed ca. 1366. Beijing: Zhonghua shuju, 2004.

Taylor, Keith Weller. *The Birth of Vietnam*. Berkeley: University of California Press, 1983.

Taylor, Romeyn. "Yuan Origins of the Wei-so System." In *Chinese Government in Ming Times*, edited by Charles O. Hucker. New York: Columbia University Press, 1969.

Thackston, Wheeler M., trans. *Rashiduddin Fazlullah's "Jami'u't-tawarikh": Compendium of Chronicles.* 3 vols. Cambridge, MA: Department of Near Eastern Languages and Civilizations, Harvard University, 1998–1999.

Thu'u bkwan chos kyi nyi ma [Tukwan]. *Lcang skya rol pa'i rdo rje'i rnam thar* [Biography of Changkya Rölpé Dorjé]. Lanzhou: Gansu minzu chubanshe, 1989.

Toby, Ronald P. *State and Diplomacy in Early-Modern Japan: Asia in the Development of the Tokugawa Bakufu.* Stanford: Stanford University Press, 1991.

Travers, Alice. "The Careers of the Noble Officials of the Ganden Phodrang (1895–1959): Organisation and Hereditary Divisions within the Service of State." *Revue d'études tibétaines* 21 (October 2009): 155–174.

Tshewang, P., Khenpo Phuntshok Tashi, C. Butters, and S. K. Saetreng. *The Treasure Revealer of Bhutan.* Bibliotheca Himalayica, ser. 3, vol. 8. Kathmandu: EMR Publishing House, 1995.

Tsiang, T. F. "China and European Expansion." *Politica* 2, no. 5 (March 1936): 1–18.

Tucci, Giuseppe. *Nepal: The Discovery of the Malla.* London: George Allen and Unwin, 1962.

———. *Tibetan Painted Scrolls.* 3 vols. Rome: La Libreria dello Stato, 1949. Reprinted in 2 vols., Kyoto: Rinsen Books, 1980. Page citations refer to the Rinsen edition.

Tumurtogoo, D. *Mongolian Monuments in Uighur-Mongolian Script (XIII–XIV Centuries): Introduction, Transcription and Bibliography.* Language and Linguistic Monograph Series A-11. Taipei: Institute of Linguistics, Academia Sinica, 2006.

Tuotuo, ed. *Song shi* [History of the Song dynasty]. Reprint, Beijing: Zhonghua shuju, 1977.

Tuttle, Gray. "A Tibetan Buddhist Mission to the East: The Fifth Dalai Lama's Journey to Beijing, 1652–1653." In *Politics, Power, and the Reinvention of Tradition: Tibet in the Seventeenth and Eighteenth Century*, edited by Bryan Cuevas and Kurtis Schaeffer. Leiden: Brill, 2006.

Uray-Köhalmi, Käthe. "Von woher kamen die Iče Manju?" In *Tumen jalafun jecen akū: Manchu Studies in Honour of Giovanni Stary*, edited by Alessandra Pozzi et al. *Tunguso Sibirica* 20. Wiesbaden: Harrassowitz, 2006.

Van Schaik, Sam. *Tibet: A History.* New Haven, CT: Yale University Press, 2011.

Van Walt van Praag, Michael. "A Legal Examination of the 1913 Mongolia-Tibet Treaty of Friendship and Alliance." *17 Lungta: The Centennial of the Tibeto-Mongol Treaty, 1913–2013* (Spring 2013): 81–100.

———. "The Simla Agreements in International Law." *Tibet Policy Journal* 1 (2014): 26–55.

———. *The Status of Tibet: History, Rights, and Prospects in International Law.* Boulder, CO: Westview Press, 1997.

Verhagen, Pieter. *A History of Sanskrit Grammatical Literature in Tibet.* Leiden: Brill, 1994.

Vladimirtsov, Boris. *Life of Chingis-Khan*. Translated by D. S. Mirsky. New York: Benjamin Blom, 1969.

———. *Obshchestvennyi stroi mongolov: Mongol'skii kochevoi feodalizm* [Social structure of the Mongols: Mongolian nomadic feudalism]. Leningrad: Akademii nauk SSSR, 1934.

Vogel, Hans Ulrich. *Marco Polo Was in China: New Evidence from Currencies, Salts and Revenues*. Leiden: Brill, 2013.

Wada Sei. "Some Problems concerning the Rise of T'ai-tsu the Founder of Manchu Dynasty." *Memoirs of the Research Department of the Toyo Bunko* 16 (1957): 51–63.

Wade, Geoff. "China's Six Wars in the Next 50 Years." *The Strategist*, 26 November 2013.

———, trans. *Southeast Asia in the "Ming Shi-lu": An Open Access Resource*. Singapore: Asia Research Institute and Singapore E-Press, National University of Singapore. http://epress.nus.sedu.sg/msl/.

———. "The Zheng He Voyages: A Reassessment." *Journal of the Malaysian Branch of the Royal Asiatic Society* 78, no. 1 (2005): 37–58.

Waldron, Arthur. *The Great Wall of China: From History to Myth*. New York: Cambridge University Press, 1990.

Walker, R. B. J. *After the Globe, before the World*. London: Routledge, 2010.

———. *Inside/Outside: International Relations as Political Theory*. Cambridge: Cambridge University Press, 1993.

Wallace, Vesna. "Buddhist Laws in Mongolia." In *Buddhism and Law: An Introduction*, edited by Rebecca French and Mark Nathan. New York: Cambridge University Press, 2014.

Walravens, Hartmut. "Das *Huang Ch'ing chih-kung t'u* als der Werk der mandjurischen Literatur." In *Tumen jalafun jecen akū: Manchu Studies in Honour of Giovanni Stary*, edited by Alessandra Pozzi et al. *Tunguso Sibirica* 20. Wiesbaden: Harrassowitz, 2006.

Waltz, Kenneth N. "Structural Realism after the Cold War." *International Security* 25, no. 1 (Summer 2000): 5–41.

———. *Theory of International Politics*. New York: Random House, 1979.

Wang Gungwu. "Early Ming Relations with Southeast Asia." In *The Chinese World Order: Traditional China's Foreign Relations*, edited by John K. Fairbank. Cambridge, MA: Harvard University Press, 1968.

Wang Gungwu, and Zheng Yongnian, eds. *China and the New International Order*. New York: Routledge, 2008.

Wang, Yong. "Offensive for Defensive: The Belt and Road Initiative and China's Grand New Strategy." *Pacific Review* 29 (9 March 2016).

Wang, Yuan-kang. "Great Qing and Its Southern Neighbors, 1760–1820: Secular Trends and Recovery from Crisis." Unpublished manuscript.

———. *Harmony and War: Confucian Culture and Chinese Power Politics*. New York: Columbia University Press, 2011.

———. "The Myth of Chinese Exceptionalism: A Historical Perspective on China's

Rise." In *Responding to China's Rise: US and EU Strategies*, edited by Vinod K. Aggarwal and Sara A. Newland. New York: Springer, 2015.

Wang Yun. *Qiujian xiansheng wenji* [Collected writings of Master Qiujian]. Siku congkan reprint ed. Taipei, n.d.

Wang Zhenping. *Ambassadors from the Islands of Immortals: China-Japan Relations in the Han-Tang Period*. Honolulu: University of Hawai'i Press, 2005.

Watson, Burton, trans. *Records of the Grand Historian: Han Dynasty*. Vol. 2. Rev. ed. New York: Columbia University Press, 1993.

Watson, Sarah, and John Chen. "Sino-Indian Border Talks Not Enough to Defuse Tensions." *Diplomat*, 3 December 2015, accessed 8 August 2016. www.the diplomat.com.

Weatherford, Jack. *Genghis Khan and the Making of the Modern World*. New York: Crown, 2004.

Wills, John E., Jr. *Embassies and Illusions: Dutch and Portuguese Envoys to K'ang-hsi, 1666–1687*. Cambridge, MA: Council of East Asian Studies, Harvard University, 1984.

———. "Great Qing and Its Southern Neighbors, 1760–1820: Secular Trends and Recovery from Crisis." Paper presented at conference "Interactions: Regional Studies, Global Processes, and Historical Analysis," Washington, DC, 3 March 2001.

Winichakul, Thongchai. *Siam Mapped: A History of the Geo-body of a Nation*. Honolulu: University of Hawai'i Press, 1994.

Womack, Brantly. *China and Vietnam: The Politics of Asymmetry*. Cambridge: Cambridge University Press, 2006.

Wong, R. Bin. *China Transformed; Historical Change and the Limits of European Experience*. Ithaca, NY: Cornell University Press, 1997.

Wood, Frances. *Did Marco Polo Go to China?* London: Secker and Warburg, 1995.

Woodside, Alexander. "Early Ming Expansionism (1406–1427): China's Abortive Conquest of Vietnam." *Papers on China* 17, no. 4 (1963): 1–37.

———. "Territorial Order and Collective Identity Tensions in Confucian Asia." *Daedalus* 127, no. 3 (Summer 1998): 191–220.

Woong Joe Kang. *Korean Struggle for International Identity in the Foreground of the Shufeldt Negotiation, 1866–1882*. Lanham, MD: University Press of America, 2005.

Wulan. *Menggu yuanliu yanjiu* [Studies on *Erdeni-yin Tobči*]. Shenyang: Liaoning minzu chubanshe, 2000.

Wylie, Turrell. "The First Mongol Conquest of Tibet Reinterpreted." *Harvard Journal of Asiatic Studies* 37, no. 1 (June 1977): 103–133.

———. "Khubilai Khan's First Viceroy of Tibet." In *Tibetan and Buddhist Studies: Commemorating the 200th Anniversary of the Birth of Alexander Csoma de Kőrös*, edited by Louis Ligeti. Budapest: Akadémiai Kiadó, 1984.

Xiao Jinsong. *Qingdai zhu Zang dachen* [*Ambans* in Tibet during the Qing dynasty]. Taipei: Tangshan chubanshe, 1996.

Xu Youren. *Zhizheng ji* [Collection from the Zhizheng era]. Siku quanshu zhenben ed. Taipei, 1978.

Yamamuro Shin'ichi. *Shisō kadai to shite no Ajia: Kijiku, rensa, toki*. Tokyo: Iwanami shoten, 2001.

Yanagisawa Akira. "Shinchō to Roshia: Sono kankei no kōzō to hensen" [The Qing dynasty and Russia: Structure and changes in the relationship]. In *Shinchō to wa nanika* [What is the Qing dynasty?], edited by Okada Hidehiro, supplementary vol. 16. Tokyo: Fujiwara shoten, 2009.

Yasufumi Toyooka. "Shinchō to kyū Min rei kokusai kankei (1644–1840)" [Qing diplomatic policy with respect to former Ming tributaries (1644–1840)]. *Chūgoku shigaku* 22 (2010): 135–152.

Yen, Sophia Su-fei. *Taiwan in China's Foreign Relations, 1836–1874*. Hamden, CT: Shoe String Press, 1965.

Yeshe Dolma and Thutob Namgyal. "The History of Sikkim." Gangtok, 1908. Unpublished manuscript.

Yi, Tae-jin. "Chosŏn's Adoption of International Law and Its Conflicts with China in the 1880s." In Tae-jin Yi, *Confucianism and Modernization in Korean History*. Ithaca, NY: East Asian Program, Cornell University, 2007.

Yokkaichi Yasuhiro. *Mono kara mita kaiiki Ajia shi: Mongoru jidai Sō-Gen jidai no Ajia to Nippon no kōryū* [Asian coastal history seen from objects: Exchanges between Japan and Asia during the Song and Yuan periods in the Mongol era]. Kyushu: Kyūshū daigaku shuppankai, 2008.

Yu Jeungah. "'Chūzō daijin' haken zenya ni okeru Shinchō no tai Chibetto seisaku: 1720–1727 nen wo chūshin ni" [On the eve of dispatching *ambans*: Qing government policy toward Tibet, 1720–1727]. *Shigaku zasshi* 113, no. 12 (2004): 59–83.

Yü, Ying-shih. *Trade and Expansion in Han China: A Study in the Structure of Sino-barbarian Economic Relations*. Berkeley: University of California Press, 1967.

Yun Ch'i-ho [Yun Qihe]. *Yun Ch'i-ho ilgi* [Diaries of Yun Qihe]. 10 vols. Seoul: Kuksa p'yŏnch'an wiwŏnhoe, 1971.

Yun, Peter I. "Rethinking the Tribute System: Korean States and Northeast Asian Interstate Relations, 600–1600." PhD diss., University of California, Los Angeles, 1998.

Zarrow, Peter. *After Empire: The Conceptual Transformation of the Chinese State, 1885–1924*. Stanford, CA: Stanford University Press, 2012.

Zhang, Feng. *Chinese Hegemony: Grand Strategy and International Institutions in East Asian History*. Stanford, CA: Stanford University Press, 2015.

———. "Rethinking the 'Tribute System': Broadening the Conceptual Horizon of Historical East Asian Politics." *Chinese Journal of International Politics* 2, no. 4 (2009): 545–574.

Zhang Tingyu, ed. *Ming shi* [History of the Ming dynasty]. Beijing: Zhonghua shuju, 1974.

Zhao, Gang. "Reinventing China: Imperial Qing Ideology and the Rise of Modern Chinese National Identity in the Early Twentieth Century." *Modern China* 32, no. 1 (January 2006): 3–30.

Zheng Hesheng and Zheng Yijun, eds. *Zheng He xia Xiyang ziliao huibian* [Collection of research materials on Zheng He's voyage to the Western Oceans]. Jinan: Qilu shushe, 1983.

Zhongguo diyi lishi dang'anguan [First Historical Archives of China], ed. *Jiaqing chao shangyu dang* [Imperial edicts of the Jiaqing reign]. 25 vols. Guilin: Guangxi shifan daxue chubanshe, 2008.

———, ed. *Qianlong chao shangyu dang* [Imperial edicts of the Qianlong reign]. 18 vols. Beijing: Dang'an chubanshe, 1991.

———, ed. *Qingdai junjichu manwen aocha dang* [Archives in Manchu of the Qing Council of State concerning boiling tea]. Shanghai: Shanghai guji chubanshe, 2010.

Zhongguo diyi lishi dang'anguan Zhongguo bianjang diqu lishi yu dili yanjiu zhongxin [Research Center of Historical and Geographical Studies of China's Frontier Regions, First Historical Archives of China], ed. *Junjichu manwen Zhungaer shizhe dang* [Documents from the Manchu-language archives of the Council of State concerning Zunghar envoys], first collection. Beijing: Zhongyang minzu daxue chubanshe, 2009.

Zhongguo junshi shi bianxiezu [Chinese Military History Writing Group], ed. *Zhongguo junshi shi* [Military history of China]. Beijing: People's Liberation Army Press, 1986.

Zhongyang yanjiuyuan jindaishi yanjiusuo [Academia Sinica, Institute of Modern History], ed. *Qingji Zhong-Ri-Han guanxi shiliao* [Materials concerning China-Japan-Korea relations in the Qing period]. Taipei: Zhongyang yanjiuyuan jindaishi yanjiusuo, 1972.

Zhou Rongbing. "Lun Jiaqingdi dui Xizang difang de zhili" [On Emperor Jiaqing's rule over the Tibetan region]. In *Xianzhe xin yan*, edited by Wang Yao. Shanghai: Shanghai guji chubanshe, 2007.

INDEX